Mike Berry is creator of the website www.419eater.com

With well over 20,000 registered users from every part of the globe, it hosts the largest scambaiting community on the internet. Currently receiving average daily hits of 10,000 plus, 419eater.com is one of the major resources for scambaiting activities.

The author practising his 'no photos please' pose.

Harbour Books Ltd
20 Castlegate
York YO1 9RP
www.harbourbooks.co.uk

Represented in Great Britain & Ireland by
Signature Book Services

First published in Great Britain by
Harbour Books 2006

A catalogue record for this book is
available from the British Library.

ISBN 13: 978 1905128 08 2
ISBN 10: 1905128 08 8

Typeset by Donkeystone
Printed and bound in Finland by WS Bookwell

Greetings in Jesus Name!

The Scambaiter Letters

Mike Berry

aka Shiver Metimbers

Harbour

This book is dedicated to the memory

of my father Brian A. Berry.

He was, and continues to be, the greatest inspiration in my life.

Thank you to my mother, Pat, for being the best.

To my wife, Trisha, for being perfect and so patient with me!

And finally to my son, Michael. I am a very proud father.

I would like to thank the following people for their help and support.

The administrators and moderators of 419eater.com who work so hard maintaining our forums and keeping the members out of trouble. In no particular order a big thank you to: Rover, Leccy, Kleindoofy, Eight, Nurse Nasty, Lotta, Meyer, Mr Fishe, SamV, Winelight, Old Coaster, Zen, Breddan Butter, Nigerian419, The False Italian, Max Power, Lew Skannen, Heinousmoz, Dr Who, Don, Daimon, Crimson Sapien, Chester, Cherrie, Spathi.

A. Skinner for his help with the scambaits, *Bonnie Scotland* & *The Road To Nowhere*, and Charlie Fake for his video skills on *The Road to Nowhere*.

To the thousands of people who have contacted me with their messages of support and, especially, for all their efforts to help rid the world of internet scams. It's a massive hill, but we're slowly climbing it.

And last, but not least, to the many, many thousands of members of 419eater. You have all helped make the site as popular as it is today, and kept untold numbers of scammers busy chasing rainbows over the years!

Thank you all.

Contents

Introducing The 419 Scam

The advance fee fraud scam is commonly known as the Nigerian scam or the '419' scam after the section of the Nigerian Criminal Code that it violates. It's a simple, but beguiling scam, extracting money from victims who believe that they will receive a certain percentage of cash for simply allowing the scammer to transfer a large amount of money into the victim's bank account. Unfortunately, during the course of the transaction, the victim is required to pay various 'local charges' (fees to fake lawyers or bankers, or back-handers to supposed government officials) to secure the successful transfer of the funds into the victim's account.These advance fees are the primary way that money is extracted from victims. Variations of the advance fee fraud scam have been around for well over 100 years. One of the earliest versions was known as the 'Spanish Prisoner' scam. The alleged prisoner was trapped in a Spanish castle and, to be released, required money to bribe the jailers. The letters were written by the fictitious prisoner who promised a share of their treasure chest in return for help. Today, with the advent of fast, efficient electronic mail, and the rise of the cybercafe, the Spanish prisoner is busier than ever.

The vast majority of advance fee fraud scams have been associated with Western Africa and in particular Nigeria. It would be wrong to assume that these places are the only source of such scams. Although a large majority of these particular scams do indeed originate from Western and, indeed, Southern Africa, advance fee fraud scammers operate from all over the globe including Asia, America, Canada, the United Kingdom and, still, Spain.

The amount of money lost to such scams varies from source to source. One figure puts the amount scammed at well over a billion pounds every year. In truth, however, it's a figure that defeats calculation. Generally, I've found that most victims are simply too embarrassed to report that they have fallen for what is perceived by many as an 'obvious' scam.

There are dozens of variations on the standard 419 scam. Let's take a look at the most common.

The victim is contacted via unsolicited mail, usually email. A scammer, claiming to be a government official, a member of a royal family, a lawyer or a banker, will explain that they have access to a large amount of money, previously belonging to perhaps a deposed government official or to a client, now deceased. These funds need to be quickly and discreetly moved overseas for safekeeping. The scammer will request the victim's help in transferring the money into the victim's own bank account. For doing this great favour, the victim is offered a percentage of the fund to be transferred, typically between 20% and 30%, which will usually add up to a few million pounds at least. Very tempting.

If the victim agrees to help the scammer, a variety of documents and certificates will arrive to back up the scammer's story. The documents are all bogus and, in a large majority of cases, are amateurish efforts which don't stand up to close scrutiny. Nevertheless, it is surprising just how many victims take these documents at face value.

Right at the start, victims are usually asked for their personal details, plus their bank details. It is a common misconception that the victim's bank details are then used to drain his account. Not so. Personal and banking details are included on the documents to lend an extra air of legitimacy to the proceedings. Nothing impresses a victim more than seeing their name and details on a document showing them that they are a hair's breadth away from raking in millions.

Early on in the scam the scammer will enlist the help of a lawyer to handle the more technical side of the transfer. The lawyer doesn't work for free and guess what - the scammer is a bit short of cash, so, if it's not too much trouble, please could you pay his fees? You will get the cash back, of course, and a lot more, once the fund has been transferred into your account!

But, as we all know, the path of true love and covert money transfers never runs smoothly. Inevitably there are problems with the transfer: certificates need to be paid for, clearence fees need to be settled, people need to be bribed to help grease the financial wheels and, you guessed it, the victim has to pay for all these fees and all the bribes. This continues *ad infinitum* until either the victim runs out of money or creduality, whichever comes first.

Throughout all this, the scammer will keep bombarding the victim with pleas to agree speedily to everything the lawyer demands. The scammer will say his life depends on it; his sick mother has minutes to live; he's had to sell his house and all his belongings just to help finance this deal; he's borrowed from moneylenders to help finance the deal and they are getting impatient to do a little bone breaking if he doesn't pay them back quickly. The psychological pressure is piled onto the victim. Daily, they will be harassed by email, telephone and fax. Throughout the scam there is always a sense of urgency and a demand for absolute secrecy. This is to avoid friends who may know better telling the victim what a *schmuck* they've been for falling for such a con.

Another variation on the advance fee fraud scam that is popular with scammers is tell their victim that a distant and forgotten rich relative of theirs has died - usually in some ghastly road or air accident - and the lawyer has been fortuitous enough to trace you after many months or years of trying. The will leaves you with millions of pounds and a life on Easy Street, but - the rub - to claim it you need to hire the services of the very same lawyer. Cue more fees!

A relatively new entrant is the lottery scam. Once again the victim receives an unsolicited 'winning notification' email congratulating him/her on their fantastic luck in having the winning numbers in a lottery they never actually entered. Of course to collect the many thousands of pounds of winnings the victim needs to pay 'processing' or 'clearance' fees to have the cash released. They have to keep paying more and more fees to try to claim non-existent money.

It's very simple to avoid falling into the clutches of scammers; if ever you

3

receive an unsolicited email offering you millions or hundreds of thousands of pounds for apparently doing very little at all, delete it and forget about it.

Never be tempted to reply to such emails, even if your intention is to give them a piece of your mind and describe in vivid detail exactly what they can do with their offer. Scammers are well used to receiving abuse and adding your own piece of vitriol to their ever-growing collection will have absolutely no effect on them. More than likely, your email address will find its way into the hands of many more scammers. Before you know it, you'll have an inbox flooded with more dead relative scams than you can shake a stick at!

It's not all bad news though.

Whilst scammers relentlessly send out many thousands of emails a day to possible victims, there are sporting people out there in cyberspace just waiting to receive them and ready to play the scammers at their own game. These people, and I'm proud to count my alter ego, Shiver Metimbers, as one of them, are scambaiters.

A scambaiter will actively communicate with a scammer, pretending to be a real victim, with the sole objective of trying to waste as much of the scammer's time and resources as possible. If some humiliation can be thrown into the mix along the way then that's all the better - my own personal prediliction to is have the scammer pose for a 'dumb pic', holding a placard with some nonsense or puerile double meaning on it. I've a collection of them. They're not big and they're not clever, but the setting up of them does keep the scammer busy, distracting them from taking money off the compassionate and gullible.

By publishing these actual email correspondences between myself and various scammers, my hope is that not only will people be entertained by them, but that it will help to raise awareness of such scams. I would hope that any person who reads this book will be armed with the knowledge of how to recognise scam emails in the future. If this book prevents just one more victim from falling for such scams then my time has been well spent.

Please do not try scambaiting at home.

Whilst antagonising fraudsters can be a harmless sport, it is worth remembering that the 419ers are criminals who persistently prey on the vulnerable and the financially desperate. Oddly enough, they might not see the funny side of being taken for a ride. Though it is unlikely that any of them would be so angry as to jump on a plane to try to find you, they may have helpful friends nearer to you.

Finally, don't be inveigled into feeling sympathy for any of the scammers in this book, no matter how harshly I treat them! There are innumerable stories of the greed of the 419 scammers, and of their heartlessness.

George Makronalli, 29, from Greece was a victim of a 419 fraud scheme. A syndicate issued a statement on the internet in which they claimed that they had stolen about R150m from the South African government by submitting false claims for 'contracts'. They were looking for help from overseas to get the money out of the country: anyone willing to help would receive a percentage of the money. Makronalli was caught with the scam. He went to South Africa on the invitation of the scammers and was kidnapped. His family were emailed with a ransom demand. The demand was not paid. A day later his body was found in Durban; his legs and arms had been broken and his body set alight. No-one was ever arrested.

I should point out that all the scambaiting characters in this book, and their views, are fictional, and not related to living characters. That they sometimes share their names with celebrities is not a coincidence, it is a joke, and should be read in that spirit.

OK, let's go! Here's a few of my personal favourite anti-scams. I hope you enjoy them.

Mike Berry
(aka Shiver Metimbers)
August 2006

The Incredible Shrinking Artwork

Here's one of my regular anti-scams, pretending to be an art dealer. I manage to secure two pieces of artwork, but, unfortunately, due to the temperature and humidity fluctuations between the UK and West Africa, as well as rogue rodents, there are problems.

John Boko is a 419 scammer. Initially he sent out a standard sitting-on-millions 419 scam email under a different name. I gave him my Derek Trotter Fine Arts reply:

Thank you very much for your very interesting email. However, I am afraid that I will be unable to help you at this time. These next three months are by far the busiest and most profitable period for my company and I cannot give any time to anything other than finding new artwork for our galleries especially wooden carvings.

You may already know of me since it was you that contacted me. My name is Derek Trotter and I am the director of Derek Trotter Fine Arts & Artist Scholarships. We are dealers in fine art and ethnic art from all over the world. We run eight art galleries and two scholarship centres here in the UK. We also offer scholarship donations to aid up-and-coming new artists who may otherwise not have the financial means to be able to produce or improve upon their work. Our scholarship payments range from between $25,000 and $150,000 depending on the potential of the artist.

I am sorry but I am unable to enter into your business proposition at this time. However, if you have any contacts in your part of the world who may be artists that you think may benefit from our financial help then I would be very interested to be put in touch with them. We are especially very keen on promoting new artists with experience in wood carving and will be happy to offer a very generous $25,000 to $150,000 scholarship package to young or old artists with good potential who may benefit from our help.

If you know of an artist who could benefit from our financial help and who would be prepared to produce work for us to sell or promote then please do let me know.

Again I am sorry that I am unable to help with your proposition at this time but I wish you luck in finding somebody to help you.

Sincerely,

Derek Trotter
Director
Trotters Fine Arts

He never responded to that email. Instead, John Boko waited a few days and got back to me under his new name, and strangely enough knew all about my company even though we don't advertise anywhere!

From: John Boko
To: Derek Trotter
Date: March 3, 2006
Subject: Special appeal

Sir - I wish to write you this message after going through your company profile in the internet. I am a graphic designer and I am currently working with a group of four young men who are artistic and talented in art work.

After going through your web, I decided to write to know if your company could be helpful in the develoment of our career in art work design.

We are currently working as a team in a small village in Abidjan Ivory Coast, West Africa. At your demand, we shall be obliged to send to you some copies of our work.

Thanks and best regard
Mr John

So I make out I don't have a clue who he his and reply as usual.

From: Derek Trotter
To: John Boko
Date: March 5, 2006

Dear Mr. Boko - Thank you for your email. Please note that we are not looking for work that has already been completed. If you require a donations/scholarship payment then you need to create a new piece of work to submit to us.

Before we proceed, let me introduce myself and tell you about my company. You may already have this information but I shall repeat it to you just in case not:

My name is Derek Trotter and I am the director of Trotter Fine Arts Dealer and Art Scholarships. We are dealers in fine art and ethnic art from all over the world and we supply many business and private customers we are a multimillion dollar company. We also offer scholarship donations to aid up-and-coming new artists who may otherwise not have the financial means to be able to produce or improve their work. Our scholarship payments range from between $25,000 and $150,000 depending on the potential of the artist.

The way our programme works is that we seek out new or up-and-coming artists all over the world who may not otherwise be financially able to promote or sell their work and then we help them to realise their full potential. We aid them by presenting them with a scholarship payment ranging from $25,000 to $150,000 which again is entirely dependent on their potential, but the minimum payment we award any artist willing to supply work for us is $25,000. Presently we are seeking artists who specialise in wooden sculptures.

HOW OUR DONATION/SCHOLARSHIP PROCEDURE WORKS:

1. Before we could make any kind of monetary payment to any artist we would of course require proof of your abilities. We do not ask artists to send in prepared samples of their work because, of course, there is no way for our foundation to know if the carving is indeed the artist's own work, therefore we would require you to provide a brand new sample for us to evaluate your abilities.

2. My company will submit to you (by email attachment) a sample photograph or photographs. This may be of a person, an animal, a building or other such item. You would then be required to carve a representation of the image we send to you. Once your have completed the work it is to be sent to us for evaluation and then a donation amount

would be awarded according to your skill or potential. Our donation payments range from between a minimum of $25,000 up to $150,000.

3. On receipt of a satisfactory piece of artwork my 4 board members will then gauge the quality and therefore the size of the donation/ scholarship amount to send to you. The payment is sent by whatever means suits you best and is made within 24 hours of receiving your work.

IMPORTANT: The artwork will have to be shipped to us for evaluation. Please note that no payments whatsoever can be given in advance of receiving the artwork. It is very important that you understand this completely. Your shipping charges WILL be refunded in full. However, they will only be refunded once we receive the sample.

I hope that is clear to you, and if you are in agreement to the terms above please let me know as soon as possible and I will arrange for a sample picture to be sent to you by email attachment.

Kind regards,

Derek Trotter - Director
Trotters Fine Arts

From: John Boko
To: Derek Trotter
Date: March 7, 2006
Subject: Special appeal

Thank very much for your prompt reply and explanations. Actually, I will like to work with your company if you must remain faithful to your bond and I promise that I will give out my best as well. I will be looking forward to receive the sample.

thanks and best regard.

John

From: Derek Trotter
To: John Boko
Date: March 7, 2006

Dear Mr. John - Instructions for you or your artist can be found below. Please let me know if you have any questions.

INSTRUCTIONS FOR ARTISTS

As mentioned on my previous email to you, before we can send you the donation/scholarship payment, you will have to submit a piece of work to our requirements. This serves to ensure the work is indeed your own artists work, and also so that we can gauge the quality of your artists workmanship.

Please find attached to this email the sample images. We have taken great care to photograph the sample images from various angles so that your artist can see the sample from every possible angle and know exactly the layout of the object, which in this case is a dog and a cat sitting on a chair. The artist will be required to make a carving of this piece in the wood of his/her choice. The sample we send has been specially selected to show off various skills. Please note the following rules:

1. The carving can be any size you choose but must be a MINIMUM of 10 inches along the longest length. Obviously you will need to take into consideration the weight of the carving so that the shipping cost is not too great for you. However, remember that we will of course reimburse your shipping costs in full on receipt of the artwork. As an example to you, the normal LENGTH of this particular carving along the longest length is 14 inches.You may make yours bigger or smaller but no bigger than 20 inches along the longest length.

2. The carving can be in any type of wood that you choose, and must NOT be painted. Obviously the quality of the wood, and, if possible, a polished smooth finish will increase the chances of your donation payment being larger. Hard woods such as ebony, mahogany, walnut or cherry would be preferable woods to use however we are happy to leave the choice of wood up to your artists.

Attention to detail is important and will help my board members to judge the skill of the artists. You will see that the attached picture has many small details. Try to capture as much detail as possible.

NOTE: An exact duplicate of the sample is not required as we are presently uncertain of your skills. However, the closer your work is to the supplied sample then the higher the donation payment is likely to be. We realise of course that to exactly duplicate the carving would take an artist of exceptional skill, so we do not expect the carving to be of such detail and quality. However, the closer to the original artwork that your artist can reproduce the sample in wood - again, the larger the donation amount will be.

Please bear in mind that the artwork will have to be shipped to us for inspection before the donation payment is given, so obviously you must take into consideration the weight of the artwork so that the shipping cost is not too high for you.

You will need to ship the completed sample to us by a courier such as FedEx or DHL. All your shipping fees will be refunded in full but your fees will only be refunded AFTER we receive the completed sample. It is not our company policy to pay for work that we have not yet received.

On receipt of satisfactory artwork, we will then judge the skill level of the artist submission and will reward you with a monetary donation depending on the quality of your work. As mentioned previously, the minimum donation amount per artist is $25,000 but this can rise up to $150,000 per artist.

Note that my board members will usually pay higher amounts for carvings which have obviously taken great skill and time to produce. Donation payment are usually given within 24 hours of us receiving the sample artwork.

Should your artists be of some skill, we would then like to make arrangements to have some more work produced by you after we have received your sample. If this is the case we will, of course, pay your full fees in advance. As a guideline, for good quality carvings we tend to pay between $8,000 - $15,000 per item, so you can see that if your work is of the required quality you could benefit greatly from our partnership.

I hope that is of help to you and I look forward to hearing from you soon. If you have any further questions, please do not hesitate to ask. Please note that once you receive this email and agree to our terms your artist must have his carving ready to submit to us within 4 weeks.

Also, please let me know when you expect to have the artwork ready for shipping. In the meantime, please can you tell me what your preferred method of payment is?

Kind regards,

Derek Trotter - Director
Trotters Fine Arts

I attach 10 sample pictures of the item I want carving. A small example image is shown here. The pictures I sent to Boko were very large and detailed.

UK readers will probably recognise the pictures as the animals from the UK TV series 'Creature Comforts'. Meet Trixie and Captain Cuddlepuss. I'm sure you can work out which is which. This particular piece is from my personal collection of 'Creature Comforts' collectibles!

From: John Boko
To: Derek Trotter
Date: March 7, 2006
Subject: Re: Special appeal

Thank for your quick reply.

I have only but one questions after going through the sample you gave to me. Could the items on top of the chair be attached to it when doing the calving or could they be separated from the chair? Can they be calved saperately?

Thanks

John

From: Derek Trotter
To: John Boko
Date: March 7, 2006

Dear Mr. John - Thank you for your email and for checking with me. I see that you are very thorough with your work. This is most encouraging. The cat, dog and chair can be carved separately, if you so wish.

Kind regards,

Derek Trotter - Director
Trotters Fine Arts

10 days go by without any contact. John then gets in touch.

From: John Boko
To: Derek Trotter
Date: March 17, 2006
Subject: Re: Special appeal

Sir - I will like to know the shipping address for my sample.

Best regard.

John

I give John the details of my non-existent secretary's address.

From: Derek Trotter
To: John Boko
Date: March 17, 2006

Dear John - As you have requested, the address of our head office is below.

Please mark the package for the attention of my secretary, Miss Paula Jervis. I am usually out of the office most of the day so Miss Jervis will advise me the moment your package arrives so that I can see to your case immediately. Note that we have several different departments in our building so it is very important that you address the shipment exactly as below:

Miss Paula Jervis
D.T.F.A.
16 xxxxx Street
xxxxxxxx
xxx xxxx, United Kingdom

Please advise me of the tracking number and carrier so that I will know when to expect the delivery of the package.

Payments usually require 24 hours notice to process . However, if I am aware of the probable date of arrival, I can ensure that your particular payment is processed as soon as possible.

VERY IMPORTANT: Mark the item value as US $20 and also as a gift because if not the import tax may be very substantial in which case we will be unable to collect the package.

Please do take great care in packaging the item. In the past we have had items delivered to us that have been damaged due to poor packing.

If possible please forward us a photograph of the sample before you ship it. This is not important, but if you send us a picture before you ship it then it will help my board members prepare more efficiently for your donation/scholarship payment.

Sincerely,

Derek Trotter - Director
Trotters Fine Arts

Good news. The package is on the way.

From: John Boko
To: Derek Trotter
Date: March 21, 2006
*Subject: Re: Special app*eal

Sir - I have been able to package and send the sample today by FedEx with tracking 8564746XXXXX

I was told by fedex agent here that it ought to arrive by wednesday. They also said that the tracking will start functioning when the package has arrived on transit in France. So I believed it will start tracking before the end of today otherwise the number is ok.

I attached a photo of the sample for your view.

John

John attaches a photo of the carving. Looks promising.

From: Derek Trotter
To: John Boko
Date: March 20, 2006

Dear John - Thank you for your email. I shall check the details later this evening on the Federal Express site.

Thank you also for sending the photograph. The piece does look very nice.

Please can you send me the following information so that we can start the process of getting any payment ready?:

1. Full name and address of the person that the payment is to be made to

2. The type of payment you require (bank transfer, cheque, Western Union etc.).

Thank you for your work so far. Sincerely,

Derek Trotter - Director
Trotters Fine Arts

From: John Boko
To: Derek Trotter
Date: March 21, 2006
Subject: Re: Special appeal

sir - Thank very much for your quick reply as well. I am sory that the picture does not appear very well it is poor photographic production. As you can see, here in Africa, it is rare to get a photographer with sophiscated camera. Haa!! haa!! africa is still too behind compare to your technology over there.

Meanwhile, I will prefer to receive my payment through western union money transfer in the name of

Mr John Boko
Abidjan Cote d'Ivoire

Thanks and best regard

I'll leave John hanging on for a reply.

From: John Boko
To: Derek Trotter
Date: March 23, 2006
Subject: Re: Special appeal

Dear sir - How are you today? I hope you are alright? I'm worried why the sudden silence since yesterday. Please let me know if you are alright if so has the package arrived to you? Please send me your phone numer.

Wishing for urgent reply.

John

From: Derek Trotter
To: John Boko
Date: March 24, 2006

Dear John - I did send you a message yesterday but it appears that you did not receive it.

Anyway, the package was delayed at customs yesterday so I did not receive it. I have checked the FedEx site today and it now seems that it will be delivered at my location sometime today.

At the moment I am helping with some aerial photographs of Blackpool Tower and shall not return to my office until later this afternoon. My secretary will alert me the moment that your package arrives and then I shall contact you ASAP.

Sincerely,

Derek Trotter - Director
Trotters Fine Arts

The package arrives, but there's a problem - well, a problem for John that is!

From: Derek Trotter
To: John Boko
Date: March 25, 2006

Dear John - I think you must be having a problem with your email.

I sent an email to you yesterday to explain in full the problems but you do not seem to have been receiving my messages. It may help if you can supply me with a more reliable email address to contact you on for faster and more secure communications.

Here is the problem.

You will recall in my email to you of 7th March that the MINIMUM length for the carving must be 10 inches along the longest length. I quote from the instructions:

1. The carving can be any size you choose but must be a MINIMUM of 10 inches along the longest length. Obviously you will need to take into consideration the weight of the carving so that the shipping cost is not to great for you. However, remember that we will, of course, reimburse your shipping costs in full on receipt of the artwork. As an example to you, the normal LENGTH of this particular carving along the longest length is 14 inches. You may make yours bigger or smaller but no bigger than 20 inches along the longest length.

When the carving arrived there seemed to be a small amount of damage. However, this is not the problem. During the shipping process something must have happened to the wood (perhaps the temperature changed?) because when the carving arrived and I inspected it, the length of the carving is very small, at only five inches along the longest length. This is half the minimum size as stated to you on 7th March.

The strange thing is that the box you shipped the carving in seems to be much bigger than the carving inside, which leads me to think that there has been some kind of shrinkage due to either temperature changes or a combination of this and the type of wood used.

I will of course be most happy to supply you with photographs of the carving to show you exactly what I mean.

I do not know if the board members will be prepared to accept this. However, I cannot tell you for certain now until Monday morning (we do not work over the weekends obviously).

Please let me know if you need any photographs and also let me know if you have some explanation for what may have happened.

Sincerely,

Derek Trotter - Director
Trotters Fine Arts
www.deltrotter.co.uk

Of course, the carving didn't shrink at all. It arrived in perfect condition, but John doesn't know that. Though, oddly, it is still a couple of inches short of the minimum requirement.

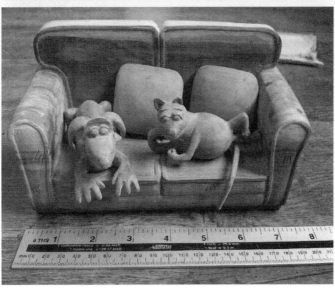

From: John Boko
To: Derek Trotter
Date: March 25, 2006
Subject: Re: Special appeal

I will wait till Monday. Bye

John

Monday arrives... and passes without my reply. Now it's Wednesday.

From: John Boko
To: Derek Trotter
Date: March 29, 2006
Subject: Re: Special appeal

Sir - I hope all is well with you. I am still waiting to hear from you as you promised in your last email. Do I have any hope as a consideration.

John

From: Derek Trotter
To: John Boko
Date: March 30, 2006

Dear John - I have attached photographs of the carving as it arrived with us. I am sorry but the board members will not accept such a small sample.

As you can see, the item is less than half the minimum size.

The submissions rules are extremely strict and we cannot change them to suit any individual person as we have to operate under strict guidelines as a UK registered scholarship centre.

You have two choices. Please let me know which of the two you want:
1. We can return this item back to you and once you have confirmed receipt of it we can refund your shipping.

2. Your artist can submit a new sample which meets the size guidelines.

I must tell you that had this item been of the required size then you artist would most definitely have been eligible for a donation payment. It is obvious that he has good skills but unfortunately there is nothing I can do unless the submission rules are observed.

If you artists wished to resubmit some work in the correct size then do let me know.

He would have to submit a different carving though. So if he wishes to resubmit then do let me know so that I can forward you some new images.

As for my contact telephone number I can be reached on (UK) +44 8707 65X XXX

Sincerely,

Derek Trotter - Director
Trotters Fine Arts

I attach three photos showing the 'shrinkage', one of which is below. Of course, the carving is fine but the images are fake. With a bit of photo manipulation I reduced the apparent size of the carvings by about three inches in length.

Looks like John is going to submit a new sample. Excellent!

From: John Boko
To: Derek Trotter
Date: March 30, 2006
Subject: Re: Special appeal

Sir - The sample instruction was misunderstood before my calving. It was after the shipment that I discoverred that the instruction reads inches while I had my measurement in cm.

However, I wish that you will still have some considerations while proper care will be taken in further edition.

I'm glad to read your message. I will prefer taking another chance. If you can send me another sample, then I will do my best to give you the required calving. I will call you later while I expect the new sample.

Thanks and God bless

John

I send more sample images to John to work from. I'm a big fan of the Commodore 64 computer, so let's see if John can make me one!

From: Derek Trotter
To: John Boko
Date: March 30, 2006

Dear John - Thank you for your telephone call a short while ago.

I have just had discussions with my art department and they have decided to send a more technical sample for your artists. It is quite obvious, even from the small carving that your artist has produced, that he has some very good skills, so they would like to test him on a more technical type of carving - in this case reproducing as near as possible a computer keyboard in wood.

We are holding a new art exhibition which we are planning for the middle of this year. The exhibition theme is 'New From Old'. Basically it is a representation of new technology created by old methods. So, for instance, we are looking for artists capable of carving or sculpting copies of modern technology, such as computer keyboards, computer mice, mobile phones etc. Judging by your artist's previous work we are quite sure that he would be of sufficient skill to reproduce such work for us.

I shall repeat the previous instructions for you again John, but this time with a few small changes. Please note that all dimensions are still though in INCHES:

INSTRUCTIONS FOR ARTISTS

Please find attached to this email the sample images. In this case they are photos of a computer/keyboard. You may recognise this machine as the Commodore 64 computer. This is what we require you to carve as a sample of your work. We have taken great care to photograph the sample from various angles so that you know exactly the layout of the object. The artist will be required to make a carving of this piece in the wood of his/her choice. The sample we send has been specially selected to show off various skills. Please note the following rules:

1. The carving can be any size you choose however the MINIMUM size must be 10 inches along the longest length. Obviously you will need to take into consideration the weight of the carving so that the shipping cost is not too great for you. However, remember that we will, of course, reimburse your shipping costs in full on receipt of the artwork. For your information, the real LENGTH of this object is 18 inches, the DEPTH is 8 inches, and the HEIGHT at the highest point is 3 inches.

2. Again the carving can be in any type of wood that you choose, and must NOT be painted. Obviously the quality of the wood and, if possible, a polished smooth finish will increase the chances of your donation payment being larger. We recommend a quality hardwood such as rosewood or similar, but of course we will leave the choice entirely to you.

3. Notice that there are letters on TOP of the keys of the keyboard as is normal. If possible, we would like you to include these letters on the carving sample. The letters must be carved into the wood, not drawn/painted. You may, however, completely ignore the other symbols that appear near the front edge of the keys. If you need a clearer explanation of this, please do contact me either by telephone or email for clarity.

NOTE: As before an exact duplicate of the sample is not required. However, the closer your work is to the supplied sample then the higher the donation payment is likely to be. We realise, of course, that to exactly duplicate the carving would take an artist of exceptional skill, so we do not expect the carving to be of such detail and quality, though the closer to the original artwork that your artist can reproduce the sample in wood, the larger the donation amount will be..

Sincerely,

Derek Trotter - Director
Trotters Fine Arts

From: John Boko
To: Derek Trotter
Date: April 1, 2006
Subject: Re: Special appeal

Sir - I want to tell you that the work is in progress and immediately it is finished, I will alert you.

Wishing you happy weekend.

John

I don't bother to reply and decide to let John get on with the work. A week later I get the expected 'give me some cash' message.

From: John Boko
To: Derek Trotter
Date: April 8, 2006
Subject: Re: Special appeal

Sir - Thanks for your letter. The work is almost finishing. I expect to ship it before wednesday next week.

If you wouldn't mind, I am presently in poor financial state as this sample will cost me higher amount due to the size this time around. as you suggested before this second sample to either send me the shipping cost of the first sample and to return of it to me, i will appreciate if you can send me the money so as to help me in shipping this new sample.

I don't think sending the sample to me will be of any use, rather if you can calculate the cost of sending it with the shipment expenses which I spent about $150 and send it to me through western union in the name of John Boko. It will help me a long well in shipping the new sample to your office.

I will appreciate your kind understanding in this regard.

Thanks and best wishes.

John

Time to frighten John into thinking he may have pushed his luck too far.

From: Derek Trotter
To: John Boko
Date: April 8, 2006

Dear John,

Two things:

1. The shipping charge would not be anywhere near $150. The last item you shipped cost less than $50 according to the Federal Express receipt I have, so where you are getting the $150 price from I do not know. Even if the second sample was three times the weight of the first sample then the shipping charge would be approximately $72. I have sent and received many many items (approximately 200+ a year) by Federal Express all over the world, so I am well aware of what the shipping charges are likely to be.

2. Again I must repeat that we do not send any money in advance of receiving a correct sample.

I am sorry, John, but as you appear not to be able to send the new sample, I will have to close your donation case.

I shall make arrangement to have your first sample returned to you by Federal Express on Monday morning.

Please inform your artist to cease all work on the second sample.

Sincerely,

Derek Trotter - Director
Trotters Fine Arts

As expected, John quickly changes his tune at the prospect of losing thousands of dollars.

From: John Boko
To: Derek Trotter
Date: April 8, 2006
Subject: Re: Special appeal

Sir - I read your message and understand that you sound bad about my request.

I want to tell you here that I was charged about 56000 cfa while $100 is about 45000 cfa. I can scan the receipt to you if you wish to see it. so I did not in anyway lie to you but I asked for only a favour. remember *according to your instruction before I shipped the item, the worth of the good is understimated to be $10 which i know you did not base your estimation on that.*

I never wished that you will sound so aggressive on this request. Nevertheless I will send the package as early promised unless you do not desire that the relationship continues.

John

That's more like it John. A couple of days later, John lets me know the second sample is nearly ready for shipping.

From: John Boko
To: Derek Trotter
Date: April 10, 2006
Subject: Re: Special appeal

Sir - I will update you asap. I never meant to delay it but due to several other works we are doing for our customers, that was why it was delayed up to this 11 days.

The finishing touches is going on and by the grace of God I will send it tomorrow.

Thanks and God bless

John

From: Derek Trotter
To: John Boko
Date: April 10, 2006

Dear John - Thank you for keeping me updated.

If possible, are you able to let me know the dimensions of the carving? A photograph before you ship it would be appreciated. However, this is not too important.

Sincerely,

Derek Trotter - Director
Trotters Fine Arts

John contacts me to let me know the carving is ready to ship.

From: John Boko
To: Derek Trotter
Date: April 11, 2006
Subject: Re: Special appeal

Sir - I have completed the sample but was unable to ship it today due to public holidays here. I don't know if it effected London too. I have attached a scan photo of the sample from three different views.

I will make sure it is sent by tomorrow and by the Grace of God it will reach you before Friday.

Thanks and best regard.

John

The photos look promising, though as an aficionado of the Commodore 64 I am slightly disappointed that the function keys are the same size as the normal keys!

From: Derek Trotter
To: John Boko
Date: April 12, 2006

Dear John - Thank you for sending me the image. The carving looks very impressive and I am sure the board members will be pleased with the result. I am sorry I was not able to speak with you on Tuesday as myself and my colleagues were at an art exhibition and did not return to the office at all until today.

Thank you for all your efforts so far and I will of course contact you immediately that the sample arrives.

Sincerely,

Derek Trotter - Director
Trotters Fine Arts

John sends me the tracking details.

From: John Boko
To: Derek Trotter
Date: April 14, 2006
Subject: Re: Special appeal

Sir - this is the tracking number:85647474XXXX

Please try and let me know when you get it as promised.

regards

John

A quick check on the Federal Express site reveals the package is indeed on its way.

The package arrives. There was a slight delay due to the UK Bank Holiday, but at least it arrived undamaged. John must have checked the FedEx site to see if it had arrived as I receive the following email from him at the same time.

The carving weighs just under 6 kilos and is larger than a real Commodore 64. It's a big beast! According to the FedEx shipping info the cost to ship this was UK £121.

From: John Boko
To: Derek Trotter
Date: April 18, 2006
Subject: Re: Special appeal

Sir - How are you today? I hope you had a nice easter holidays.

Please I want to find out if you have received the sample. From the tracking information, it is ready for clearance.

Pls update me when it is through.

Regards

John

And here are a couple of photos of the carving I received.

Time to let John know the package has arrived so that he can start to make plans to spend his money.

From: Derek Trotter
To: John Boko
Date: April 19, 2006

Dear John - Just to let you know that I have now taken possession of the package which you sent to me and I will be examining it later today, along with my board members. I shall be in touch with you very shortly.

Sincerely,

Derek Trotter - Director
Trotters Fine Arts

From: John Boko
To: Derek Trotter
Date: April 20, 2006
Subject: Re: Special appeal

Sir - How are you today? Hope there is no problem. My effort to reach you on phone was not successful uptil now. Pls update me on the statue.

Regards, John

Derek is away on business, so his brother takes over the case.

From: Rodney Trotter
To: John Boko
Date: April 20, 2006

Dear Mr. Boko - My name is Rodney Trotter and I am the brother of Derek Trotter. I am also the head of sales for our company.

My brother is unfortunately unavailable at the moment as he is attending an art exhibition in Blackpool, Germany and will not return until the end of next week. My apologies if you have tried to contact him and received no reply. His attendance was needed at very short notice.

I have been given charge of your application.

I am just letting you know that the board members are currently examining your work and I hope to be able to report back to you later today.

Yours faithfully,

Rodney Trotter - Sales
Trotters Fine Art

From: John Boko
To: Derek Trotter
Date: April 20, 2006
Subject: Re: Introduction

Dear Mr Rodney - I'm pleased over your message of introduction and update. Actually, I have tried several times without success to reach Mr Derek; both on phone and email. Nevertheless, I'm glad to hear that your company is in the process of examining my sample. I hope for better and favourable report.

Thanks and best regard as I wish that you will keep me updated until the return of your brother.

Best Regard

John

From: Rodney Trotter
To: John Boko
Date: April 21, 2006

Dear Mr. Boko - Thank you for your reply yesterday. I am sorry for the slight delay in my reply. However, I have been trying to investigate the latest 'problem' with your submission and I have had to make a few calls.

It appears that your package was infiltrated by a rodent, more accurately a hamster. We have, for discussion purposes, named it 'Bert'. Unfortunately, Bert must have been caught inside the packaging during shipping somewhere between your location and our head office.

Initial veterinary reports point to Bert being an African hamster, so I can only assume that Bert chewed his way into the packaging shortly after you posted it.

I am afraid Bert has badly damaged the carving as can be seen in the attached photographs. Bert has gnawed a hole all the way through the carving as well as creating many smaller holes around the piece.

Before my brother left for the Blackpool exhibition, he and I managed to capture Bert so that we could take him to the vets to have him examined to try to find out exactly where he came from.

To my shame I have to admit that I was extremely disappointed and indeed angry with Bert for the damage that he caused to your impressive work. I was ready to shoot him.

However, my brother is a very active animal rights campaigner and would not allow it. He made me promise to take Bert to our local hamster sanctuary which is indeed what I have done.

Under normal circumstances. items which arrive damaged are usually disqualified by us, but under these exceptional circumstances the board members have decided to try to come to some agreement on a donation payment as soon as possible.

I shall contact you again hopefully later today to let you know the outcome of this meeting.

Sincerely,

Rodney Trotter - Sales
Trotters Fine Art

I attach two photos of Bert, including one showing the damage he caused. The damage is, of course, faked. No Commodore 64 computer was harmed during this scambait.

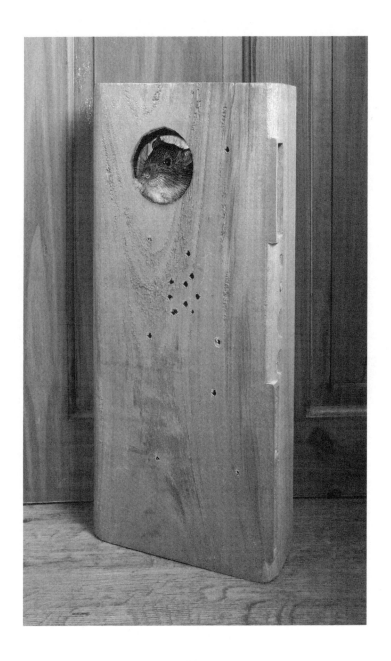

A short and sweet reply from John.

From: John Boko
To: Derek Trotter

Date: April 21, 2006
Subject: ok

OK!

And later after no reply from Rodney Trotter.

From: John Boko
To: Derek Trotter
Date: April 22, 2006
Subject: Re: ok

Sir - Still waiting

And again:

From: John Boko
To: Derek Trotter
Date: April 23, 2006
Subject: Re: ok

Till date no more comment.

John

Time for some bad news I think.

From: DCI Roy Slater - UK Police
To: John Boko
Date: April 24, 2006

Dear Sir.

Ref. Case No. #1312212/132

According to our information you have recently had dealings with a
person calling himself Derek Trotter and a company called Trotters Fine
Arts. Please can you confirm to me that this is the case?

I am afraid to have to report to you that Mr. Trotter is in fact not who he
says he is. In fact Mr. Trotter's real name is Hercules Poirot, and he is a
known art forger and fraudster who we have been closely watching for
nearly seven months. Mr. Poirot has been arrested and is currently in
our custody along with three of his accomplices.

We are seeking information on Mr. Poirot's recent dealings and also
witnesses who can provide detailed facts and dates that may help us in a
future criminal prosecution against him and his associates.

According to some of the information we have found on Mr. Poirot's
computer, you recently communicated with him and sent some pieces of
artwork in order to claim a donation payment. I am sorry to say that the
story that Mr. Poirot gave to you about providing a scholarship and
donation scheme are entirely false, and items which were sent to him by
artists have been sold on to collectors at vast profits. For instance the
first carving that you sent to him (a cat and a dog on a chair) was
recently sold to an dealer on the underground market for £32,700.
Unfortunately, the poor artists who supplied these works are not
receiving a single penny for their work. To date Mr. Poirot has
defrauded over 200 artists, none of which have received any payment
whatsoever. As far as we are able to calculate, Mr. Poirot has illegally
sold artwork to the total value of £1.7 million pounds.

The address that you were given for Trotter's Fine Arts is, in fact, that
of a post office. Mr. Poirot gave artists this address and then he
collects the items from the post office using false identification.
Trotters Fine Arts does not, and has never existed at any real location.

If you wish to pursue a claim against Mr. Poirot, then please do get back to me at this address, quoting the case reference number above. I can also pass your details onto the criminal compensations department and possibly have some compensation sent to you.

I am sorry to give you such distressing news. However, you have my personal assurance that Mr. Poirot and his cohorts will suffer the full force of the law.

In good faith.

DCI Roy Slater
UK Met Police

A day goes by. John senses he is being played for a fool, and decides to contact Derek Trotter with a proposition.

From: John Boko
To: Derek Trotter
Date: April 25, 2006
Subject: attn mr derek

Sir - How are you today? Without doubt you are doing well. I know it will be difficult for you to reply my last messages. It is really nice to know that the game was for fast lane. I'm not in any way against your plight but know that I have known what is involved, why not make it a win, win game.

Even before I got the strange mail from slatter which I send copy to you, the game was clear to me. I know he himself has his own motive which might not be far from gaining his own interest.

I thought of our correspondence and I found that that we can be useful to each other. Now, you are convinced that I can offer the product you need and I'm sure you have the moving market for the product.

Why can't we forget the donation of a thing and when I work out an art work you will sell and pay me according to price we agreed on. The amount you make out it should not be my concern but what covers my expensse with small coin will be surficient and satisfactory. Think about!

John

DCI Slater did tell John that the Trotters Fine Arts email system had been shut down...

To: John Boko
Date: April 25, 2006

*** AUTOMATED MESSAGE - PLEASE DO NOT REPLY AS YOU
WILL NOT RECEIVE A REPLY ***

Dear Sir or Madam.

This is the automated mailserver system for: **deltrotter.co.uk**
Please note that this system is now no longer in use. The account that
you are trying to contact has been closed until further notice.
Please do not reply to this automated email because you will not receive
a reply. A copy of your message has been included below.

Thank you.

*** AUTOMATED MESSAGE - PLEASE DO NOT REPLY AS YOU
WILL NOT RECEIVE A REPLY ***

>mailbot.rev.191221<

**To date there has been no word from John. Game over, I think, but
I'm keeping his file open just in case!**

Question: How do you get a scammer to burst into fits of rage and threaten you with a rather nasty demise?

Answer: You get him to board a plane and travel a few hundred miles to meet you and you don't turn up!

A scambaiting friend of mine, 'A. Skinner', is contacted by a 419 scammer posing as a doctor working on behalf of a desperate widow. As time goes by, the opportunity of causing some real scammer aggravation arises and Shiver Metimbers is called into the proceedings!

A. Skinner is playing the part of Mr. Ed Shanks. Shiver Metimbers (aka me) is playing the role of his rich partner, Max N. Paddy.

From: Mohamed Lucien
To: Ed Shanks
Date: Tue, 8 Feb 2005
Subject: MEDICAL DOCTOR FROM GHANA .....quick response needed.....

Dear Ed Shanks - My name are Dr Mohamed Lucien, a medical Doctor. and the sole proprietor of the above specialist Hospital. (SAHARA CLINIC & MATTERNITY)

I understand that through Internet is not the best way to link up with you because of the confidentiality which the transaction demands.

However, I have already sent you this same letter by post one month ago, but I am not sure if it did get to you since I have not heard from you, hence my resending it again.I have a widow here in my Clinic who is on a political Asylum in ACCRA GHANA WEST AFRICAN Refugee Camp,she has been so ill for some couple of months now.

This woman confided in me based on the free medical attention I have been giving to her and her children. She had revealed to me of her lifehistory and about her late husband who was a top military officer in one of the west African country(liberia) before his death during the civil war and the fortune she inherited from her latehusband. She has asked me to source a credible and trustworthy partner abroad who will manage her funds for investment, the sum of $40 Million us dollers which is all ready in Texas in USA with adeplomat. It was to be deliver to mr. Wood klark in califonia in USA, but due to the Earth weak that incue in Indonesia,unfortunately, mr Wood Klark travelled there for a business era, and he was dealth by the accedent of the Earth weak.

So Mr. Ed Shark, I please you in the Name of ALLAH ,for you to represnt the post of MR WOOD KLARK TO ME WITHthe deplomat in Texas to Clear the consignments from the deplomat ,and you must not allow him to know that the consignment content ok, for him not to raise his eye brown on you and your family untill the Widow and her daughter come over to me you and your family.

you for this venture and I believe you will be in the position to assist in managing this large sum in a profitable venture and also to help create a safe heaven for her and her children by making a residence arrangement for them in your country. After she had disclosed this information to me, I saw the reason to request from her to all the documents relating to this deposit of which she did, now I have the documents covering the deposited in a package consignment which I will not hesitate to fax to you the copies as a prove for your confirmation as soon as i receive your response via email. I am obliged to assist this lady knowing too well that she has a limited knowledge in the business world and as such she can not manage this funds herself in Africa inorder to avoid any trace of her by the government, I will need from you a mutural understanding and then we shall make plans on how the funds would be secured into an account in your name, after which you will arrange and travel immediately to meet with the deplomat for clearing.This amount is contained in a sealed trunk box and it is registered and declared as containing family treasures and

39

preciouse items, so even as I am writing you now the security company and it's Agent is not aware that there is cash money in the trunk box, let me assure you that this transaction is 100% hitch and risk free, from my discussion with her, she has agreed to give you a reasonable amount of percentage for your involvement in this and this has to be discussed upon the receipt of your quick response.

Thanks and God bless for your understanding,

Best regards,
Dr.Mohamed Lucien.
00233 244 937082

A. Skinner, taking on the role of Ed Shanks, steps in to save the day.

From: Ed Shanks
To: Mohamed Lucien
Date: 9th Feb 2005

Dear Sir - Of course I would be willing to help in this situation. I am aware of the unfortunate circumcision in Indonesia.

Sincerely,

Ed Shanks

From: Mohamed Lucien
To: Ed Shanks
Date: 9th Feb 2005
Subject: THANK YOU FOR YOUR RESPONSE

SAHARA CLINIC & MATTERNITY,
P.O.BOX 333, SAVANA MARKET
ROAD ,ACCRA GHANA.
00233 244 937082

DEAR MR.ED SHANKS - THANKS FOR RESPOND AND YOUR CONCERN,OF BEEN TO HELP THE WIDOW TO BE HER BENEFICIARY SINCE HER FIRST BENEFICIARY HAS BEING KILLED AT INDONESIA BY THE EARTH WEACK INCIDENT A MONTH AGO.

THE WIDOW CAME TO THE CLINIC TODAY AND SHE WAS VERY WORRIED ABOUT HER CONSIGNMENTS NOT TO BE RETURN TO AFRICA BECAUSE OF DELAY.

BUT I EXPLAIN TO HER AND ADVICE HER THAT I HAVE HEARD FROM YOU, THAT YOU SAID YOU WILL MAKE ARRANGEMANT TO HELP HER TO MEET WITH THE DIPLOMAT AND CLEAR THE CONSIGNMENTS FROM THEM.

AFTER I HAVE EXPLAIN SHE WAS VERY HAPPY AND SAID SHE WILL KEEP ASIDE FEAR PERCENTAGE FOR YOU AFTER YOU HAVE RECEIVED THEM TO YOU HOUSE AND YOU SHOULD SEEK FOR A LIVING HOUSE TO BUY WHEN SHE HAS ARRIVED TO YOU WITH HER DAUGHTER TO USA.

BUT SHE SEE REASON WHY SHE ASK ME TO TELL YOU THAT YOU SHOULD TRY YOUR POSSIBLE BEST TO SEND YOUR FIRST PAGE OF YOUR INTERNATIONAL PASSPORT OR YOUR DRIVING LICIENCE FOR HER TO KNOW WHOM SHE IS DEALING WITH MORE BETTER.

HELLO MR. ED SHANKS, I WILL ADVICE YOU RIGHT NOW FOR YOU TO SEND YOUR DATA SUCH AS YOUR

(1) YOUR HOUSE ADDRESS
(2) PHONE NUMBER AND FAX
(3) YOUR COMPANY ADDRESS.
(4) YOUR PICTURE

THIS 4 INFORMATIONS WILL ENABLE THE DEPLOMAT TO ABLE TO DELIVER THE CONSIGNMENT TO YOU AT YOUR DOOR STEP OR YOUR HOUSE.IMMEDIATELY YOU SEND THE INFORMATION. THEN I CAN SEND IT TO THE DEPLOMAT BOARD IN TEXAS TO DELIVER THE CONSIGNMENTS TO YOU AT YOUR DOOR STEP AS I HAVE SAID.

YOU SHOULD SEND THEM VERY FAST FOR THEM TO MEET WITH YOU, BECAUSE THE WIDOW WILL NOT BE HAPPY IF THE CONSIGNMENTS RETURN HERE IN AFRICA BECAUSE OF THE REASONS I TOLD YOU IN MY FIRST MAIL TO YOU. IF POSIBLE SEE BACK PAGE AGAIN.

CALL ME AS SOON YOU RECEIVED THIS MAIL. I AM DR. MOHAMED LUCIEN THE SOLE PROPRIETOR OF THE ABOVE CLINIC 00233 244 937082.

URGENT REPLY NEEDED .

THANKS. ALLAH BLESS YOU

DR. MOHAMED LUCIEN

From: Ed Shanks
To: Mohamed Lucien
Date: 10th Feb 2005

Dear Sir - Here is the information attached:
404 Second Avenue West
Seattle, Washington 98119
Telephone and Fax: 206-350-6523

Shanks

From: Mohamed Lucien
To: Ed Shanks
Date: 10th Feb 2005
Subject: Re: THANK YOU FOR YOUR RESPONSE

DEAR SHANKS

WHAT IS THE PROBLEM WITH YOUR PHONE???? YOU GAVE ME A NEW NUMBER TODAY AND I CALL YOU BUT SOME ONE TOLD ME THAT IT IS A WRONG NUMBER WHY????????.

YOU HAVE TO BE SERIOUS WITH THIS REGARD AND COMPOSE YOUR SELF AND SEND THE ORIGINAL NUMBER SO THAT I CAN REACH YOU EVEN THE DEPLOMAT OK. BECAUSE I WILL BE VERY BITTER WITH YOU IF I SEE THAT THE DEPLOMAT RETURN THE CONSIGNMENT TO AFRICA FOR THE SAKE OF NO RECIPENT OR DELAY.

PLEASE TELL ME NOW THAT YOU ARE NOT READY TO HELP THE WIDOW, BECAUSE I CAN NOT UNDERSTAND YOU NO MORE. YOU LIE TO ME THAT YOU CALL MY HOT LINE NUMBER BUT IT WAS NOT GOING THROUGH .

CALL MY NUMBER AGAIN 00233 244 937082. I HAVE NO TIME TO CRAKE A JOKE WITH YOU NOW BECAUSE THERE IS NO TIME TO WASTE AFTER ALL THE DELAY.

DO YOU SUGGEST THAT I SHOULD LOOK FOR ANOTHER BENEFICIARY WHO CAN HELP THE WIDOW???? THERE IN USA.

I DONT WANT THE WIDOW CONSIGNMENT TO GET LOST, THAT WAS WHY I SEEK FOR YOUR ASSISTANT OK.

IF YOU KNOW YOU CANT CALL ME THEN YOU ARE NOT READY TO HELP HER.

CALL ME NOW SO THAT THE DEPLOMAT CAN UPDATE YOU .

I AM DOING ALL THIS BECAUSE I GARANTEE THE WIDOW THAT I HAVE A RELIABLE FRIEND WHO CAN HELP HER THERE WHICH IS YOU. CALL ME AND GIVE YOUR NUMBER AGAIN WHICH IS THE CORRECT ONE.

THERE IS NO TIME TO WASTE BECAUSE THE CONSIGNMENT IS ABOUT TO COME BACK TO AFRICA.

THANKS

DR MOHAMED LUCIEN.

And another plea.

From: Mohamed Lucien
To: Ed Shanks
Date: 10th Feb 2005
Subject: PLEASE RESPOND

SAHARA CLINIC & MATTERNITY,
P.O.BOX 333, SAVANA MARKET
ROAD ,ACCRA GHANA.
00233 244 937082
DEAR MR. SHANKS,

I WAS IN RECEPIENT OF YOUR DATAS, AND BE ADVICE THAT I HAVE FORWARD YOUR INFORMATINS TO THE DEPLOMAT ,IN REGARD OF THE DELIVERY OF THE CONSIGNMENT TO YOU. AND WITH THIS DATA I HAVE FROM YOU I KNOW YOU CAN NEVER RUN AWAY WITH THIS MONEY. I HAVE BEING TRYING TO CALL YOU ALL DAY ON THE SAME PHONE AS YESTERDAY BUT IT HAS AN ANSWERING MACHINE, WHY ????. WHEN YOU KNOW THAT YOU HAVE A VERY IMPORTANT BUSINESS WITH ME.

ALSO I ASKED YOU TO CALL ME, BUT YOU FAILED. WHY????

YOU HAVE TO PREPARE NOW BECAUSE THE DEPLOMAT WILL CALL YOU AND YOU HAVE TO ARRANGE ON HOW THINGS WILL

GO VERY SMOOTHLY TO MAKE SURE YOU RECEIVED THE CONSIGNMENT, YOU HAVE TO KEEP THE SECRET TO THE DEPLOMAT BECAUSE THEY DO NOT KNOW THE CONTENT OF THE TRUNK BOX (CONSIGNMENT).

SO OPEN YOU PHONE NOW BECAUSE YOU HAVE TO EXPECT THE CALL OF THE DEPLOMAT FROM TEXAS OK, AND YOU HAVE TO CALL ME ALSO TO UPDATE ME THAT YOU HAVE OPEN YOU PHONE SO THAT I CAN STILL TALK WITH YOU.

I HAVE SHOWN YOUR PICTURE TO THE WIDOW THIS MORNING WHEN SHE CAME FROM THE REFUGEE CAMP FOR TREATMENT, AND SHE WAS VERY HAPPY TO SEE YOU FOR THE FIRST TIME.

TRY AND OPEN YOUR PHONE AND MEET WITH THE DEPLOMAT NOW BECAUSE I WILL NOT BE HAPPY IF THE CONSIGNMENT SHOULD BE RETURN BACK TO AFRICA.

CALL ME IMMEDIATELY .

THANKS
DR. MOHAMED.

From: Ed Shanks
To: Mohamed Lucien
Date: 11th Feb 2005

Dear Dr. - Try me at the other number which is 254-741-XXXX. I can't get thru on your number. Or say the pass phrase which is my church name of the Church of the Holy Mackerel.

Ed Shanks

Mohammed tries to call Ed Shank on the new number he has been given - it's a bad number though! He sends an abusive email to Ed Shanks who is not all all impressed.

From: Ed Shanks
To: Mohamed Lucien
Date: 11th Feb 2005

Dear Mo - You are a disgrace speaking to me that way. I accidentally gave you the wrong number. The correct one is 254-741-XXXX.

Ed Shanks

From: Mohamed Lucien
To: Ed Shanks
Date: 11th Feb 2005
Subject: I AM SORRY

SAHARA CLINIC & MATTERNITY,
P.O.BOX 333, SAVANA MARKET
ROAD. ACCRA GHANA.
00233 244 937082

DEAR MR. SHANKS - I AM VERY SORRY TO USE THAT ARSH
WORDS ON YOU, BE INFORM THAT I CALL YOU WITH THE
NUMBER TODAY BUT UNFORTUNATELY NO BODY PICK THE
CALL UP.

PLEASE I HAVE SEND THE NEW NUMBER TO THE DEPLOMAT
AGAIN, AND I THING THAT BY THE GRACE OF GOD, THEY WILL
CALL YOU TODAY TO DELIVER THE CONSIGNMENT TO YOU OK.

PLEASE FORGIVE ME AND LETS BE ONE AS BEFORE. HELP
THE WIDOW AS YOU HAVE PROMISE EARLIER, SHE IS EVEN
ARRANGING ON HOW SHE WILL COME OVER VERY SOON YOU
CLEAR THE CONSIGNMENT TO YOU HOUSE. PLEASE KEEP THE
SECRET TO THE DEPLOMAT THAT THE CONTENT IS NOT
MONEY SO THAT THEY MAKE NOT RAISE EYE BROWN ON
YOU OK.

I WILL CALL YOU AGAIN IF YOU HAVE MEET WITH THE DEPLOMAT.
THANKS KEEP ON UPDATING ME...

BEST REGARD

DOCTOR MOHAMED LUCIEN

From: Ed Shanks
To: Mohamed Lucien
Date: 11th Feb 2005

Dear Mo - I should be in most of the day. Please call.

Ed Shanks

Mohamed's scamming partner, Peter Corey, telephones and explains that there is a 'fee' necessary to pay before the consignment can be cleared.

From: Peter Corey
To: Ed Shanks
Date: 11th Feb 2005
Subject: PAYMENT INSTRUCTIONS

Dear Shanks - As discussed on phone awhile ago, i would need the sum of $7,500 in order for me to get your consignment cleared so as to come immediately to make delivery to you.

Please, i would advise you send the above amount to me by western union money transfer to the following names:

1) Mr.Peter Corey

address: Houston Texas.
amount to be sent: : $2500

2) Mr.Scott Lake

address: Houston Texas.
amount to be sent: : $2500

3) Mr.Tony Andrew

address: Houston Texas.
amount to be sent: : $2500

As soon as the money is collected i'll proceed to get your consignment cleared and come to you for the delivery.

Please, let me know the nearest airport to you so that i'll route my ticket there.

You can give me a call on my phone number: 1-713-478-9116 as soon as you receive this mail.

Regards,

Peter

Mohamed checks to see if the payment has been sent yet.

From: Mohamed Lucien
To: Ed Shanks
Date: 12th Feb 2005
Subject: HAS THE MONEY BEEN SENT???

SAHARA CLINIC & MATTERNITY,
P.O.BOX 333, SAVANA MARKET
ROAD. ACCRA GHANA.
00233 244 937082

DEAR SHANKS,

HAVE YOU HEARED FROM THE DEPLOMAT ? PLEASE KEEP ME UPDATED .

YOU HAVE TO SEND THE $7,500.00 TO THE DEPLOMAT MR PETER COREY AND CLAER THE CONSIGNMENT TO YOUR HOUSE OK

THANKS
DOCTOR MOHAMED LUCIEN.

From: Ed Shanks
To: Mohamed Lucien
Date: 12th Feb 2005

Dear Mo - I have talked to Peter Corey. He wants me to send money to him and 2 others named Mr. Scott Lake and Mr. Tony Andrew at $2,500 each.

I will be away from home this weekend, but am not sure if I should send the cash. I would feel better meeting them somewhere and handing it over.

Then Peter Corey could send me the consignment later.

Sincerely,

Ed Shanks

From: Mohamed Lucien
To: Ed Shanks
Date: 13th Feb 2005
Subject: DO NOT DELAY

DEAR SHANKS - YOU CAN GO ON, ON WHAT SO EVER YOU
WANT BY SENDING THE MONEY OR FEELING TO MEET THEM
TO HAND OVER THE CASH TO THEM, ALL I WANT, IS YOU TO
RECEIVE THE CONSIGNMENT TO YOUR HOUSE THEN THE
WIDOW CAN START READY TO COME OVER TO MEET YOU OK.
I WILL ADVICE YOU TO SEND THE MONEY IF POSSIBLE BECAUSE OF
SECURITY REASON.

I PRAY TO GOD TO GIVE YOU MORE KNOWLEDGE TO TAKE
CARE OF THE MONEY UNTIL THE WIDOW COME.

PLEASE DONT DELAY THE PAYMENT BECAUSE IT MAY CAUSE
THE RETURN OF THE CONSIGNMENT TO AFRICA.

PLEASE TAKE CARE AND BE HUMBLE TO THEM SO THAT THEY
CAN TAKE THING LIKELY WITH YOU.

THANKS

DR. MOHAMED

At this point ,we will have to skip a few emails as they were accidentally lost, but they are not integral to the correspondence.

Mohammed informs Ed Shanks that the poor widow he represents is suffering and near death. Money is her only salvation!

From: Ed Shanks
To: Mohamed Lucien
Date: 17th Feb 2005

Dear Mo - I am a kind man. Please do not tell me of the widow's suffering as it makes me sad. I am torn between not doing the deal, going to Houston, or having the meeting with the diplomat somewhere else. Let me pray on it.

Ed Shanks

Even meeting the diplomat elsewhere, it seems, has a price tag.

From: Mohamed Lucien
To: Ed Shanks
Date: 17th Feb 2005
Subject: URGENT

DEAR SHANKS - I RECIEVED YOUR EMAIL TODAY AND I WLL
ADVICE YOU NOW THAT I CAN NOT MAKE THE CHANGE OF
THE AGREEMENT WITH OUT THE $2700 AT THE THE SECURITY
COMPANY OFFICE .

THE COMPANY WRITE ME A LETTER TODAY VIA MY HOSPITAL
EMAIL ADDRESS TO THE WIDOW, THAT HER CONSIGNMENT
WILL BE LEAVING TEXAS AFTER SOME DAYS FROM NOW TO
LONDON SINE NO BENEFICIARY TO CLEAR THE FEE OF
CLEARANCE, THAT TEXAS IS NOT SECURE ENOUGH FOR THE
ABORDING CAGO, THAT ANY CONSIGNMENT THAT ARE IN
TEXAS WILL BE CARRY TO LONDON TO THE HEAD BRANCH IN
LONDON.

MR. SHANKS , I AM VERY SORRY FOR THE DELAY FROM YOUR
SIDE. I WILL HEAR FROM YOU IF YOU CAN SEND THE MONEY
BEFORE THE CONSIGNMENT TO TO LONDON.

THE SECURITY STATED IN THE LETTER TO THE WIDOW THAT
IF THE CONSIGNMENT SHOULD LEAVED TO LONDON ,ANY
BENEFICIARY TO CLEAR IT WILL PAY THE SUM OF $11,000
BEFORE THEY CAN GIVE OUT THE CONSIGNMENT TO HE OR
SHE, BUT IT ALSO STATED THAT THERE IS NO SENDING OF
LEARANCE FEE BUT HAND TO HAND PAYMENT, WHEN I READ
THIS LETTER I REMMBER THAT YOU SAID YOU LIKE THAT,
HENCE I WILL WANT TO KNOW IF YOU CAN TRAVELL TO
LONDON TO CLEAR IT TO USA AS WELL.

THE WIDOW FEELED SO PITY BECAUSE HER CONSIGNMENT
IS GETTING DELAY WHICH SHE WAS AFRAID FOR THE
CLEARANCE FEE IS GETTING HIGH AS THE DELAY ARE
INCURING FROM HER SIDE,

I WILL ADVICE YOU AS THE DOCTOR FOR YOU TO CHOSE ONE
OF THE ALTARNATIVE IF YOU CAN SEND THGE MONEY, OR YOU
CAN PAY FOR THE CHANGE OF THE AGREEMENT OR YOU CAN
GO TO LONDON TO MEET WITH THE DIPLOMAT TO PAY THEM
HAND TO HAND AS YOU WANT EARLIER.

SINCE WE HAVE NO CHANCE NO MORE I AM NOWA FRAID OF THE WHOLE THINGS THAT IS HAPPENING TO THE WIDOW IF I SHOULD REMMBER THE DEATH OF HER LATE HUSBAND, WHO WAS A TOP MILITARY MAN IN LIBERIA, WEST AFRICA,

SHE CRIED TODAY WHEN SHE WAS THING ABOUT THE HER CONSIGNMENT. SHE REFUSE TO TAKE TREATMENT AND SOME MEDICINE I GAVE TO HER .

MR SHANKS TRY TO HELP THE WIDOW OUT OF THIS PROBLEM VICTIM, IF THIS CONTINUE IT MAY CAUSE HER EARLY DEATH AS A RESULT OF HIGH BLOOD PRESSURE.

I WILL TOP FROM HERE TO HEAR FOR YOUR CO OPERATION AND YOUR KINDLY RESPONSE TO HELP AS WELL.

THANKS

DOCTOR MOHAMED LUCIEN.

At this point scambaiter A. Skinner contacted me, Shiver Metimbers, to tell me that there was a possibility of baiting a scammer based in London. Of course I was definitely up for that, and told A. Skinner to pass on to Mohamed the information that he had a partner in the UK who was only too happy to hand over $11,000 in cash!

From: Ed Shanks
To: Mohamed Lucien
Date: 19th Feb 2005

Dear Dr. Mo - This news about the widow's health has me in a fit of discomfort. There is no way I can travel to London due to my cashflow and other various reasons.

However, I have a very good friend in Glasgow, Scotland by the name of Mr. Max N. Paddy. This gentleman and I have been business partners and friends for years. I spoke with him this weekend and he would be willing to make the payment of $11,000 USD on my behalf. He will pay it in person and in cash if you will have a representative come to Glasgow to meet him there. London is only a 5 hour train journey from Glasgow.

Mr. Paddy N. Max can be reached at +44 8707 659 XXX or by email on max@the-dark-side.co.uk. Max is a director of a large communications company in the UK called Dark Side Communications.

Sincerely,

Ed Shanks

Mohamed gives us an update on the widow's health problems, and also agrees to accept payment in the UK. Looks like the game is on!

From: Mohamed Lucien
To: Ed Shanks
Date: 20th Feb 2005
Subject: AGREEMENT CHANGES

Dear Shanks - The widow was rushed down to my clinic from the refugee camp yesterday, Because she refused to eat and take her drugs i gave her, she is about to die but only GOD who save her yesterday.

But now she was admitted in the clinic, i gave her some drips to give her strengt. Be advice that she is geeting better. It was so disapointed that you were unable to pay the money to the diplomat in USA. Since you have a partner in LONDON who is realiable like you, it will be better .

I will be happy very well since he is ready to clear the consignment. Since you dont have chance to go to LONDON, It will be better for your partner to go and PAY THE $11,000 to the doplomat head branch office in london. give me your partner email, name and phone number so that i can contact him immediately as well.

i agree with your suggestion ok. i am happy , let try all our best to help the widow ok. i want you to call me and advice the widow not to worried please, she think too much, advice her to take her drugs and try to eat ok.

when i hear from you can can call the dilomat to tell me the time the conignment will leaved for london to the head branch office of the security company as you know.

thanks
DOCTOR MOHAMED.
SAHARA CLINIC & MATTERNITY,
GHANA ACCRA

Mohamed attempts to persuade Max N. Paddy to come to London with the cash.

Date: 21st Feb 2005 - Mohamed calls Max N. Paddy.

Max N. Paddy:	Hello.
Mohamed:	Hello and good afternoon. Could I speak to Max N. Paddy please?
Max N. Paddy:	Yes this is Max Paddy speaking. Who is calling please?
Mohamed:	Yes, yes. This is Dr. Mohamed Lucien. How are you?
Max N. Paddy:	Oh hello doctor. Thank you for your call. What can I do for you?
Mohamed:	Oh very good. Eh, Mr. Shanks has told me that you are not ready to receive the consignment in London but I am afraid I have made all arrangements and the diplomat cannot come to Scotland. Can you meet him in London and give him the $11,000 and collect the consignment from him?
Max N. Paddy:	No I'm afraid that will be impossible. You will have to send a representative to Scotland to collect the money or else I cannot make the payment.
Mohamed:	You cannot come to London to make the payment?
Max N. Paddy:	No. As has already been explained to you, the money must be collected from me at my location.
Mohamed:	Listen, listen, listen. When the diplomat arrives in London I will tell him to give you a call so that you can discuss this with him.
Max N. Paddy:	That's fine. So that we are not wasting each other's time I want to make it perfectly clear that if the cash cannot be collected from me in person then I will not be paying it. If the diplomat cannot come to Scotland then tell him not to bother coming to the UK at all.
Mohamed:	OK I will see what I can do on my own end. How am I not sure that you do not have a different motive for wanting the diplomat to come to Scotland?

Max N. Paddy:	How do I know you are not going to steal my money?
Mohamed:	(laughing) OK! Let's keep our fingers crossed and I will try to make the necessary arangements. The widow is relying on me.
Max N. Paddy:	OK.
Mohamed:	Now I want you to immediately send me a scan of your international passport so that you can identify yourself fully to me.
Max N. Paddy:	No problem. I will do that as soon as you send me your own identification.
Mohamed:	(getting angry) Listen to me. Why should I be sending you... what do you want from me? What identification you want? Why? Listen to me; I am only trying to assist... I should be scared of you because... the widow is...
Max N. Paddy:	(interrupting) Just one moment. One moment, one moment, one moment. Who is making the $11,000 payment here?
Mohamed:	You are making the payment but...
Max N. Paddy:	(interrupting) Yes I am making the payment. I am the one giving you many thousands of dollars. I am the one who should be concerned about security, not you.
Mohamed:	(shouting!) WHAT ABOUT... WHAT ABOUT THE WIDOW'S MONEY? WE ARE TALKING ABOUT MILLIONS OF DOLLARS!
Max N. Paddy:	I don't care about the widow's money. I am not going to get any of that money. This deal has nothing to do with me. I am doing a favour for my good friend Mr. Shanks and I am not getting any money out of this deal.
Mohamed:	(calming down now) OK... OK. Now I understand. There is no problem. I will see what the diplomat can do. I will tell him...
Max N. Paddy:	OK Mr. Mohamed. I am going to have to go now as I am wanted in a meeting. Goodbye.
Mohamed:	OK. Goodbye.

Mohamed is a little disappointed that I cannot make the trip to London, and emails Ed Shanks to tell him.

From: Mohamed Lucien
To: Ed Shanks
Date: 21st Feb 2005
Subject: PLEASE SPEAK WITH PADDY

SAHARA CLINIC &MATTERNITY,
P.O.BOX 333,SAVANA MARKET ROAD,
ACCRA GHANA. TELL.+233 244 937082.

21 FEBUARY 2005.

DEAR SHANKS, THANKS FOR YOUR KINDLY CONCERNED. I WAS
SO GRAETFULL WITH YOUR ASSISTANT, I HAVE CALL MR. MAX
N. PADDY TODAY. I DISCUSS WITH ME VERY WELL, HE WAS SO
KIND LIKE YOU, BUT HE IS NOT IN LONDON. THAT IS THE ONLY
PROBLEM, HE PROMISE TO CLEAR THE CONSIGNMENT FROM
THE DIPLOMAT. BUT HE TOLD ME THAT HE CAN NOT GO TO
LONDON AS WELL, REMMEBER THAT YOU WERE AWARE OF
THE AGREEMENT WITH THE WIDOW AND THE COMPANY. IT
DOSE NOT STATED THAT THE CONSIGNMENT WILL GO TO ANY
COUNTRY ACCEPT LONDON, THE BRANCE OFFICE.

TRY AND TALK TO YOUR PARTNER TO TRAVEL TO THE SECURITY
COMPANT BRANCH OFFICE IN LONDON. SINCE IT IS NOT
WRITTEN, IT CAN NOT BE CARRY TO ANY OTHER COUNTRY
SINCE NO ONE CAN CLEAR IT FROM USA. I DONT KNOW HOW
TO EXPAIN TO THE WIDOW NOT BECAUSE SHE IS UNCONCIOUS.

TELL YOUR FRIEND TO TRAVELL TO LONDON IMMEDIATELY.
FEARLY PERCNTAGE WILL BE GIVEN TO HIM, I HAVE NO BODY
IN LONDON EVEN THE WIDOW, SHE ONLY WANT TO INVEST IN
USA NOT LONDON, SHE WILL WANT YOU TO COME TO LONDON
AND CARRY IT BACK TO USA, PLEASE CONTACT YOUR FRIEND
TO TRY ALL PASSIBLE BEST TO COME TO LONDON, TELL HIM
THE CONDITION OF THE WIDOW AS YOU KNOW, THIS IS HER
LIFE, HELP HER, MAKE HER DREAM COME TRUE, SHE WILL
COME OVER TO MEET THE SPECIALIST DOCTOR IN USA.

NEVER ALLOW THE WIDOW TO DIE AND LOST HER CONSIGNMENT
FOR NOT THING SAKE. I WHICH I CAN HELP I WOULD HAVE
TRY, BUT NO FRIEND I HAVE IN LONDON. THE CONSIGNMENT
WILL BE DELIVER TO HIM WHEN HE COME TO LONDON BY
MICHAEL DANNIS

THANKS

DOCTOR MOHAMED.

From: Ed Shanks
To: Mohamed Lucien
Date: 22nd Feb 2005

Dear Dr. Mo - Well, this is a fine state of affairs. Here the widow is suffering and unconscious with her trunk boxes in London and no one to claim them.

As I explained earlier, all I want to do is make sure the security company is paid NOW for the widow. That is what Mr. Max Paddy agreed to do for me. I did NOT expect the diplomat to deliver the trunk box. I will take care of receiving the box later through some other form of shipment to the USA. I simply want the diplomat to be paid before someone else lays claim to the box.

Mr. Max Paddy has the cash ($11,000 which can be converted to British Sterling if you like), but it will be necessary for someone to meet him in Glasgow, Scotland. That is a simple task that diplomats do all the time. It would be the same thing if Mr. Max Paddy came to London to meet Mr. Michael Dannis or an associate. Please get this done as quickly as possible so we can quit wasting time.

Sincerely,

Ed Shanks

From: Mohamed Lucien
To: Ed Shanks
Date: 22nd Feb 2005
Subject: i will try to get the diplomat to glasgow

Sahara clinic & Matternity,
P.o.Box 333. Savana Market
road, Accra Ghana.
Tell : +233 244 937082
22 Febuary 2005.

Dear Shanks - I received your email and i quit understand the basic fat. As you know the consignment is now in london, I have try all my possible best to explain to the diplomat office in london, that they should give me the last favour by still try again to take the consign to scotland, in Glasgow. That Mr. Max N. Paddy, will be the recipient this time, and he will help the Widow to pay the clearance fee ($11,000) only.

The diplomat office has agreed to to delived the consignment to scotland, in Glasgow, to Mr. Max N .Paddy, and the deplomat who will deliverd the consignment is MICHAEL DANNIS.

You have to contact him immediately : Tell +447876467826 Fax: +447092860142

Name : MICHAEL DANNIS.

The consignment will be carried to Mr. max N. Paddy immediately you have call him for details to mandate you what day he will arried at scotland in Glasgow.

Please you have to keep the secret to the deplomat because he do not know the content of the trunk box. because i dont want any diplomat to raise eye brown on you for the widow consignment ok.

Call me immediately when you have hear from the diplomat traveling to scotland with the consignment as you know. It is only $11,000 you have to pay him for the clearance. immediately you received the consignment, you have to make special arrangement to ship the consignment to USA, BEFORE the widow will come over the investment to seek for a specialist doctor for her health. fairly percentage will be given to you after the clearance has been done .

May almighty Allah be with you for the consigned and all the enfort done to not allow the widow die on unconcious and not allowing her consignment get lost in london. Get back to me when you have concluded with MICHAEL DANNIS.

Thanks
Doctor mohamed Lucien.

From: Ed Shanks
To: Mohamed Lucien
Date: 22nd Feb 2005

Dear Dr. Mo - This is excellent news for all of us, the widow especially. Please advise Mr. Dannis that a meeting on Friday or Saturday would be most convenient with Mr. Max N. Paddy. Have diplomat Dannis contact Mr. Paddy by telephone or email to work out the details. You have both his telephone and email address. Certainly the contents of the box will NOT be revealed to the diplomat.

Sincerely,

Ed Shanks

Are you all sitting comfortably? We're now going into a long series of telephone calls and very little in the way of emails!

WARNING: Some of the language in the latter part of these calls is of a very adult nature. PLEASE do not read too much further on if you are easily offended, though I hasten to add I , Max N. Paddy, behave impeccably!

Shortly after mailing Ed Shanks, Mohamed gives Max N. Paddy a call to try to worm his way out of sending a diplomat to Scotland. That just isn't gonna happen Mo!

Date: 22nd Feb 2005 - Mohamed calls Max N. Paddy.

Mohamed:	Hello?
Max N. Paddy:	Good morning.
Mohamed:	Hello, good morning is that Max N. Paddy?
Max N. Paddy:	Yes it is.
Mohamed:	Oh Max N. Paddy, how are you?
Max N. Paddy:	I am fine thank you. What can I do for you?
Mohamed:	I am calling to explain in detail, what exactly and where exactly the diplomat is going to deliver.
Max N. Paddy:	Right. As long as he is going to deliver in Scotland then there isn't going to be a problem.
Mohamed:	No listen to me. I am afraid he cannot go, he cannot come to Scotland, he...
Max N. Paddy:	(interrupting) OK, OK, OK, OK, in that case we have no deal.
Mohamed:	Do you know about Blackpool? Is Blackpool close to Scotland?
Max N. Paddy:	No. Not it is not.
Mohamed:	It is not?
Max N. Paddy:	No. It is halfway.
Mohamed:	Halfway?

Max N. Paddy:	Yes.
Mohamed:	Oh what a pity because your partner just sent me an email pleading that the diplomat Michael Dannis should deliver to you in Scotland but I'm afraid the diplomat say he cannot go there because he had a bitter experience before in Scotland.
Max N. Paddy:	In that case I will inform Mr. Shanks that he will have to find somebody else to help him because I will not go to Blackpool.
Mohamed:	You will not go to Blackpool?
Max N. Paddy:	No.
Mohamed:	Oh! In that case please inform your partner of the situation. I don't know. I don't know because the consignment... the consignment is presently in London. It is presently in London.
Max N. Paddy:	Yes I know, you keep telling me.
Mohamed:	OK. You can call me later after you have had a discussion with your partner.
Max N. Paddy:	Why do I need to call you? I have already told you if somebody cannot come to Scotland then I cannot pay you the money, it is that simple.
Mohamed:	OK, OK there is no problem, bye bye.
Max N. Paddy:	Bye.

The 'diplomat' Michael Dannis calls just a few short minutes later. What a coincidence! Michael doesn't fancy the trip.

Date: 23rd Feb 2005 - Michael Dannis calls Max N. Paddy:

Max N. Paddy:	Good afternoon. Max N. Paddy speaking. Who is calling please?
Michael:	Hello Mr. Paddy this is diplomat Mr. Dannis.
Max N. Paddy:	Hello Mr. Dannis. I have been expecting your call.
Michael:	I... You in Scotland?
Max N. Paddy:	Yes, that is correct.
Michael:	I have arrived in London and I will like to come

	to you but I am having to pay some fees to UK customs.
Max N. Paddy:	That's no problem. I can reimburse any expenses once you get here.
Michael:	You wanna come to London?
Max N. Paddy:	No. I will pay you the money when you come to meet with me in Scotland.
Michael:	No, but you must pay me the custom fee now before I come beca-
Max N. Paddy:	(interrupting) No. I am not going to pay any fees in advance of the meeting in Scotland. If you cannot get to Scotland then please get yourself back on the plane and...
Michael:	(interrupting) No, no, basically I have to give the payment to customs before I can proceed.
Max N. Paddy:	I am not going to pay the fees in advance, I am going to pay the fee in person. If I cannot pay the fee in person then I am n....
Michael:	(interrupting) OK why not come to London and -
Max N. Paddy:	(interrupting) No. No. No.
Michael:	Listen carefully. You don't expect me to use my personal funds to pay the customs fees? This is not how I work.
Max N. Paddy:	(slowly and deliberately) I am willing to pay you the money that you require. However, you must collect it from me in person at my location. If you cannot do that then please get back on the plane. I have informed four different people of the same story.
Michael:	OK I will fly to Scotland to collect the fees from you in person. Is that OK with you?
Max N. Paddy:	Yes that's fine. You can also catch a train directly to Scotland.
Michael:	OK. I talk to you again soon. Bye bye.
Max N. Paddy:	Goodbye.

Michael called again shortly after that to tell me his partner Ken Wilson would be flying to Scotland to meet with me the next day. Michael passes me onto his partner Ken Wilson, who calls me on the day of the meeting to let me know he is on the way.

Date: 24th Feb 2005 - Ken Wilson calls Max N. Paddy.

Max N. Paddy:	Hello.
Ken:	Hello. Is that Mr. Paddy?
Max N. Paddy:	Yes it is.
Ken:	Yes, this is Ken Wilson. My partner Mr. Dannis told you yesterday about me. I am at the airport right now and I will be flying up to meet with you in Scotland shortly.
Max N. Paddy:	OK, that's fine.
Ken:	And... erm, the flight is gonna be leaving for 2.45pm and I will call when I arrive there.
Max N. Paddy:	Right.
Ken:	So what I'll do... how many minutes drive from your office to the airport?
Max N. Paddy:	Five, maybe ten minutes at the most.
Ken:	So we can make the meeting at the airport so I can quickly get the next flight back to London?
Max N. Paddy:	That's not a problem. Give me a call when you arrive and I will be there within a few minutes.
Ken:	OK Mr. Paddy. Nice talking to you. I will call you later. Bye.
Max N. Paddy:	Thank you. Goodbye.

It has to be noted at this point that, of course, I am nowhere near Scotland. I am sat in the comfort of my home here in Manchester!

After a 5 hour trip, Ken has arrived at Glasgow airport! A little bit of research gives me the names of various cafés that are in the Glasgow airport terminal. My plan is to get him to a café and then call the café itself to confirm Ken IS actually there before giving him the good news!

Date: 24th Feb 2005 - Ken Wilson calls Max N. Paddy.

Max N. Paddy:	Hello.
Ken:	Good afternoon Mr. Paddy, it is Ken Wilson speaking.
Max N. Paddy:	Hello Mr. Wilson.
Ken:	I am just outside Glasgow Airport at the moment.
Max N. Paddy:	Oh that's great. I will be on my way to you very shortly.
Ken:	OK I will wait.

Max N. Paddy:	There are plenty of small bars and cafés where you can wait for me, and in fact there is one that I always use when I am in the airport. That would be a good place to meet. It is called *The Ritazza* coffee house. I will meet you there in 15 minutes.
Ken:	OK, no problem. I will speak to you soon. Bye.
Max N. Paddy:	Thank you. Bye.

Over the next half an hour (yes, I was 'delayed'), I arrange with Ken that he move to three other meeting places within the airport, giving him various excuses as to why this was necessary. I decided to test if Ken really was at the airport by getting him to suggest a café at which to meet.

Ken called me to tell me he had found a cafe called *Delice de France*. A quick call to *Delice de France* confirmed to me that Ken was indeed standing there waiting for me. I had managed to get Ken to fly a few hundred miles from London to Scotland for absolutely no reason. Time to give Ken the bad news.

Date: 24th Feb 2005 - Ken Wilson calls Max N. Paddy.

Ken:	Hello?
Max N. Paddy:	Hello is that Ken?
Ken:	Paddy?
Max N. Paddy:	Hi. Is that Ken?
Ken:	Yes, it's is Ken.
Max N. Paddy:	OK. Where are you Ken?
Ken:	I told you, I am in *Delice de France*.
Max N. Paddy:	Why are you there? What are you waiting there for?
Ken:	Sorry?
Max N. Paddy:	What are you waiting there for?
Ken:	(aggravated) What am I waiting here for?
Max N. Paddy:	Yeah.
Ken:	(aggravated) What am I waiting here for?
Max N. Paddy:	Yes.
Ken:	(long pause) Why you asking me this question?
Max N. Paddy:	I'm just asking because I was just wondering; did you really think I was going to let you steal $11,000 from me?

At that point the phone went dead! So I called Ken back, but all I got was his answering service.

Ken:	(answerphone) You are getting through to the right number. Just leave you name and your telephone number and I will get back to you.
Max N. Paddy:	Hello Ken, this is Max N. Paddy. Just to say thank you for making the long flight to Scotland. It was pleasant speaking to you. You've got my telephone number anyway, so any time you want to discuss any other scamming matters then please do give me a call. Bye.

Ken wasn't quite as abusive as I'd hoped, but don't worry readers it gets worse! Mohamed Lucien calls to ask for an explanation. This is where the rich language starts folks.

Date: 24th Feb 2005 - Dr. Mohamed Lucian calls Max N. Paddy.

Max N. Paddy:	Hello, good afternoon.
Mohamed:	Hello Max N. Paddy how are you?
Max N. Paddy:	I'm fine. What can I do for you?
Mohamed:	Erm... Erm. I am surprised. I do not know what is happening.
Max N. Paddy:	I know exactly what is happening.
Mohamed:	What have you done to my, my, my deputy?
Max N. Paddy:	Your deputy is a thief.
Mohamed:	What? What do you mean he is a thief?
Max N. Paddy:	He is a 419 scammer.
Mohamed:	Why do you say so?
Max N. Paddy:	I know exactly what he is and you are a thief as well.
Mohamed:	Sorry?
Max N. Paddy:	You are a thief as well.
Mohamed:	(angry now) You are a bastard. You will die.
Max N. Paddy:	Oh dear. Is that the best you can do?
Mohamed:	Listen, listen, listen. I will take your life, you are a bastard.
Max N. Paddy:	Yes.
Mohamed:	I'll take your life bye bye.
Max N. Paddy:	Is that all you have to...

The phone goes dead. No problem, I call Mohamed right back.

Max N. Paddy:	(after a very long silence!) Dr. Mohamed! Hello... ?

Mohamed:	Don't call me in your life!
Max N. Paddy:	What!
Mohamed:	Bastard! Don't call me in your life.
Max N. Paddy:	I'll call you when I want to. You are a -

The phone goes dead again! Just when I was recovering from the disappointment of the rather lame threats, a great call comes in quite late the same evening. Apologies for my rather juvenile behaviour, I was trying to wind these guys up!

Date: 24th Feb 2005 - Mohamed Lucien & Ken Wilson (tired after a long trip) call Max N. Paddy.

Max N. Paddy:	Hello.
Mohamed:	You fool! You are gonna die soon. I am very close to you and I am watching you OK.
Max N. Paddy:	OK, no problem.
Mohamed:	We are Mafia's. We are all over the world. We are going to kill you.
Max N. Paddy:	OK.
Mohamed:	You think you are smart eh?
Max N. Paddy:	Yes.
Mohamed:	You fucking bastard. Fucking bastard.
Max N. Paddy:	Did you e-
Mohamed:	(interrupting) You fool! You are dead! I am gonna fuck you man. You are dead!
Max N. Paddy:	(laughing)
Mohamed:	FUCK YOU. FUCK YOU. I'M GONNA KILL YOU MAN!
Max N. Paddy:	Are you going to let me talk?
Mohamed:	I'M GONNA TAKE YOUR LIFE VERY SOON.
Max N. Paddy:	Hey, do yo-
Mohamed:	(interrupting) When you are dead it wi-

I interrupt Mohamed here to call him a 'mugu'. This is basically the scammer equivalent of fool, or idiot.

Max N. Paddy:	Hey mugu! Mugu. Let me talk please.
Mohamed:	WHO IS A MUGU! WHO? I AM A MUGU?
Max N. Paddy:	Yes.
Mohamed:	I AM NOT A MUGU, YOU ARE THE MUGU. I AM THE MAFIA. I am going to fuck you up, man.

Max N. Paddy:	Yeah, yeah, yeah...
Mohamed:	I'm the head of the Mafia. I'm gonna fuck you up.
Max N. Paddy:	All righty then.

Mohamed then passes the phone over to Ken.

Ken:	Hello.
Max N. Paddy:	Hello.
Ken:	You're dead, mate.
Max N. Paddy:	OK.
Ken:	You're a dead dog, mate.
Max N. Paddy:	OK.
Ken:	You better leave Scotland because we gonna blow your fuckin' arse off. I'm a yardie you know. I'm gon-
Max N. Paddy:	You idiot! I'm not even in Scotland!
Ken:	You're fucking dead. You're gonna die. We are coming to you.
Max N. Paddy:	Did you enjoy your flight today?
Ken:	We are coming for you.
Max N. Paddy:	And where are you going to come to kill me?
Ken:	We're going to burn down your house...
Max N. Paddy:	And where are you going to come to?

Ken gives the phone back to Mohamed.

Mohamed:	You are a fool!
Max N. Paddy:	Why doesn't anyone want to list-
Mohamed:	(interrupting) I'll give you 24 hours to die. I'll-
Max N. Paddy:	(interrupting) Excuse me, excuse me, excuse me, excuse me...
Mohamed:	You are a fool. Fool. Fool.
Max N. Paddy:	Your phone is going to be very busy for the next few weeks!

...one of the fun things I do is to post scammers' phone numbers on my website and invite people to call them!

Mohamed:	This is just an old mobile phone. This phone is clear for, for, it is clear for, for fo...
Max N. Paddy:	For, for, for, for, for, for, for, for, for!
Mohamed:	FUCK YOU! FUCK YOU, BASTARD!
Max N. Paddy:	Can I ask you a question? Hello...

The phone goes dead. Time to call them right back!

Max N. Paddy:	You shouldn't put the phone down on people. That's very rude!
Mohamed:	Is that you fool?
Max N. Paddy:	Yeah. I need to ask you a question.
Mohamed:	You are going to die soon.
Max N. Paddy:	Listen to me please.
Mohamed:	OK, go ahead.
Max N. Paddy:	Where are you going to come to kill me - can you tell me please?
Mohamed:	We know where you live. We have been following you for the past four days.
Max N. Paddy:	(laughing very loudly and annoyingly!)
Mohamed:	You are laughing?
Max N. Paddy:	Yes.
Mohamed:	I'm coming to kill you now.
Max N. Paddy:	You fool. You don't even know where I am.
Mohamed:	Where are you? Are you....
Max N. Paddy:	(interrupting) I am in the USA.
Mohamed:	You are in the USA?
Max N. Paddy:	Yes.
Mohamed:	Then you are finished.
Max N. Paddy:	(laughing) Is that right, you little boy!
Mohamed:	You are a fool.
Max N. Paddy:	You are the fool. You are the ones who wasted money on a flight to Scotland!
Mohamed:	Your death comes. We are Mafia. We are Mafia.
Max N. Paddy:	No, you are not Mafia, you are idiots.
Mohamed:	Fuck you!
Max N. Paddy:	(laughing)
Mohamed:	Bullshit, bullshit. BULLSHIT! BUUULLLLSHIT! FUCK YOU! FUCK YOU! FUCK YOU!

The phone goes dead!

NOW we're getting somewhere. Pity that they didn't give me much of a chance to taunt them some more! I call the guys back just before midnight to try to provoke them some more.

Date: 24th Feb 2005 - Max N. Paddy telephones Mohamed Lucien.

Max N. Paddy:	Hello. (very long silence) Hello Mr. Mugu....... Hello coward. Are you too scared to talk? Mafia man. MAFIA MA-

Mohamed:	(interrupting) YOU FOOL! YOU FOOL!
Max N. Paddy:	(laughs) Anyway, seriously. I'm ringing you for a reason. I need to know what time you will be killing me tomorrow because I have got some appointments. (Long silence) Can you tell me? I'm quite busy, you see, so I don't want to die when I'm in a meeting or som-
Mohamed:	(interrupting) You are dying today.
Max N. Paddy:	I'm dying today! Oh, excellent! What time?
Mohamed:	(sounding really tired and pissed off) Fuck you. Fuck you. Fuck you.
Max N. Paddy:	Look. All I wan...

The phone goes dead. I try to call back but it's turned off.

The next morning Ed Shanks sends a message to Dr. Mohamed to try to explain what the hell is going on!

From: Ed Shanks
To: Mohamed Lucien
Date: 25th Feb 2005

Dear Dr. Mo - I just got the word from Mr. Max N. Paddy that he thought you were a crook and scammed you. I had no idea that he was thinking something like that and would trick your diplomat into coming to Glasgow Scotland, then not show up himself. Max N. Paddy thought this would protect me from getting cheated, but I wanted to transfer the boxes for the widow. I believe you and he didn't. He said you were very upset.

I still want to transfer the box. However, if you don't trust me anymore that is fine also.

Ed Shanks

Dr. Mohamed, suitably unimpressed with the day's proceedings, decides to contact Ed Shanks for an explanation!

From: Mohamed Lucien
To: Ed Shanks
Date: 25th Feb 2005
Subject: EXPLAIN

SAHARA CLINIC & MATTERNITY,
P.O.BOX 333, SAVANA MRKT

ROAD, ACCRA GHANA
+233 244 937082.
25TH FEBUARY 2005

DEAR SHANKS,/ MAX N.PADDY,

I RECEIVED YOUR EMAIL AND MR.MAX N.PADDY TODAY IN MY OFFICE. BUT I WAS SURPRISED, I DONT UNDERSTAND ANY MORE, WHAT IS WRONG, I BELIVED YOU ALL DAY LONG. PLEASE CAN I HEAR MORE BETTER FROM YOU HOW THE DIPLOMAT DEAL WITH YOUR FRIEND IN SCOTLAND.?????.

I AM NOT SO SURE OF WHAT YOUR FRIEND TOLD ME ALL ABOUT. IF THAT IS THE CASE , I WILL ADVICE YOU THAT YOU AND YOUR FRIEND TO COME TO GHANA TO MY CLINIC AND SEE WITH YOUR EYES . IT WILL BE BETTER FOR ME TO RETURN THE CONSIGNMENT FROM SCOTLAND OR LONDON TO GHANA. SO THAT YOU CAN COME AND CARRY THE WIDOW TO YOUR COUNTRY WITH THE CONSIGNMENT AS WELL.

I AM NEVER A CROOK OK. I AM A GOOD ISLAMIC MAN WHO HAVE THE FEAR OF ALLAH. IF THE DIPLOMAT DISAPOINTED, LET GIVE THE GLORY TO ALLAH, ALL I KNOW THE CONSIGNMENT MUST BE GIVEN TO YOU. WHAT PAINS ME ALOT IS THE NAME YOUR FRIEND TRY TO CALL ME. I DONT KNOW IF HE HAS FORGOTTEN THAT I AM NOT THE DEPOSITOR OF THE CONSIGNMENT, I AM ONLY DOING A FAVOUR FOR MY CLIENT / PATIENT AS YOU KNOW. AS YOUR FRIENT IS A DIRECTOR TO A COMPANY, THAT IS HOW I AM STILL SOLE PROPRIETOR / DOCTOR TO MY HOSPITAL. I WONDER WHY HE SHOULD ADRESS ME LIKE I AM A CHILD. OH OH MY GOD.

NEVER WORRIED SHANK EVERY THING WILL BE IN CONTROL OK. I CAN NOT BECAUSE OF MONEY POLUTE MY RELATIONSHIP WITH YOU AND MR MAX N.PADDY, OK. THE MATTER IS THAT LET US REASON TOGETHER. I WILL WANT YOU TO COME TO GHANA AND MEET ME AT MY HOSPITAL WITH YOUR FRIEND MAX N. PADDY.

SINCE I HAVE CONTACTED YOU TO HELP THE WIDOW, I KNOW IT SHALL COME TO PASS .

TRY AS MUCH AS POSSIBLE TO BUY YOUR TICKET TOGETHER WITH YOUR FRIEND TO COME OVER, THEN I WILL

CONTACT LONDON TO RETURN THJE CONSIGNMENT TO MY HOSPITAL THEN YOU CAN MAKE ARRANGEMENT TO TRAVELL WITH THE WIDOW. PLEASE I AM REAL........ NOT A SCMAMER....... AS YOU THOUGHT....... I AM.......... I JUST WANT TO HELP........

I WAIT FOR YOUR URGENT REPLY AS A MATTER OF URGENTCY.

THANKS
DOCTOR MOHAMED.

No reply sent!

From: Mohamed Lucien
To: Ed Shanks
Date: 25th Feb 2005
Subject: i am waiting

Dear Shanks - i have been waiting .....

i am confused ok, please get back to me ....the widow cried about you and your partiner. but i try to tell her that i have invited you and your friend to come to my hospital then they can see her, that makes her stop cring today. she said you should come that she want to see you.

please shanks and co. dont feel tied about the business, i pray to God that you will received the consignment here in ghana very safty as well.

thanks

Doctor Mohamed.

awaiting to hear from you.

From: Ed Shanks
To: Mohamed Lucien
Date: 25th Feb 2005

Dear Dr. Mo - I have been in touch with Mr. Paddy Max and have scolded him severely for making fun of you and causing all that trouble. Needless to say he will not travel to Ghana or anywhere else to meet you. For all the trouble he has caused you in my name, now I am fearful of meeting you also. You may still be mad. He mentioned that you have the Nigerian Mafia after him. Mr. Paddy is quite crazy and will do some weird things. I should never have trusted him.

However, perhaps you and I and the widow can still do business. I am considering sending you the cash required by Western Union. Mr. Paddy advises against it, but for some reason I find you a trustful person. I could send you part of the money, then the rest later. We would have to have some sort of agreement. What do you think?

Sincerely,

Ed Shanks

From: Mohamed Lucien
To: Ed Shanks
Date: 26th Feb 2005
Subject: PAY FOR THE CONSIGNMENT

SAHARA CLINIC & MATTERNITY,
P.S.BOX. 333 ,SAVANA MART
ROAD, ACCRA GHANA.
+233 244 937082
26 FEBUARY 2005.

DEAR SHANKS - I AM IN RECIPIENT OF YOUR EMAIL TODAY IN MY OFFICE.

YOUR PARTNER MR. PADDY N. MAX, I SUGGESTED THAT HE IS NOT HAPPY OVER THE BUSINESS BECAUSE THE WIDOW SAID THAT SHE DONT WANT HER CONSIGNMENT TO BE INVESTED IN UK, BUT IN USA. I THINK THAT IS THE REASON WHY MR. PADDY WAS DOING THAT. HENCE I WANT YOU AND HIM TO COME TO MY CLINIC TO SEE THE WIDOW.

I AM A GENTLE MAN WHO HAVE THE FEAR OF ALLAH, I NEVER HAVE PROBLEM WITH YOU OR MAX. BUT I WAS STILL SURPRISE WHY MR PADDY REFUSED TO RECIEVED THE DIPLOMAT AND CLEAR THE CONSIGNMENT AT SCOTLAND.......

I HAVE NO NIGERIA MAFIA PLEASE, I AM A GENTLE MAN WHO ONLY HAVE GENTLE MEN FRIEND AS I AM.

ACCORDING TO THE AGREEMENT, I WILL CONSULT MY LAWYER FOR THE LETTER OF TRUST ON MONDAY OK. BUT YOU

*HAVE TO KNOW THAT MR PADDY WANT TO POLUTE OUR
RELITIONSHIP, I AM READY TO FINISHED THE BUSINESS WITH
YOU OK.*

*YOU HAVE TO TELL ME HOW MUCH YOU HAVE NOW TO SEND
SO THAT THE ATTONEY CAN PREPARE IT VERY WELL. I AM
HAPPY FOR THIS IDEA BECAUSE I WANT EVERY THING I WANT
TO DO NOW MUST BE LEGAL AND LEGITIMATE AS WELL
BECAUSE MR PADDY HAS DISAPOINTED ME..*

*I HAVE FORGIVEN HIM OK, AFTER YOU HAVE SEND THE
MONEY THEN I CAN PAID THE DIPLOMAT HEAD OFFICE HERE
TO DELIVERD THE CONSIGNMENT TO YOU IN USA AS IT WAS
DONE IN SCOTLAND.*

*DONT BE TIRED, EVERY THING IS IN CONTROL, MR. PADDY IS
NOT A RIGHT PERSON BECAUSE HE REFUSE TO GIVED ME IS
PASSPORT OR ID CARD, I DONT KNOW IF HE WANT TO RUN
AWAY WITH THE WIDOW MONEY/CONSIGNMENT... PLEASE
STATE THE MONEY FOR THE WESTERN UNION SO THAT EVERY
THING CAN BE DONE WELL.BUT BE ADVICE THAT THE TOTAL
MONEY FOR THE CLEARING IS $11,000 .*

*PLEASE MR SHANKS TRY FOR THE WIDOW LIFE NOT TO DIE
WITH HEART ATTACT, NOT THE MONEY IS THE MOST PRECIOUS
BUT HER LIFE,*

*SHE IS CRING TO MEET YOU THEN YOU CAN TAKE HER TO THE
SPECIALIST DOCTOR IN USA.*

I WAIT TO HEAR FROM YOU URGENTLY .

*THANKS
DOCTOR MOHAMED LUCIEN.*

**Myself and A. Skinner decide it would be fun to try to persuade Dr.
Mohamed to apologise to me (Max N. Paddy) for the abusive threats.
Not only would it be a good thing to hear, but after having given an
apology, if we screw him over again it will make him even more angry!**

**Ed Shanks sends the following email to Mohamed, along with a copy
of an email I am supposed to have sent to Ed.**

From: Ed Shanks
To: Mohamed Lucien
Date: 25th Feb 2005

Dear Dr. Mo - I was certainly glad to receive your mail. During our conversations you always came across as a kind and gentle man.

Let me explain the situation to you. Some years ago Mr. Paddy was scammed out of several thousand dollars and thought you were trying to scam me. We have had a long talk and I have convinced him that you are a truthful and honest man who just has the widow's welfare at heart.

Therefore, we will both be available to fly to Ghana to meet the widow and your kind self, and hand over the $11,000 USD. There is only one hitch to us coming to Ghana. Mr. Paddy Max insists that the person who gave him the death threats must call him and apologise. He must apologise and promise not to kill either of us.

Let me know what you think of this idea ASAP, so we can make our travel arrangements.

Your Friend,

Ed Shanks

My made up message from Max N. Paddy to Ed Shanks, which is also sent to Mohamed.

Max N. Paddy.
Managing Director: Dark Side Communications Inc.

Dear Ed - Thanks ever so much for your email. You have certainly put my mind at ease. I am sorry that I reacted in such a way to Mr. Mohamed and his partners but, as you know, I have in the past lost over $29,500 dollars to a scammer in the Netherlands.

This hurt me very much and I have been suspicious of such business deals ever since.

However, your long talk today has convinced me that I was wrong about Dr. Mohamed. Maybe I was too quick to judge this poor man. From what you have told me he seems like a very humble person, so I will help you by giving you the $11,000. You stated that Dr. Mohamed wants the payment by Western Union? If this will make the deal faster for you Ed, I will be happy to make the whole payment this way. However, I must insist that Dr. Mohamed speaks to me in person over the phone to apologise for his actions against me.

This is the only condition that I have. Once I have heard Dr. Mohamed's apology with my own ears I will then make the transfer for you.

Dr. Mohamed will need to tell me to whom I am to make the payment. Once I have made the payment I will fax/email him with the payment receipt. If Dr. Mohamed still requires a copy of my passport, I will be happy to send it to him.

Thank you again for our long talk today, Ed. It was nice to speak with you again.

Take care my good friend,

Max.

Max N. Paddy.
Managing Director: Dark Side Communications Inc.

After a slight delay, the apology from Dr. Mohamed comes in.

Date: 1st Mar 2005 - Mohamed Lucien apologises to Max N. Paddy.

Max N. Paddy:	Hello.
Mohamed:	Hello. How are you Paddy Max?
Max N. Paddy:	Who is that speaking please?
Mohamed:	This is Dr. Mohamed Lucien
Max N. Paddy:	Oh hello Mr. Lucien. Nice to hear from you.
Mohamed:	Yes. I am very sorry for the way that I addressed you. It was that I was very angry and er, things like that but really the whole thing was explained to me that now I am very sorry about our misunderstanding and please, please let us move on.
Max N. Paddy:	OK that is fine. If you can forward me the information by email to make the payment I will try to get the money to you this afternoon.
Mohamed:	OK. I will send you the name to make the payment, OK?
Max N. Paddy:	Yes. I will make the payment after 2pm this afternoon.
Mohamed:	I am going to send the information right now.
Max N. Paddy:	That's fine.
Mohamed:	OK. Thank you and bye bye.
Max N. Paddy:	Goodbye.

Short and to the point, but it's one-up for the good guys!

Dr. Mohamed contacts Max to send the payment information (the poor deluded fool!).

From: Mohamed Lucien
To: Paddy N. Max
Date: 1st Mar 2005
Subject: NAME TO SEND THE MONEY

Sahara clinic & matternity,
p.o.box 333, savana mart road,
Accra Ghana .
+233 244 937082.
29 febuary 2005.

Dear Paddy N. Max - thanks for your co operation during our brif conversation on the phone today.

I am very happy to get you on the phone today, i have been calling all day but no one picks the call. But mr. ED told me that it wes your office line. may be you are not on site by then, so sorry.

I will give you the name right away to send the money toay as you know, there is no time to be wasted from you, immediately you have send the money to day,i will rushed over to the head office and pay the money immediately ok, then you can tell me where i will order the diplomat to do the delivery as you know.

I have told the WIDOW that her consignment will be cleared to from the diplomat, she was so happy and she was full with joy, but right now she has gone to bed for a relaxation.

She pray for you and ED SHANKS, SHE SAID SHE WILL BE WITH ED VERY SOON, BECAUSE SHE NOW KNOWS RIGHT NOW THAT EVERY THING HAVE BEEN IN CONTROL. SHE is a good christain, God has answered her prayer all day.

TH NAME TO SEND THE MONEY IS GODSTIME AGOBA . PLEASE IMMEDIATELY YOU HAVE DO THE SEND, YOU HAVE TO CALL MY ATTENTION ON THE PHONE AND GIVE ME ALL THE SENDING DETAILS AND YOUR PASSPORT.

I WILL STOP HERE TO WAIT FOR YOU OK AS SOON AS POSSIBLE.

THANKS

DOCTOR MOHAMED LUCIEN..

Mohamed lets Ed Shanks know the deal is near to an end (or so he thinks).

From: Mohamed Lucien
To: Ed Shanks
Date: 1st Mar 2005
Subject: I HAVE SPOKEN WITH PADDY

Sahara clinic & matternity,
P.O.Box 333,Savana Mart.Road,
Accra Ghana,
+233 244 937082
29 Febuary 2005.

Dear Shanks - Thanks for your email, i was so glad when i heared from you all day, i have spoken with mr. MAX N. PADDY, today and he has agreed to send the money via western union today.

I will not forget to say thank you very much. immediately this money has been sent, i will rushed over to the diplomat head office here to pay the money immediately so that the company can delivered the consignment to you in your house in america .

I understand your words of travelling, i wiches you safe jonney. i will advice you to always have a contact with MAX N.PADDY ALWAYS to be updateing you alday,

Please i will advice now to please wait for the diplomat at your house, because immediately the money is paid today, you are going to recieved the consignment this week.

Please i am begging you to do me the favour by checking your email untill you are back ok.

I will email you immediately i have recieved the money today. **(Don't hold your breath, Doc!)**

I will stop here to hear from paddy Max N. inregard of the sending of the fund today.

Thanks
Doctor Mohamed Lucien..

Time to send Mohamed his payment.

Max N. Paddy.
Managing Director: Dark Side Communications Inc.

Dear Mr. Mohamed - The payment has now been made and you should be able to collect the money immediately.

The control number is 8173911753. As you requested I have also attached a copy of my passport.

Unfortunately my scanner was not working correctly to send you a scan of the Western Union receipt but I was able to take a good quality photograph of it for you so that you can view the details.

Sincerely,
Max N. Paddy.
Managing Director: Dark Side Communications Inc.

I attach a copy of Max N. Paddy's passport (UK readers will recognise the photo as that of comedian Peter Kay!).

I also included a photograph of the Western Union payment I sent to Mohamed. Note the American Express Corporate Platinum card added for extra effect, and the Rolls Royce car keys!

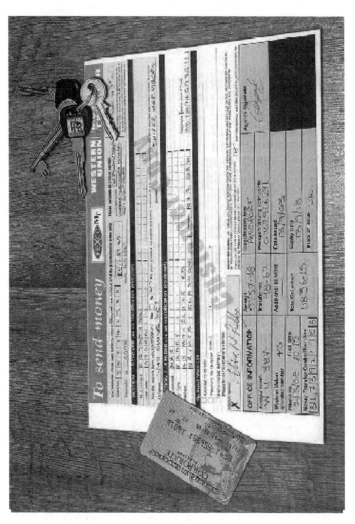

I think the fake Western Union payment pushed Mohamed over the edge. Mohamed and Co. never got back to either Max N. Paddy or Ed Shanks.

The Tale of the Painted Breast

'Prince' Joe Eboh contacts me with a classic 419 opening letter. I decide to make him jump through a few hoops before I'm prepared to agree to his proposition, and the results are amusing and profitable, to the tune of $80 + $49 DHL shipping. The result is our scammer is down a painful total of $129.

From: Prince Joe Eboh
Date: Wednesday, April 21, 2004
Subject: TRANSFER

Prince Joe Eboh

Dear Sir/Madam - I am fine today and how are you? I hope this letter will find you in the best of health. I am Prince Joe Eboh, the Chairman of the "Contract Award Committee", of the "Niger Delta Development Commission (NDDC)", a subsidiary of the Nigerian National Petroleum Corporation (NNPC).

The Niger Delta Development Commission (NDDC) was set up by the late Head of State, General Sani Abacha who died on 18th June 1998, to manage the excess revenue accruing from the sales of Petroleum and its allied products as a domestic increase in the petroleum products to develop the communities in the Niger Delta Oil producing areas. The estimated annual revenue for 1999 was $45 Billion US Dollars Ref. FMF A26 Unit 3B Paragraph "D" of the Auditor General of the Federal Republic of Nigeria Report of Nov. 1999 on estimated revenue.

I am the Chairman of the Contract Award Committee, and my committee is solely responsible for awaiting and paying of contracts on *behalf of the Federal Government of Nigeria. My Committee Awarded Contracts to foreign contractors for Drilling and Ecological Matters in the oil producing areas of Niger Delta. We overshot the contract sum by US$25,000,000.00. We have paid the contractors and withholding the balance of US$25,000, 000.00. But, because of the existence of some of the domestic laws forbidding civil servants in Nigeria from opening, operating and maintaining foreign accounts, we do not have the expertise to transfer this balance of fund to a foreign account.*

However, this balance of US$25,000, 000.00 has been secured in form of Credit/Payment to a foreign contractor, hence we wish to transfer into your bank account as the beneficiary of the fund. We have also arrived at a conclusion that you will be given 20% of the total sum transferred as our foreign partner, while 5% will be reserved for incidental expenses that both parties will incur in the course of actualizing this transaction, and the balance of 75% will be kept for the committee members.

If you know that you will be capable of helping us actualize this transaction, you should send to me immediately the details of your bank particulars or open a new bank account where we can transfer the money US$25,000, 000.00, which you will be holding in trust for us until we come to your country for our share. Your nature of business does not matter in this transaction. The required details includes your company's name, address, your private personal telephone/fax numbers, your full name and address, including your complete bank details where the transferred fund will be routed by the Apex Bank.

Note that this transaction is expected to be actualized within 21 working days from the day the required details are forwarded to the Federal Ministry of Finance who will approve the needed foreign exchange control allocation for the release of this money to your account. Please, treat this as top secret. You should contact me urgently.

Thanks for your cooperation.

Yours faithfully,

Prince Joe Eboh

From: Father Hector Barnett
To: Prince Joe Eboh

Father Hector Barnett
Financial Development
London SW

Dear Sir - My thanks for your very interesting email below. I would
dearly love to help you. However, my ministry forbids me from entering
any business deal with partners who are not part of our faith. I am sorry
but there is nothing more I can do for you.

If you ever decide to join our faith then of course I could help you both
with my experience and financial support. I wish you well in your
endeavour my brother.

Father Hector Barnett
Financial Development - Holy Church of The Order of The Red Breast.

From: Prince Joe Eboh
Date: Friday, April 23, 2004
Subject: Re: I'm ready to join your faith.

Dear Father Hector - If joining your faith is what it takes to help me of
course, I am ready to joing you. I'm from a good christian family. I will
do anything you want me to do in the faith. Don't forget that I have to
transfer the money to your account as urgently as possible. Send me
your account details. I hope to read your mail soon.

Prince Joe Eboh.

Time to put my dastardly plan into action.

From: Father Hector Barnett
To: Prince Joe Eboh

Dear brother Eboh - Bless you for your prompt reply and may the Lord
God Almighty send you many blessings (Amen). My brother, it is
wonderful that you are considering joining our church, you will be most
welcome in our holy order.

My brother, of course you will have to prove your commitment to our
ministry. This will require you to send us a photograph of yourself
showing part of the commitment ceremony that we require (this is very

simple), and you will also have to sign our Order of The Red Breast induction agreement form. The agreement form is very simple and only requires your name and signature.

If you are in agreement to our terms above, please signify it to us as soon as possible and I shall arrange to give you the complete instructions for the photograph and agreement form.

As soon as you have been inducted to our order then we can proceed with your business proposition immediately. Please note that we cannot agree to any form of communication other than email until after you have been inducted to our church.

Father Hector Barnett
Financial Development - Holy Church of The Order of The Red Breast.

From: Prince Joe Eboh
Date: Tuesday, April 27, 2004
Subject: Agreement

Dear Father Hector - Peace be unto you in the name of our lord and saviour Jesus Christ Amen. I'm in agreement with your terms. I will adhere strictly to your instructions. Send me a comprehensive instruction for the photograph and agreement.

Stay blessed.

Prince Joe Eboh.

From: Father Hector Barnett
To: Prince Joe Eboh

Dear brother Eboh - Bless you for your interest in our church, and herewith you will find the complete induction procedure. First of course you will need to know a little more about our ministry.

Our ministry was founded in 1774 by a wonderful lady by the name of Betsy Carrington (I have attached a photograph of her for your records). She spent many of her first preaching years in Kenya, spreading the holy gospel amongst the local people there.

She was the first person male or female to promote Christian texts and beliefs to the Masai warrior tribe. The most famous account is when as a test she had to remove the top part of her clothes and paint the top half of her body and breast with the red Masai warpaint as a gesture of faith and belief to them so that they would accept her and trust her. She was almost immediately accepted by them and was one of the most trusted westerners known at that time.

In her later years she returned to England and started her own ministry, Holy Church of The Order of The Red Breast, and was very active until her sad death in 1861.

As a qualification to enter the Holy Church of The Order of The Red Breast, all followers must go through the initiation procedure that Miss Carrington made so famous. Of course in these modern times, female members do not have to paint their breast. They only need to make the symbol on their stomachs. However, all males must still show commitment to the church by having the symbol of the church marked on their breasts.

My brother, this is what you will need to do in order to complete the church induction ceremony:

You must remove your shirt and then paint/draw in red, the symbols of our church. So that you know exactly how the symbol must look, I have attached a photograph of four of our young inductees going through the procedure. Please use this picture to enable you to make the same marking on yourself. I have also attached a small picture showing the design in more detail.

Next you will need to have a HIGH QUALITY photograph taken and sent it to us my email attachment.

Once your photograph has been received we will then forward you the induction certificate. All this requires is your name and signature. Once you have signed and dated it, please send it back to me by email attachment.

After that you will then be a full member of our beloved ministry and as well as being able to do business with you we can also offer financial help to you in the future if you ever need it. Our church is committed to helping any members in whatever way is possible. If you ever need money for charitable purposes, then you just need to contact us and quote your member number and we can arrange payments to you within 24 hours.

I look forward to welcoming you into our membership my brother.

Father Hector Barnett

Financial Development - Holy Church of The Order of The Red Breast.

Our Most Holy Betsy Carrington   **The Red Breast logo**

**Courtesy of Photoshop - A Church of The Painted Breast
induction photograph.**

From: Prince Joe Eboh
Date: Monday, May 04
Subject: Re: Agreement

Dear Father - Sorry for the delay in sending my photograph. I was away from office to the capital city on official assignment. Attached is my photograph. I'm not only interested in becoming a member of this church but to also establish a branch of the church here in Nigeria.

I'm looking forward to receive the forms so that I can fill it and send back to you immediately. Remember father that this business is to be rounded up as soon as possible after which we will now talk on how to have a brach established here in Nigeria. I hope to hear from you soon. Thanks

Prince Joe Eboh.

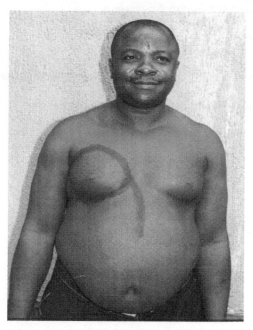

The 'Prince' attaches his induction photograph, and it's a doozy!
Looks like you had a few too many burgers there Joe.

From: Father Hector Barnett
To: Prince Joe Eboh

Dear brother Eboh - My thanks for your picture which has been received and confirmed this morning.

I am very happy to tell you that now you are halfway through your induction procedure. All that is required is that you sign and return the induction agreement form.

Unfortunately, as you may know, today May 3rd is a Bank Holiday here in England, so the holy fathers are not assembled today. I will send you the agreement form tomorrow. Once you have signed the form and returned it to me then we can more swiftly on to your business proposition.

Expect to hear from me tomorrow morning.

God bless you.

Father Hector Barnett
Financial Development - Holy Church of The Order of The Red Breast.

The day after, I send Eboh his induction agreement form.

From: Father Hector Barnett
To: Prince Joe Eboh

Dear Brother Eboh - Good afternoon to you my brother, and I hope that this email finds you in good health.

My brother, please print out the attachment to this email. This contains your final agreement form. Once you have completed the agreement form then you will become a full member of our holy order. You have been assigned what we call a "guru" to help you in the future if you need it.

He will offer you advice and help whenever you need it. His name is Father Metimbers, and he will contact you when we have finished our business together.

Please sign your full name on all the areas of the agreement form which are underlined. This includes the 7 rules also. Then, write the date in the area provided and send the agreement for to us.

Please ensure that you send the agreement back to us scanned to a good and clear size.

Once we have received the form and checked it over, you will then receive a welcome letter to our church, and, of course, we can quickly proceed onto your business proposition.

I look forward to hearing from you soon.

Blessings.

Father Hector Barnett
Financial Development - Holy Church of The Order of The Red Breast.

AGREEMENT FORM ATTACHED

From: Prince Joe Eboh
Date: Thursday, May 06, 2004
Subject: Agreement Form

Dear Brother Hector - I want to thank the almighty God himself for the opportunity I have to be a member of this great church The Holy Church Of The Painted Breast. I'm looking forward to establishing a branch of the Church here.

But I'll like us to finish everything about the business proposal, which I sent to you earlier. I'm a government functionary my status is very delicate that's why I'm careful about any business I engage myself in.

I will need a Bank Account where I will transfer the money as soon as we are through with the induction. Attached is the Agreement Form.

Thanks for your cooperation.

Brother Joe Eboh.

Joe attaches my signed agreement form, which looks like a scan of a fax. It's almost unreadable but it'll do!

INDUCTION AGREEMENT

Agreement No. 172114

The Holy Church of The Painted Breast

This is an agreement secured in good faith between Father Hector Barnett on behalf of The Holy Church of The Painted Breast, _____.

This is to certify that I, _____ do solemnly swear on oath that I will ensure that I shall abide by the rules and regulations of **The Holy Church of The Painted Breast**. I will serve my ministry and fellow man to the best of my ability.

As discussed this day 4th May 2004, I, _____ agree to abide by the rules and conditions contained within the document known henceforth as "_The Agreement_". Upon the signing of The Agreement and the presentation of **photographic identity**, I will then be granted entry into the holy order of the Painted Breast. I shall also agree to abide by the following rules:

1. I shall not eat the meat of a pig _____

2. I shall not listen to Hip Hop _____

3. I shall not covet my neighbours ass _____

4. I shall not touch the one-eyed trouser snake _____

5. I shall pray to the memory of Miss Betsy Carrington daily _____

6. I shall honour the holy gnu _____

7. I shall honour the words of guru Shiver Metimbers _____

I promise in the presence of Almighty God himself that I shall abide by the rules above, lest I be cut down asunder and suffer the trial of a thousand baiters.

The Holy Church of The Painted Breast does hereby promise to take care of our new brother in all ways possible within our means and within the laws of our ministry.

Signed on behalf of the Holy Church of The Painted Breast: _____
Father Hector Barnett

Beneficiary: _____ Dated: 4/5/2004

86

From: Father Hector Barnett
To: Prince Joe Eboh

Father Hector Barnett
Financial Development
London SW

Dear brother Eboh - May I take this opportunity to welcome you officially as a member of Holy Church of The Order of The Red Breast. Please send me your full mailing address and I will post you some detailed information and brochures about our church.

Now to your business proposition. Please will you forward me instructions on exactly how you wish to proceed with this deal.

Father Hector Barnett
Financial Development - Holy Church of The Order of The Red Breast.

From: Prince Joe Eboh
Date: Monday, May 10, 2004
Subject: Re: Agreement

Dear Brother Hector - I must thank you for your swift response. Here is the mailing address:

297 IKORODU ROAD,
LAGOS, NIGERIA.

Send the brochure I'll receive it. About our deal, I'll like you to send me a name that will serve as your company's name or a letter headed paper that serves as your company's name. I will register the name with the corporate affairs commission Federal Republic Of Nigeria after which the ministries of finance will approve the payment. Second, send me a bank account where the money will be transferred.

I will also need your bank's phone/ fax numbers, your personal phone/ fax numbers. I'm processing the necessary documents that will facilitate this deal as urgently as possible. This money will be in the account in two weeks, after which I will come to England so that we can sit-down and discuss some important issues. Thanks for your cooperation.

Brother Eboh.

From: Father Hector Barnett
To: Prince Joe Eboh

Father Hector Barnett
Financial Development
London SW

Dear brother Eboh - Thanks for your email and it was rather super to hear from you again. God Almighty, is it really that time? Anyway, please find attached my details which you asked for. I hope they are to your satisfaction.

I'd just like to say, on a personal note, that I am thrilled that you have now joined our church brother Eboh, and I look forward to meeting with you and here's hoping we can get stoned together.

I must end this email now as my brother Pastor Risedmilc needs some urgent help with a housing project that we are partners together with.

Blessings,

Father Hector Barnett
Financial Development - Holy Church of The Order of The Red Breast.

I attach my details

 Father Hector Barnett
Financial Development
The Holy Church of the Painted Breast
21-27 Bayted Way
Strung-a-Long
London SW21

Tel: +44 7092 037387

Bank details:

Plunder & Flee Incorporated
103 Penny Lane
London SW12

Tel: +44 206 2020153
Fax: +44 206 2026155

Account No: 1006291
Sort Code: 77 21 99

From: Prince Joe Eboh
Date: Saturday, May 15, 2004
Subject: Re: I NEED ANOTHER EMAIL ADDRESS AND & YOUR FAX
NUMBER

Dear Father Hector - Thanks for your mail. I have forwarded your application for approval of this payment in your name to the Central Bank Of Nigeria and other ministries. The most important thing is that I am going to register your name with Corporate Affairs Commission Federal Republic Of Nigeria to enable me obtain your certificate which will be sent to you. The certificate will cost money and which will enable me to get some approvals from the ministry of finance and NNPC / NDDC. All these documents will be backdated to show that you executed this contract in the year, 1990.

The contract number has been given to me and it is as follows: NNPC/ NDDC/PED – 10 / 470 / 1990. I received the number days ago from Nigerian National Petroleum corporation (NNPC). As you can see, we have come to the heart of this business. I want you to cooperate with me so that we will have a platform where we are both beneficiaries of this transaction. I have received your Bank details and phone/fax numbers but I'll still need your personal fax number. Thanks for your cooperation.

Brother Joe Eboh.

From: Father Hector Barnett
To: Prince Joe Eboh

Dear Brother Joe - God bless your little cotton sox and how are you this glorious day? Thank you for fixing the email problem, and now I am sure that we can proceed briskly.

Please can I ask that if any one of your representatives contacts ask them to quote the password "Pappa's Got a Brand New Bag" on all future emails so that I will know for sure that the email is associated with you. This is very important because I do receive many emails every day, and especially now as it is the Tribble season things get very busy indeed.

My personal FAX number is 44 7012 674 XXXX

Brother Joe, I thank the good Lord JC himself for allowing me to introduce you to our wonderful church (amen). For your contemplation, here is a prayer which we in the Church of The Red Breast always say twice a day. It helps to ease the mind and clear our thoughts for the day ahead:

When all around you is misery and pain.
When you are caught in wind and rain.

When people stare and gaze with fear.
When people say things rather queer.

When the love of Betsy fills your soul.
When Shiver Metimbers scores a goal.

When the love of doom hangs nearby.
When the end of modalities makes you wonder why.

When all above seems a great test.
Get on down with the Holy Red Breast.

Thus endeth the lesson.

I look forward to your next communication brother Eboh.

Blessings,

Father Hector Barnett.

From: Prince Joe Eboh
Date: Tuesday, May 18, 2004
Subject: Password: Pappa's Got a Brand New Bag

Dear Father Hector - I'm very happy to hear that you received my last e-mail to you. I'm also thankful to God for the official introduction of my ownself to our wonderful church. I have said the prayer this morning and immediately I finished, something like a fountain went down my system making me to feel strong & happy. **(That would be complete bullshit, wouldn't it, Joe?)** *As a matter of fact, I can't wait to round up this deal so that I can come over to England to see you face to face. Can I have your photograph?*

I have spent money to process all the necessary documents for the transfer of this fund. Note that the documents bear your name as the contractor. What remains now is the registration of your name as the contractor who executed the contract. The ministry of finance will not approve this payment until I'm able to register your company's name with the corporate affairs commission Federal Republic of Nigeria who will issue a certificate to certify that your company executed this contract in the year, 1990.

The registration will cost $18,000.00. Which I need urgently because everything about this transaction and the draft is in your name. I've spent a lot of money already to process the relevant documents. I will need your assistance this time around as regards the registration. The commission will register your name and then, the ministry of finance will approve the payment and the cash will be in your account in less than two weeks. The contract number is NNPC/NDDC/PED – 10 / 470 / 1990. Every thing about this deal should be strictly confidential until we round up please. Thanks for your cooperation.

Brother Joe Eboh

Let's see if there's any chance I can get some cash out of the Prince.

From: Father Hector Barnett
To: Prince Joe Eboh

Dear brother Joe - Many thanks for your email and I do apologise for the late reply but we have been inducting many new members to our church. As you have requested, please find attached my photograph. The lady in the photograph with me is Sister Annette Kurtain.

I think I understand your explanation of the facts brother Eboh, but may I ask one question? Will I be required to pay the full amount of $18,000.00? The money is not too much of a problem for me as I am in the financial development section of our church. However, all withdrawals of $10,000.00 and above require a clearance certificate and clearance fee ($80).

Because the money you require will not be spent on a church project, I am not allowed to pay the clearance fees. If you wish me to pay the entire $18,000.00 registration costs, then I am afraid that I will have to ask you to send me the clearance fee. Once I have the clearance fee, sending you the $18,000.00 registration fee will be a very simple matter, and can be done within 8 hours of receiving the clearance fee.

Obviously to keep things secret and confidential it will be better not to have any paperwork at my end associated with this transaction, so I would suggest that the most secret and secure way to pay clearance fee would be in cash - that way no paperwork will be discovered here that may possibly ruin this deal.

Please let me know your thoughts.

Blessings, Father Hector Barnett.

I send Joe a quickly edited picture featuring David Hyde Pierce, aka Niles Crane, from the TV show *Frasier*.

From: Prince Joe Eboh
Date: Wednesday, May 19, 2004
Subject: Re: Password: Pappa's Got a Brand New Bag

Dear Father Hector - Thanks for your prompt response. I have been saying the prayer as instructed by our great church and it will interest you to know that each time I say the prayer, I feel rejuvenated. I received your photograph as well as that of Sister Kutain. I decided to attach my personal photograph again for your view.

Father, I want you to understand the fact that I have invested a lot of money into this deal, whatever expenses you incur shall be given back to you. I will at this point implore you to assist me. You can pay/send this money on two installments so that there wont be much need for the clearance fee. All the documents have gone through the appropriate legal progressions and they all bear your name. what remains now is the certificate of incorporation and that's where the money I requested plays an important role. Find below the account where you are to send the money. The account was given to me yesterday by the coporate affaires commission. According to them, that is the agent that receives money on their behalf. **(At this point, Joe supplies me with details of a bank account in which to transfer the $18,000.)**

Thanks for your cooperation.

Brother Joe Eboh.

Joe sends me a picture of himself, which I have seen before - it was sent to a fellow scambaiter a few days earlier.

You're not getting your cash so easily Joe.

From: Father Hector Barnett
To: Prince Joe Eboh

Dear brother Joe - Thank you so much for your wonderful photograph and bless you for your quick reply.

My brother, the content of your email is fully understood, but I must point out some things to you before we can proceed in this deal.

The total amount that you are requiring me to invest is $18,0000.00. Now this is absolutely not a problem, and I can easily gather this amount. However, even in two instalments as you advise, the total withdrawal amount will be over $10,000 so the clearance fee has to be paid. Let me try to explain to you exactly how the church withdrawal system works.

As an example, if I needed to withdraw $12,000 I would have to pay the clearance fee. If I pay the clearance fee in anything other than cash, I have to fill out another certificate which is called a "Usage & Certification certificate". The Usage & Certification certificate states in great detail what the payment is to be used for. I have to get every stage of the payment stamped and authorised, and the money has to be proven to have been used for the original purpose. The person to whom the money is being provided MUST sign the Usage & Certification certificate IN PERSON at our church headquarters in London. This is an added security measure to ensure the payment is going to be used for its intended purpose.

Now, if the clearance fee is paid in cash, then there is no need to complete the Usage & Certification certificate. Also, I do not need to explain to the church committee for what purpose the funds are for. This will give us both a much higher level of security as you have already advised me that it is vital that we keep this business deal totally secret. If I have to complete the Usage & Certification certificate then there will be at least 23 other people who will know about our plans.

For amounts under $10,000 a clearance fee is still required, and the charge is dependent on the total amount required.

So you see brother Eboh, there is no way around the $80 clearance fee I am afraid, and unless you are able to come to London to sign the Usage & Certification certificate and you don't care to keep this deal secret then you will have to send the fee in cash. If you can do this, please let me know and I will forward you my private home address so that we can ensure secrecy throughout.

Once I receive the clearance fee then the transfer if the $18,000 will take only a matter of a couple of hours.

I hope that my explanation is clear for you my brother.

Take care,

Father Hector Barnett.

From: Prince Joe Eboh
Date: Wednesday, May 19, 2004
Subject: Re: Password: Pappa's Got a Brand New Bag

Dear Father Hector - Thanks for your swift reply. The contents of your mail was understood. I'll like you to forward your private home address to me. Father, we are already partners in this deal therefore, I will be glad if you use your personal money to pay for the clearance fee on my behalf. You will get back every money you invest. As soon as this money is released, I will come to London to visit our church and to discuss with you some personal issues. Give me an address where I can get you.

I want to also remind you that I've been expecting the brochure and other booklets you said you were going to send. Thanks for your cooperation.

Brother Joe Eboh.

I already guessed Joe would ask me to pay the fee myself, so I had a pre-prepared excuse at the ready.

From: Father Hector Barnett
To: Prince Joe Eboh

Dear brother Joe - Thank you for your quick reply. I am sorry, but I cannot pay the clearance fee for you. As the rector of my church, I am not given wages or salary of any kind. My home is provided by the church, and all my other utility bills (electricity/telephone/food etc.) are provided for by the church, so I am sorry but I do not have the money to make the payment for you. **(Let's scare Joe into the prospect of me giving up in this deal.)** I am sorry my brother, but it indeed seems that I will be unable to help you. I am unable to pay the $80 for you, so if you are unable to send the payment to me yourself then I do not think that we can go forward in this deal. It is a great shame, as I am sure that you would have done much wonderful and Godly work with the money. **(If you count buying televisions, stereos, computers, drugs and whores as Godly work.)**

Unless you can send the payment yourself in cash then I see no way that we can proceed. Considering that you are expecting me to send you $18,000.00 (eighteen thousand US dollars) I think that $80 is a very small amount to ask in return.

Being that you are Chairman of the Contract Award Committee I am sure you will have no problem finding such a small amount as $80.

Blessings,

Father Hector Barnett.

Joe falls for it, and it looks like I'm in the money!

From: Prince Joe Eboh
Date: Wednesday, May 19, 2004
Subject: Re: Password: Pappa's Got a Brand New Bag

Dear Father Hector - Remain blessed for your response. Tell me how I should send the $80 to you. Do not forget to send me your personal home address. Blessing.

Brother Joe Eboh.

From: Father Hector Barnett
To: Prince Joe Eboh

Dear brother Joe - Please find my personal address herewith. May I suggest that the best way to send the money would be to hide it inside something like a wedding/birthday card, maybe even one of your local newspapers, and send it by a fast courier such as FedEx, DHL or perhaps you have a local courier that you could use.

Also, if you could enclose a letter repeating the full instructions for the transfer of the $18,000 so that I can move immediately to do it as soon as your payment is received.

My private home address is as follows:

Hector Barnett
xxxxxx xxxxx
xxxxxxx
xxxxx
xxxx xxxx
UNITED KINGDOM

Please advise me of the tracking number and courier as soon as you can. I will ensure that I am home to collect the payment and your transfer instructions.

Take good care my brother,

Father Hector.

From: Prince Joe Eboh
Date: Wednesday, May 19, 2004
Subject: Re: Password: Pappa's Got a Brand New Bag

Dear father Hector - I received your instructions. I will send the money tomorrow in the morning. I hope you'll be at home to receive it. Stay blessed.

Brother Joe

From: Prince Joe Eboh
Date: Thursday, May 20, 2004
Subject: Re: Password: Pappa's Got a Brand New Bag

Dear Father Hector - I went to DHL office to send the money as you have instructed. They told me that they don't accept cash but I managed to persuade them before they accepted it. You should expect it by monday because according to them it will take two days. The tracking number is 353196XXXX.

Brother Joe Eboh

Joe attaches a manky scan of the shipping receipt, but a quick check at the DHL website shows it's legit!

97

From: Father Hector Barnett
To: Prince Joe Eboh

Dear brother Joe - Bless you for sending the information, and I will ensure I am available to you all day on Monday should the cash arrive as expected.

Father Hector.

From: Prince Joe Eboh
Date: Friday, May 21, 2004
Subject: Re: Password: Pappa's Got a Brand New Bag

Dear Father Hector - I must thank you for the support you have been giving me. The number I sent to you is the Airway bill number they did not provide any other number other than that. I'm also happy to hear thay you'll be home on monday to receive the cash. I'm still expecting the brochure you said you will send. **(Oops! Forgot about that!)**

God bless you Amen. Hope to hear from you soon.

Brother Joe Eboh.

Pay day! The cash arrives - it was, of course, donated to a local charity. I need some thinking time so I make Joe wait 24 hours for my reply.

From: Father Mike Myers
To: Prince Joe Eboh

Dear brother Joe - Good afternoon sir, and I hope this letter finds you in exquisite health?

My name is Father Mike Myers and I have been given a message to pass on to you by my friend Father Hector Barnett. Father Hector is at home today, but he has telephoned me to inform you that the parcel you sent to him has been received, and he sends his thanks. I am sorry but I was not told the contents of the parcel, but of course you will already know what that is.

Anyway, Father Hector will be back with us tomorrow morning (Tuesday) and has promised to contact you immediately on his arrival. Apparently he has some further business with you.

Please take care,

Father Mike Myers.

A happy (for now) Joe immediately emails Father Hector to praise him for staying home all day!

From: Prince Joe Eboh
Date: Monday, May 24, 2004
Subject: Re: Password: Pappa's Got a Brand New Bag

Dear Father Hector - I received your reply through Father Mike. He made me to understand that you have received my parcel, Thanks be to God almighty whom we serve. I want to also thank you for making it a point of duty to remain at home for the sake of the parcel. God bless you Amen.

I hope to read your mail soon.

Brother Joe Eboh

More delaying tactics...

From: Father Hector Barnett
To: Prince Joe Eboh

Dear brother Joe - God bless you my little mucker and how are you this glorious day.

My apologies for the late reply but we had a small accident at the church this morning. I am afraid we have had an infestation of Tribbles, and we called in the Pest Patrol people to try to remove the infestation. Unfortunately Ted, the pest patrol guy, decided to gas the Tribbles, and in the front yard of the church he got himself into his Chemical Protection Suit (CPS).

Well, as you know, here in the UK we are very wary of terrorism after our part in CRUSHING the rebel alliance in Iraq. Sadly, when the pest patrol man put on his chemical suit it created mayhem in our street. People thought there was a real chemical attack in progress. Someone mistakenly called the Police and anti-terrorism squad and the whole street was sealed off for several hours this morning. The pest control man was dragged away by the police and we have not seen or heard from him again. One officer told me that they would give Ted, "a good seeing to", so I presume that means they will be checking his credentials. It was a very troubling experience.

Because of this I have been unable to get to the processing department of our financial division, and I will be delayed until tomorrow morning. My apologies over this brother Eboh, but I will arrange the payment first thing tomorrow morning and I shall email you as soon as I have withdrawn the cashola.

Blessings,

Father Hector.

Seems like there may be some trouble at the church.

From: Father Mike Myers
To: Prince Joe Eboh

Dear brother Eboh - Please can you contact me as soon as possible? Will you please let me know the last date that Father Hector communicated with you?

This morning Father Hector withdrew $18,000.00 from our Donation Fund, and we have not had any contact with him since. We are very worried about our brother and we are contacting everybody who has recently made contact with him.

Please contact me ASAP when you receive this email.

Thank you,

Father Mike Myers.

Joe ignores Father Mike's email and sends a message to the now missing Father Hector.

From: Prince Joe Eboh
Date: Thursday, May 27, 2004
Subject: Re: Password: Pappa's Got a Brand New Bag (very urgent)

Dear Father Hector - Blessings to you in Jesus name, Amen.

Thank God you were able to arrest the situation that plagued your church environment. I thank God also for the pest control guy that did the Job.

I have been expecting your mail at least to know if there is a good development. I have just been informed by the ministry of finance that the fund has been moved to the Apex Bank in Holland.

The only thing that impedes the release of this fund to your account is the Certificate of Incorporation and that is where the money I requested of you plays an important role.

Please, contact me as urgently as possible so that I will know what is happening.

Thanks for your cooperation.

Brother Joe Eboh.

Father Mike Myers sends another appeal to Joe.

From: Father Mike Myers
To: Prince Joe Eboh

Dear brother Prince Joe Eboh - Sir, please can you tell me if you received my email of yesterday (26/05)? We are getting very worried about the sudden disappearance of brother Hector Barnett.

I know that he was in communications with you and that he withdrew $18,000.00 on your behalf.

I would appreciate it very much if you would contact me to let me know if you have made any contact with father Hector in the last 48 hours.

Kindest regards,

Father Mike Myers.

This time Joe decides to reply to Mike.

From: Prince Joe Eboh
Date: Thursday, May 27, 2004
Subject: Re: Password: Pappa's Got a Brand New Bag (Very Urgent)

Dear Father Mike - I have not heard from him since 25th because that was the last time I heard from him. I am very worried too.

Brother Joe Eboh.

From: Father Mike Myers
To: Prince Joe Eboh

Father Mike Myers
Financial Development
London SW

Dear Mr. Eboh - Thank you for your reply. It is very disturbing that we have not had any news of our brother Hector for over 48 hours. I have just this moment telephoned the police and asked them to check his home address. I am worried he may have had an accident at home that is preventing him from contacting us. I shall inform you of any news I receive.

Take care bro.

Father Mike Myers
Financial Development - Holy Church of The Order of The Red Breast.

From: Hector Barnett
To: Prince Joe Eboh

Dear Joe - This is your good friend Hector Barnett. Please do not be alarmed that I am contacting you from a different email address. I will explain what has happened.

I have been troubled recently after the death of a dear friend of mine, Minnie Mowse. She was a very very dear friend indeed. Her death has affected me greatly and started to make me question my faith. I have decided to leave the church and join a travelling circus. I have already made two very good friends, and tomorrow I will be starting my circus training with them.

Please do not reply to my barnett@xxxxxx.co.uk address because I will no longer see any emails addressed to that location. I have not yet told my brothers at the church of my decision, but I have left a letter for my good friend Father Mike Myers at my private home address. Of course now that I have left the church I can no longer live at my old home as this was provided for by the church, so now I am currently staying with my new circus friends.

Joe, regarding the business proposition; I am still wanting very much to continue with this deal, and before I left my church building I managed to withdraw the $18,000.00 to send to you.

Unfortunately there seems to be a problem. I tried to make transfer using the bank details that you gave to me. They are as follows:

Bank: Citibank, New York, 111 Wall St, New York, N.Y. 100043
Swift Code: xxxxxx
Acc No. 3614xxxx
Acc Name: Access xxxxxx
Beneficiary: xxxxxxx

Unfortunately, I was informed by Citibank that the account number you gave to me does not exist. Please can you tell me what the problem is.

I look forward to hearing from you soon Joe. Please reply only to this email address.

Take care my friend,

Hector Barnett.

According to Citibank, the account number Joe gave me REALLY does not exist. Maybe it was shut down by a good Samaritan?

From: Prince Joe Eboh
Date: Friday, May 28, 2004
Subject: Re: IMPORTANT EMAIL CHANGE - HECTOR BARNETT
(VERY URGENT)

Dear Hector Barnett - Before your mail came I was so worried being that I have not heard from you since 25th. Your friend father Mike sent a mail to me asking if I knew your where abouts. Sorry if the account has inconvinienced you.

Here is another account that the commission has provided: Mr. Micheal Nzewuka and Mrs. Martina Chikoze Onyemobi. They said those names are the people in charge of the agency that receives money on their behalf.

They have also instructed that you pay the money instalmentaly because western union here does not receive more than $5000. So, you can pay $10,000 on Mr. Micheal then $8,000 on Mrs. Martina. I hope the instruction is understood? **(?!)**

I was in formed yesterday by the ministry of finance that the fund has been moved to the Apex Bank in Holland. Therefore, send the money quick this moning so that the Certificate of incorporation will be released to you and the cash will be transfered to your account.

Why did you decide to leave our church and what about me? You know it is because of you that I joined the church. And since I've been observing the prayer you gave me there have improvements in my life.

(Again, that would be bullshit, wouldn't it Joe? How can wasting $129 be an improvement?)

Please, make it fast so that I will come over to London to see you.

Thanks for your cooperation.

Brother Joe Eboh

From: Hector Barnett
To: Prince Joe Eboh

Dear Joe - Please, now that I am no longer part of the church and I consider you my good friend, please call my what my close friends call me, which is Heccy.

So you want me to pay $18,000 via Western Union Money Transfer? That might me a problem with such a large about as I have the money in cash, and if I walk into a W.U. office with $18,000 in cash there may be some serious questions (and CCTV). I will try anyway. I will need more information to make the W.U. payment though. As well as the names (which you have supplied) I will need their addresses and contact telephone numbers, as here in the UK they will ask me for these details.

If it suits you better I could make arrangements to fly to Holland and hand over the cash in person. Now that I have left the church I am free to travel where I please and next week my circus friends are travelling to Rotterdam which is not far from the bank.

My new friend and magician, The Amazing Tossini (or Bert to his friends) has relatives in Holland also, and we will be paying them a visit.

Let me know your thoughts.

Regards,

Heccy.

Joe supplies me with some other account to which the money should be transferred.

From: Prince Joe Eboh
Date: Friday, May 28, 2004
Subject: Re: IMPORTANT EMAIL CHANGE - HECTOR BARNETT (VERY URGENT)

Dear Heccy - I understand your point. Please, find bellow another account which the comission has given to me:

BANK: ANZ BANKING GROUP LTD
MINERVA HOUSE
P.O.BOX 7
MONTAGUE CLOSE
LONDON SE1 9DH

SWIFT CODE:ANZBGB21

A/C NO: 67XXXX-USD-011(FOR DOLLAR)

A/C NAME: ACCESS BANK PLC
BENEFICIARY: CENTURY SUBSEA LTD.

They said the account is very active. Send the money via it

Joe Eboh.

I make a quick snitch call to the ANZ bank in London and alert them that one of their accounts is being used for fraudulent purposes.

From: Hector Barnett
To: Prince Joe Eboh

Dear Joe - I cannot understand what is going on. I tried to pay the $18,000 into the account you gave me the details for. They are as follows:

BANK: ANZ BANKING GROUP LTD
MINERVA HOUSE
P.O.BOX 7
MONTAGUE CLOSE
LONDON SE1 9DH

SWIFT CODE:ANZBGB21

A/C NO: 67XXXX-USD-011(FOR DOLLAR)

A/C NAME: ACCESS BANK PLC
BENEFICIARY: CENTURY SUBSEA LTD.

When I tried to transfer the cash I was given the following message from the Manager of the ANZ Banking Group:

****

Dear Mr. Hector.

Ref: Transfer application No. 118721-921

Thank you for using our services but I am sorry to inform you that your transfer to account number 67XXXX-USD-011 has been refused for the following reasons:

Error 7801: This account is being investigated

I am sorry sir, but we have recently been given information by a Canadian agent that this account is being used for the fraudulent transfer of funds and is currently under investigation by New Scotland Yard and the US FBI. Unfortunately, during the investigation procedure all transfers to and from this account are now being refused.

The account is now being carefully monitored to see who is accessing the account.

Please accept my sincere apologies for the inconvenience.

Sincerely,

Mr. Malcolm McDowell
MD ANZ Banking Group (UK) Ltd.

****

Please can you explain to me what is going on here? Why is your account under investigation? I will need a full and frank explanation. I am now extremely worried about this transaction.

Kind regards,

Heccy

From: Prince Joe Eboh
Date: Saturday, May 29, 2004
Subject: (VERY URGENT)

Dear Heccy - I will ask the same question if I were in your shoes. The truth is that the commission provided the account. According to them, that is the account they have been using to receive money. So, if there are people who have used the same account to send or receive money fraudulently, I do not know because the commission did not tell me any such thing. I was also scared and shocked to hear such a terrible news from you.

At this point, let me encourage you not to relent because we have come a long way in this transaction. I reported to them immediately, what you said about the account. I was mad at them when they now gave me the same Western Union Money Transfer on the name of Mrs. Martina Chikoze Onyemobi with the following office address and phone number:

14 Opebi Road,
Lagos Nigeria.
Tel: 234-80-33125309

They have instructed that you send the money on instalments of $5000 each. They said you should send the money $5000 until you finish paying the $18,000. This is because the don't receive more than $5000 here in Nigeria. Please, send the money as they have instructed so that we can round up this bisiness as soon as possible and I will come over to London to see you. Thanks for your cooperation.

Joe Eboh.

From: Hector Barnett
To: Prince Joe Eboh

Dear Joe - Thank you for your email and your explanation. I must say that the bank made me feel very unhappy, and I did feel like mutilating someone quite viciously. However, I did get into trouble the last time I did that so I'm wanting to stay well clear of the whole area of mutilation, it really isn't worth it.

I am glad you got mad Joe, because these things that the commission are doing to us are really delaying this whole process. I have the cash here in my hands and I cannot seem to be able to get it to you. It really is very frustrating, and I do feel for you. I am in a little town called Massachusetts and it is a beautiful little town. Myself and my fellow circus friends went out to spread the word to the townsfolk about our circus which is appearing in the town tonight. Please find attached a photograph of myself, along with a few of my clown friends. Of course you should recognise myself, I am the second from the left. I am still very new to clowning of course, so I have not quite perfected the makeup procedure. Koko The Klot (the man right next to me) has told me he will get me a green wig that will make me look much better.

I will make the first Western Union payment shortly Joe and I shall email you the receipt.

Take care bro,

Heccy.

I stick the head of David Hyde Pierce (Niles Crane) onto a clown's body and give him some clown makeup.

I send Joe a Western Union payment for $5000 - it's fake of course!

From: Hector Barnett
To: Prince Joe Eboh

Dear Joe - I'm just taking a quick break in between shows, and I managed to get your first Western Union payment made ($5000).

Please can you confirm you have received the payment and I will send the rest? Please find attached the payment receipt.

The Money Control Transfer Number is 2205499731. The security question is "Favourite clown?" and the answer is "Heccy McHec".

I hope to hear from you soon. I must go now as I am needed on the trapeze.

Your friend,

Heccy.

Oh dear. Seems like Prince Joe couldn't cash the W.U. payment.

From: Prince Joe Eboh
Date: Monday, May 31, 2004
Subject: Re: (VERY URGENT)

Dear Heccy - I gave the informations you provided to the commission only for them to go to the bank and find that the money was not there. I went to western union website to verify your informations and here is the answer i got "W0131 We do not have an order with the provided information" this is terrible.

Please, can you tell me what is happening? the money doen't seem to have gotten here. Please, reply ASAP.

Joe Eboh.

Sadly, it's time to give Joe some bad news and put this puppy to bed.

From: Hector Barnett
To: Prince Joe Eboh

Hi Joe - Sorry to learn that you were not able to receive the $5,000. I will go to the W.U. office shortly and get my cash back.

Listen buddy, I've made a decision. I'm sorry, but I got talking to my circus friends and they convinced me that the best thing to do would be to keep the $18,000 for myself. It would be a lot less trouble, and a hell of a lot more fun for me, so I'm sorry, I have decided to keep the cash.

My new circus friends, The Great Tossini and Koko The Klot want me to invest some of the money in their new snow exportation business. Tossini & Klot assure me that we can make a fortune exporting snow to Siberia. Apparently there is a huge gap in the market for snow importation in that part of the world. I really think I'm onto a winner here. I am so excited about my new business venture. We have even made up a slogan for our company, 'There's no business like snowbusiness!'. Catchy isn't it?!

We also decided to use some of the $18,000 for a big party at a local night club to celebrate our new partnership. I did feel a little guilty about keeping the cash, but after a few drinks any feelings of guilt I might have had completely disappeared.

Anyway, just so that you don't feel left out, I asked The Amazing Tossini to take a photograph of us all together on our night out, and I have attached it to this email so that you have a nice memento of your good friend Heccy. Hopefully you will be comforted by the fact that your $80 helped to change my life for the better. To be honest we had just a little too much to drink (our bar bill was over two thousand dollars alone!) so please accept my apologies for my drunken state.

After the nightclub we moved onto Pepé Le Pew's high class restaurant, and stuffed ourselves! Still it was another $3,000 well spent! Well, by the time the night was over we had blown over $6,500 on booze, food, hookers and drugs.

Joe, I never realised life outside the church was so fucking cool dude! Man, forget painting your tit red, get your ass out there and paint the mofo town red! What the hell kind of church asks you to paint a stupid symbol on your breast anyway? I never did understand that!

I gotta go now Joe, but listen, thanks so much for sending me the $80, it was really good of you. You have really made me one happy guy! Gotta go now buddy, there's a lady's ass over there with my name on it.

Heccy.

I've edited this picture quite a bit. I added Joe's birthday card that he sent me, Joe's DHL delivery package, Joe's red breast picture AND a couple of pictures of Joe which he had sent to other baiters.

Surprisingly, Joe doesn't answer back with the expected tirade of abuse.

From: Prince Joe Eboh
Date: Monday, May 31, 2004
Subject: Re: (VERY URGENT)

Dear Haccy - Thank you very much, your mail was quite surprising. I never expected that this little money will get you carried away when we have $25m which I want to send to your account. Do you think its a child's play? at my age I cannot engage in a busimess that I will not finish. I want to do this business with you.

Forget about your friends I still have trust in you and I want us to continue irrespective of what has happened. I will come to London soon. So, tell me if you're still interested in this transaction so that I will know your position on time because I've started making contacts already to have a power of attorney because the fund has left to Holland which I told you earlier and all the documents bear your name.

I received a mail from Father Mike. He was asking me if I have heard from you. Please, reply ASAP Thanks.

Joe Eboh.

Let's see if we can have a chat with Joe on the phone - at his expense of course.

From: Hector Barnett
To: Prince Joe Eboh

Hi Joe - Thanks for your email.

Look, of course I know this is serious business buddy. Try to chill out a little. Tell you what, give me a call on my mobile phone and let's see what solution we can come up with.

Please note that I will be performing later this evening, so it is vital that you call me at a pre-arranged time or I will not be able to speak with you. If you want to call me tonight, then do so ONLY between 7pm and 8pm this evening. If you call at other times I will not be able to answer the phone (leave a message). If you cannot speak tonight then let me know and I will give you a time to call tomorrow. Please reply to me ASAP to let me know if you will be calling. Remember, the time zone I am using is GMT, so make sure you use UK times.

My number is (UK) +44 7017 421 XXX. Please note that the circus is very busy (and noisy) so you will need to speak loudly so that I can hear you over the music and the crowds.

Cheers buddy,

Heccy.

Joe doesn't reply to me, instead he contacts brother Mike Myers, and he has a proposition for the good father...

From: Prince Joe Eboh
Date: Tuesday, June 01, 2004
Subject: ABOUT HECTOR

Dear Father Mike - I do not know if Hector related to you the business I have with him. Now, read this mail carefully. I am the chirman contract award committee Niger Delta Development Commission (NDDC) Federal Republic of Nigeria. There is this fund About $25,000,000.00 meant for the payment of a contract executed in the year, 1990. I want to transfer this fund to a foreign account, when I told Hector about it, he told me the church does not permit him to engage in business with people who are not members of the church. He asked me to send him a photograph of myself with the symbol of the church drawn around my breast so that he could subject me to the normal induction precess. He also sent a form I received the form signed it and sent it back to him. After doing all that, he sent me a mail telling me that I have become a member of the church that we can go ahead with the transaction when I asked him to provide me with his account information so that there wont be errors in the process of transfering the cash.

As a matter of fact, I used my money to process the necessary documents that will facilitate the registration of his name as the contractor who executed the contract. I did all that so that we could have a smooth registration of his name. The commission responsible for the registration charged $18,000 and being that I have spent a lot of money already to process other relevant documents, I asked Hector to help me send the money, he told me that withdrawal of any amount from $10,000 and above attracts a clearance fee of $80. I managed to send the $80 through DHL that was the parcel he asked you to tell me he has received on that monday if you can remember. Immediately he got the $80, he told me that he has withdrawn the $18,000 on my behalf. After he got the $18,000 cash with him, he did not send it to me *so that I will use it to register his name and the ministry of finance will approve the payment of the fund which will be transfered to his account immediately.*

All of the sudden, I received a mail from him and he told me that he is no longer a member of the church, ok what about the cash? that he has decided to use the cash to enjoy himself. I was so surprised to hear that from him having gone far in our business transaction.

I decided to tell you about this business so that you tell him that what he is doing is not good. I still have $25m to send to his account so he should not be carried away by common $80.

On the other hand, I thank God that this money was not released to his account but it has been moved to the Apex Bank in Holland. I will be glad if you give me the opportunity to continue this transaction with you. We are going to benefit from the money, The both of us. I will like to have your photograph. Blessings.

I hope to read from you soon.

Brother Joe Eboh.

OK, I know this is a long shot, but I wonder if there's any chance of reverse-scamming this idiot for a second time?!

From: Father Mike Myers
To: Prince Joe Eboh

Dear Brother Joe - Thank you for your very informative email, and I must be very honest and open with you and tell you that I am indeed very sorry for the situation that brother Hector has put you in. When we searched brother Hector's house we found a letter from him explaining to us that he had decided to leave the church. It seems he was very saddened by the death of a very close relative. In the letter he told me that he would be seeking new employment and that he promised to pay back the $18,000 as soon as possible. Father Hector's absence has left many of us very sad, because he did such wonderful work for us, and was always a very, very honest and trustworthy person. I can only imagine that the shock of his friend's death may have affected him mentally. I still hold out hope that eventually my dear brother will return to the church once he has dealt with his inner demons.

Hector did not tell me of your business, but I am not surprised that he tried to help you. Hector was a very generous and helping man, and would always try his best to help his fellow man wherever he possibly could.

Indeed, the procedure that Hector asked you to perform is the normal induction procedure of our church, and indeed, looking in the church membership files your name is duly listed as a full member, so in that respect brother Hector did everything in a most correct and honest fashion.

Hector was correct in telling you that to withdraw such a large amount of money requires a clearance fee, this is exactly how the process works.

My brother, I am bound by the laws of my church to try to help you. I am very sorry that brother Hector is at the moment not of sound mind. I am very confident that my brother will return to the church and will indeed return the $18,000. I can help you in this process if you will allow me. However, one area that I cannot help you is with the payment of the clearance fee. I do not know if brother Hector told you this, but we do not receive any payment or wages for working here at the church. All our bills are paid for by the church, and the houses that we live in are also provided free to us. Our food and other sundry items are all provided for us, so we have no need for wages. Helping our fellow man is payment enough for us here.

So the situation is this brother Joe. I can take over from brother Hector and help you by providing the $18,000 but I am afraid that I am not able to pay the $80 clearance fee. If you want me to help you by sending you the $18,000 then you must do your part by paying the clearance fee. In fact, because of all the trouble that you have been put through, I am willing to give you an extra $2,000 which should hopefully make up for your loss and the stress which this whole affair must have caused you. So, if you are willing to send the $80 clearance fee by some fast courier then I will be most delighted to send you a total of $20,000 [Twenty thousand dollars] the next working day after your clearance fee is received. However, I must warn you to keep this most secret. Because of the disappearance of brother Hector there are many people asking many questions, so it is vital that we keep this process extremely secret.

Please let me know what your decision is and, if it is a positive one, I will give you my own personal address so that you can send the clearance fee.

Take great care my brother, and blessings to you and your family,

Father Mike Myers.

Joe is, quite rightly, being more cautious now!

From: Prince Joe Eboh
Date: Tuesday, June 01, 2004
Subject: Re: ABOUT HECTOR

Dear Father Mike - Thank you very much for your kind response. Before we proceed, I'd like to have your personal photograph, your private phone/fax numbers and a detailed account information where the fund will be transfered. This is not a joke at all. The cash is there waiting for approval.

But, are you still in contact with Hector? I have included my lawyer among the crew that will be coming with me to London and I can assure you that I am going to pick Hector Barnett.

If it is possible, let me have a copy of your membership list to ensure that my name is there.

Brother Joe Eboh.

From: Father Mike Myers
To: Prince Joe Eboh

Dear brother Joe - Your email is fully understood, but one thing that you must understand here is that I am extremely busy with my church duties. I cannot afford to waste much time on this matter. Either you want my help or you do not. I am willing to help you, but please do not try to make demands on me because I have other more important matters to attend to. Also, of course I realise this is not a game. Believe me Joe, if I thought you were playing a game I would have ceased all communication with you immediately. Please treat these matters with the utmost seriousness or I can assure you that I will not proceed any further.

Now, as I have said, I am willing to help, but you must realise that my church duties come first, no matter what.

To answer your questions, no, I have not had any contact with father Hector. I have no idea at all where he is, but I pray to God that he will bring him back to us safely one day. He is very much missed.

Please find attached my photograph as you have requested. My telephone number is +44 701741xxxx. Please note I am very busy, so if I am not available to receive your call please do leave a message and I will try to call you back when I have time.

I cannot give you a copy of my membership list as details of signed up members are strictly private and are protected by the Data Protection Act of 1998. It is against the law for me to disclose anybody's information to an unauthorised third party. If you wish to examine the Data Protection Act in more detail you can view it here: http://www.hmso.gov.uk/acts/acts1998/19980029.htm. All I can tell you is that you are definitely listed as a member.

Now finally I must ask that you proceed very quickly if you require my help. In 10 days time I am leaving to do some work in Argentina, and whilst I am there I will not be able to help you further. I am able to get the $20,000 payment cleared for you within 12-24 hours, but only after you have sent the clearance fee. If you wish the payment to be made before I fly to Argentina then I urge you to waste no time in this matter. Please signal your intentions ASAP and I will forward you my address details.

With kindest regards, Father Mike Myers.

Keeping with the *Frasier* theme, I send Joe a quick cut & paste job featuring Martin Crane.

117

Time for Heccy to see when Joe is going to call.

From: Hector Barnett
To: Prince Joe Eboh

Hey Joe - I have been waiting for your phone call, or at least an email. Have you been busy? Sure has been busy here. I have been promoted to head keeper here in the circus. The money is crap but hopefully my new snow exporting business will bring in the cash pretty soon.

My partners think that we will be millionaires within 12 months.

Anyway, please let me know what day you will be giving me a telephone call so that I can arrange a time to speak with you on the phone.

Gotta go buddy,

Heccy.

Joe seems miffed, and I can't say I blame him!

From: Prince Joe Eboh
Date: Thursday, June 03, 2004
Subject: Re: (VERY URGENT)

Dear Heccy - Sorry, but I have to tell you that you decided to listen to your friends and they have succeeded in deceiving you. Do realise that you would have finished that money and that the fund would have been released into your account?

Anyway, I have been able to raise $16,000 with $2,000 still remaining. I will need you to assist me with it as soon as possible.

I need an authentic Fax/Phone numbers because I was informed by the corporation that the Apex Bank has been wanting to reach you since the fund is no longer here.

I hope to here from you soon.

Thanks for your cooperation.

Joe Eboh.

From: Hector Barnett
To: Prince Joe Eboh

Hello Joe - Sorry, but I have no cash left now. I have put all my money into the snow exportation business. Come back to me in about 6 months and I'll probably be able to help you then.

I'm sorry buddy, but I think it might be a good idea for you to find another partner to help you if you need the cash now. My advice would be to contact someone in my church again. They are always looking to invest, and as you are already a member there you should have no problem getting help. Speak to father Wayne Sworld or father Mike Myers, they are probably the best people to help you. Please do not tell them that you are in contact with me though.

Gotta go now Joe, we are moving on from Massachusetts in France to a small provincial town called Indiana, also on the outskirts of France. I'll still be able to email you as I have a new satellite laptop I bought with some of the $18,000, so I might email you again to let you know how I am getting on.

Take care fella,

Heccy.

From: Prince Joe Eboh
Date: Thursday, June 03, 2004
Subject: Re: (VERY URGENT)

Dear Haccy - I will not be happy if at the end of the day, we fail to achieve the aim of this transaction. Could you furnish me with Father Wayne Sworld's e-mail address so that I can contact him.

This business has lingered for too long. Assist me with the $2000. Do you think about what you will get at the end of this transaction?

Reply ASAP.

Joe Eboh

From: Hector Barnett
To: Prince Joe Eboh

Hi Joe - No problem. Father Wayne's email address is wayne.s@xxxx.co.uk . Please note that if he agrees to send you any payment, you will still have to forward the clearance fee to him as usual. As well as Father Wayne, I can wholeheartedly recommend Father Mike Myers also. Of all the members of our church, his is probably the most trustworthy. He is one of our church's most respected elders and does a lot of very splendid charity work. He is an extremely trusting and fastidious person.

Laterz buddy, Heccy.

Joe, now struggling to come to terms with the loss of his $80, decides to have another go at father Mike Myers.

From: Prince Joe Eboh
Date: Friday, June 04, 2004
Subject: Re: For your information

Dear Father Mike - I still need you to help me. I have exhausted all the money I have to make sure that all the documents are correctly processed. I managed to raise the money I sent to Hector which he used for a purpose other than what it was originally meant for.

Assist me with the money. I will pay back the money to you in double benefits when the fund is transfered to you. Do not let this transaction to die just like that.

Thanks for your cooperation.

Brother Joe Eboh.

Father Mike of course isn't about to be scammed quite so easily!

From: Father Mike Myers
To: Prince Joe Eboh

My dear brother prince Joe - Thank you for you email, however I am afraid I cannot help you in respect of the clearance fee. As I have explained to you, I do not have money of my own to spend.

Please believe me, I would dearly love to help you but I am afraid it is impossible at this moment in time. Any money that is awarded to me for my work is usually given directly to a good charity anyway, but sadly at this present time I just do not have the money to give to you.

So, I think that despite our best effort we have come to the end of the road my brother. I will wait for your reply just in case you have friends who are willing to lend you the clearance fee. If not I shall make plans for my flight to Argentina as explained previously.

I hope you are able to find all that you need my brother, and I will pray for you and your family today.

If I do not have a reply from you within the next 12 hours I shall presume that you no longer need my help.

God bless you,

Father Mike Myers.

From: Prince Joe Eboh
Date: Friday, June 04, 2004
Subject: Re: For your information

Dear Father - I want you to consider what you will gain at the end of this transaction. Youre about to earn a share of money that will put smile on your face and you are telling me you can't help. Anyway, if you feel you can no longer continue then give me a power of attorney so that I can continue with another person.

Thanks for your cooperation.

Brother Joe Eboh.

From: Father Mike Myers
To: Prince Joe Eboh

Dear brother Joe - Of course I understand the huge benefits my brother, but the simple fact of the matter is that I do not have the money. If I had the money, I would help you immediately, but I am sorry, I do not have it. I can turn the argument around and say the same thing to you Joe. For a tiny investment you could receive the $18,000 you require, but unfortunately you do not seem willing to help yourself. That is a pity, but of course it is your choice entirely.

There is no need for me to give you power of attorney as I have signed nothing with you, and you have signed nothing with me. You are free to do as you please my brother.

Thank you for replying to me so quickly, and I do wish you luck finding help from somebody else. I will book my flight tomorrow morning. I will return home in 3 months, so if you need any help or advice then please contact me again after August 16th.

God bless you,

Father Mike Myers

Looks like Joe has given up on Father Hector and Father Mike, and so now moves on to Father Wayne Sworld!

From: Prince Joe Eboh
Date: Friday, June 04, 2004
Subject: Membership (REPLY ASAP)

Dear Sir - I am a member of your church The Holy Church of Painted Breast. Attached is my induction photograph. I joined the church in the light that I will be channeled to the path of righteousness and also, to render assistance me when the need arises.

I am the chairman, contract award committee NDDC. I have some money, which I want to transfer to a foreign account. The amount is $25,000,000.00. When I came in contact with this church, I was told that except I am a member, I would not be assisted. I signaled to them immediately my willingness to become a member. I was subjected to the church's induction procedure after which an agreement form was sent to me via the Internet. I signed the form as instructed by the church and sent it back. At the heel of this, I received a mail from one Father Hector Barnett that I have been made a full member of the church. He assured me that we could go ahead with the transaction without cracks since the church authorities have approved of my membership. I asked Hector to send me his bank details so that I will have an idea of where I am transferring the fund. He sent me his bank details, his personal phone and fax numbers address and everything that is needed for a successful transfer of this fund which is presently in the Apex Bank Holland. After sending those details, I spent a lot of money to process documents that will facilitate the quick release of this fund to his account. All of the sudden, Hector stopped communicating to me.

The reason I decided to relate all these to you is because I don't want this transaction to be Jeopardised. I will need your assistance. I want to continue with you in this transaction since you are a member of our church. Please, if you are willing to help, send me the following details:

Your account details

The name of your bank and address

Your bank's phone and fax numbers

Your full name and address

Your private phone and fax numbers

All these are very important in this transaction as all the documents are going to bear your name.

After this fund has been transferred to your account, I will come over to London immediately. You have a lot to gain from this transaction.

Reply ASAP, Thanks for your cooperation.

Brother Joe Eboh.

Incredibly, even after seeing my Photoshopped image of all the different pictures of himself that he sent to different scambaiters, Joe STILL thinks this church is real and attaches the 'painted breast' picture I originally talked him into taking for me!

From: Father Wayne Sworld
To: Prince Joe Eboh

Dear brother Prince Joe Eboh - Thank you for the very interesting email that you send to me. Sorry for my delay in replying to you but I had to make a check to see if you are listed with our church. Of course, as I expected you are indeed one of our overseas members. Welcome brother Joe and I hope that you are well this wonderful day?

You proposition is indeed a most interesting one, and at once I am alerted to the much good that I could do for my church with such money. I think I will be able to help you with the transfer, but please, I will need to know the answers to these questions.

I am unable to ask Father Hector about your proposition because some days ago I am very sorry to say that he left our church, and we do not know there whereabouts of our brother, so please, can you answer me the following questions true and full:

a) Will I be required to travel to meet with you to finalise this deal?

b) How long will the procedure take to complete?

c) Will I be required to help finance part or all of this operation?

d) Once the fund has been transferred will you be coming to live in the UK or will you go back to you own country?

Please let me know the answers to these questions my brother so that I may be able to make a clear decision if I can help you.

God bless you and your friends and family.

Father Wayne Sworld.

From: Prince Joe Eboh
Date: Friday, June 04, 2004
Subject: Re: Membership (REPLY ASAP)

Dear Father Wayne Sworld - I want to thank you first for your swift response. I also appreciate your understanding concerning the mail I sent to you. You asked some interesting questions in the later part of your mail. Now, here are the answers to your question:

(a) You will not be required to travel to meet with me to finalise this transaction except if you want to come.

(b) This transaction will take two weeks at most three weeks.

(c) You will be reqired to finance part of this operation if need be.

(d) Once the fund is transfered I will come over to the Uk to mainly to have my share of the fund and to get acquainted with our church members.

Could you send me your photograph?

Thanks for your cooperation.

Brother Joe Eboh.

From: Father Wayne Sworld
To: Prince Joe Eboh

Dear brother Joe Eboh - I am happy to receive your prompt reply. Thank you for answering my questions.

As you have requested of me, you will see attached a photograph of me with my wife Edwina, and my mother-in-law. This picture was taken two months ago at a birthday party for my mother-in-law.

Two or three weeks to complete the transaction will not be a problem. My friend Father Mike Myers is leaving to do some charity work in Argentina, and I am taking over from him for the three months he is away.

My brother, it is important to me that you are able to tell me what amount of money I will be required to put into this deal?

God bless you and your family,

Father Wayne Sworld.

Continuing once more with the *Frasier* theme, I introduce Bulldog Briscoe's head to the proceedings.

From: Prince Joe Eboh
Date: Saturday, June 05, 2004
Subject: Re: Membership (REPLY ASAP)

Dear Father Wayne - Glory be to God for another new day. The photograph you sent is a nice one. You are all looking good. **(Bulldog**

will be pleased.) *You will need to send me your account details like I told you in my previous mail. It is very important in this transaction. Account number*
Name of bank and address
Bank phone and fax numbewrs and telex of the bank

Your address
Your private phone and fax numbers

Your full name which I will register with the corporate affairs commission

Send the information to me immediately and i will forward it to the corporate affairs commission after which I will now update you on any further development. It is the corporation that will issue your certificate of incorporation before the ministry of finance will approve the release of the fund to your account.

Please, this transaction should be kept strictly confidential

Thanks for your cooperation.

Brother Joe Eboh.

From: Father Wayne Sworld
To: Prince Joe Eboh

Dear brother Joe Eboh - Thank you once again for your email. My details are below. Please remember that I will need to know how much money I am expected to need for this business transaction, this is very important.

My bank details are.

NotWest Bank PLC
1 St. Phillips Place
Birmingham
West Midlands
B3 2PP United Kingdom

Account number is 2045213 and the Sort Code is 44 81 42

My personal home address is: **(I give Joe a real second postal dropping address)**

Wayne Sworld
193 xxxxx
xxxxxx
xxxxxxx
xxxxxx xxxx
United Kingdom

My private telephone number is (country code 44) 70174 1xxxx

Again, please note that is it very important that you let me know the
total cost of this transaction. I do not know if you are aware of this my
brother, but all employees of the church do not receive money for their
services, so we are not rich men. There should be no difficulty getting
money for the transaction but I will have to borrow it from the church
and pay the money back once the fund has been transferred.

Take good care brother Joe.

Father Wayne Sworld.

For a third time, Joe brings up the need for a $18,000 fee.

From: Prince Joe Eboh
Date: Monday, June 07, 2004
Subject: Re: Membership (REPLY ASAP)

*Dear Father Wayne - Thanks for your mail. I have forwarded your
application for approval of this payment in your name to the Central
Bank Of Nigeria and other ministries. The most important thing is that
I am going to register your company with corporate affairs
commission Federal Republic Of Nigeria to enable me obtain your
certificate which will be sent to you.*

*The certificate will cost some money $18,000 and which will enable me
to get some approvals from the ministry of finance and NNPC / NDDC.
All this will show that you executed this contract in the year, 1990. The
contract number has been given to me and it is as follows: NNPC/
NDDC/PED – 10 / 470 / 1990. I received the number today from
Nigerian National Petroleum corporation (NNPC). As you can see, we
have come to the heart of this business.*

*I want you to cooperate with me so that we will have a platform where
we are both beneficiary of this transaction. I have received your Name/
Bank details but I will still need your Bank's fax & phone numbers
which will enable the Apex Bank to follow them up until the money gets*

to your account . As soon as you are able to send the money today or tomorrow then the fund will be in your account in a week's time. I have seen your phone number, I will still need your private fax number because the minister of finance may need it to send you some fax messages.

Thanks for your cooperation.

Brother Joe Eboh

You just don't get it do you Joe? You know we are not gonna get very far until you pay those damn clearance fees!

From: Father Wayne Sworld
To: Prince Joe Eboh

Dear brother Joe Eboh - Thank you for your email. I am afraid that I do not personally have that kind of money. Please remember that church employees to not receive payment for their services. As reward from our work our housing and day-to-day bills are paid for by the church.

The good news is that I can get the funds from church funds, but to withdraw such a large amount a clearance fee will have to be paid in advance, and it will also have to be paid in cash, that is if you want to keep this deal secret as you have asked. For an amount such as $18,000 the clearance fee will be $80.00.

You see my brother, if the fee is not paid in cash, a form called a Usage & Certification certificate will have to be completed. I have to write down in great detail on this form and explain every single part of the payment procedure, which includes the details of who is requesting the money, exactly what they are to do with is, and I need signed and stamped authorisation letters from the 8 member Funds Committee. Then the details have to be given forward to the Charity Commission department for final clearance (chaired by 15 members). This is a long process and can take up to 4 weeks to complete, and also more than twenty people will know the full details of this transaction by that time.

If, however, the clearance fee is paid in cash then the above procedure can by bypassed completely. The payment could then be paid within 6 to 8 hours depending on the time of day the request was put in.

My brother, I cannot pay the $80 for you. If you require the

$18,000 then you will need to send me the $80 in cash as soon as possible.

I shall await your urgent reply.

Father Wayne Sworld

Later that day, I get a message from the 'Honourable' Minister of Finance, of Nigeria, Mrs. Iwealan, saying that the fund has been approved. Attached to her email is a certificate to prove it. I email her back, confirming receipt of the document. After all, good manners cost nothing.

Meanwhile, Joe is learning fast. He realises if he asks for less money that will mean less clearance fees!

From: Prince Joe Eboh
Date: Monday, June 07, 2004
Subject: Re: Membership (REPLY ASAP)

Dear Father Wayne - I received your mail and everything you said was understood. The commission sent me a message a couple of hours ago to inform me that there is a new development. That left me almost uncomfortable, I left my office immediately to go and what out about the development, on reaching there the executive officer told me that they have forward all the documents to the ministry of finance with your name all over it. I gave the minister of finance a call immediately of course. She has to give heed to my call because of my office. As a matter of fact, she told me that the money has been approved but, she cannot authorise the release of the cash to your account because your stamp duty & certificate of incorporation which I told you about doesn't seem to be in your documents. She went further to tell me that we have to finish everything about the stamp duty first before proceeding with certificate of incorporation.

Believe me, I have spent $95,000 to process all the necessary documents which are already bearing your name. The minister told me openly that the stamp duty will cost $3000. **(Amazing - from $18,000 to $3,000 inside a couple of hours!)** *You can see that this amount is not up to the amount that requires a clearance fee of $80. Please, I want you to assist me with the money urgently so that we can get that done and proceed ok?*

Keep record of every money spent on this transaction. I am keeping record of mine too. When the money is finally transfered, I am going to make sure we get back all what we've put in before the money will be shared.

In case you receive any document, send it to me so that I can see what it is all about.

Take care. Brother Joe Eboh.

You're not gonna wriggle off paying these fees so easily Joe.

From: Father Wayne Sworld
To: Prince Joe Eboh

Dear Brother Joe Eboh - Thank you for your email. You are correct that $3000 does not require a clearance fee of $80. In fact, $3000 only requires a clearance fee of $65 which is the minimum clearance fee amount. So, you can have two choices brother. If you still need the $18,000 then I can still get that for you but the clearance fee is $80, or, if you only need $3,000 then the clearance fee is $65.

I have received a document from a Mrs Iweala and I have attached the document to this email.

So Joe, if you can send me the $65 or the $80 as soon as possible I shall make preparations to withdraw the $18,000 or the $3,000 as soon as your fee is received.

Take care,

Father Wayne Sworld

Wriggle... Wriggle... Wriggle...

From: Prince Joe Eboh
Date: Monday, June 07, 2004
Subject: Re: Membership (REPLY ASAP)

Dear Father - I told you earlier that I have spent a lot of money in this transaction. Please, I beg you in the name of God Almighty assist me with the $3000. You can borrow from any of your friends outside the church. I will give back to you every money you spent in this transaction.

The attachment from Iweala did not open. Please send it in such a way that I will be able to open and read it.

Thanks for your cooperation.

Brother Joe Eboh.

From: Father Wayne Sworld
To: Prince Joe Eboh

Dear Brother Joe Eboh - I am sorry, but you are asking me to do something that is against the rules of my church and also of my conscience. I am sorry but I cannot possibly borrow from my friends or fellow church members.

I suggest you take your own advice and borrow from your friends. Surely a man such as yourself who is chairman of contract award committee NDDC will have no problems getting either $80 ($18,000) or $65 ($3,000)? I would be extremely surprised if an important man such as yourself cannot raise such a small amount of money.

Brother Joe, it seems that if you are unable to send either the $80 ($18,000) or $65 ($3,000) then we have no further business together. I am willing to help you by providing $18,00 or $3,000 but you MUST help yourself here. I cannot do any more for you as raising the $18,000 or $3,000 is already a very hard thing for me to do.

If you ask any other person in my church they will tell you exactly the same this. It is your responsibility alone to pay the clearance fee. If you cannot pay the clearance fee then our partnership is now at an end.

God bless you,

Father Wayne Sworld.

Joe didn't reply to that email, so I try a familiar tactic of introducing a fake scammer to the plot.

From: Father Wayne Sworld
To: Prince Joe Eboh

Dear brother Joe Eboh - I hope this email finds you in good health?

Brother, I am writing to ask if you have changed you mind and decided not to apply for the financial aid?

The reason that I need to get a reply from you is that on Friday I received an offer from one of your fellow countrymen who required my help, and he had a similar offer to yours. He has agreed to become inducted to our church and although he only requires $14,650 he has also agreed to pay the $80 clearance fee that is required.

Unfortunately, until I know for sure that you do not need our help, I cannot help this other poor person. So please, let me know if you will no longer be requiring my help so that I can arrange to send financial help to your fellow countryman who contacted me.

Remain bless always.

Father Wayne Sworld.

I have to give it to Joe - he's full of bright ideas!

From: Prince Joe Eboh
Date: Monday, June 14, 2004
Subject: I await your reply

Dear Father Wayne - Thanks for your mail. We have come a long way in this transaction. I really need your help if not I would have not spent the amount of money I have invested in this business so far.

I agreed to be inducted as a member of the church because of the way I was approached initially. They assured me that they would give me the maximum support that I need only for them to turn their back on me all of a sudden.

Father, there is no point prolonging this business, I am a civil servant and the fact remains that I have spent a lot of money to actualise this transaction. Remember that my intentions are to use part of the money to support the church, you will also have your percentage because the cash will be in your account.

My self and family are virtually living from hand to mouth as a result of the amount that has gone out of me hoping that things will be alright.

Let me suggest an idea I think will be helpful to us. Since that other person from my country has agreed to pay a clearance fee of $80, I advocate that you make use of his clearance fee to clear the money amount that I have requested of you after that, you can now replace his $80 from what you have cleard. Do you understand? this is a sure means to get things done easily. Remember that you are my last resort, assist me and we will both smile at the end of the day.

Thanks for your cooperation.

Brother Joe Eboh.

I'll try to force his hand here, but I have a feeling that Joe doesn't want to budge. What Joe doesn't realise is that I know that, as well as

myself, Joe is in communication with another victim who he hopes to get a few thousand dollars out of. Trouble is for Joe, I know who the 'victim' is; he is a fellow scambaiter who is passing information back to me. In short, Joe is wasting his time if he thinks he can drop me and get cash out of his other contact!

From: Father Wayne Sworld
To: Prince Joe Eboh

Dear brother Joe - My thanks for your quick reply, it is very much appreciated.

I am sorry brother Joe, but finally I think we must end our relationship here and now. I cannot use the other person's $80 fee; this would go totally against my church rules and my own moral rules. I would be doing wrong in the face of God Almighty (amen) and I will never do that.

I will contact our new brother Kofi Nkrumah tomorrow and tell him that I am now able to arrange for his payment.

I am sorry that I could not help you my brother. It is a great pity you have no friends to lend you the money, but I do wish you well for the future. Take care.

Your friend, Father Wayne Sworld.

Shortly after sending the above email, I decide to contact Joe as Father Hector, Joe's original tormentor!

From: Hector Barnett
To: Prince Joe Eboh

Hi Joe - This is your good friend Heccy, how are you?!

I decided to write to you just to ask how you are getting on with your project? I hope all is going well for you, and if you need any advice about handling those dudes at the church please let me know.

Everything is going fine with me. At the moment myself and the circus are in Portugal, and we will be here for the next three weeks. As you may know Portugal is hosting Euro 2004 and we have many shows planned to entertain the football fans and keep them happy, especially when their team loses!

Great news on the snow importation business. We managed to secure a three year contract with the Siberian government to supply fresh ice to them. Unfortunately, they will not pay us until the end of the three year contract, but it is worth 2.7 million UK pounds, so if you are still available in three years time Joe then let's do some business together.

So, what is your situation with your business proposition Joe? Did you contact Father Wayne or Father Mike? I hope they are giving you much help. I know that father Wayne is a very honest man, and is also very efficient when it comes to business matters, Between father Mike and father Wayne I think that father Wayne would be able to complete your business proposition the most quickly.

Hopefully by now you will probably have received the $18,000 you need, and you will have got the deal into operation by now. I wish you much luck with it Joe.

I have now finished my trial period with the circus and have now been promoted to head dung handler. While we had a short break from training I took a photograph of me for you so that you can see how well I am doing

I will write again soon my friend.

Heccy.

I knock up a quick picture featuring Niles Crane once more.

From: Prince Joe Eboh
Date: Thursday, June 17, 2004
Subject: I await your reply

Dear Haccy - Thanks for your e-mail and for having me in your mind.

Could you assist me by sending $80 to father Wayne? I have spent nothing less $115,000.00 to process this transaction. I am exhausted already and Wayne is asking for another $80 which I cannot afford for now. Please, do something to assist me.

Prince Joe Eboh

Joe seems to be really digging his feet in and really doesn't want to pay the $80 fee, so I'm going to try and force his hand.

From: Hector Barnett
To: Prince Joe Eboh

Hello Joe, - Thanks for the reply good buddy, but I am sorry to have to tell you that I cannot afford to send you the $80 just yet as I have invested all my money into the snow exportation business. Dude, if I had the cashola I would give it to you, but sadly it's all gone.

I have to say that it surprises me greatly that you cannot afford to raise the $80 fee yourself Joey; I thought you told me you were the Chairman of the Contract Award Committee? I would expect that an important person such as you would not have any problem raising such a tiny fee.

I do have some good news though. Remember Ted, the Tribble exterminator? Well he was released from hospital yesterday. Apparently he had a bad accident in the police cells the day he was arrested, and managed to hit himself severely on the back of the head 27 times. Anyway, word on the street is that he's fine now and will be back at work in the next week. I'm sure that has brightened your day up.

Just to let you in on some inside information Joe, you know that the church donation period is nearly over? The end of the church financial year is on July 4th, the same day as American Independence Day? Well, just to let you know that if your $18,000 is not paid to you before July 4th then you will be unable to get any payment from the church until the new financial year starts which is on September 25th, so if you need the $18,000 then I urge you to act very fast or you will miss your opportunity.

Who are you in contact with at the church? Is it Father Mike or Father

Wayne? They will both know that the final date for your payment application is July 4th, so I would advise you not to waste any time Joe, because if you delay much more then the chance for you to get the $18,000 will disappear very quickly, and I would not like that to happen.

Please contact your church partner ASAP Joe. Don't miss out on such a great opportunity. Hopefully when you have finally transferred the fund you can come to visit with me at the circus.

Take care buddy, and I'll write again soon.

Heccy.

From: Prince Joe Eboh
Date: Friday, June 18, 2004
Subject: I await your reply

Dear Haccy - Yes, I am the Chairman Contract Award Committee. The fact remains that I have spent a lot of money to bring this transaction to the postion where it is today. I have lots of other projects that require my financial attention. You are asking me to send another $80 even when you did not use the one I sent earlier for the purpose it was mearnt to serve.

You are my friend, therefore, if you see it necessary to help me fine.

Thanks.

Prince Joe Eboh.

From: Hector Barnett
To: Prince Joe Eboh

Dear Joe - It is very simple. Please understand this. I have no money, so I cannot help you. Even if I wanted to help you I couldn't because I have no money. I lack money, therefore I cannot help. I am helpless because I have no money. This fact will not change.

I am not asking you to send me anything. Nobody is asking you to send anything. YOU are the one waiting for the $18,000 payment, and it is YOU that will lose out if you do not act quickly. All I am doing as your friend is telling you that if you do not get things sorted out before July 4th then you will lose the $18,000.

My advice to you is to be very quick and contact Father Wayne or Father Mike and arrange their clearance payment as soon as you can because if you do not then you will definitely lose the chance of ever receiving the $18,000.

My friend, it is no use to keep making excuses and trying to find ways for other people to pay the $80. It is a complete waste of time believe me. No one will be able to pay the $80 only you. I am sorry, but that is just the way it is.

All your delay and attempts to get other people to pay is doing only one thing; it is making your chance of ever getting the $18,000 disappear.

My friend you are very quickly running out of time. It is very very important that you act very quickly now. I do not want you to lose out on the opportunity of a lifetime, but unless you send the clearance fee to Father Mike or Father Wayne then you WILL lose the $18,000, this is a very real and very hard fact.

The church has many millions to spend on good causes, but after July 4th then they will not give one single penny to anybody until their new financial year starts.

I advise you to contact Father Wayne or Father Mike immediately and get something in motion fast.

I wish you good luck buddy.

Heccy.

Desperation.

From: Prince Joe Eboh
Date: Friday, June 18, 2004
Subject: I await your reply

WHAT ABOUT THE $80 I SENT TO YOU?

Time to see if I can take Heccy out of the equation and get Joe back to Father Wayne or Father Mike.

From: Hector Barnett
To: Prince Joe Eboh

Yo Joe - The $80 is gone dude. I told you that I would pay you the $80 back, but it won't be for a while yet as I have more important things to take care of. I need to buy my friend Koko The Klot a birthday present (he's 30 years old next week) and I've thought a great present for him. I decided to buy him a juice extractor because in every town we visit he tells me the girls are always after his juice, so I thought that buying him a juice extractor would be a great idea!

Anyway, once the cash starts to flow in from the snow exportation business I'll send you the $80 back. I reckon we should start to get some cash in about 10 or 12 months time, so that's not too bad is it Joe? I'll send you a bit extra for your trouble. Hey, you wouldn't want a juice extractor would you?

I have some sad news Joe. Apparently the circus owners didn't sign a long stay application form for our stay in Portugal, and we have been told that we don't have permission to stay here any longer. We are moving out today and going to Von Richthofen in Germany. Unfortunately Von Richthofen is a very small and remote town and does not have any electricity supply, so while I am there for the next 6 weeks I will not be able to contact you. It is very sad I know, but Von Richthofen is a beautiful place, even though it is a very red and barren land.

So Joe, this is probably the last email I will be able to send to you until sometime in August, so I wish you well with your venture, and I hope that you do eventually receive your $18,000 payment.

Laterz buddy,

Heccy McHec.

Father Mike Myers gets back in touch.

From: Father Mike Myers
To: Prince Joe Eboh

Dear brother Joe - This is father Mike Myers. How are you brother?

I am writing to you because I have not had any reply from you since June 1st. I do not know if you are still requiring my help but I need to inform you that all donation/payment applications must be completed in the next two weeks. You see my brother, our church is nearing the end of our financial year, and if applications are not approved in time then no more payments can be made.

It is quite possible that perhaps you have managed to raise the $18,000 you required from somewhere else. If this is the case, please ignore this email, and I shall not bother you again. However, if you are still expecting the $18,000 payment from us then you will need to get the $80 clearance fee to me as soon as possible because time is running out quite quickly.

God bless you brother.

Father Mike Myers.

From: Prince Joe Eboh
Date: Saturday, June 19, 2004
Subject: I await your reply

Dear Father Mike - Thank you very much for your concern. Like I stated earlier, I do not have another $80 to send to you people. I sent $80 to Hector and he did not use it in accordance with our plans and you are asking me to send another?

I have other projects that require my financial attention, I have been investing. Please, if you are still interested in our transaction then, do something to help actualise this business.

Thanks.

Brother Joe Eboh.

From: Father Mike Myers
To: Prince Joe Eboh

Dear Brother Joe - I am sorry that you do not have the payment. I will therefore close your application request and wish you well for the future.

Goodbye,

Father Mike.

As has been mentioned earlier, Prince Joe is also scamming another 'victim', but unknown to Joe the other victim is one of the noble order of scambaiters. Joe has made a request for $18,000 from this

other scambaiter and is expecting it any day. I think this is the reason Joe hasn't sent me any more cash yet. I am sure he is just waiting to receive his $18,000 from his other 'victim' then he can ignore me. However, I know that Joe is going to get a nasty surprise from my scambaiter friend in the next few days, so I don't want to leave Joe thinking he has burnt his bridges with me.

My hope is that once Joe has been slapped by his 'victim' he might become more compliant. A few days after my email above, I send this...

From: Father Mike Myers
To: Prince Joe Eboh

To whom it may concern:

Please note that this email is being sent to the following potential payment benefactors:

Mr. Simon Phillips
Doctor John Adverse
David Jenkins
Suzanne Patterson
Jackie Fitzimmonds
Prince Joe Eboh
Peter North
Simon Conton
Deborah Kanks

Dear Sir or Madam - You are receiving this email because you recently applied for church funds for your various organisations.

Please note that the final date for receipt of your clearance payments has now been extended to July 18th NOT July 4th. This is due to new UK charity laws which come into effect on June 26th. Therefore if you have not yet paid your clearance certificate fees you now have a two week extension on the final date required for your clearance fees payment.

It is duly noted that we have now received clearance fee payments from three of the persons names above (David Jenkins, Peter North and Deborah Kanks). These three people please be advised that your payments of $13,720, $8,450 and $15,550 respectively, have now been cleared and the payment will be forwarded to you on Friday 25th June.

I would like to take this opportunity to congratulate Franklin Mynt, Simon Sez, and Georgina Mina who all successfully received their payments last week. On behalf of my church I would like to thank each and every one of them for the letters of thanks they sent to us.

If you have any questions, please do not hesitate to contact me.

God bless you all.

Father Wayne Sworld.

Joe didn't reply (I didn't expect him to), but a couple of days later I send some 'good news' from Father Mike about Hector Barnett. Joe will be so pleased for him!

From: Father Mike Myers
To: Prince Joe Eboh

Dear Prince Joe Eboh - I realise of course that our business is over but I just had to share the WONDERFUL NEWS which I received today.

Joe, our dear dear brother, Father Hector Barnett has finally made contact with me, and I am so very happy to tell you that he is safe and well. It seems that brother Hector has entered into a business partnership with two new friends that he has met up with, and a couple of days ago they signed a contract which is to earn our brother and his friends more than three million pounds! This is fantastic news, isn't it Joe?

Father Hector has of course apologised both to me and the church and although I am sad to report that our brother will not be returning to us, he has promised us a very generous donation of £400,000.00 (four hundred thousand pounds). He said that he would send us the donation when his payment has cleared in a few weeks.

Isn't it fantastic that our brother is safe, Joe? I thought that you would of course be most happy to hear this great news because I know that you were very worried when Father Hector went missing. Brother Hector sent me a photograph of himself and his partner Mr. Tossini accepting the first part of their three year payment from the Siberian Trade Commission. Apparently brother Hector has set up a snow exportation business, and Siberia is their first government customer.

Take care Joe, and God bless you and bring health and wealth to you.

Father Mike Myers - Donation Committee.

Hector and Tossini accept their cheque for £3,457,000 from the Siberian Trade Commission.

Result! Joe replies. Short & sweet, but at least it's a reply.

From: Prince Joe Eboh
Date: Saturday, June 26, 2004
Subject: Re: FANTASTIC NEWS!!

Dear Father Mike - I am glad that Hector has finally contacted you. Send my greetings to him. What about father Wayne? I hope he is fine.

I have not been able to raise the $80. Please, if Hector contacts you again, tell him that I am asking for the $80 I sent to him.

Thanks.

Brother Joe Eboh.

From: Father Mike Myers
To: Prince Joe Eboh

Dear brother Joe - Unfortunately I have no way to contact Hector. He told me he was in a remote part of Germany where there is no telephone or electricity.

Apparently a friend who was leaving the area said that he would deliver the message to me. What do you need to know about Father Wayne? He is still here in the church with me.

Take care,

Father Mike Myers.

No reply from Joe for quite a few days now. However, my scambaiting friend has now dropped the bombshell to Joe that he has been wasting his time! Can I resurrect his interest?

From: Father Mike Myers
To: Prince Joe Eboh

Dear brother Joe - I am duty bound to pass on news of our dear brother Hector Barnett. This morning he sent me an email, and also a photograph. Brother Hector is now in Siberia after taking the first steps importing the snow there. As you can see by the photograph attached, he is doing very well and is in good health.

Hector asked me to send you his regards and said that he would contact you sometime later this year once he returns to England. He enquired about the $18,000 but of course I had to inform him that you were unable to supply the fee required. However, I am sure you will be filled with happiness to learn that brother Hector is doing so well.

Blessings,

Father Mike Myers

From: Prince Joe Eboh
Date: Tuesday, July 13, 2004
Subject: Re: FANTASTIC NEWS!!

Dear Father Mike - Thank you so much for the information about Hector. I am happy to hear that he is doing good. Please, extend my regards to him and tell him that the business I have with him still lingers as every document about the deal is already bearing his name.

How are the rest members of the church? I hope everyone is fine.

God bless you!!

Prince Joe Eboh.

From: Father Mike Myers
To: Prince Joe Eboh

Dear brother Joe - Thank you for your very swift reply. I will indeed pass on your regards to him the next time that I am in touch..

Regarding the business, even though the documents may be in Father Hector's name, we can still process the $18,000 payment to you if required. However, I must stress that you will still need to send the $80 clearance fee, but you must ensure that it arrives on of before July 28th. The final date for processing documents and payments is July 14th, but as your induction documents have already been processed, all that is needed to pay you the $18,000 is your clearance fee.

I was given the impression that you no longer wanted to receive the $18,000 donation brother Joe. If you have changed your mind then please let me know quickly because time is very short.

With our blessings,

Father Mike.

From: Prince Joe Eboh
Date: Saturday, July 24, 2004
Subject: Re: FANTASTIC NEWS!!

Dear Father Mike,

I thank you for your time and interest in having us do this business. I should have replied you earlier but I was on official trip the capital city. I arrived yesterday in the evening.

I am still very much interested in finishing this business with you but the problem is the clearance fee. It is said that we should be our brother's keeper and if you have belief in being your brother's keeper, why don't you help me? Do not forget that I have already sent a clearance fee to Hector. Unfortunately he used it to serve his personal purpose. Remember also that as a member of the church of the painted breast, I am entitled to financial help from the church because that was the impression I had initially.

Like I stated in one of my early mails, I have embarked on a lot of other projects that are capital intensive so I do not have another $80 to send. Whenever you are in touch with Hector again, do not hesitate to tell him that due to his diversion of the $80 I sent to him we have not been able to round up this transaction up till now. Tell him I have instructed that he should send the money to you so that the $18,000 will be processed and sent to me and we will round up this transaction as soon as possible.

I hope to receive your favourable response.

Thanks for your cooperation.

Brother Joe Eboh.

From: Father Mike Myers
To: Prince Joe Eboh

Dear brother Joe - Thank you for your email. I was worried that something had happened to you because of your long delay in replying to me. Thank God that you are safe and well.

Regarding the clearance fee - I am sorry but this is something that must be paid if you need to keep this deal secret as you have already advised. Of course you are correct that the church is obligated to offer you financial support, and I have agreed to offer you the financial support by sending you the $18,000 you require. You must agree that this is indeed very generous support, and more than we usually give.

I am afraid that I do not have any contact with brother Hector any more so I cannot ask him to help. I believe his business in Siberia will be keeping him away until the end of this year. Hector has promised to visit us at Christmas.

Joe, there are two things I can do to help you:

I can make OFFICIAL arrangement to provide you the $18,000 without you having to pay a clearance fee. However, this will mean that you will have to sign the Usage & Certification Certificate in person at our offices (perhaps brother Barnett explained this to you already?). Please note that by accessing the money via this means it will require that you present in writing a full explanation of what you intend to use the money for. I know that you told me this needs to be secret my brother, but if you want the money processed in this way, at least 20 to 30 other people will have to be informed about your plans in advance of your payment, thus the secrecy of this deal will be lost. If you are happy to do this, then please make your arrangements to meet me at our offices in London and we can get the payment processed within 24 hours.

There is one final way that I can help you, but this will still require that you send a payment.

I can use some of my own money towards the clearance fee. I only have $40, but if you promise to reimburse me the money once the deal is finalised then I will be happy to give it to you. So, if you are able to raise the other $40 required and send it to me then we can easily complete the transfer with no one else involved. If you are able to send the $40 cash then please let me know and I will forward you my own private home address for you to send the payment to. Once I receive the payment I can access the funds within 6 hours.

I await your urgent reply.

Take care my brother.

Father Mike Myers.

Joe isn't quite as dumb as he seems. He thinks he has come up with a solution.

From: Prince Joe Eboh
Date: Saturday, July 24, 2004
Subject: Re: FANTASTIC NEWS!!

Dear Father Mike - It appears we now have a solution to the situation we are in. I believe the $40 will be able to give us a clearance of $9,000 out of the $18,000. Why don't you help by using the $40 in your posession to get that out of the money so that the commission can start *working on our documents and we'll complete it along the line.*

Alas, Joe has forgotten about a previous email...

From: Father Mike Myers
To: Prince Joe Eboh

Dear Joe, - Unfortunately $65 is the minimum clearance fee amount. I believe you were told this in a email by one of my brothers on June 7th. Please check your email and you will see. This means that we are still $25 dollars short, so you will need to send me the $25. There is no way around this Joe.

I must say that I am surprised that you are making such a simple thing so difficult. Considering that you have such a responsible position/job you are delaying things quite considerably. So you have two final choices brother Joe:

1. Send me the $25 so that I can pay the minimum $65 clearance fee or:

2. Come down to London and sign the Usage & Certification Certificate. This does not require a fee of any kind.

Your brother,

Father Mike.

Joe hasn't replied to my email for quite a while. I think he's had enough. However, I haven't! Time to bring back Hector.

From: Hector Barnett
To: Prince Joe Eboh

Dear Joe - Good news! Dude, I'm back in England after my partner Tossini and Klot agreed that we should all take a three week holiday away from work.

Joe, I think I may now be able to help you with the $18,000 now buddy as I have taken out some cash from our snow exportation business to use for the holiday and I have quite a lot of money spare, so I should be able to get the cash over to you quite soon.

However, there is one problem that we need to fix. For reasons of security I do not want to be seen sending email to your joeXXXX@yahoo.ca account. You MUST try to find another email address to reply to this email. This is very important, and when you reply to me from your new email address I will explain it to you.

Your friend, Heccy.

I need Joe to contact me from another email address. I have a cunning plan. Joe dutifully gets a new email account.

From: Prince Joe Eboh
Date: Friday, July 30, 2004
Subject: God's good news!

Dear Hector Barnett - Good to hear from you after a long time. This is Joe Eboh, Let me give you the new email address as demanded by you. Jacksonxxxxxx@yahoo.co.uk . It is the same box I used to send you this e-mail. With this new box, I hope that by the special grace of God we will finalise this transaction soon.

According to your mail you have some good news for me, What is it all about?

I hope to hear from you soon.

Thanks for your cooperation and God bless.

From: Hector Barnett
To: Prince Joe Eboh

Dear Joe - I must apologise for my late reply. There has been some trouble here in the last 24 hours.

Apparently some members of my church have not been happy that I left them, and sadly I have to report that I have received threats from some of them. I will not go into detail about what the threats were, but it involves a large cucumber and my rectum.

Anyway, I have had to hire some security to look after me whilst I am on my short visit to the UK. As you can see by the attached photograph, they are bad mofos, so I think my rectum is safe.

To get back to business I can now give you the good news that I will be able to send the fees your require. The snow exportation business has really paid off in a big way, so I have plenty of cash spare to get this deal over and done with. Please let me know the exact amount you require and how I can make the payment to you.

Laterz buddy,

Heccy.

Heccy with his bodyguards.

From: Prince Joe Eboh
Date: Saturday, August 07, 2004
Subject: Re: God's good news!

Dear Heccy - I must apologise also for my late response to your mail. I have been on transit recently carrying out my official assignments.

It is important I let you know that I am happy for your success in the snow exportation business. You really look good in the photograph.

I believe in dialogue and that's the reason I will advise you to try and settle whatever dispute between you and the church to avoid further threats from them ok?

About our transaction, the amount the commission required of you was $18,000. This money as you already know is needed to get your name registered so that the certificate of incorporation can be issued and the ministry of finance will now authorise the central bank to release the fund to your account.

My brother Heccy, I will not fail to tell you that this money is needed urgently this time around because we've wasted a lot of time. It even got to a point that the secretary general of the commission started asking me what was happening that I was not responding to the business the way I should.

The corporate affairs commission advises that you send the money via western union money transfer Lagos Nigeria. Here is a name they have provided: MRS MARTINA CHIKOZE ONYEMOBI, this is the lady in charge of the agency that receives money on their behalf. You are to send the money in her name. Added to this, you are to send the money on three or two installments because western union does not receive more that $10,000 here.

You are my trusted partner in this business and anything that affects you negatively affects me too so, I'd like to hear the details about what you said you would tell me.

Thanks so far until I hear from you.

Joe Eboh

I'm sad to say, but I'm sure now that there's little chance of getting any more money out of Joe, but hey, that doesn't mean we can't have fun with him!

From: Hector Barnett
To: Prince Joe Eboh

Hello Joe - I hope you are in good health, and I am looking forward to finalising this fookin' deal at long last. Buddy, it is been a long and winding road, but I feel now we are coming to the end. Soon this business will be completed, and hopefully we will meet and be good friends. Perhaps you can come to meet my parents Alice and Jennifer, they have been eager to meet you ever since I told them about you.

Joe, before I can send the payment there is one last thing that must be done. In London there are new restrictions on sending money to Nigeria and other West African countries. I do not know why this is. To be truthful to you, I am a simple man, with simple pleasures, and I know nothing much about international business. Anyway, apparently you have to complete a Security Validation Form for any large amounts of money that you are receiving. I have attached the form for you to complete and return to me. Once I have received it I can take it to the Western Union Office and make the first payment to you. It is VERY important that the form is returned fully completed and VERY clear. The lady at the Western Union office told me that she would not accept unclear forms. She was a bit of a bitch, but I would certainly give her one.

Brother Joe, I am sorry that the secretary general of the commission started asking you what was happening, and that you were not responding to the business the way you should. Tell that arsehole that I will mutilate his mofo gonads if he is rude to you again. My apologies for my outburst, but I will not accept people talking to my dear friends like that. If the secretary general gives you any more trouble just let him know that he's not dealing with a goddamn clown here.

Are you sure that Mrs. Onyemobi can be trusted Joe? She isn't your girlfriend is she Joe? You know what these damn women are like; once they get their hands on your cash their knickers turn to cast iron - I think you know where I'm coming from?! So, as long as you are sure I can trust her then your word is good enough for me.

I will leave you to fill in the form now Joe. Please try to get it back to me as quickly as possible.

Laterz buddy. Heccy.

[SECURITY VALIDATION FORM ATTACHED]

Joe is getting impatient. Can't see why -   he's only been waiting since April!

From: Prince Joe Eboh
Date: Tuesday, August 10, 2004
Subject: Re: God's good news!

Dear Heccy - I have received your last mail and the form attached to it. Unfortunately, what is contained in the form isn't clear to me at all. Therefore, I want to advise that you send the form again in such a way that it will be clear to me so that I will know exactly what to do.

This transaction as you already know has taken a long time. I want you to go to the western union and pay $2500 so that we can get going because everything has been on the stand still since all these months. I will be waiting to receive the $2500 soon. The corporate affairs commission does not have to be asking me questions again over my reluctance in this business.

Honestly I did not know that you would delay this business up till now but I'm happy still that you are back so that we can get it rounded up.

Thanks for your cooperation.

Joe.

From: Hector Barnett
To: Prince Joe Eboh

Yo Joe - Sorry to learn you are having a prob with the form. I have attached two different versions for you. Hopefully this will fix the problem.

Please remember that Western Union will NOT let me make the payment to you without the completed form, so please do not delay in sending it back to me. The only thing now that delays this payment is you sending the form.

PLEASE NOTE: It is vital you act fast Joe as I will be leaving England very soon to return to the circus troupe.

Cheers bud, Heccy.

From: Prince Joe Eboh
Friday, August 13, 2004
Subject: Security Form

Dear Heccy - I'm so sorry for the delay. I was engaged in a fieldwork management some few days ago. Nevertheless, attached is the completed security form. Act fast so as to round up this business before your departure.

Joe Eboh.

The scan of the security form is so small, and therefore unacceptable.

From: Hector Barnett
To: Prince Joe Eboh

Dear Joe - I took the form to the W.U. office a short time ago and they refused to accept it. Apparently it is too small, and you did not complete the bottom part of the form (your email address etc.).

Please can you scan the form again to be larger and clearer. If you can get the form back to me today before 5.00pm I should be able to make the payment.

Cheers dude, Heccy.

There's a delay in Joe's reply, so I decide to introduce a scamming competitor into the game, my own Barrister Kim Diko. Apparently, the good barrister sent me a warning about Joe, from Joe's own email account!

From: Hector Barnett
To: Prince Joe Eboh

Dear Joe - What is going on?! I received the message below which came from your email address. It was very disturbing and I do not know what is going on here. Please explain this to me immediately. Heccy

—— Original Message ——
From: jacksonXXXXXXX@yahoo.co.uk
To: heccy@XXXXXX.co.uk
Sent: Tuesday, August 17, 2004
Subject: STOP TALKING THIS MAN!!!!!

Compliments of the day my dear fried Mr. Hector Barnett.

I am sending this esteemed email to you in the vain hope that you will take my advice as given to you as a good frind soon to be. The man PRINCE JOE EBOH is not to be trustd. He is a bad man. I can help you better in this deel if you talk to me. Please reply to me soonest at this most private email address barriXXXXXXX29@yahoo.com

Have a nice day and god bless

Barrister Kim Diko

Joe replies, but does not even mention my email to him about Barr. Diko. He also sends me a new scan of the security form. It's larger but still a poor scan. When printed even my typeset questions aren't legible. It looks like he has printed my scan on a fax. (Just for the record Joe answers No to if he is a member of the Mafia, has he ever been a communist, is the money going to be used for international terrorism, is the money going to be used for local terrorism, has he ever been committed to a lunatic asylum and has he ever killed anyone. He answers Yes to does he enjoy the refreshing taste of Pepsi and also to did he find the form easy to complete. To the question: 'Why do birds suddenly appear, every time you are near?', he answers, 'Don't Know'.) I want him to send back a decent scan of my original form so I can post the form on my website. I'm going to chase him for this.

From: Prince Joe Eboh
Date: Wednesday, August 25
Subject: I await your reply

Dear Heccy - I'm not happy with the way you delayed before replying my last mail. I hope all is well anyway?

Well, I have attached the security form again so that you can make the payment immediately.

We can't afford to let this business elude us at this point. Let me give a suggest, if paying the money in London seems difficult, you can go to Paris and make the payment so that we can round up before you go back. Better still, if you are not interested you can then give me a power of attorney to continue with another person.

Hope to read your mail soon. Thanks for your usual cooperation.

Joe Eboh.

Seems that Joe needs to be taken down a peg or two. I don't like his attitude.

From: Hector Barnett
To: Prince Joe Eboh

Joe - What are you talking about with the delay? It is YOU that is delaying these mofo matters by not answering my emails for a week at a time. If you cannot communicate effectively and on time then you can shove this damn deal up your sorry ass. Don't you DARE speak to me like that again. I have ALWAYS answered your emails VERY quickly, yet I have to wait DAYS and DAYS to get a single reply out of you. Why are you taking so long to reply?!

Now, do you want this $18,000 or don't you? If you want it then you had better damn well apologise and apologise FAST because I won't put up with your bloody whingeing. THAT FORM YOU SENT ME IS NOT THE FORM I SENT TO YOU. Send me back the ORIGINAL form I sent to you or this deal is OFF. You have 24 hours to send me the original form or you can forget everything. WHY ARE YOU WASTING MY TIME?!!!

I can send you a Power of Attorney RIGHT DAMN WELL NOW if you want it. I have better things to waste my money on.

Now come on Joe - get your fookin' act together for Christ's sake.

Heccy.

Did I go too far?! Nope!

From: Prince Joe Eboh
Date: Saturday, August 28
Subject: I await your reply

Dear Heccy - How can you say the form I sent to you is not the original one you sent? Please Heccy, it is high time you stopped playing with my acumen. You sent me a form, I printed it, filled it and got it sent back to you and you're telling me the form I sent is not the original copy you sent.

I do not want this deal to start having cracks at this point of conclusion. I still have the form in my box if you want me to forward it to you good. I couldn't have gone to get another form to send to you other than the one you sent.

If you want me to forward the form exactly the way you sent it I will, with your mail attached to it so that all this delay will stop.There's no point wasting time in this process.

Thanks for your cooperation.

Joe Eboh.

From: Hector Barnett
To: Prince Joe Eboh

Dear Joe - One question on the form I sent was: "Why do birds suddenly appear every time you are near?". This question was NOT on the latest form that you sent to me. Where did you get that form from? Are you trying to get money from somebody else? Is Barrister Diko correct when he tells me you are a thief?!!!!!!!

I am VERY mad now. You are wasting my time.

You MUST get the original form to me QUICKLY or my money will go to somebody else more worthy. You have a good copy of the original form I sent to you. You must get it back to me and stop fooling about. I do not have time to waste now.

Heccy.

Time for my fake Barrister Diko to contact Joe with an offer to help swindle me!

From: Barrister Diko
To: Prince Joe Eboh

My guy - I don dey speak with your maga and im day think say you dey play wayo. I go just take am go my side unless say you want make we share the money. I don sabi everything for this maga, I even collect

155

im password to im email (heccy@XXXXXs.co.uk)l. I don sabi all of im people and know say this maga and im friend get plenty money.

My guy, make you reply tell me waetin you want do.

Markus
barriXXXXXXX29@yahoo.com

Many thanks to Double-O, who translated the original English text into the above scammer-speak . The English text reads...

Hey - I am in contact with your [victim] and he is now suspicious of you. I have told him you are a [thief] and that you are ready to steal his money. I will be taking over from you unless you want to share this [victim's] wealth with me. I have plenty information about this [victim] which can help us.

I know this [victim's] email password and I can see all the emails that he is sending and receiving to his friends. He also has MUCH money and rich contacts.

Mail me now to discuss your terms.

Markus

Let's see if Joe is willing to pair up to rob me! No reply from Joe yet, so I fire off another complaint.

From: Hector Barnett
To: Prince Joe Eboh

Dear Joe - Who is this Barrister Diko? Do you know him? Why does he keep sending me warnings about you? What is going on? Where did he get my email address from? Do you know him? What are you intending to do with my money? Who shot J.R.?

Barrister Diko sent me another email to tell me bad things about you. I am very confused now Joe. You seem to be taking much too long to reply to me and then all of a sudden another person contacts me to tell me not to trust you. Do you know this Barrister Diko? He tells me that he is in Lagos also. Have you been to his office? What is this game he is playing?

Joe, it is VERY important that you stop wasting time now. Please read the email from barrister Diko below and explain to me what the hell is going on.

Heccy

I attach a copy of an email that Barr. Diko supposedly sent to me.

—— Original Message ——
From: barrxxxx29@yahoo.com
To: heccy@xxxxx.co.uk
Sent: Monday, August 30 2004
Subject: EBOH WILL STEAL YOUR MONEY I CAN HELP YOU!!!

COMPLIMENTS OF THE DAY TO YOU AGAIN MY GOOD
FRIEND HECTOR BARNETT. MY FRIEND I AM VERY WORRIED
THAT YOU ARE STILL TALKING TO THE CRIMONAL EBOH.
BELIVE ME HE IS ONLY WANTING TO STEAL MONEY FROM
YOU AND KEEP IT FOR HIMSELF. PLEASE BELIEVE ME THAT I
WANT TO HELP YOU. JOE EBOH IS TRYING TO TAKE
BUSINESS AWAY FROM ME AND THE INVESTMENT THAT HE
IS TELLING YOU ABOUT IS IN FACT MY OWN INVESTMENT

I URGE YOU TO SEEK GUIDENCE FROM GOD ALMIGHTY
(AMEN) AND LET ME HELP YOU INVEST THE $18000 IN A
TRUE AND TRUSTED VENTURE. PLEASE CONTACT ME ON
THE TELEPHONE NUMBER I GAVE TO YOU BEFORE AND LET
US TALK MY FRIEND.

JOE EBOH WILL NOT TALK WITH YOU ON THE TELEPHONE
BECAUSE HE KNOW THAT HIS VOICE IS THE VOICE OF
EVIL. IF YOU ASK HIM TO TALK WITH YOU HIS ANSWER
WILL ALWAYS BE NO.

PLEASE LET US HURRY AND INVEST THE MONEY QUICKLY
IN MY PROPOSAL IT WILL MAKE US BOTH VERY RICH MEN

REPLY TO ME ALWAYS ON MY EMAIL ADDRESS
barristerdioi@yahoo.com

MAY GOD BLESS YOU

BARRISTER DIKO

Joe replies at long last.

From: Prince Joe Eboh
Date: Thursday, September 02, 2004
Subject: Re: security form

Dear Heccy - If you allow yourself to be deceived by Diko or whatever
you call him, you'll have your self to blame because that guy is only

trying to reap where he did not sow. He sent me a mail to tell me that he knows you including members of your family and that he has access to your box heccy@xxxxx.co.uk. I want to ask you a question, why should you relate the stipulations of this business to a fraud you call your friend knowing that we've come a long way in this deal? Well, I must tell you at this point that I'm disappointed in you because what you've just done is an abuse of trust.

The success of this business lies in your hands therefore. If you want us to move ahead send this money so that we can round up quickly and we'll both have our shares out of the money.

Heccy, I urge you to be wise!!!

Thanks for your co-operation.

Joe Eboh.

From: Hector Barnett
To: Prince Joe Eboh

Dear Joe - Will you send the security form CLEAR & LARGE as I FIRST REQUESTED? Will you send the security form THAT I SENT YOU, THE ORIGINAL ONE?

I CANNOT SEND THE MONEY UNTIL YOU SEND ME THE Original COMPLETED AND CLEAR FORM

I CANNOT SEND THE MONEY UNTIL YOU SEND ME THE Original COMPLETED AND CLEAR FORM

I CANNOT SEND THE MONEY UNTIL YOU SEND ME THE Original COMPLETED AND CLEAR FORM

I CANNOT SEND THE MONEY UNTIL YOU SEND ME THE Original COMPLETED AND CLEAR FORM

I CANNOT SEND THE MONEY UNTIL YOU SEND ME THE Original COMPLETED AND CLEAR FORM

I CANNOT SEND THE MONEY UNTIL YOU SEND ME THE Original COMPLETED AND CLEAR FOR

I CANNOT SEND THE MONEY UNTIL YOU SEND ME THE

Original COMPLETED AND CLEAR FORM

I CANNOT SEND THE MONEY UNTIL YOU SEND ME THE
Original COMPLETED AND CLEAR FORM

I CANNOT SEND THE MONEY UNTIL YOU SEND ME THE
Original COMPLETED AND CLEAR FORM

I CANNOT SEND THE MONEY UNTIL YOU SEND ME THE
Original COMPLETED AND CLEAR FORM

I CANNOT SEND THE MONEY UNTIL YOU SEND ME THE
Original COMPLETED AND CLEAR FORM

I CANNOT SEND THE MONEY UNTIL YOU SEND ME THE
Original COMPLETED AND CLEAR FORM

I CANNOT SEND THE MONEY UNTIL YOU SEND ME THE
Original COMPLETED AND CLEAR FORM

I CANNOT SEND THE MONEY UNTIL YOU SEND ME THE
Original COMPLETED AND CLEAR FORM

Do you get the message now? If you don't, please do not bother me
again. I am sick of having my time wasted and getting emails from
stupid barristers. I do not know who to believe now. All I do know is
that you will not get a single dollar until the ORIGINAL form is sent
back to me completed and LARGE and CLEAR.

Do it QUICKLY or forget everything.

Heccy.

**Sadly, I have to report that there was no further contact from
Joe. I suspect I was rumbled, since he abandoned his email account.**

**Well, it was a great five months worth of scambaiting, and Joe provided
me with a lot of laughs.**

**I'll miss Joe - probably not as much as he will miss his $80, but what
the hell.**

Harry Potter & the Well of Scammers

One of the golden rules of scambaiting is 'make your scammer do all
the work'. Tie the guy up. Make his life miserable by dragging out the
dealings for as long as humanly possible. What better way to keep a
scammer busy than to make them copy an entire book by hand?

First of all, I get the standard 419 scam introduction from Barrister
Issah.

From: Barrister Musa Issah
To: Arthur Dent
Date: January 23, 2006
Subject: If you will be interested to act upon on receipt of this mail

My Dear - Greetings. I know this mail may come to you as a surprise,I
am Barrister Mussa Issah the solicitor/counsel to the late Sanni Abacha
who was then before his death, the President/Head of State of the
Federal Republic of Nigeria.

Just yesterday his widow wife Mrs. Mariam Abacha called to intimate
me of the condition of her family over the pursuance of fund by the
Government over the husbands alleged loot.

In fact, she conferred in me that her son was working with a German
National only for the German to take advantage of the situation, there
by setting her son up in Germany where he went to claim his father
deposit. You can verify this fact your self through the German Embassy
over an alleged Abacha's Son, Mr. Abba Abacha trying to pull out the
sum of (US$40 M) Forty Million Dollars from the Bank.

At this point in time, she solicited my humble self to look for a reputable gentleman who will be of great assistance to the family and somebody who can take over the sum of $27M (Twenty Seven Million United States Dollars Only) which is presently deposited in a Security Company, for investment. I will later on the course of this transaction disclosed to you the Security Company accordingly.

If you will be interested to act upon on receipt of this mail, please do contact me on the enlisted contact adress and more so be kind to issue me with your current Telephone Number for prompt conversation.

Thanks for your sincere understanding while looking forward to your positive response/cooperation.

Regards,
Barrister Musa Issah

I run my handwriting routine by the barrister.

From: Arthur Dent
To: Barrister Musa Issah
Date: January 23, 2006

Dear Mr. Issah - Thank you very much for you interesting email, it was kind of you to contact me with your proposition.

Unfortunately I am not in a position to help you at this point in time as my company are conducting a very important 4 year long research project on Advanced Handwriting Recognition and Graphology systems.

Our work is extremely intensive and vitally important for our clients. They have committed over eight million dollars to our project and we are nearing the final stages.

After nearly 4 years of research and development we are now only three months away from the conclusion and I am afraid I can allow nothing to interfere with the project until its completion.

We are always looking for paid volunteers to help with our project. If you are aware of anyone who would like to earn money by helping with our project by providing samples of their own handwriting to us then please do read the submission information below. We pay US $100.00 per page of handwriting samples.

Sincerely,

Arthur Dent BSC. HHGTTG. PhD.
Director
Singlesideband Systems

YOUR HANDWRITING SAMPLES WANTED TO HELP OUR RESEARCH PROJECT

We are looking for people to submit samples of their own handwriting to add to our database of hand written text. Currently we have over three hundred thousand handwritten pages from people all over the world and we are looking for more all the time. All the handwriting is analysed by computer and the data will then be used to facilitate the completion of advanced artificial intelligence systems for our client, Cyberdyne Systems.

We are currently looking for people to submit by email attachment, scans of their handwriting samples so that we can increase the size and thus the computational power of our preliminary database.

NOTE: We will supply the text for you to copy by email attachment. You do not have to write your own story, poem etc. All that is required is that you duplicate the text we send to you in your own handwriting on paper and then scan it and return it to us by email attachment.

Handwriting samples are very valuable to our project so Singlesideband Systems are prepared to pay US $100 (one hundred dollars) for every sheet of handwritten text that is submitted to us.

However, please note that the MINIMUM number handwriting sample pages you can submit is 100 (one hundred). Of course, you may submit as many as you wish above that number. We would certainly take as many handwriting samples as you are able to provide.

If you think you may know anyone who may be able to help us in this project, please contact me at my email address below and we will forward you very simple instructions on how to submit your handwriting samples by email attachment.

Thankfully Barrister Issah knows just the people for my project.

From: Barrister Musa Issah
To: Arthur Dent
Date: January 26, 2006
Subject: Re: If you will be interested to act upon on receipt of this mail

Dear Arthur Dent - I write to acknowledge the receipt of your mail.
Sorry for the late response.

Thanks very much for your response, I quite appreciate despite your
very busy schedule, you still make out time from no time to correspond
with me.

I spoke with staffs after going through your massage this morning and
all aspects of your reguest was fully deliberated on.

I gave them go ahead to arrange things with you without further delay.

Contact them with below contact information as to discuss all
modalities.

Mrs Joyce Ozioma esq
tel. :234-802-306-xxxx
e-mail: lawxxxxxxx@consultant.com

Mr Maurice Dim esq
Tel. :234-803-307-xxxx
E-mail: lawxxxxxxx@consultant.com

(Though the telephone contact numbers are different, the email
addresses are identical.)

Your urgent response with the required informations/instruction will be
required in order to make the project successful.

Yours faithfully,
Barrister Musa Isah

I fire off the information to both addresses and also confirm to the
barrister that contacts have been made.

From: Arthur Dent
To: Barrister Musa Issah
Date: January 23, 2006

Dear Mr. Issah - Thank you for your reply and I can confirm that I have sent an introduction to the persons you specified.

Sincerely,

Arthur Dent BSC. HHGTTG. PhD.
Director
Singlesideband Systems

Introducing Mrs. Joyce Ozioma who steps up to the plate and offers her services.

Strange. Her emails are coming from exactly the same location and computer as the barrister's. I sense that I am being deceived!

From: Mrs. Joyce Ozioma
To: Arthur Dent
Date: January 26, 2006
Subject: If you will be interested to act upon on receipt of this mail

Sir - We got your mail and the contents well noted. We were told about the handwriting research project this morning by chief Musa.B.E Isah esq and We would like to know how many samples you may require from us.

Presently, my colleagues and I are ready to sample ours, we can as well provide as many as we can from friends in various universities here in Nigeria. Kindly advice on how we will receive our reword

We anticipate the copy of the text sample by email attachment with other necessary informations.

Regards
Mrs Joyce Ozioma

From: Arthur Dent
To: Mrs. Joyce Ozioma
Date: January 26, 2006

Dear Mrs. Ozioma - Thank you for your reply and your interest in my company's project.

Basically we are after as many samples as possible of your handwriting. As outlined in my previous email, the MINIMUM number of pages we can accept is 100. However, we would be most delighted to receive as many as you and your colleagues are able to supply.

I have supplied some sample text to this email in the form of a book in PDF format, which is the most common format for presenting text. If you have any problem reading the file then please get back to me for more information.

If you decide to duplicate the WHOLE book in your handwriting then we pay an additional bonus payment of $4,000 as well as the standard $100 per page. Here are the rules for submission:

SUBMISSION RULES

The MINIMUM number of pages we can accept is 100. However, you may submit as many as you wish.

It is very important that each A4 page matches the book pages as closely as possible, so for instance if you are copying up to page 120 of the book, you should have 120 A4 pages of your own text.

The number of your pages/scans must match the page numbers of the book.

1. Payment is made only on receipt of the full 100 or more pages. Note that we do not pay any money in advance of receiving the completed pages.

2. You may if you wish submit to us one page so that we can inform you if you are producing the work correctly.

3. The paper must be lined and the layout of the A4 page must match as closely as you can the layout of each page you are copying.

4. All writing MUST be in BLACK ink/pen.

IMPORTANT: Note that we can only make one payment to you, so for instance you cannot submit 100 pages, then get paid, then submit more pages. You are only allowed to submit work once and once only.

Once you have completed your handwriting, you will then need to scan each page and then send it to us by email attachment.

It is very important that the scans are large and clear. Small or unclear scans will not be accepted and payment will be refused. As a guide we generally ask that the scan width be 1200 pixels wide.

If you are not sure of any part of these instructions, please do get in touch with me for clarification by email or telephone.

Also, please let me know by what means you prefer your payment to be made.

Sincerely,

Arthur Dent BSC. HHGTTG. PhD.
Director
Singlesidband Systems

I attach the PDF file for Joyce. A few days pass and then Joyce gets back in touch.

From: Mrs. Joyce Ozioma
To: Arthur Dent
Date: February 1, 2006
Subject: Re: If you will be interested to act upon on receipt of this mail

Good day sir - I am writing to inform you that I have opened the attached book and I have commence work on the writing. I will be sending you a copy by tomorrow for approval.

Meanwhile, in my message of yesterday, I requested your telephone number(s) and your office address, as I have gone through your website and there was no telephone contact in it.

I read from the site that you are currently upgrading your website, as such there was no address or telephone/fax contacts.

I will appreciate you include them when replying this message.

Please respond to enable me send the first pages for approval by tomorrow.

Do have a nice day.

Mrs. Joyce Ozioma

Joyce wastes no time in starting on the project and sending me a sample page.

From: Arthur Dent
To: Mrs. Joyce Ozioma
Date: February 2, 2006

Dear Mrs. Ozioma - Thank you for your very rapid response, it is most appreciated and I congratulate you on your professionalism.

I can confirm that the sample you sent to me is 100% acceptable, thank you.

Please will you advise me how many pages you are considering to duplicate and also by what means you wish your payment to be made?

Sincerely,

Arthur Dent BSC. HHGTTG. PhD.
Director
Singlesidband Systems

From: Mrs. Joyce Ozioma
To: Arthur Dent
Date: February 2, 2006
Subject: handwriting project

Dear Sir - Thank you too for your immediate response, this gives me confidence that I am on the right track.

As I earlier informed you, I am imploying other hands to make sure that the poject is successfully completed and right on time.

I am anticipating copying the entire book as you said in one of your messages that it attracts a bonus of US$4,000.00.

Regarding receiving of the payment, I will prefer western union money transfer. I will issue you with names for the collection of my payment.

I will like you to advice on how the scanning should be send. Am I to send the entire pages on your email box or are there alternative email boxes?

I am contemplating sending about 20 pages through one email box, which will be about 15 email boxes for the entire book. All the same your candid advice will equally be appreciated.

Waiting for instructions from you.

Regards,

Mrs. Joyce Ozioma

From: Arthur Dent
To: Mrs. Joyce Ozioma
Date: February 2, 2006

Dear Mrs. Ozioma - Thank you for your email and your payment option is entirely agreeable. Are you able to receive the payment amount in one single payment? I am asking because I know that in some countries there are restrictions on the size of Western Union payments. Please advise me.

It would be preferable to me if you send the completed scans to a spare email address rather than my normal email. Therefore please send the scans to the following address: singlesideband.dent@xxxx.com. Any normal email should of course be addressed to this email address.

Sincerely,

Arthur Dent BSC. HHGTTG. PhD.
Director
Singlesidband Systems

From: Mrs. Joyce Ozioma
To: Arthur Dent
Date: February 2, 2006
Subject: Re: handwriting project

Dear Sir - Your mail is well received and content well noted. Regarding the scanning, I will send them to the provided email box while other correspondence will be directed to this mail box as usual.

Paying me through western union as I earlier suggested will be ok as I will provide as many names as possible for the collection since it can not be sent in bulk but on a second thought, I am considering the charges etc, so I am contemplating sending one of my relatives in the UK there to pick up the payment for me, that is why I earlier demanded for your address. I will appreciate you forward you address to me where the person can come for collection of my payment.

Advice me on how the charges will be paid if I provide names for sending the payment through western union to Nigeria here.

Thanks and best regards.

Mrs. Joyce Ozioma

From: Arthur Dent
To: Mrs. Joyce Ozioma
Date: February 3, 2006

Dear Mrs. Ozioma - Thank you for your email.

We will be paying any charges that are incurred so you need not worry about that. However, if you have contacts in the UK who would like to collect your payment from our offices then that is completely agreeable also.

Sincerely,

Arthur Dent BSC. HHGTTG. PhD.
Director
Singlesidband Systems

From: Mrs. Joyce Ozioma
To: Arthur Dent
Date: February 9, 2006
Subject: urgent response required

Dear Sir - I will appreciate you call me through my number which is 234-802-306-XXXX tonight so that we can discuss as am about scanning the jobs across to you.

The scanning can not be completed in a day, that was why I asked if the total 293pages can be scanned and sent within 2 days.

As I earlier notified you, I employed capable hands to complete the writing. I want you to advice on how long it will take to make payment upon your receipt of the total 293 pages.

I request for your urgent response and kind advice on the above.

Yours faithfully,

Mrs. Joyce Ozioma

I didn't bother to call, but a few days later Joyce sent me the completed work - as 289 attachments. And in case you're wondering what the pages look like...

Christopher Little
Literary Agency

CJL/mm/01

24th July 2006

<u>"Harry Potter & the Chamber of Secrets"</u>

Thank you for your recent letter and enclosures, requesting permission to use a handwritten extract from the above Harry Potter title in a book about email scammers entitled "Greetings in Jesus Name".

I am sorry to say that this is not something we would grant permission for. Furthermore, 'Harry Potter' and other names, images and places from the series are subject to complex contractual commitments and trademark restrictions, and all publishing rights to and in the Harry Potter series are reserved by J K Rowling. Kindly note that Ms Rowling does not wish to pursue any other companion books or adaptations of her books at this point in time and that it is her wish that if and when any accompanying 'spin-off' books to the Harry Potter series are published, she will be the author.

We are sorry for this disappointing response but would like to thank you again for taking the time to write, and for your interest in the Harry Potter series.

With best wishes

Yours sincerely

The Christopher Little Literary Agency
(Agents to J K Rowling)

10 Eel Brook Studios, 125 Moore Park Road, London SW6 4PS • Telephone: 44 (0)20 7736 4455 • Fax: 44 (0)20 7736 4490
e-mail: info@christopherlittle.net   www.christopherlittle.net
VAT Reg No. 245 0585 66

Recycled paper

Well, anyway...

Shortly after, Joyce emails me with her payment details.

From: Mrs. Joyce Ozioma
To: Arthur Dent
Date: February 11, 2006
Subject: urgent

Sir - This is to notify you that I have completed the scanning and sent the total copies of 293 to the email box you gave to me. I urge you to check it and get back to me.

Below is the information for the payment through western union money transfer, please the names, address, text questions and answers must be exactly as it is written:-

1. NAME : PRINCE UCHENNA OLOLO
ADD : PLOT 47 TRANS AMADI LAYOUT PORTHARCOURT, RIVERS STATE, NIGERIA
Question : NAME & WHAT
ANS : OLOLO & BUILDING
AMOUNT US$8,000.00

2. NAME : DIM JUDE OKECHUKWU
ADD : 15 OLADIPO FAFORE STREET, AKOWONJO LAGOS STATE, NIGERIA
Question : COLOUR
ANS : BLACK
AMOUNT US$2,300.00

3. NAME : NGOZI OGUGUA
ADD : AMADI AMA- PORTHARCOURT, RIVERS STATE, NIGERIA
Question : NAME & WHAT
ANS : OLOLO & BUILDING
AMOUNT US$8,000.00

4. NAME : JOY OZIOMA OLOLO
ADD : 1st Avenue, plot 265, 122 Rd., Gowon Estate, Ipaja - Lagos State, Nigeria.
Question : NAME & WHAT
ANS : JOYCE & WRITING
AMOUNT US$4,000.00

5. NAME : CHUKWUNONSO ANENE
ADD : WOJI ROAD, WOJI - PORTHARCOURT, RIVERS STATE, NIGERIA

Question : NAME & WHAT
ANS : OLOLO & BUILDING
AMOUNT US$8,000.00

6. NAME : DIM JUDE OKECHUKWU
ADD : 15 OLADIPO FAFORE STREET, AKOWONJO LAGOS STATE,
NIGERIA
Question : COLOUR
ANS : BLACK
AMOUNT US$3,000.00

Note that it is very important that you include senders name and full address when sending.

Call me through my number 234 - 802-306-XXXX immediately the payment is sent and do not for get to give me the sender's name, address and the control number through this email box.

Expecting your response.

Thanks and best regards,

Mrs. Joyce Ozioma

Hmm. Looks like there are going to be six disappointed people waiting for their payments.

From: Arthur Dent
To: Mrs. Joyce Ozioma
Date: February 11, 2006

Dear Mrs. Ozioma - Thank you for your telephone call this afternoon and also for sending in the completed work which I confirm has now been received. I shall ensure you get what you deserve as soon as possible.

Unfortunately as it is the weekend I cannot authorise your payment until Monday morning as our accounts department do not work on Sat/Sun. However, I shall arrange your payment for some time on Monday afternoon (13th Feb).

Thank you once again and I shall contact you soon.

Sincerely.

Arthur Dent BSC. HHGTTG. PhD.
Director
Singlesideband Systems

After a delay of a couple of days, a frustrated Joyce gets in touch.

From: Mrs. Joyce Ozioma
To: Arthur Dent
Date: February 13, 2006
Subject: Anticipating the fulfilment of your words

Dear Sir - I am writing to remind you that I am still in anticipation of the payment information. From your correspondence of Saturday, I was meant to understand that the payment will be made "sometime on Monday afternoon (13th Feb)."

Sir, I will appreciate if you give me a call as soon as the payment is made on 234 - 802-306-0032 . Please while sending the payment information, do not forget to include the sender's name, complete address and the control number through this email box.

Anticipating the fulfilment of your words.

Thanks.

Mrs. Joyce Ozioma

I'll make her wait just a little longer!

From: Arthur Dent
To: Mrs. Joyce Ozioma
Date: February 13, 2006

Dear Mrs. Ozioma - My apologies for the delay in getting back to you. We had an emergency with one of our clients' computer systems and had to send a four man team, including myself to repair a very serious problem. Unfortunately this took much longer than I had estimated and kept me away from my office for nearly two days. I shall contact you again later today to arrange payment.

Sincerely.

Arthur Dent BSC. HHGTTG. PhD.
Director
Singlesideband Systems

From: Mrs. Joyce Ozioma
To: Arthur Dent
Date: February 14, 2006
Subject: Re: Anticipating the fulfilment of your words

Sir - Your message of 14th February 2006 was received and content understood. I do hope that you have successfully completed the repairs.

I honestly expected the payment information just as you stated you will be arranging later today.

Mr. Arthur, to be candid with you, I am not pleased with your delay in paying me for a work I have completed for you. If you can remember, I severally asked you when my payment will be made upon completion of the project from my side, which you specifically told me 24hrs. Sir, I do hold people by their words, as such I will not want yours to be reverse. I completed my work and sent to you exactly the time I told you, which you confirmed was ok.

Please I will appreciate if you make my payment and send the transfer information to me through this email box by tomorrow.

I was even expecting we would have completed this and if possible you give me another one to handle, which I am arranging different people to do the writing as you stated in your previous correspondence that you need different handwritings. All the same, keep to your word, I have kept to mine by completing the work and sent same to you accordingly.

Meanwhile, I have been wondering why you don't pick your calls. I have tried severally in geting across to you by telephone without success, the phone will ring althrough without anyone picking, does it mean that you don't go out with your mobile phone or that you don't answer calls while working? Why is it that you don't call me on phone, at least to explain the situation of things?

Please do keep to your words regarding my payment.

I will sincerely appreciate receipt of the payment information by tomorrow.

Thanks and God bless.

Mrs. Joyce Ozioma

Let's see what Joyce has to say when I accuse her partner - the original

Barrister Musa who first contacted me - of being a scammer.

From: Arthur Dent
To: Mrs. Joyce Ozioma
Date: February 14, 2006

Dear Mrs. Ozioma - Please would you explain to me why you are associating with a known 419 scammer? I have been contacted by Inspector Morse of the UK Police (morse@xxxxpolice.co.uk) to tell me that the person known as Musa Issah is a known felon and has been sending out many hundreds of scam emails and apparently there have been many complaints and reports about him.

I would like you to explain to me why you are connected to such a person. My company cannot be allowed to be associated with such people.

Sincerely

Arthur Dent BSC. HHGTTG. PhD.
Director
Singlesideband Systems

From: Mrs. Joyce Ozioma
To: Arthur Dent
Date: February 14, 2006
Subject: No information from your side yet....... why?

Dear sir - Thanks for your mail, you are well understood. I commend your intelligence but sincerely advice you to be more careful with your choice of words when dealing with people mostly nationals of countries not within your continent less it be assumed that all from your base are abusive which I know they are not having dealt with many in the past.

But if I may ask, why is it that you have not said this all these while I have not submitted the hand written samples? If you feel Mr Mussa is a known felon as you and your inspector claimed, don't you thing is better you confront him rather that seeking explanations from me..Do you feel my explanations about him will be accaptable to you?

I can not but care less of your impression about me or the body I represent but all things being equal I must not fail to make you understand that I don't have an idea of all these accusation you and your so called Inspector Morse of the UK Police is levelling against your fellow man.

I'm a sabbatherian and I so much believe in law of cammah that was why I did the job for you without asking of mobilizing fee from you couples with love and respect I have for Mr Issah. If you feel you can eat my money and get away with eat well, that is for you but I'm assuring you that you can run away in the sight of man but can never run away in the sight of the Almighy God whom I serve.

Mr Issah you are talking about is well known personality here in Nigeria and I would'nt know your reason of passing your judgment without hearing from him, my advice is for you confront him as he is in position to clear himself from the alligations .

I am only concerned with securing the payment evidence of the job I did for you to enable me pick up the money and will appreciate you go ahead and arrange the payment to day please, then you can offer me jobs next time you want upon your confirmation of truth about Mr Issah.

Thanks.

Mrs. Joyce Ozioma

From: Arthur Dent
To: Mrs. Joyce Ozioma
Date: February 15, 2006

Dear Mrs. Ozioma - I am afraid you do not grasp the importance of the information that was given to me. It is not up to me to investigate Mr. Mussa, I am not a policeman or detective. I shall leave such work to the experts. I was just given a warning not to deal with him as apparently there is an imminent arrest of him and his associate due very shortly. The fact he is a scammer and a thief are not my words madam, but the words of a high ranking police officer. I would advise you to choose your own words more carefully.

I am glad that you state that you could not care less about my impression of you Mrs. Ozioma because I suspect that you are more closely associated with Mr. Musa and his activities than you are admitting to, therefore I am going to refuse to accept any work from you and the samples you have sent in to me so far shall be destroyed. You shall be receiving no payment from my company. We do not associate ourselves with criminal activity in any way, large or small.

Good day.

Arthur Dent BSC. HHGTTG. PhD.
Director
Singlesideband Systems

From: Mrs. Joyce Ozioma
To: Arthur Dent
Date: February 15, 2006
Subject: sorry

Sir - I received this your message with heavy heart and could not really figure out what is actually going on, why would anyone scam or steal from you? please your urgent answer to this question will highly be appreciated.

Of course I'm closely associated with Mr. Musa and some of his activities but that does not mean I must know every of his activities. Since you have made up your mind about the informations you claimed inspector forwarded to you and based on it passed the concluded without caring to know the truth, I will not question your judgement.

However, I still can not but care less over your impression about me why because I don't see anything wrong in working for you. If you think the words I used while expressing my feelings about the whole thing is bad then I'm sorry but that is the basic truth. Clear consience they say fears no accusation. You are suspecting Mr Issa to be one of the scammers as you and your inspector claims will not make me deny the fact that Mr Issa is a good man. I don't know him as a fraudster and can not tell you nothing but the truth. As a matter of fact, I don't know what went wrong between you and him and will not tell what I don't know.

I don't have any option than to let him (Mr Issah) know about the situation of things now before taking the matter to God in prayers since it is the only way to go about it for now. But do have it at the back of your mind that no one takes what belong to me forcefully and get away with it without having a bitter story to tell unless the God I serve is not alive. Sir, this is not a threat but a very sound warning.

Thanks.

Mrs. Joyce Ozioma

From: Arthur Dent
To: Mrs. Joyce Ozioma
Date: February 15, 2006

Dear Mrs. Ozioma - Thank you for your reply. However your talk of God is wasted on me. I am not a believer in such fairytales.

Good day.

Arthur Dent BSC. HHGTTG. PhD.
Director
Singlesideband Systems

Sadly, that was the last I ever heard from Joyce. Perhaps she and Mr. Musa have gone into hiding, suspecting a real imminent arrest?

Date: Mon, 25 Aug 2003
From: <drahmedibrahim@tiscali.co.uk>
Subject: URGENT

FROM:
DR. AHMED IBRAHIM
HEAD OF ARCHIVES / RECONCILIATION
BOND BANK NIG. LTD.
VICTORIA ISLAND, LAGOS.

RE: NEXT OF KIN.

DEAR,

DO NOT BE SURPRISED AT RECEIVING THIS MAIL. I BELIEVE THAT THERE IS NO HARM IN TRYING SOMEONE TRUSTWORTHY AT HEART. A NEW RELATIONSHIP WILL GO A LONG WAY TO HELP ME.

I NEED YOU TO COME AND STAND AS 'NEXT OF KIN' TO ONE MR. MANSOUR RAHBANI WHO DIED IN 1999 OF A HEART CONDITION HERE IN LAGOS. SOME YEARS AGO, MR. MANSOUR MADE A NUMBERED (OR FIXED) DEPOSIT OF US$27,000,000.00 MILLION IN MY BANK. UNFORTUNATELY, HE DID NOT MENTION A NEXT OF KIN IN ANY OF HIS PAPERS WITH US OR HIS CONTRACTORS - TEXACO OIL.

SINCE THEN, THERE HAVE BEEN NO RESPONCE TO OUR INTERNATIONAL ADVERTORIALS CALLING FOR ANY RELATIVE

*TO CONTACT US. IT IS FOUR YEARS NOW AND STILL NO
RESPONCE. BY AUGUST ENDING, THE INTEREST WILL BE
ROLLED OVER, BRINGING THE TOTAL CLAIMS TO
US$28,000,000.00 MILLION.*

*MY DEPARTMENT HAS THE MANDATE TO OVERSEE THE
INTERNAL CLEARANCE FOR CLAIMS SUCH AS THIS AND THE
FINAL APPROVAL SIGNATURE FOR PAYMENT IS MINE. YOU
HAVE NO RISK. BY LAW, YOU ONLY NEED TO SHOW-UP ONCE
BEFORE THE MONEY WILL BE PAID INTO YOUR ACCOUNT
ABROAD. HOWEVER, PLEASE KNOW THAT THE MONEY WILL BE
SHARED BETWEEN US; I WILL TAKE 60% AND YOU: 40%.*

*THERE ARE REASONS WHY WE NEED TO CLAIM THIS MONEY
FAST. I WILL GIVE YOU MORE COMPREHENSIVE DETAIL WHEN
YOU REPLY.*

THANK YOU.

DR. AHMED IBRAHIM

And so it starts...

From: Klench Mychiques
To: drahmedibrahim@tiscali.co.uk

Dear Dr. Ibrahim - Many thanks for your splediforous email. I do not
know how you came to find my private business address, but I have to
confess that I am extremely interested in your offer. Please tell me more.
Do you like stunts?

Your friends,

Mr. Klench Mychiques - Stuntman Extraordinaire

Date: Wed, 27 Aug 2003
From: <drahmedibrahim@tiscali.co.uk>
Subject: RE: URGENT I AM WAITING FOR YOUR RESPONSE NOW
(THIS BUSINESS IS 100% LEGAL AND IS CONFIDENCIAL)

DEAR KLENCH MYCHIQUES,

*HOW ARE YOU TODAY. THANK YOU FOR YOUR RECENT MAIL IN
REGARD TO YOUR COMMENT IN THIS BUSINESS, I AM HEREBY*

*TO EXPLAIN TO YOU THE WAY FORWARD. I AM MANAGING
DIRETOR OF BOND BANK NIGERIA LTD. THEN THERE WAS A
GOOD CLIENT WOH DIE ON HEARTH CONDITION.*

*MR.MANSOUR RAHBANI HAS A CHAIN OF COMPANY LIKE
TEXACO OIL AND DIAMOND MINING COMPANY AND HE
DEPOSIT US$27M(TWENTY SEVEN MILLION UNITED STATE
DALLARS). SINCE FOUR YEARS INTERVAL NOBODY OR
RELATIVE COME FOR THE MONEY AND THE MONEY HAVE
ROLLED OVER TO US$28M BY THIS AUGUST 2003. RIGHT NOW,
FOR YOUR EFFORT TO STAND IN THIS BUSINESS, I WILL TAKE
60%FROM THE TOTAL AMOUNT WHILE YOUR RATIO WILL BE
40%FOR PROVIDING AN ACCOUNT TO SECURE THE FUND.(WE
NEED TO CLAIM THIS MONEY FAST). NB:MR RAHBANI DID NOT
MENTION NEXT OF KIN,WHO WILL STAND AS THE BENEFICIARY
OF THIS FUND. SO, THAT IS WHY I WANT A CAPABLE CLIENT TO
STAND AS THE BENEFICIARY OWNER OF THE MONEY.*

*I WILL BACK YOU UP WITH EVERY NECESSARY DOCOUMENT IN
RESPECT OF THIS TRANSACTION. BESIDES,I WILL DIRECT YOU
TO A CAPABLE LAWYER WHO WILL HANDLE THE TRANSFER
PROCESS THIS FUND WILL BE REMITTED INTO YOUR ACCOUNT
ABROAD WITHOUT ANY PROBLEEM.I WOULD LIKE YOU TO
PROMISE ME THAT YOU WILL NOT BETRAYED ME. IF THE
MONEY COMES IN YOUR CUSTODY. AFTER THE END OF THIS
BUSINESS WE ARE GOING TO SMILE TOGETHER. I NOW LOOK
FOWARD TOWARDS YOUR QUICK REPLY AND CO-OPERATION.*

THANKS.

DR AHMED IBRAHIM,

From: Klench Mychiques
To: drahmedibrahim@tiscali.co.uk

Dear Mr. Ibrahim - Many thanks for your prompt reply, and your
proposal is indeed very interesting to me. I would like to see if I can
help you out with this matter.

A couple of things you need to know before I proceed:

If you offer requires travel, this will be impossible for the next 7 days as
both of my arms are in plaster as a result of a motorcycle jump which
went badly wrong (I was still paid my usual $120,500 for doing it
though, so who gives a shit!).

I am due on the set of the new James Bond movie on the 13th of September until the 15th of September (I am the stunt double to the actor Pierce Brosnan who plays James Bond), so should any travel be required I will be unavailable during those two dates. However, I will have my laptop with me, so email communication will not be a problem, providing I am not doing a stunt at the time.

Also note that due to a disastrous stunt I performed some years ago, my hearing is 95% impaired, so I cannot use a normal telephone. As you have probably realised by now I am a professional stuntman by trade, and my hearing was damaged by a large explosion in my shorts (I was doing a scene for a low budget porno movie called Ball Busters). I am able to speak via a TextPhone which converts your words to text so that I can read it. If you have a TextPhone then I will be happy to communicate via that. If you do not have a TextPhone then all communication will have to be via email I am afraid. I hope that is not too great a problem for you?

One final note: Before I am prepared to do business, I would of course require some proof of your identity. I am able to email to you my passport picture on receipt of your identifications details.

I look forward to your reply.

Sincerely,

Klench Mychiques - Stuntman Extraordinaire

I am contacted by Ibrahim Ahmed's barrister, Gbamuda.

Date: Fri, 29 Aug 2003
From: "gbamuda nngida">
Subject: UPDATE FORWARDED.

Dear Sir - I am directed by my client Dr.Ibrahim Ahmed to make an official contact to you in respect to the transaction of fund (USD$28.million) from his serving bank (Bond Bank Nig Ltd).

I have also been mandated to forward to you his passport photograph as requested please stanby. I wish to comment here that your traveling date or schedule might not fall into the seventh day as stipulated by you. It will come upon your confirmation date, due to your health problem. Surfice to say, that arrangement will be concluded with the BOND BANK OVERSEA OFFICE when the time comes.

My contact phone 234-80-33165253 AND Email as above. Due to the confidentiality that this transaction demands we shall adopt a communication code "PEACE". This shall also known to my client Dr Ahmed I. Any communication without this code should be disregarded. The code shall only be known to the three of us concern.

Yours Sincerely,
Barrister N.Gbamuda.
CODE:"PEACE"

From: Klench Mychiques
To: Mr. Gbamuda

Dear Sir - Many thanks for your email, but before I proceed with further negotiations I must ask the following: before I go any further, I have to tell you that I am going to have to make a request for you to prove your identity to me. The reason for this is that some months ago, I made a deal with a very ungodly man who was a liar and a thief. After putting my trust and good Christian faith in him, he stole US $23,773 from me, the miserable bastard. So, please forgive me if my request seems strange to you.

I am well aware that in situations like this, false images are freely available. Sir, I am not accusing you or Dr. Ibrahim of being dishonest, but I am afraid I cannot accept a passport photograph as proof of identity. Of course, if I were to see it in person then its validity would be certain, but as I will only be receiving an image of it, it can be easily forged. Therefore, I request that you, Mr. Ibrahim, or a representative make arrangements to send me a photograph holding a sign with my name and company logo written upon it. On seeing this, it will prove to me 100% that I am dealing with a totally honest person as this image will not be able to be forged. If yourself, Mr. Ibrahim, or representative is agreeable to this then I will forward a suitable image as an attachment for you to print out. I hope you will agree that this is a small thing to ask in return for my help in this matter.

(I like to let my victim know that the upcoming fees shouldn't be a problem - it sets their mind at ease)

May I presume that processing fees may be required to facilitate the release of these funds? In the UK I have to deal with such fees on a regular basis. This is not a problem, and on receipt of proof of your identity (the photo) I will be happy to release any necessary funds of my own should they be needed. If it is at all possible, it would be of great benefit if you would be able to calculate the total amount that may be required to facilitate the urgent completion of your proposition.

My sincere regards,

Klench Mychiques - Stuntman Extraordinaire

Surprisingly, the barrister seems to accept my request without any argument!

Date: Sat, 30 Aug 2003
From: "gbamuda nngida"
Subject: Re: ACCEPTED CONDITION.

Dear Mr Klench - Many thanks for your mail.

Your condition is quite acceptable,because this days alot of things happens around the world, and that makes someone doubt who is GOOD or BAD,i will not be surprise to hear that the sum of $23,773 was taken away from you,so Please do forward the attachment to me.

I like to use this medium to expantiate that the identity of DR.IBRAHIM AHMED meant was not his photograph picture as you thought, but DR AHMED'S INTERNATIONAL PASSPORT,i hope the international passport will serve to your request.Incase it is not enough please get me informed ASAP while i expect your attached picture and details/ specimen of how you want the holding of sign with your names.

Finally,the fees mentioned in your mail is not known to me yet,except as we progress.

Barrister N.Gbamuda.
CODE:"PEACE"

From: Klench Mychiques
To: Mr. Gbamuda

Dear Barrister N. Gbamuda - Many thanks for your prompt response. You email has been read and is fully understood.

I have decided to send an attachment with my name printed upon is so that you are able to print it out. On the image I have also included my personal password. When I see this printed with my name, then I will be 100% sure of the source of the image, for I will give this password to nobody else. If I ever ask you for my password, please use the word 'TIGHTLY', this way I will be certain the message originates from your good self.

A final few words about the image that I am requesting you send; please ensure that the image you send is LARGE and CLEAR, and be sure to print out my sign large and clear enough to be seen clearly. This will eliminate any chance of forgery. As soon as I receive an acceptable photograph of you or a representative holding my name and password I will proceed with your instructions IMMEDIATELY.

As a gesture of good faith I have also attached a scan of my passport to this email for your perusal. I would appreciate it if you would keep my image private or I may have to have plastic surgery.

May God bless you, and I hope that once I receive the image I require we will be able to expedite the completion of this deal to a very successful conclusion.

My sincere regards,

Klench Mychiques - Stuntman Extraordinaire

The guy in the picture is American actor Gregory Harrison.

185

Date: Sat, 30 Aug 2003
From: "gbamuda nngida"
Subject: Fwd: passport attached Peace and Tightly.

Dear Klench - I am sending my pasport as demanded.Please,now you can make move to contact the paying center in holland as directed by Ahmed Ibrahim.Please negotiate with the officer in charge Mr Amanda Williams **(MISTER Amanda Williams?)** *on your preparation for visit for the claim of the fund.All necessary documents has been forwarded to the paying institution in holland.*

Yours Sincerely,

Barrister N.Gbamuda.

A rather crappy passport from Barrister Gbamuda.

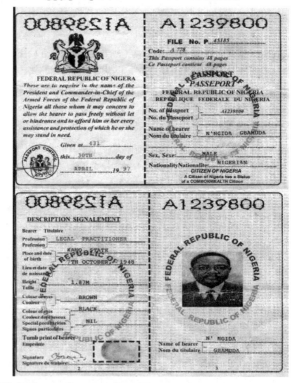

NOT the image I was wanting. Time to complain.

From: Klench Mychiques
To: Mr. Gbamuda

Dear Mr. Gbamunda - Please Sir, where is the image I asked for with my name and password ('TIGHTLY')? I sent you an image to have taken with you or a representative to prove your honesty but instead you sent to me your passport. What the blazes is going on?

On a further note: I will be unavailable for the next 24-48 hours. This is due to a television appearance I am making. My friends and colleagues have organised a televised tribute show to celebrate my 500th stunt (see attached photo). I will get back to you ASAP, provided I am not totally whacked out.

Klench Mychiques - Stuntman Extraordinaire

The guy in the image is stuntman Dar Robinson. He looks enough like Klench Mychiques for me to get away with it!

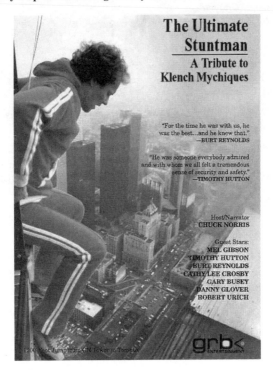

Date: Mon, 1 Sep 2003
From: "gbamuda nngida"
Subject: Re: YOUR PASSWORD: PEACE - MY PERSONAL
PASSWORD: TIGHTLY(UNDERSTOOD)

Dear Mr Klench - Many thanks for your mail. It is certainly clear to me now and i will do as demanded so that there will be a 100% trust in me and what we are doing for finalization of this transaction.This of course will certainly put confidence in you when making any form of transfer payments as mentioned earlier by you in the course of this transaction.

Please note that i will be going to the photographer today and hopefully,the picture might be ready between tomorrow or next. I hope that your tribute show is well.

Yours Sincerely,

Barrister N.Gbamuda.
PEACE.

From: Klench Mychiques
To: Mr. Gbamuda

Dear Mr. Gbamuda - Thank you for your email, and I look forward to receiving your next communication.

You will be pleased to learn that the TV show went well. Me and Burt Reynolds had a little too much to drink and got caught humping one of the female car-park attendants - I don't think we will be allowed in that theatre for some time yet!

Kindest regards,

Klench Mychiques - Stuntman Extraordinaire

Date: Wed, 3 Sep 2003
From: "gbamuda nngida"
Subject: Fwd: pic(Peace for me Tightly for you)

Dear mr Klench - I am sending by attachment the picture as demanded. Now i have satisfied you and proved myself.It is your

*turn to fulfil your promises to assist in bringing this transaction to a
successful conclussion.*

*As a start,you are advised to make contact to the name and address
stated below for your visit arrangement to sign the neccessary
documents for the release of the fund:*

*MR AMANDA WILLIAMS
GLOBAL FINANCIAL NETWORK,
PO BOX 4243,1103 CN
AMSTERDAM-THE NETHERLANDS.
PHONE:31-615-465438.
E-mail: amawils2001@yahoo.ca*

*Yours Sincerely,
Barrister N.Gbamuda.*

**Not quite Mario Testino. The camera flash has bounced off the white
page and screwed up the contrast.**

Ibrahim Ahmed pops in to ask how things are going.

Date: Wed, 3 Sep 2003
From: drahmedibrahim@tiscali.co.uk
Subject: RE: PROGRESS NEWS FROM GBAMUDA TODAY

DEAR KLENCH MYCHIQUES - HOW ARE YOU TODAY.I AM SO
HAPPY TO HEAR FROM GBAMUDA THAT ALL IS GOING
SMOOTHLY. HE TOLD ME ABOUT THE PICTURE AND PASSPORT
ISSUE.I BEG YOU TO BE HONEST TOUS WHEN THIS MONEY
COME TO YOUR ACCOUNT.AND TO GIVE US YOUR HIGHEST
UNDERSTANDING AND MUTUAL COOPERATION.

I HOPE TO HEAR FROM YOU AS YOU ARE DEVELOPING.
PROGRES.WHEN DO YOU INTEND TO TRAVEL TO HOLLAND
FOR FINALIZATION?

THANKS,

DR AHMED IBRAHIM.

From: Klench Mychiques
To: drahmedibrahim@tiscali.co.uk

Dear Ahmed - Good to hear from you again.

Yes, everything is going smoothly. I intend to travel to Holland to settle
the agreement very soon, and I will notify you of my flight date when I
have it, if I can be bothered.

Kind regards,

Klench Mychiques - Stuntman Extraordinaire

Now back to the barrister.

From: Klench Mychiques
To: Mr. Gbamuda

Dear Mr. Gbamuda - Many thanks for your picture, which has been
received and is approved. Now that I have seen you are a large
man to be trusted I will destroy the image for security purposes. **(You**

wish!) I am now happy to continue to follow through with your proposition.

My sincere regards,

Klench Mychiques - Stuntman Extraordinaire

Now to contact 'MISTER' Amanda Williams. Thought I'd try out some gobbledegook on him/her? Reader note: these are the actual words I typed.

From: Klench Mychiques
To: Amanda Williams

Dear Amanda Williams - I am contacting you on behalf of Ahmed Ibrahim/Gbamuda. Blah blah blah, necessary documents. Blah blah, release forms etc.

Ready to sign etc. ZZzzz.

Yours sincerely,

Klench Mychiques - Stuntman Extraordinaire

Ahmed Ibrahim replies.

Date: Wed, 3Sep 2003
From: drahmedibrahim@tiscali.co.uk
Subject: RE: URGENT

DEAR MYCHIQUES - HOW ARE YOU TODAY? BARRISTER GBAMUDA HAS TOLD ME THAT YOU PEOPLE HAVE COMMUNICATED EACH OTHER.

I AM PLEASED TO INFORM YOU THAT NEWS REACHING ME TODAY IS THAT A PROTOCOL OFFICER BY NAME MR J.P PHILIPS WILL BE WITH YOU IN AMSTERDAM TO WITHNESS THE ENDORSEMENT AND WILL BE WITH YOU AT THE AIRPORT WITH IDENTIFICATION TO ACCOMPANY YOU.

PLEASE COMMUNICATE WITH MR AMANDA FOR PROPER ARRANGEMENT. **(I have done, but he/she hasn't replied to me yet.)**

THANK YOU,
DR.AHMED IBRAHIM.

At last, Amanda replies, and hits me with the inevitable fees.

Date: Thu, 4 Sep 2003
From: amanda williams
Subject: RE: VERY URGENT

Dear Sir - I am sorry that for not contacting you on mail since your file came to my desk because of the board meeting i was attending. These are the rules and regulations that you should abide immediately for this transaction.

(A) INDENTIFICATION PROOF(an international passport or Driver's Lincense)
(B) NOTIFY TO US WHEN YOU ARE COMING TO AMSTERDAM FOR THE NECESSARRY ENDORSMENT.
(C) THE COST OF RELEASE ORDER FORM IS———12,300 Euros
OUR HANDLING/ADMINSRATIVE COST IS——— 5,500 Euros
The Total cost of Seveenteen Thousand Eight Hundred Euros are for all the charges on this transaction. You are now advice to come down immediately for the signing of the Release Form. Waiting to hear from you through the above E-mail for the confidentiality of the transaction.

Best Regards

Amanda Williams
Director/Release Officer

From: Klench Mychiques
To: Amanda Williams

Dear Mrs. Williams - Please find attached my current passport image.

The administrative costs seems fair, considering the total amount that will be freed by this minuscule payment. Please tell your representative that I will bring the full amount in cash, if I can be bothered.

I will make flight arrangements ASAP and then contact you with the flight details, if I don't get to a bar first.

I look forward to meeting with Mr. Philips in Amsterdam. I hope he is not homosexual, as I plan a visit to the Red Light area for some good old adult fun.

Sincerely,

Klench Mychiques - Stuntman Extraordinaire

Date: Fri, 5 Sep 2003
From: "gbamuda nngida"
Subject: Re: YOUR PASSWORD: PEACE - MY PERSONAL
PASSWORD: TIGHTLY

Dear Mr Klench - I have been informed that all preparations are in top place for your final visit and completion.Mr philips,a protocol officer has been asigned to the Global Financial Network Amsterdam for this purpose.

It is partinent to note also that correspondence reaching shows that you have contacted by Mr Williams Amanda for your requirements.

Please comply and forward me detail of your arrival.

Yours Sincerely,

Barrister N.Gbamuda.
PEACE.

From: Klench Mychiques
To: Mr. Gbamuda

Dear Mr. Gbamunda - I have indeed contacted Mr. Amanda.

I am still however waiting for an email from the person who is to actually meet me at the airport (Mr. Philips).

I need him to email me to verify his identity to me. Once verification is complete I will proceed to book my flight and then forward the details onto him and Mr. Amanda.

Please note I will be unavailable for the next 24 hours as I am doing a motorcycle stunt at a local superstore (I am attempting a world record motorcycle leap over 127 shopping trolleys).

Attached is a photograph of me practising for the big event.

Sincerely,

Klench Mychiques - Stuntman Extraordinaire

An image taken from the Net, but with my name added for impact!

Date: Fri, 5 Sep 2003
From: "gbamuda nngida"
Subject: Re: YOUR PASSWORD: PEACE - MY PERSONAL
PASSWORD: TIGHTLY

Dear mr klench - Many thanks for prompt respond and present effort towards contacting mr Amanda.

Please i like to advise that you send him another remind incase there is any waste of time or delays from his side in responding,please bear with me.Like i mentioned earlier,mr Amanda or mr J.P Philips will be meeting with you at the airport or any place of meeting/your arrival before proceeding to their office.

Yours Sincerely,

Barrister N.Gbamuda.

What? No good wishes for my big jump?!

From: Klench Mychiques
To: Mr. Gbamuda

Dear Mr. Gbamuda - It is with a heavy heart that I (try to) email you today. Unfortunately, both of my arms and right leg are in plaster (again) and I am finding it extremely difficult to type. I do not know if anything is broken, but the doctors told me to wrap myself in plaster just in case. Good doctors are so hard to find.

As I informed you yesterday, I was making an attempt at the world record for jumping over shopping trolleys, but the stunt went badly wrong.

Although my stunt co-ordinator set up my jump ramp perfectly, during the night some bastard moved it up against a brick wall. As I have so much faith in my stunt co-ordinator I asked no questions and performed the jump with disastrous consequences, hence my trip to Amsterdam may be delayed slightly.

Please find attached a photograph showing my failed attempt. I would not like you to think I am trying to delay you. I will make my flight booking ASAP and then I will await the contact from your representatives.

Sincerely, and in no small pain,

Klench Mychiques - Stuntman Extraordinaire

My accident! Will Gbamuda notice the 419?

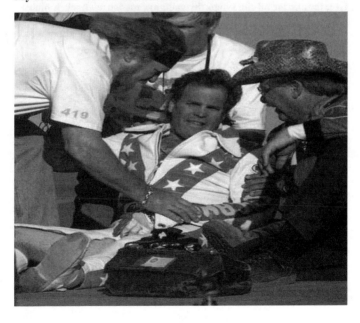

Nope! And it looks like Gbamuda hasn't a clue what's going on with his own crew either.

Date: Sat, 6 Sep 2003
From: "gbamuda nngida"
Subject: Re: YOUR PASSWORD: PEACE - MY PERSONAL
PASSWORD: TIGHTLY

*Dear mr klench - I am in receipt of your mail.I wish to advise that each time you correspond to mr Amanda,please copy me by bcc or cc which ever one you prefer for transparency purpose,because i am still wondering what must have been delaying Mr Amanda in replying to your mail you said you sent to him.***(Come on man. You're seeing everything anyway!)**

I am looking forward to fast conclusion of this deal.

Yours Sincerely,
Barrister N.Gbamuda.
PEACE.

Gee, thanks for all the sympathy you gave me for my broken limbs!

From: Klench Mychiques
To: Mrs. Williams

Dear Mrs. Williams - Please find attached a copy of my booking receipt for my flight to Amsterdam. Also attached is a copy of my passport.

The flight No. is BA0434 (British Airways) and will arrive in Amsterdam at approximately 1.30pm in the afternoon of the 15th of September.

I am hoping my plaster will be removed by then.

Please ask the person who is to meet me to hold a large sign with my name at the arrivals lounge (Klench Mychiques) so that I am able to recognise the person I am meeting (Mr. Philips).

I would appreciate confirmation of receipt of this email.

Sincerely,

Klench Mychiques - Stuntman Extraordinaire

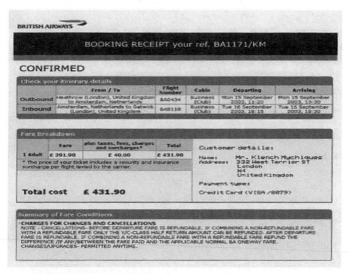

A cooked up flight receipt.

Date: Sat, 6 Sep 2003 06:05:06 -0400 (EDT)
From: amanda williams
Subject: Re: VERY URGENT

Dear Sir - I saw what you sent on mail pertaning to your arrival here in Amsterdam. Everything has been taken note about receving you. The person will show you the photocopy of your passport that was forwarded to us as well for you to be rest assured about him. We will be expecting your arrival on 15 september as you said, but before that i will e-mail you again.

Thanks and God Bless.

A. Williams.

Date: Sat, 6 Sep 2003
From: "gbamuda nngida"
Subject: Re: YOUR PASSWORD: PEACE - MY PERSONAL PASSWORD: TIGHTLY

Dear mr klench - I am happy to hear that at last you people have been able to communicate each other.It is also nice to hear from you that you have booked your flight for 15th and have advised Amanda accordingly. Please always get me informed of every step as soon as you arrive for the completion. I will advise you after the completion on how the fund will be kept and managed after my meeting with Dr Ahmed. Has Amanda acknowledged your booking scheduled you sent to him?

Finally have you people agreed on meeting and identification? **(Nope.)**

Yours Sincerely,
Barrister N.Gbamuda.
PEACE.

From: Klench Mychiques
To: Mr. Gbamuda

Dear Mr. Gbamuna - Thank you for your email.

Mr. Williams had returned my email, BUT I am still waiting for the person who is to meet me to email me. Please STRESS to Mr. Amanda Williams that until I have received identification from the person who is to meet me I will not make the flight, and I will spend the time seeking out prostitutes in London instead.

Sincere regards,

Klench Mychiques - Stuntman Extraordinaire

Ibrahim gets in touch.

Date: Mon, 8 Sep 2003
From: drahmedibrahim@tiscali.co.uk
Subject: RE: GOOD NEWS.

DEAR MYCHIQUES KLENCH - HOW ARE YOU TODAY?I RECEIVE GOOD NEWS FROM MY LAWYER THIS MORNING.HE TOLD ME EVERYTHING IS MOVING SUCCESSFULLY,HE TOLD ME ALSO YOU WILL BE TRAVELLING ON THE 15TH OF THIS MONTH,A WEEK TODAY FOR COMPLETION.MAY GOD BE WITH YOU AS YOU ARE HELPING.I AM SO HAPPY,I MUST CONFESS.

(YOU'RE happy?! I still haven't got the identification yet.)

THANK YOU,

DR AHMED IBRAHIM

A. Amanda (?) gets in touch to let me know how things will proceed - or so she/he thinks.

Date: Mon, 8 Sep 2003
From: amanda williams
Subject: Re: VERY URGENT

Dear Sir,

Every arrangement about your arrival has been taken care. The are going to hold a placard with your name on it. J.T Philips will receive you and he is going to show you a photocopy of your passport for you to be sure of the person receiving you.

There is nothing again that we can do because of Security reasons that is why we are always careful with our clients. **(We'll see about that, Mr. Williams.)**

God Bless and wishes you safe arrival to Amsterdam, The Netherlands.

Best Regards,

A. Amanda

Gbamuda has a little whinge at me for continually requesting identification.

Date: Mon, 8 Sep 2003 21:22:47 +0100 (BST)
From: "gbamuda nngida"
Subject: Re: YOUR PASSWORD: PEACE - MY PERSONAL PASSWORD: TIGHTLY

Dear mr klench - Many thanks for your mail.I like to say that you are bring back issues,i told you that your passport copy has been forwarded to Mr Amanda Williams for documentation,which can as well be used for identification upon your arrival. Note that you gave me a condition of sending you a photographed picture which i did,and the reason for that was to maintain trust in what we are doing and to prove to you that i am not hidding my identity.

Moreso,because i believe you and i are one and are working with one spirit to achieve our goal. The issue of Amanda doing same as i did should not arise because they are different body only concern in making payment to us.I believe they should have their mode of operation.Your passport copy sent to them is enough for identification,except you have another motive. **(Well spotted, Ahmed!)**

Finally,i like to suggest that you ask mr Amanda williams or colleague (J.T philips) whomsoever will be seeing upon arrival to present your passport copy which i sent to them and identity of the person before following the person.This is to be sure you are meeting with the right person.Alternatively,a code can be given to Amanda williams or his partner just like we are communicating with"tightly and peace" for easy identification to support your passport copy they are having.

Yours Sincerely,
Barrister N.Gbamuda.
PEACE.

Time to get stroppy.

From: Klench Mychiques
To: Mr. Gbamuda

Dear Mr. Gbamuda - And I told you that BEFORE I travel to Amsterdam I require proof of identity from the person I am meeting. If the person I was meeting was to be you then there would not be a problem as you have already proved yourself to me. However, I now am expected to travel hundreds of miles to meet someone I have never seen. Sir, honestly, would you do this without any proof of identification? Everyone in this deal so far has seen my identity. I have sent evidence to EVERYONE when asked. YOU are the only person whose identity I have seen.

If you do not like the way I work sir, please let me know and I will cancel my flight and close the deal. I have other business affairs I can be attending to.

Sincerely,

Klench Mychiques - Stuntman Extraordinaire

Gbamuda tries to call my bluff.

Date: Tue, 9 Sep 2003
From: "gbamuda nngida"
Subject: Re: YOUR PASSWORD: PEACE - MY PERSONAL PASSWORD: TIGHTLY

Dear mr klench - Many thanks for your mail. For you to have taken my identity is enough to believe what i am telling you and to follow whonsoever i introduce to you. Well,the identity issue with mr Amanda or mr phillips **(make your damn mind up how you are spelling his name)** *can be discussed very well with mr Amanda,so contact him and ask him how this can best be resolved. This is not enough for foryou to decide to cancel your flight or back out of helping, except you* *actually do not want to continue.If you insist on withdrawing,well that is your decision because i have done all you required.*

Yours Sincerely,
Barrister N.Gbamuda.

From: Klench Mychiques
To: Mr. Gbamuda

Dear Mr. Gbmuda - I have asked and asked and asked and asked for identification from Amanda, but I have not received it. I have so far spent £431 on airline tickets AND I am required to bring with me SEVENTEEN THOUSAND EIGHT HUNDRED EUROS, the total cost to me so far in US Dollars being TWENTY THOUSAND THREE HUNDRED AND TWELVE ($20,312).

If I am to spend $20,312 then I must INSIST that I receive identification BEFORE I board the plane on the 15th. I suggest you contact Amanda and tell him that he will be wasting Mr. Philips's time at the airport waiting for me, as I will not be arriving until I receive OFFICIAL identification.

Mr. Gbmuda, please note that all further emails will be ignored until I receive what I want. **(So there!)**

Sincerely,

Klench Mychiques - Stuntman Extraordinaire

Mr. Gbamuda won't have any of it... for now.

Date: Tue, 9 Sep 2003
From: "gbamuda nngida"
Subject: Re: YOUR PASSWORD: PEACE - MY PERSONAL
PASSWORD: TIGHTLY

Dear mr klench - This decision is not mine.You can contact Amanda for all these arrangement.I am not a staff of Global Financial Network and as such will not dictate their working ability or modus operandi.I believe they should have their working skills.

If you decide to drop here because of identity from Holland office,well like i said before,that is your decision.I have proven myself to you as demanded. We are working as one body and co and only a paying body. I have never done a business with a bank and demand the bank to

201

send me a picture of the director and i have never heard it before.Like i said except you have a different motive.

Contact Amanda for this request.
Barrister N.Gbamuda.
peace.

Klench doesn't take any crap.

From: Klench Mychiques
To: Mr. Gbamuda

Mr. Gbamuda - OK, fine. DEAL FINISHED. Tell Amanda that my flight is being cancelled this afternoon. Bye,

Klench Mychiques. - Stuntman Extraordinaire

Is this the end then?

Date: Tue, 9 Sep 2003
From: "gbamuda nngida"
Subject: Re: YOUR PASSWORD: PEACE - MY PERSONAL PASSWORD: TIGHTLY

Dear klench - Thank you,i will report back to Dr Ahmed. You can inform that to Amanda so that he can put a stop to their documentation.

Barrister Gbamuda.

I do not bother contacting Amanda. I'll let them stew.

Date: Tue, 9 Sep 2003
From: amanda williams
Subject: Re: VERY URGENT

Dear Sir - I am not surprise that the way you authoritave write on e-mail can jeorpadise this transaction. You wrote to us about the person meeting you to hold a large sign on your arrival, which we agreed. The name of the person to meet you, which we agreed. The next step is your withdrawal which you think you are doing for us or Gbemudia.Since i started working, i have never seen a client behaving this way.Anyway, Thank you and God Bless.

A. Williams

From: Klench Mychiques
To: Amanda Williams

Bye then.

Ahmed Ibrahim finally gets in touch to see what's going on!

Date: Tue, 9 Sep 2003
From: drahmedibrahim@tiscali.co.uk
Subject: RE: URGENT

*DEAR MYCHIQUES - HOW ARE YOU TODAY? I AM HIGHLY
DISAPPOINTED WITH THE NEWS I JUST GOT FROM MY
LAWYER THIS AFTERNOON. YOU SHOULD KNOW THAT IT IS
NOT THE DUTY OF MY LAWYER TO MAKE SUCH DEMAND TO
AMANDA, BUT YOURS.*

*I SINCERELY ASK THAT YOU REQUEST AMANDA TO FORWARD
YOUR DEMAND WHICH I KNOW HE WILL PERFECT, DEPENDING
ON YOUR GOOD RELATIONSHIP WITH HIM.*

DR. AHMED IBRAHIM.

I ignore his email. Ahmed demands an explanation again.

Date: Wed, 10 Sep 2003
From: drahmedibrahim@tiscali.co.uk
Subject: RE: WAITING YOUR REPLY.

*DEAR MYCHIQUES - I SENT A MAIL YESTERDAY OVER THIS
CONTROVERSY AND I AM YET TO HAVE YOUR REPLY. REPLY
NOW SIR STATING YOUR DESIRE.*

DR AHMED IBRAHIM.

From: Klench Mychiques
To: drahmedibrahim@tiscali.co.uk

My desire sir, is to have PHOTOGRAPHIC IDENTIFICATION from
the person who is to meet me at Amsterdam. This must happen
BEFORE my flight on Monday. If I do not have SATISFACTORY
identification my 10am GMT TOMORROW MORNING you will never
hear from me again.

I do not want any more excuses, and I do not want you to tell me to
email somebody else to ask for the identification. This is the last email I
send to ANYONE until identification arrives. NO-NEGOTIATION.

Pissed-off,

Klench Mychiques - Stuntman Extraordinaire

As expected, they buckle under pressure.

Date: Thu, 11 Sep 2003
From: amanda williams
Subject: Re: Confidential

Dear sir - Since yesterday, we have been having problem with the server. I apologised of not mailing you after receiving a mail from Dr Ahmed Ibrahim of Bond Bank Nigeria, instucting an indentification of the person to receive you. We are now forwarding it to you with your passport picture with him as well.

Thanks and God Bless.

A. Williams

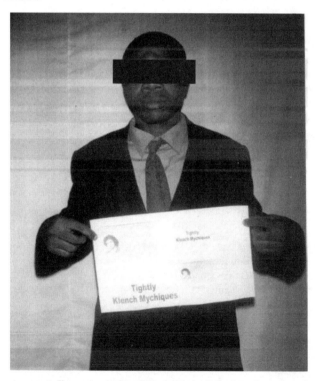

In retrospect, I'm not convinced that this isn't just an innocent chap roped in for the photo - so I've given him letterbox anonymity.

From: Klench Mychiques
To: Amanda Williams

Dear Mrs Williams - Thank you for the email, and the photograph you sent to me is acceptable. That wasn't so hard was it?

I presume your representative (Mr. Philips) will be at the airport arrivals lounge to meet with me on Monday?

Sincerely,

Klench Mychiques - Stuntman Extraordinaire

Ibrahim is a happy guy.

Date: Thu, 11 Sep 2003
From: drahmedibrahim@tiscali.co.uk
Subject: RE: PROGRESS NEWS FROM HOLLAND TODAY

DEAR MYCHIQUES - HOW ARE YOU TODAY.

I AM HAPPY TO INFORM YOU THAT THE NEWS REACHING ME TODAY AFTER MY MAIL TO THE HOLLAND OFFICE AS I PROMISED YOU, IS THAT YOUR DEMAND FOR THE IDENTITY HAS BEEN GRANTED.PLEASE CONFIRM THIS NEWS TO ME.

I THINK YOU CAN NOW MAKE YOUR MONDAY TRIP.

I HAVE INFORMED MY BARRISTER ACCORDINGLY,PLEASE REACH HIM FOR ISSUE RECONCILIATION.

THANK YOU.

DR AHMED IBRAHIM.

From: Klench Mychiques
To: drahmedibrahim@tiscali.co.uk

Dear Mr. Ibrahim - Yes, I can now confirm I have received the identification I require. I shall be arriving in Amsterdam on the afternoon of the 15th (Monday).

Sincerely,

Klench Mychiques - Stuntman Extraordinaire

Date: Fri, 12 Sep 2003
From: drahmedibrahim@tiscali.co.uk
Subject: RE: THANK YOU AND SAFE FLIGHT.

DEAR MYCHIQUES - HOW ARE YOU TODAY. I THANK YOU SO MUCH FOR THE CONFIDENT.

PLEASE I WILL LIKE THAT YOU COMMUNICATE MY LAWYER FOR RECONCILIATION PURPOSE BECAUSE WE ARE ALL ONE AND MUST WORK IN ONE SPIRIT THE WAY WE STARTED.

IT WAS NEVER HIS FAULT AS I EXPLAINED BEFORE TO YOU.

YOU SHOULD UNDERSTAND HE HAS CONTRIBUTED ALOT TO BRING US TO THIS STAGE,WE CANNOT PUSH HIM ASIDE. **(I'll push whoever I want to mate.)**

I WISH YOU GOOD LUCK AND SAFE FLIGHT. **(It's extremely safe sat here in my front room, thank you.)**

THANK YOU,

DR.AHMED IBRAHIM.

The day of the Amsterdam meeting arrives. But what's this? - Klench isn't there!

Date: Mon, 15 Sep 2003
From: drahmedibrahim@tiscali.co.uk
Subject: RE: UPDATE SITUATION IN HOLLAND TODAY

DEAR MYCHYQUES - HOW ARE YOU TODAY.IT IS EXACTLY 3.30PM HERE AND OFFICE IS ABOUT TO CLOSE.

I WRITE TO KNOW WHAT THE SITUATION IS,BECAUSE THE NEWS REACHING ME HERE IS THAT YOU ARE YET TO BE SEEN AFTER A LONG WAITING FOR YOU AT THE AIRPORT AND THE ARRIVAL OF THE FLIGHT YOU GAVE TO THEM. **(I'm gutted.)**

I AM WORRIED HERE BECAUSE I THOUGHT WE AGREED AFTER THE RECEIPT OF THE IDENTITY YOU REQUESTED.

THANK YOU,

DR AHMED IBRAHIM.

From: Klench Mychiques
To: drahmedibrahim@tiscali.co.uk

Dear Dr. Ibrahim - I think there has been some mistake. I mailed your Amsterdam contact to tell him that I would be meeting with him at the Amstel Botel Hotel in Amsterdam (Oosterdokskade 2 Amsterdam 1011 AE). **(Actually, I didn't, but what the hell.)** I am here now as I write this, waiting for your contact to arrive. My room number is 117. I have told the person at the booking desk that I am expecting a visitor.

Your contact was told not to arrive until after 4.00pm today as I needed to sleep with a prostitute for a short while before I meet with anyone.

Sincerely,

Klench Mychiques - Stuntman Extraordinaire

I feel it can only be so long before I am rumbled. Ibrahim contacts me from a new email address.

Date: Tue, 16 Sep 2003
From: drahmedibrahim1@tiscali.co.uk
Subject: NEW EMAIL.

DEAR MYCHIQUES - FOLLOWING MY MESSAGE TO YOU FROM THE OLD EMAIL BOX,I AM WRITING FROM HERE AS PROMISED INCLUDING YOUR LAST MESSAGE OF HOTEL DETAILS TO ME. PLEASE WE SHALL ONLY COMMUNICATE FROM HERE.

THANK YOU,

DR.AHMED IBRAHIM.

A new day dawns, and it's the day of my departure from Amsterdam. Mr. Amanda Williams gets in touch.

Date: Tue, 16 Sep 2003
From: amanda williams
Subject: Re: Confidential

*Dear Sir - I acknowlage your arival here in Amsterdam. We are coming to see you today for the finalization of the transaction. We waited yesterday to collect you at the Airport but could not see you. So, bear with us for the delay in coming to the Hotel.***(Didn't Ibrahim explain the story to you?)**

A. Williams

From: Klench Mychiques
To: Amanda Williams

Dear Amanda - My apologies for the mix-up. I did email to confirm my change of plan and to meet at the Amstel Botel Hotel in Amsterdam (Oosterdokskade 2 Amsterdam 1011 AE). I suggest you chastise Mr. Ibrahim severely as I did tell him of my plans 24 hours ago.

Please note: I am due to return to the UK at 6.00pm this evening, so time is running short. Better get your ass into gear.

Sincerely,

Klench Mychiques - Stuntman Extraordinaire

It must be starting to dawn on the Lads that they are been screwed with.

Date: Tue, 16 Sep 2003
From: drahmedibrahim1@tiscali.co.uk
Subject: RE: NEW EMAIL.

DEAR MYCHIQUES - THE INFORMATION REACHING FROM HOLLAND IS THAT THEY WENT TO THE HOTEL AND WERE TOLD YOU HAVE CHECKED OUT,PLEASE GIVE INSTRUCTION TO THE HOTEL ATTENDANT THAT YOU ARE EXPECTING A VISITOR AND NOTITY THEM OF WHERE YOU ARE.

IF YOU DECIDE TO LEAVE AMSTERDAM BY 6.00PM TODAY WITHOUT COMPLETING THIS SIGNING,I TELL YOU THAT YOUR COMING IS USELESS.

PLEASE MAIL TO AMANDA NOW FOR A BETTER APPOINTMENT INSTEAD OF MISSING YOURSELVES. THANK YOU.

AHMED.

Let's start some blatant bullshitting.

From: Klench Mychiques
To: drahmedibrahim1@tiscali.co.uk

Dear Ahmed - I think something is seriously wrong. I HAVE NOT checked out of the hotel. I ordered room service ten minutes ago (a big beef burger, fries and a chocolate shake) and I am still most definitely here. Are you sure the contact came to the correct hotel? What is his name? **(Of course, I know it's supposed to be Mr. Philips, but sometimes it's good to play dumb.)**

I am leaving Amsterdam today at 6.00pm, whether your contact arrives or not.

I will forward this email to Mr. Amanda Williams. **(Duly done.)**

Klench Mychiques - Stuntman Extraordinaire

Date: Tue, 16 Sep 2003
From: drahmedibrahim1@tiscali.co.uk
Subject: RE: HOTEL

DEAR MYCHIQUES - THANK YOU FOR THE MAIL.PLEASE YOU CAN INSTRUCT THE HOTEL ATTENDANT TO CALL MR AMANDA WILLIAMS ON HIS PHONE NUMBER:31-615-465438 SINCE YOU CANNOT CALL HIM DUE TO YOUR EAR PROBLEM.

HE HAS SENT ANOTHER PROTOCOL OFFICER TO FETCH YOU. **(He's gonna have a LONG walk, friend.)**

THANK YOU,

AHMED.

From: Klench Mychiques
To: drahmedibrahim1@tiscali.co.uk

Dear Ahmed - I'll see what I can do. These attendants seem pretty busy to me. I ordered a prostitute 45 minutes ago, and I'm still waiting (and throbbing).

Klench Mychiques - Stuntman Extraordinaire

Sure is busy in my inbox today - Mr. Amanda Williams has a word.

Date: Tue, 16 Sep 2003
From: amanda williams
Subject: Re: Confidential

Dear sir - I dont know where this problem is coming from. This is the hotel AMSTEL BOTEL HOTEL (Oosterdokskade 2, Amsterdam 1011AE) There Telephone Number given to us by the receptionist is 0206264247. I have send back the Protocol Officer to the Hotel again

Kindly, do this favour by given the Receptionist my Number—
0615465438 to call me immediately for more clarification.

Thanks

A. Amanda

I can't understand who A. Amanda is supposed to be. I'm presuming
they mean Amanda Williams! Well, of course, I didn't get to meet
anyone at the Botel - it's a lovely place BTW! The next day dawns, as
does the realisation that something is drastically wrong for the Lads.

Date: Wed, 17 Sep 2003
From: drahmedibrahim1@tiscali.co.uk
Subject: RE: SOMETHING WRONG

DEAR MYCHIQUES - WHAT IS GOING ON? THIS IS STRANGE.

Time to 'fess up.

From: Klench Mychiques
To: drahmedibrahim1@tiscali.co.uk
CC: Amanda Williams

Dear Mr. Ibrahim (and friends) - Here is what is going on:

By now you will probably have guessed that you have been fooled into
believing that I was coming to meet your mugu friend in Amsterdam. I
never left the country. Whilst your foolish friends were running around
in Amsterdam trying to find me, I was sat in my very comfortable chair
at home, drinking coffee and checking my emails!

How did you think that my name of Mr. Klench Mychiques was real?!
You must do your homework before you try to steal money from
people! Your introductory documents were full of spelling and grammar
errors, and your communication skills are plain awful.

Ibrahim , or whatever your real name is, from your very first email I
knew you were a 4-1-9 advance fraud fee scammer. There is NO
$28,000,00.00. I know it, and of course YOU know it. I'm not sure if
Mr. Amanda Williams knows it though. Going by the communication
between you two I'd be surprised. Also, what the hell is with a name
like Mr. Amanda Williams? Don't you know that Amanda is a GIRL'S
name?

I know you have been using false names and details, and of course I
know that you and your friends are thieves.

All the documents and photos I sent to you were of course false. Do not worry though, your time with me has not been wasted completely. I run a web site where your pictures and all the letters will be displayed for all my readers to see, so you are going to be quite famous soon.

Of course I have saved ALL the emails and pictures you sent to me, along with ALL the email headers. Soon they will all been sent to the Nigerian Police's fraud section, and also the FBI's advance fee fraud department. Hopefully you will be hearing from them very soon.

Do not bother to reply to me with your excuses Ibrahim, I have heard them all. I KNOW you are a THIEF, and I KNOW your friends are THIEVES also. Do not try to convince me your proposition was real because it was ALL A COMPLETE LIE!

(Let's see if Ahmed's up for a bit of tuition.)

I'll tell you what I will do. I will make a deal with you. You send me US $8,000 by wire transfer, and I will show you where all your mistakes have been made, and show you how to produce REALISTIC documents and wording. Being a businessman myself (a REAL one!) I know how such things SHOULD look. I will also keep your activities out of the news and police files!

(Scamming $8,000 from a scammer would be a MAJOR coup. I suspect that it just isn't going to happen though.)

I hope we meet again soon Ahmed. I look forward to making a fool of you again!

From Shiver Metimbers

Would Ahmed reply? You bet your ass he would!

Date: Thu, 18 Sep 2003 11:45:37 +0200
From: drahmedibrahim1@tiscali.co.uk
Subject: RE: BIG FOOL YOU ONLY WASTED YOUR TIME NOT MINE

DEAR FRIEND AND PARTNER, **(I think not, Ahmed.)**

I SUSPECTED YOUR MOVE TO BE TRICKY,BY MENTIONING FIRST THAT YOU ARE JAMES BOND ACTOR.YOU MAY THINK YOU ARE SMART,YOU ARE NOT,I HAVE ALSO FOOLED YOU WITH THOSE PHOTOGRAPHS,IF YOU HAD GONE YOU WOULDN'T HAVE SEEN THAT SECOND FACE I SENT TO

YOU,COMPUTER WORK CAN BE HELPFUL .LET ME TELL YOU NOW THAT I AM ONLY 22 YEARS OF AGE.THANK YOUR GOD YOU DID NOT ENTER MY TRAP,I WOULD HAVE BECOME A BILLIONAIRE WITH YOUR MONEY.

IF YOU HAVE BRAIN ENOUGH YOU CAN COME TO ME WHILE WE TEAM UP TO DUPE MORE PEOPLE. I AM AS WELL WRITING YOU FROM COTE'D IVOIRE. BIG FOOL.

From: Klench Mychiques
To: drahmedibrahim1@tiscali.co.uk

Mr/Mrs/Dr/Barrister (delete as applicable) Ibrahim - Please do not for one moment think I believe you about your knowing that I was messing with you. That is simply not true. You were completely fooled for every second, right up to my last email to you.

I am not the fool here Ibrahim (if that is your real name), YOU are the fool!

YOU are the one who sent the VERY BADLY made passport.

YOU are the one who sent me the picture of the FAT MAN on the sofa!

YOU are the one who sent me the picture of the IDIOT in the suit!

It does not matter if these pictures are not you or your real people. The fact is that I FOOLED you into going to the trouble of TAKING the pictures and wasting your time! It does not matter to me if the pictures are really you or not. YOUR TIME WAS WASTED MAKING AND SENDING THEM!

You NEVER suspected me for one second. You were fooled every step of the way.

I will leave you for now Ibrahim. I have plenty of other scammers to deal with.

Also, if you are supposed to be in a non-UK country, try not to use a UK based email address like the one you have now. This is VERY amateur. Just because you are using a tiscali.co.uk email address, do not think that you cannot be traced back to your origin because you can. It is very easy to do. This is a very basic mistake that most 419 scammers make.

Bye!

Shiver Metimbers

He just won't give up.

Date: Thu, 18 Sep 2003
From: drahmedibrahim1@tiscali.co.uk
Subject: Re: THANKS FOR THE MISTAKES,GOOD FRIEND.

DEAR BIG FRIEND - I LIKE YOU,YOU ARE VERY BRILLIANT AND SMART.THANK YOU FOR THE LITTLE ADVISE AND MISTAKES CORRECTED.I WILL WORK ON THAT.BUT I TELL YOU THAT YOU CAN NEVER TRACE MY STATION VIA YOUR COMPUTER,WHY DID YOU NOT TRACE THAT I WAS SENDING THOSE MAILS FROM ABIDJAN.

SECONDLY,I TELL YOU THAT THESE: YOU are the one who sent the VERY BADLY made passport. FOR SURE IT WAS MADE BY A COMPUTER EXPERT. **(Thanks for the compliment... I think!)**

YOU are the one who sent me the picture of the FAT MAN on the chairs..I TELL YOU THAT NO ONE EVEN KNOWS IF THE FAT MAN IS DEAD OR ALIVE CREATURE. **(Sorry readers, he's completely lost me.)**

YOU are the one who sent me the picture of the IDIOT in the suit! SAME WAS DONE TO THIS PERSON.ACTUALY,HE MIGHT BE CALLED IDIOT BECAUSE HE IS SOMEWHERE ELSE WHILE PEOPLE ARE USING HIS IMAGE TO FRAUD.(?)

THANK YOU,I LIKE TO BE YOUR FRIEND.WE CAN DISCUSS ON FRIENDLY BASIS.TO BE FRANK WITH YOU,I AM BASED IN ABIDJAN.AND A CITIZEN OF GHANA. IF YOU ARE TRUELY RICH,PLEASE YOU CAN HELP ME.WE ARE POOR IN OUR FAMILY.

Barefaced cheek.

From: Klench Mychiques
To: drahmedibrahim1@tiscali.co.uk

I made the passport my friend, and I can prove it. Send me a picture and I will duplicate the quality for you!

Your mistakes are not corrected because you have just repeated them in your email to me.

Ibrahim. I am sorry, but I think you are a little crazy. The picture of the fat man was sent to me by YOU. The man holding the KLENCH MYCHIQUES TIGHTLY page WAS sent by you. You may need your memory fixing! Stop lying to me Ibrahim, it will make me respect you more!

No, the IDIOT in the suit picture was sent to me by your 'Mr' Amanda Williams! Don't you don't even know what your own dumb partners are doing?!

I am happy. I know the truth. No matter what lies you give me.

Bye.

Shiver Metimbers.

Nearly a month later, I receive the following email from Ahmed Ibrahim.

Date: Wed, 15 Oct 2003
From: drahmedibrahim1@tiscali.co.uk
Subject: Re: hello

Good friend - i just remembered today and say i should say hello to you.i am now a good born again christian.i wish to thank you for your advise which i gave a very big thought and decide to quit this unfaithful game.i now attend one of the biggest churches in Abidjan,i have been made a church worker.

thank you, remain bless.
jude(my real name)

From: Mike
To: Jude

Hey Jude, (Sorry, I couldn't help myself!)

Thank you for your email. I hope what you are telling me is the truth. If it is the truth then I congratulate you on your decision, and I hope you do well for yourself.

Regards,

Mike.

Hey, it's just my job.

A Mark of my Respect

I'd had a bad couple of months! Added to the regular influx of between 60 and 100 normal scam emails a day, I seem to have had far more than my fair share of donation scammers. Ahmed Sadiq is one such scammer.

When I received Ahmed's introductory email, I was a bit too busy to indulge him and decided to tell him exactly what I thought of him. Ahmed made the mistake of continuing his correspondence with me, probably under the delusion that he could extract money from me.

I take on the identity of two different 'victims' in this particular scambait. Lance Myboyle is the Managing Director of a large communications company, and then we have Father Bruce Corbin, head of the accounts department of the Holy Church of The Tattooed Saint!

A tip for any prospective scammers who may be reading this: please do your research!

From: Ahmed Sadiq
To: Lance Myboyle
Date: Sunday, October 09, 2005
Subject: Good day

Good day, May the innumerable peace that Allah brings be and remain with you. **(Yeah, yeah, Ahmed. Whatever.)** *I know this might be the first of its kind. Please bear with me.*

I am Ahmed Sadiq, a university undergraduate of Weister City University, London **(?!)**. *Ever since I was a boy, I have dreamed of visiting the Holy Ground , Mecca . It has been my utmost heart desire*

215

that one day I will make it to be part of the struggle for Allah's sake. Having the burning sensation of working for Allah to a great height, I feel that this vision will only be complete if I finally reach there.
(Careful, Ahmed. I'm sure that burning sensation is probably a urinary tract infection. Better get it checked out.)

This was why four (4) of us were chosen in my school to be part of this year's fasting. So preparations are been made now for our travel but there is a little problem. And this problem is my main aim of writing. The school sponsored us partly and had told us to complete the money for our flight tickets. I have sourced for funds everywhere; I have even sold some of my new books but all to no avail. So I resorted to this means. And I pray that this little sum wont hold me back in the fight for Allah's supremacy.

All I need is, please, a support towards this dream. The travel tickets are ready and preparations are almost complete for our travel. Please I beg of you, may Allah replenish abundantly anything you can sacrifice for his service. Anything you can offer me will be highly appreciated I look forward to hearing from you soon.

Sadiq

If you get an unsolicited email similar to this ladies and gentleman, please remember it's a scam, plain and simple. I'll let Ahmed know exactly what I think.

From: Lance Myboyle
To: Ahmed Sadiq
Date: Friday, October 14, 2005

Dear Mr. Sadiq,

1. There is no Weister City University in London.

2. You are located in Nigeria. My gut feeling is that you are a scammer.

3. Goodbye.

Lance Myboyle
Managing Director: Dark Side Communications
www.the-dark-side.co.uk

Ahmed is not put off by my previous email. Like most scammers, they believe their own hype.

From: Ahmed Sadiq
To: Lance Myboyle
Date: Monday, October 17, 2005
Subject: thank you

Good day, I am so happy to see your reply. Thanks. **(If you're happy to be called a scammer Ahmed, I can do that all day.)**

Concerning your enquiries about my genuinety, sorry maybe you are not aware of the university because it's new and its publicity is not that wide. My set is the second set after the pioneer set. So you can see the university is still new and growing.

About my nationality, yes I'm a Nigerian; I opened this e-mail box while in Nigeria before coming over to London for my studies.

Please, I beg of you, anyhow you can help promote the fight for Allah's sake by coming to my aid will be appreciated and I pray that Allah will not leave you unrewarded. Also any information you seek of me to still ascertain my confidentiality will be forwarded to you.

I earnestly wait for your reply. Thanks.

Sadiq.

I try to get rid of Ahmed once more.

From: Lance Myboyle
To: Ahmed Sadiq
Date: Monday, October 17, 2005

Dear Mr. Sadiq - I know the university is not there because I live in London. When you are in London, email me again, because your email is still not coming from here.

Lance Myboyle
Managing Director: Dark Side Communications
www.the-dark-side.co.uk

Ahmed replies again, and comes up with an excuse why his email is coming from Nigeria and not London as he first insisted.

From: Ahmed Sadiq
To: Lance Myboyle
Date: Friday, October 21, 2005
Subject: thank you

Good day sir, now i am on vacation that is why i mail from my home. and my second semester is resuming next year january thats when i will come back to london.

217

But sir, the exercise will finish by the end of november so i plead for your help. as our lecturer normally quotes that only the wise uses opportunities before they become obvious. so this opportunity i have now, i hope to utilise it efficiently

i beg of you sir, please accord me the trust, i wont dissappoint

bye

I give Ahmed one more chance to leave me alone and spare his sanity.

From: Lance Myboyle
To: Ahmed Sadiq
Date: Friday, October 21, 2005

THE

UNIVERSITY

DOES

NOT

EXIST

THEREFORE

YOU

ARE

A

LIAR

Lance Myboyle
Managing Director: Dark Side Communications
www.the-dark-side.co.uk

Ahmed comes clean.

From: Ahmed Sadiq
To: Lance Myboyle
Date: Sunday, October 24, 2005
Subject: sorry

Good day sir - I have one reason for writing this mail. It is to plead for your forgiveness for telling you lies. I thought by so doing, I would gain your help.

Truly, I am a Nigerian, schooling in Nigeria but because of the upsurge of crime and corruption in Nigeria, I reasoned that mere mentioning of my nationality as Nigeria will scare you aware and thereby prevent my dreams.

That was why I faked London. Still you found out. Once more I plead that you forgive me.

Please sir, believe me, it was because of the bleakness in achieving this dream that resorted me to this. Yes we are given the opportunity for the travel on the condition of funding ourselves. I have tried immensely sir but all my efforts still plead for a support. And as I told you, long since I have nursed the ambition of visiting the Holy Ground.

So all I ask from you is to forgive me because condition made me to do it. And if you find it in your heart to forgive me, anything you tell me, I will take it.

Please I'm sorry.

From: Lance Myboyle
To: Ahmed Sadiq
Date: Sunday, October 24, 2005

Dear Mr. Sadiq - Well I am grateful at least that you have come to finally tell me the truth, and you are to be respected for that. I know nothing of Nigeria so why you should try to hide the fact that you are there is a puzzle to me.

Unfortunately, even though you have been truthful to me finally, I am not in a position to help you. My business already funds many charities already and we cannot really take on any more cases.

However, I can give you the contact details of Father Bruce Corbin, who is the head of the church that I am a member of. I do know that they do indeed give financial and spiritual help to people from all over the world. I must warn you however that I am unsure if Father Corbin will be able to help you as I know donations are usually only given to church members.

You can contact him if you wish, and if you tell him that Lance Myboyle has given you his contact details he may look on you more favourably.

His email address is corbin@xxxxxchurch.co.uk

Father Corbin is head of the accounts department for the Holy Church of The Tattooed Saint of which I have been a member of for nearly 18 years. I wish you good luck, and in future try not to hide your roots, be proud of them.

Sincerely,

Lance Myboyle
Managing Director: Dark Side Communications
www.the-dark-side.co.uk

From: Ahmed Sadiq
To: Lance Myboyle
Date: Thursday, October 27, 2005
Subject: please sire

Good day sir - I am so grateful to have seen your help in alleviating my need especially for the fact that you have forgiven me. It takes one in a million to understand as you have done. Thanks. **(You're quite welcome.)**

As you told me sir, since your business helps the poor, I beg and plead that you add me to be the last in your charity list. Please I will make do with anything at all. Right now I am hopeless and as I have told you the stark truth, please consider me because of it. Please I don't have any other place to go to.

As for Father Corbin, thanks for going the extra mile of giving me his details. I will also plead for his support, I also beg of you to help me and explain more to him. I guess he will listen to you more.

Honestly sir, I appreciate your concern once more. You have taught me never to deny my roots; I promise I will never again.

Sadiq

Ahmed fires off his first introductory email to Father Corbin.

From: Ahmed Sadiq
To: Father Bruce Corbin
Date: Thursday, October 27, 2005
Subject: good day father

Good day Father Corbin, - Please bear with me. I know you don't know me. A member of your church by name Lance Myboyle, the Managing Director: Dark Side Communications (www.the-dark-side.co.uk) linked me up to you.

I am Ahmed Sadiq, a university undergraduate from Nigeria. Ever since I was a boy, I have dreamed of visiting the Holy Ground, Mecca. And graciously, last month, due to the burning sensation in us to achieve this dream, my school gave four of us the opportunity to travel on the condition that we will sponsor ourselves. Father, to be candid, I have sourced for funds everywhere; I have even sold some of my new books but all to no avail. So I resorted to this means. All my efforts are still pleading for support.

That was why I reached Lance Myboyle for help and he helped me by re-directing me to you of the view that his church, the Holy Church of The Tattooed Saint of which you are the Head of the Accounts Department can help me. He told me you give spiritual and financial help to people all over the world, so I decided to plead for your concern. Father Bruce, please, right now I am hopeless and the exercise will be terminating soon.

Please Father, notwithstanding the distance, I beg of you, anything you will offer me to achieve this my lifetime dream, I will never forget. I am pleading father.

Once more, I commend your spirit of philanthropism. As Lance Myboyle has talked much good about you and your church, I pray that you consider my situation, as posterity will not relent to reward you.

Thanks.

Sadiq.

I let Ahmed know there will be no help forthcoming from me.

From: Lance Myboyle
To: Ahmed Sadiq
Date: Thursday, October 27, 2005

Dear Mr. Sadiq - I am sorry but my company has given all we are able to charities this year and we cannot really afford to help any further.

Hopefully Father Corbin may be able to help you. I know his church hand out many many donations all over the world and their church is

extremely generous. I am sorry I cannot help you at this time but I wish you good luck for the future.
Sincerely,

Lance Myboyle
Managing Director: Dark Side Communications
www.the-dark-side.co.uk

Not to worry Ahmed. Father Corbin is on the case!

From: Father Bruce Corbin
To: Ahmed Sadiq
Date: Thursday, October 27, 2005

Dear brother Sadiq - Thank you so much for your email it is very nice to receive your message. Yes I do know Lance Myboyle very well. He has been with our church for nearly 18 years and is a very generous man. Please pass on my regards to him the next time you speak with him.

I know the Mr. Boyle's company do help many many charities in the UK so I must say that it is little surprise to me that he is unable to help because I do know that his company spend many many hundreds of thousands of dollars a year to help the less privileged. I would urge you not to take any rejection from him too hard. I know from experience that he is a very good and caring man.

Regarding your request and what you seek. It is a very noble cause that you are striving for and I will pray for you this evening that you find what you are seeking. I would usually be in a position to offer you much help in your current situation, but I am bound by certain rules of our church. I can see that you are in great need of help, and believe me I do feel for you. Under normal circumstances I would be willing to authorise my church to send you a donation of perhaps $15,000.00 or $20,000.00 to help you. However, I am afraid that such financial help is only given to members of our own church.

If you were a member of our ministry then I could help you financially. However, because that is not the case I am very sorry but there is nothing I can offer you except my prayers. Of course if you were to join our church then of course we could offer you immediate help. However, I would not expect an outsider to be willing to complete our church induction procedure as it required considerable commitment.

I will however wish you much luck finding a benefactor and you will be remembered in our prayers this evening. God be with you,

Father Bruce Corbin
Accounts Department
Holy Church of The Tattooed Saint

From: Ahmed Sadiq
To: Father Bruce Corbin
Date: Saturday, October 29, 2005
Subject: good day father

Good day father - Really, I didn't believe that there could be such generous minds until I saw your reply. It means Lance Myboyle was not mistaken in directing me to you. And because of this I pray that may your spirit of generosity not cost you anything, may it lead you to greater heights and opportunities in life.

As you confirmed it, Lance Myboyle also is good, charitable and helps the less privileged but he explained to me that his company has finished for this year's charity help. He would have helped me but he said they cannot help any further this year. That was why he re -directed me to you. **(Actually Ahmed, I redirected you to Father Corbin because you're a gullible ass.)**

Please Father, judging from your last reply, I know left for you alone, you would help me if not for the sake of your church's rule. Lance Myboyle also told me that. But father I plead for your consideration, the exercise is fast terminating, that is why I sound desperate. What ever you want me to do to make sure I attract your sympathy, I will do it, just find it in your heart to help me please.

Father, I hold you in high esteem considering your reply, please don't let me down I beg. More especially continue remembering me in your prayers

I pray you consider me.

From: Father Bruce Corbin
To: Ahmed Sadiq
Date: Saturday, October 29, 2005

Dear Brother Sadi - Bless you for your very kind response to my email, thank you.

Brother Sadiq, I have to tell you that I am extremely thrilled that you are indeed considering joining our church. Your commitment is to be admired greatly. However, you must understand that in order for me to be able to help you it means you will have to join our church, and you must (like all our members) prove your absolute devotion to our cause and church. The induction procedure is simple, but you must be warned that it must not be taken upon lightly.

I must tell you that to join our church you must show great commitments. Nevertheless, the rewards are great. Once you have become a member and have completed the induction procedure I am sure that my board members can help you with a most generous donation, especially if you are in agreement to help spread the word of my church in your country. I cannot give you a firm commitment as to the amount of the donation we can send to you to help others, but it is normal in these types of cases for my church to offer sums of between $20,000 to $40,000. Of course, in order to receive such a donation you must become a full and willing member of our church.

Again I must repeat I that to enter our ranks does take great commitment. All members of our church (myself included) must bear the tattoo mark of our saint, Saint Bartholomew Shiver. This mark of faith is tattooed on to each individual member of our church. Not only does this serve as a graphic reminder of our commitment to our faith, but all over the world it helps us to recognise our brothers and sisters. It is a golden rule of our church that our members must do everything in their power to help and aid fellow members.

So, to be inducted into our church, you must agree to the following:

1. Agree to have a tattoo showing the mark and name of Saint Bartholomew Shiver. This can be placed on any part of your body. Most of our members have this placed on their arms.
2. Provide photographic proof of the tattoo mark.
3. Complete our church induction form. This is a very simple form which you need to sign to agree to our rules, regulation and devotion to our patron saint Bartholomew.

4. Agree to use any donations sent to you for the good of your fellow men & women.

If you can agree to the above requirements then I see no reason why we cannot start your induction procedure immediately. On receipt of the photographic proof of your tattoo mark of St. Bartholomew and on receipt of the completed induction form we can provide you with a generous donation and regular help within 24 hours of receiving the photographic proof.

We will also of course send much information by post, containing our scriptures, information about the church, and how we would like you to help spread word of our church and cause.

Let me know if you are in agreement to the above requirements and I will forward you more detailed information and also a picture of the tattoo mark of St. Bartholomew so that you can make your own arrangements to have the tattoo applied at your place of choosing.

Of course agreeing to have a tattoo placed upon your body is a very important one, and committing yourself to this is a great request, but it is exactly this which will show us your willingness to be a part of our ministry.

Please note that you must be able to fund the tattoo and photographs yourself. We will of course refund you all your costs as well as provide the donation to you. However, this can only be given once the induction procedure has been completed successfully.

God be with you,

Father Bruce Corbin
Accounts Department
Holy Church of The Tattooed Saint

Ahmed has some questions. Don't you just hate that?!

From: Ahmed Sadiq
To: Father Bruce Corbin
Date: Tuesday, November 01, 2005
Subject: good day father

Good day father - I am so happy to have seen your reply. Really I have been thinking of what to do next. I understand your mail but I am a bit puzzled. Yes I will do whatever you say so that this my lifetime dream will be actualized but these are my worries.

1. We don't have that kind of church down here in our country so how can I be following your proceedings

2. Tattooing is not common in my country and hardly can you see the tattoo markers.

3. Father as I told you earlier, I am desperate because of time factor, how long can the induction take.

I commit all to your hands, as you have promised to help me. I believe you, please don't let me down.

I wait for your reply.

Thanks.

From: Father Bruce Corbin
To: Ahmed Sadiq
Date: Tuesday, November 01, 2005

Dear Brother Sadiq - Thank you for your message.

My brother, I have given you my offer of help. My church can help you financially with a donation of perhaps $18,000 to $20,000 but in order to receive it you must be a member of our church. It is totally up to you whether you have the willingness and ability to do this. I would not under any circumstances want you to feel forced to join us. However, I must reiterate that if you require our financial help then that is what you must do.

I shall try to answer your questions as much as I can:

1. We realise there is no church branch of ours in your area, which is why the donation amount will be so much. With some of the money we send to you we hope that you will aid us in setting up a church or information point in your areas. If you forward me your full mailing address I will be most happy to post you some of our literature and brochures explaining all about our church.

2. I cannot help you in the respect of tattoo markers. If you are unable to get the tattoo mark then of course we cannot help you.

3. The induction time is totally up to you. The sooner you are able to

supply photographs of your tattoo process then the sooner we can make the donation payment to you. We can forward the donation payment to you within 24 hours of receiving the photographic evidence of your tattoo mark. As an example we had a gentleman in Nairobi, Kenya by the name of Akeem Franklin who completed the procedure in three days and he received a $23,750 donation payment immediately. He is now using the payment to spread the word of our church in his township (Westlands), and next year he is coming to meet with us at our annual members gathering in London.

I hope that help you brother Sadiq, and if you decide you wish to proceed then let me know as soon as possible and I will forward you more detailed instructions.

Please note that under no circumstances whatsoever can I offer you any financial help unless you have completed the induction procedure. If you cannot do this then I am very sorry but I cannot help you. It is not my decision, it is the way that my church has been run for many years.

God be with you,

Father Bruce Corbin
Accounts Department
Holy Church of The Tattooed Saint

From: Ahmed Sadiq
To: Father Bruce Corbin
Date: Friday, November 04, 2005
Subject: good day father

Good day father - There is no problem, after due considerations, I have decided to join your church. To be a member of a growing church at least with a member from my neighboring country, Kenya.

So I hope the detailed information you said would be forwarded as soon as possible and the induction process completed.

Thanks once more for your concern.

It's all part of the service, buddy.

From: Father Bruce Corbin
To: Ahmed Sadiq
Date: Friday, November 04, 2005

Dear Brother Sadiq - Thank you so much for your reply.

I am very excited that we are soon to have a new member from your country. Indeed, so far we have no members at all in your area and we would be thrilled if you are able to help spread the word about our ministry there.

As you have requested, the induction information is as follows. Please take care to follow the procedures very carefully. The four church board members will decide on your donation amount which depends on how strictly you have kept to our procedure.

The induction procedure, which we call "the baiting of the faithful" should take very little time to complete. How long this takes is completely up to you and how quickly you are able to present the photographic evidence that you have completed our procedure to the satisfaction of the four church board members. As I told you previously, the faster that you are able to complete the procedure the faster you will receive our financial help.

INSTRUCTIONS

1. I have attached a sample image of our induction logo. It bears the name of our Saint, St. Bartholomew Shiver. Phase one of the induction procedure is to have a copy of this logo tattooed onto a part of your body.

2. You may choose the part of the body which you feel comfortable with having the tattoo. However, you must ensure that the completed tattoo is large and clear so as to be able to be photographed clearly. To aid you, I have also included a photograph of one of our recent inductees, Mary Jane Branson. As you can see, Mary chose to have the induction logo tattoo on her right shoulder.

3. You must ensure that photographs of as much of the tattooing procedure are taken as possible. Take photographs of the various steps of having the tattoo applied.

4. You must supply various photographs of the tattoo from different viewing angles, and also a photograph of yourself for identification, and if possible, showing the tattoo at the same time.

*** VERY IMPORTANT - PLEASE READ CAREFULLY ***

You must understand that the tattoo MUST be a real tattoo, not a drawing or other type of fake tattoo. In other words, being a real tattoo you will of course have it with you for life, so it is important that you are absolutely sure and happy about your decision to join our church.

Of course, as you will know, real tattoos leave slight scarring for the first few days until they heal. Photos MUST be supplied so as to provide proof that a real tattoo has been applied.

Sadly, some people have tried to fool us by applying fake tattoos, but I must warn you that our four man board are extremely diligent and can recognise a fake tattoo very easily. If your tattoo shop need it, we are happy to provide them with payment for their services and allowing you to take photographs. Payment to the tattoo shop can be up to US $1,000. If you provide us with a receipt after the tattoo has been applied we will send payment to them immediately the photographs have been received.

We require at minimum for you to send by email attachment HIGH QUALITY PHOTOGRAPHS of the following:

1. The first stage of the tattoo being applied to the inductee. If possible, photographs showing the tattoo artist actually applying the tattoo would give great encouragement to the board members.

2. Photographs of the tattoo immediately after it has been completed, so that the board members will be able to ascertain it is real because of normal scarring or marking.

3. Photographs taken 24 hours later, showing the healed tattoo.

It is your decision what colour to make the tattoo, but please ensure you choose a colour which can be photographed clearly. Most of our members choose to have a black tattoo applied.

Again, it is entirely your decision what part of your body to have the tattoo applied to. All you need to do is ensure the tattoo is large and clear enough to be photographed clearly. Places that our members usually choose are: arms, top of the legs, or back shoulders.

I must stress to you again that the tattoo must be real, and the photographs you send will be inspected very carefully to ensure that they are. I am sorry that I have to keep repeating this to you brother

Sadiq but as I have already told you, sadly there are ungodly people out in the world who try to take advantage of our church by applying for donations by sending in fake photographs. This is why it is very important that the photographs you send by email attachment are very large and clear so that the validity of the tattoos can be checked easily. Poor quality or small images will be rejected by the board members.

Once we have received satisfactory photographs from you, we will then send you a copy of the church induction application form. This is a very simple form which the applicant must complete and sign with their name and date. Once the form has been returned to us then your donation payment can be processed within 24 hours and sent to you by whichever method best suits your means.

I offer one piece of advice brother Sadiq; the board members usually give larger donations depending on the size of the tattoo. So the larger the tattoo the larger the donation payment is liable to be, but the very minimum we send to help is $20,000, so as you can see you will be able to do a lot of very good work with such an amount.

Of course, once you become a member you will be invited to our yearly gathering here in the UK (your flight fees and expenses will of course be paid by us) and you will be able to meet many of our members as well as myself.

I hope that explains things clearly to you brother Sadiq, and if you have any questions please feel free to contact me any time.

Please will you reply to this email as soon as possible to let me know when you expect to be able to email me the photographs. The four board members work all across the UK so they will need to be gathered to examine your photographs and make the donation payment. This may take 2 or 3 days, so if I know in advance when you are likely to be ready to send the photographs I can ensure that the board members are gathered together in readiness for your photographs.

Please also let me know by what means you would prefer the donation payment to be made.

God be with you,

Father Bruce Corbin
Accounts Department
Holy Church of The Tattooed Saint

I attach the church logo, and a sample (Photoshopped) picture of one of our inductees. The girl's picture was taken from the internet so I have covered her face a little to protect her innocence!

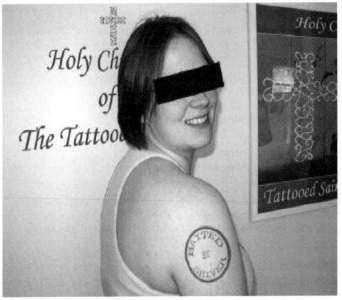

From: Ahmed Sadiq
To: Father Bruce Corbin
Date: Sunday, November 06, 2005
Subject: good day father

Good day father - I received your mail. As I told you, tattooing is not rampant in my area so it will take me a little time to source for the markers. I will try to complete the whole exercise not later than this week.

As for the authenticity of the tattoo, I guarantee you that.

Thanks.

I decide to ignore this email.

From: Ahmed Sadiq
To: Father Bruce Corbin
Date: Wednesday, November 09, 2005
Subject: good day

Good day father - As I told you, I am still on the efforts to accomplish the task. I finally located the venue for the tattoo markers in the new state I told you of. So on a happy note I will commence the marking tomorrow.

But the problem is that the amount is too exorbitant. I have pleaded with them for sympathy considering my plight but all to no avail. So as a last resort, I had to deposit my flight documents as a collateral because I told them you promised to offset the bills after.

I am so happy for your concern. Expect the pictures this week and I hope all these my efforts will be acknowledged.

Thanks once more. I count on you father.

From: Father Bruce Corbin
To: Ahmed Sadiq
Date: Saturday, November 12, 2005

Dear Brother Sadiq - Thank you for your email and I hope you are well. It was nice to hear from you again.

Please do not worry. You may tell your creditors that the church will be happy to pay any additional costs for the tattooing process, and if they wish they may write to me personally and I shall confirm that with them.

I am happy to learn that you will soon be joining with us.

Please remember that it is important to arrange as many photographs of the process and tattoos as possible so that the board members can easily examine the evidence of your process. I am sure that they will be impressed by your commitment so far.

Thank you again brother Sadiq, and God bless you.

Take care.

Father Bruce Corbin
Accounts Department
Holy Church of The Tattooed Saint

A week later the photographs finally arrive...

From: Ahmed Sadiq
To: Father Bruce Corbin
Date: Saturday, November 19, 2005
Subject: It is done father

Good day father, on a happy note, after all the stresses of locating a place and the financial setbacks to the actualisation of this, i have finally done it. its been sent alongside this mail. Father, as you said, i chose a portion of my thighs/laps for clarity purposes. Since the inscription on thursday, i have not gotten strenght to send the pictures because since then, it has been so painful. **(Oh what a shame. How will I sleep tonight?!)** *i didnt know its so painful as this but all the same, i am happy to have met your requirements.*

The tattoo and its markers are the best we can boast of down here in my country having 4 pictures to show for the 4 stages. they are all attached.

Finally Father, graciously, i have done my part.All is now left for you. considering all my efforts in this pursuit, my travel documents being deposited, my great commitment to every principle of yours right from the inception, all i plead now is for a favourable consideration. i have always trusted in you, i know you will not fail me. **(I can't guarantee that I'm afraid Ahmed.)**

thanks a lot

The original pictures Ahmed sent were pretty small, so I demanded larger ones, which you see here - OUCH!

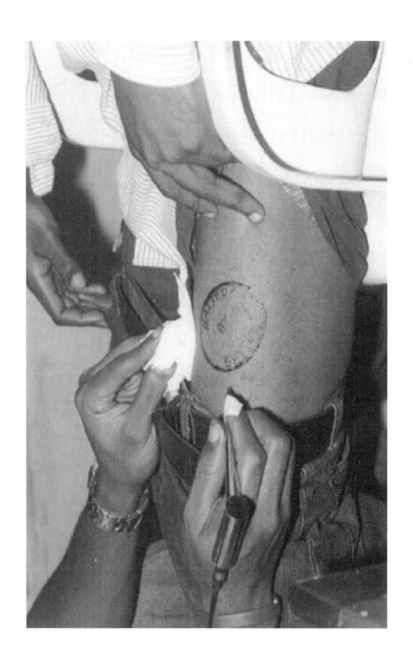

234

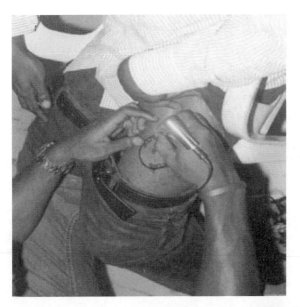

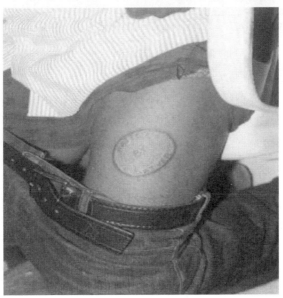

From: Father Bruce Corbin
To: Ahmed Sadiq
Date: November 28, 2005

Dear Brother Sadiq - Thank you for sending in the newly scanned pictures. I can confirm to you that the size and quality are now acceptable to us.

My apologies for the late reply. However, I had to pay a short visit to our local hospital as I have not been feeling very well for the past few days and it was discovered that I had managed to contract a serious tribble infection in my stomach. Fortunately I received treatment in time and I am now feeling almost back to normal. This is the reason for my delay in replying back to you.

Now that you have sent in acceptable photograph I am now passing your case over to father Jack Hackett who is head of the charity awards division of our church. He will be the person in charge of making the payment to you and he will contact you soon to make arrangements for the payment. I expect him to contact you in the next 24 hours.

Blessings,

Father Bruce Corbin
Accounts Department
Holy Church of The Tattooed Saint

From: Ahmed Sadiq
To: Father Bruce Corbin
Date: November 28, 2005
Subject: good day

Good day father - i am so happy to have heard from you again it really shows that you care. sorry for the ill health. i am happy you are well again.

about my case i am also happy how you are forwarding it, please father, help speed it up, people down here are on my neck especially the tattoo people. so please do it for me, i have always trusted you. help make it a reality soon please

thanks once more

The street cred Father Jack Hacket gets in touch wiv (sorry, *with*) Ahmed.

From: Father Jack Hackett
To: Ahmed Sadiq
Date: November 30, 2005

Alo bruva felix - My name is old Father Jack Hackett. Please excuse my
poor english, I am a man from Atlantis and I am still well new to
writing and speaking English. I ope yous can understand me well.

I apologise dat I ain't contacted yous earlia, oweva father Bruce Corbin
as bin admitted to our local hostipal wiv a bad Tribble infecshun and I
ave bin visitin im there. I ave spent da last two days by is bedside as he
is quite ill. Da doctors oweva tell me dat he will be fit and well quite
soon.

Onto your photographs: I thank yous fo sendin da enlargements and I
can confirm to yous dat myself and da other board members is now
entirely satisfied wiv the pictures. Tomorrow mornin I ave to visit
Father Corbin fa a few hours, but once I return I will send yous by
email attachment da induction form which just requires your signature.
Once yous ave signed it and returned it to me then we can process your
payment immediately.

Kind regards,

Father Jack Hackett
Charity Awards Department
Holy Church of The Tattooed Saint

From: Ahmed Sadiq
To: Father Jack Hackett
Date: November 30, 2005
Subject: good day

*Good day - i am so happy to hear that it was accepted favourably. i
look forward to your induction letter as time is no more on my side.
please help procees it fast. i am indebted to many down here considering
the actualisation of this*

i thank you once more.

my regards to father bruce

**Father Hackett hasn't replied for a couple of days and Ahmed is
worried.**

From: Ahmed Sadiq
To: Father Jack Hackett
Date: December 2, 2005
Subject: still waiting

Good day father - i am still waiting for your reply

thanks

A few days later, Father Hackett gets in touch, but there's sad news.

From: Father Jack Hackett
To: Ahmed Sadiq
Date: December 5, 2005

Alo bruva felix - Mi apologies fa da long delay in replyin to your email but I am afraid I ave some wicked news concernin fatha Corbin.

Unfortutanely old Fatha Corbin died from da Tribble infection he caught, and passed away in da early ours of Decemba 2nd.

I ope yous can understand dat we ave bin busy takin care of old father Corbin's funeral arrangements and last wishes, ence da delay in gettin back to yous. I apologise fa da delay and I will be contactin yous again well shortly to finalise your donation payment.

kind regards,

Father Jack Hackett
Charity Awards Department
Holy Church of The Tattooed Saint

From: Ahmed Sadiq
To: Father Jack Hackett
Date: December 7, 2005
Subject: Such bad news

Good day father - what a terrible news to have heard that my lovely friend father bruce is dead. its so painful considering all the help he has been rendering. i wish i would have been around to confort the whole church. anyway am sorry. may his soul rest in peace.

i still wait for your concern towards my case. **(Hey, thanks for such a long mourning period, Ahmed!)** *time is almost up down here thats why i sound desperate. please in good faith like that of father bruce, i wish you would help me actualise this.*

as i have always trusted father bruce, i trust you dont let me down

i wait for your reply

Father Jack doesn't bother to reply.

From: Ahmed Sadiq
To: Jack Hackett
Date: December 7, 2005
Subject: urgent please

Good day father - i think it is the best to tell you my predicament and the need why i have gone this extent of joining your church and having on me the mark of shiver.

as i explained to father bruce, i needed help to achieve my long time dream in life. i was introduced to father bruce by a member of your church Mr Lance and since then, having complied with every of your requirements to recieve your concern, all i get now from you is silence. i have been so straight forward to you, i have trusted your church for good only for me to start having double mind about the whole thing. tell me where have i gone wrong.

please all i ask for is just little money to retrieve back my travel documents wilth my international passport from the tattoo markers here. as i explained to father bruce, there wasnt any money at hand for the tattoo but as i explained to the markers, they understood and did it on the basis that on payment, i will get back my documents.as father bruce promised.

with a sincere heart, i plead for just the little to get back my things please. its about 450 dollars. i will ever remain grateful if you appreciate my sincerity to you by granting me this token.

there is no much time for me for my travel, i want to get through this and seek assistance else where.

i need your reply soonest please.

From: Father Jack Hackett
To: Ahmed Sadiq
Date: December 9, 2005

Alo bruva felix - Dude, ya wanna chill for a few minuts bro. Dunno if yew know but we have a frikkin' funeral to arrange ere.

You'll get da dosh as soon as possibul, but be pashent cos we gotta get Fathe Corbin stuck in an ole before da maggots cum callin, ya get mi? Da induktion form wil be wiv ya in a few hours time.

Latersz,

Father Jack Hackett
Charity Awards Department
Holy Church of The Tattooed Saint

The next day I send Ahmed his induction form.

From: Father Jack Hackett
To: Ahmed Sadiq
Date: December 10, 2005

Alo bruva felix, As I promised attached is da induktion form. Please print it out and complete it then send it back to us by email attachment. Make sure dat the scan is LARGE and CLEAR to avoid any delays.

Latersz,

Father Jack Hackett
Charity Awards Department
Holy Church of The Tattooed Saint
INDUCTION FORM ATTACHED

Ahmed finally sends the completed form back to me.

From: Ahmed Sadiq
To: Father Jack Hackett
Date: December 16, 2005
Subject: Such bad news

Good day father

Now i wait for the payment, consequent on your reply, i will forward the mode of payment, and how it will be sent.

your better opinion is still welcome

i am happy the way you are concerned

thanks

HOLY CHURCH OF THE TATTOED SAINT

INDUCTION AGREEMENT

Please complete the required information below. Failure to provide complete information may result in your payment being delayed.

Please write your full name and address in the box below:

AHMED SADIQ
P.O. BOX 6660,
ALADINMA POST OFFICE
OWERRI, IMO STATE.
NIGERIA

I, **AHMED SADIQ** do herby promise on the Holy Bible that I shall use my donation payment only for the good of my fellow people and to help to create awareness of the Holy Church of The Tattooed Saint in my country.

I, **AHMED SADIQ** promise that I shall abide by Saint Shiver's teachings of The Basted, and will endeavour to follow his example for fear of the Slapping of The Unruly.

I, **AHMED SADIQ** shall use some small percentage of my Donation Payment to aid the encouragement of The Baiting of The Faithful in my area.

Please explain in the box below what you intend to do with the Donation Payment:

I WILL USE THIS DONATION (PART OF IT) FIRST. FOR MY FLIGHT TICKET (SINCE IT HAS BEEN MY LIFETIME DREAM).

SECONDLY AS STATED ABOVE, FOR THE PROPPAGATION OF THE AFFAIRS OF THE HOLY CHURCH OF THE TATTOOED SAINTS.

FINALLY, CHARITY ORGANISATIONS DOWN HERE WILL BENEFIT RICHLY FROM IT.

THANKS.

I decide not to bother replying.

From: Ahmed Sadiq
To: Father Jack Hackett
Date: December 21, 2005
Subject: Such bad news - Good evening father, i thought by now i have received your reply. what next is remaining, i think i have met all your demands

please i wish for a favourable consideration from you at least for meeting all your requirements and having on me the mark of shiver.

i pray to hear from you soonest

I think it has escaped Sadiq's attention that for the past three weeks or so I have been referring to him as 'Felix'. Why he hasn't pulled me up on this I don't really know. I guess he's only taking notice of the lack of payment so far. Anyway, back to his real name as there's no comedy value in continuing getting his name wrong if he isn't going to notice!

From: Father Jack Hackett
To: Ahmed Sadiq
Date: December 22, 2005

Alo bruva Sadiq - Sorry fa da delay in replyin to yous oweva were do get well busy comin up to da Christmas period and of course we ave did ave to deal wiv da remembrance service fa Fatha Corbin. Dat went very well, thank yous fa askin.

Please can yous reconfirm to me da details of ow yous dwant da payment to be made. It is important dat dis is done without any errors whun angin wiv such a large amounst of money.

Latersz,

Father Jack Hackett
Charity Awards Department
Holy Church of The Tattooed Saint

From: Ahmed Sadiq
To: Father Jack Hackett
Date: December 23, 2005
Subject: clarify me

Good day father - thanks for the reply

first i need to know the total amount to be sent because in my country, money through western union money transfer allows for only 5,000 dollars a time. so i need to know the exact amount so that i will know how to split it for the sending. also i wish you a prosperous new year in your good works

From: Father Jack Hackett
To: Ahmed Sadiq
Date: December 25, 2005

Alo bruva Sadiq - Da total wamount dat as been awarded to yous is $42,772

Latersz,

Father Jack Hackett
Charity Awards Department
Holy Church of The Tattooed Saint

From: Ahmed Sadiq
To: Father Jack Hackett
Date: December 27, 2005
Subject: i am happy

Good day *father - now that you have clarified me, i will now go to the bank to sought out how and the means of your payment*

once concluded, i will reach you immediately. once more i am so grateful for your concern. thanks a million times

I'll let Sadiq stew for a week before I reply.

From: Father Jack Hackett
To: Ahmed Sadiq
Date: January 07, 2006

Alo bruva Sadiq - Sorry for da layte reply to your massage but becos of da Christmas break we have ad sum dely wiv our payment scheme.

I am hopin to get yower payment sent in da next 24/48 hours

Latersz,

Father Jack Hackett
Charity Awards Department
Holy Church of The Tattooed Saint

From: Ahmed Sadiq
To: Father Jack Hackett
Date: January 09, 2006
Subject: i understand

Good day father - i saw your reply and i understood the delay there's no problem. as you said, i wait for the first part of the payment. what you have to send is a control pin which i will present to the bank here in nigeria

thanks

A couple of days go by and Sadiq hasn't had his payment yet.

From: Ahmed Sadiq
To: Father Jack Hackett
Date: January 11, 2006
Subject: please father

GOOD DAY FATHER - thanks for your long time concern i still wait for the details as you said as this is a new year, i expect a rapid response to this course. by now i should have seen the details to collect the money.

please try and help me out in this

i have been patient all day.

Sadly, Father Hackett has caught the same bug that killed Father Bruce Corbin...

From: Father Bungdit Upp
To: Ahmed Sadiq
Date: January 11, 2006

Dear brother Sadiq - Good afternoon and I hope you are well?

My name is Father Bungdit Upp and I am the personal assistant to
Father Hackett.

Unfortunately Father Hackett is ill in bed with a slight Tribble infection
which we believe he caught from one of our members. I am afraid he
will be unavailable for the next few days because of this.

However, I am informed that payment information was sent to you
earlier this morning and you should have all the details you require to
collect your payment.

Please let me know when you have received the payment.

God be with you

Father Bungdit Upp
Charity Awards Department
Holy Church of The Tattooed Saint

Sadiq is starting to get a little impatient.

From: Ahmed Sadiq
To: Father Bungdit Upp
Date: January 13, 2006
Subject: tell me

Good day father - to be candid i dont understand what is going on. i have met
all your requirements, what then do you want me to do. since december last
year, i was promised of the payment, till now, all is in vain. please where have i
gone wrong or dont i deserve it

about the information for the payment, i didnt receive anything and i
think you have not sent it, if am worthy, please kindly do it for me pls,
am at a fix now

my sympathey to sick father thanks and i earnestly wait for the payment
details pls

From: Father Bungdit Upp
To: Ahmed Sadiq
Date: January 13, 2006

Dear Sadiq - Please don't give me a hard time. I am only following bloody orders from my boss Father Hackett. I don't know what has gone on between you two but again all I am doing is following orders. I have only been working with the church for the last few weeks so I haven't really been given the fully story about you, so please chill dude.

To be truthful to you Sadiq buddy, I am sick of being ordered around. I know I'm new here, and yes, maybe as a former sex offender I should be thankful for this crummy job, but being the new guy, all I get all day is ordered about by everyone. It's stuff like, 'Hey Bungdit, get me a drink'. 'Hey Bungdit, fetch me my cross'. 'Hey Bungdit, show us your knob'. You know, stuff like that gets pretty boring after a while and the last thing I need is some wise-ass who doesn't even know me to start ordering me about and whingeing over a few measly dollars.

Now, I'm sorry if you did not receive your payment information. I was told by father Hackett that it was sent to you yesterday, So don't go bustin' my balls over some mistake that I was not part of. As you will see I have repeated the payment information for you below.

Now, once you have collected your cash please get back to me and let me know you have collected it.

And please, don't give me any more damn grief. I get enough of it from these idiots I work with. I'm considering a new career in the circus, but please keep that to yourself.

Payment Amount: $42,772 split into the following payments: 8 x $5,000 and 1 x $2,772

Name of Payee: Ahams Chidiebere
Secret Question: Who is Lance Myboyle?
Answer: Dark Side Communications
MTCN Number: 9318262251

Bye for now.

Father Bungdit Upp
Charity Awards Department
Holy Church of The Tattooed Saint

Strange. For some reason Sadiq can't collect his money!

From: Ahmed Sadiq
To: Father Bungdit Upp
Date: January 16, 2006
Subject: urgent

Good day - sorry for my harsh letter, it was because time wasnt on my side again. i hope you have accepted my appologies. about the number, we went to the bank only for them to reject it that the no is invalid. please i dont understand. just cross check to know where the problem is from i wait for your reply.pls am not ordering

bye am waiting now

A short time after, the same day...

From: Ahmed Sadiq
To: Father Bungdit Upp
Date: January 16, 2006
Subject: I am waiting

i tried again, it didnt work.

the no was invalid, so do help me by re sending a valid one, i hope to collect it tommorrow

also who is sending it, is it the church or father hackett

thanks once more

From: Father Bungdit Upp
To: Ahmed Sadiq
Date: January 16, 2006

Dear Sadiq - Dude, is there really any reason to send me two emails one immediately after the other. Yeah I know you are in a rush for the payment but winding me up when I'm already stressed out just isn't going to help matters.

I don't know why you are saying the payment number is wrong. I'm looking at the note that Hackett gave to me and I've double-checked the email I sent to you and the numbers are correct.

Unfortunately I cannot speak to Father Hackett today to get the correct numbers as the old loon is still taking it easy in his hospital bed, whingeing on an on about being in pain with Tribble fever. Let me tell you, I think he's swinging the lead. I had a bout of Tribble fever a couple of years ago when I was doing drug runs between Bolivia and Alaska, and I can't say it affected me all that much. I reckon Father Hackett is just using it as an excuse to have a few days rest and try to chat up his nurses. He's a randy old sod really. Perhaps I'm being a little harsh on the guy, he is 79 after all and he did put in a good word for me that night I was arrested for suspected wire fraud. I wasn't me I tell you, the money was just resting in my account. I always meant to give it back.

To get back to the point Sadiq, I will go and check on Father Hackett's computer to discover what the correct payment number is. Father Hackett's handwriting is not very clear so it is quite possible that a mistake may have been made. I have checked and your payment is definitely here waiting for collection.

Leave it with me for a few hours and once, I have checked the old git's machine, I will send you the amended details later this evening.

Cheers,

Father Bungdit Upp
Charity Awards Department
Holy Church of The Tattooed Saint

I took a little too long to get back to Sadiq,

From: Ahmed Sadiq
To: Father Bungdit Upp
Date: January 17, 2006
Subject: re: i am waiting

i wait for the correct nos pls do check and reply me

thanks so much

From: Father Bungdit Upp
To: Ahmed Sadiq
Date: January 17, 2006

Dear Sadiq - Sorry for the late reply dude but I could not get to speak with Father Hackett until late in the evening. By that time the church was closed and I could not get access to his computer.

Father Hackett is gravely ill I'm afraid. It seems the Tribble infection has greatly affected him and he is finding it very hard to speak. After some time and a lot of prodding, he was able to give me the password for his computer so that I could try to figure out the correct payment code to send to you.

I spent four hours this morning searching the files and luckily I managed to find the payment codes. At least I think they are yours. There was a 10 digit number which was referenced with our name and labelled as "Ahmed's back-hander".

As I suspected, Father Hackett wrote down the code for you the other day incorrectly. As you know I sent you the payment code 9318262251 but in fact Father Hackett mistakenly wrote the number 1 when he should have been writing number 7 so the correct number is 9378262251. Hopefully that number will work for you.

I found a lot of interesting information on Father Hackett's computer too.

For instance, some photographs of all the Fathers at the recent Christmas party, including myself. I thought you might enjoy seeing a picture of me. Attached you will see myself, and behind me Father Hector Barnett. We had plenty of fun at the party as you can see. We were playing blind man's buff at the time. I was playing the part of the blind man, and father Hector was in the buff. It was great, though unfortunately my clothes had a small stain on the back. Not sure where that came from.

Anyway, back to the point: As I said, the correct pay number is 9318262551 and hopefully you will at long last finally be able to get what you so richly deserve.

(Will Ahmed notice I wrote three different numbers there?)

Cheerio,

Father Bungdit Upp
Charity Awards Department
Holy Church of The Tattooed Saint

I attach a Photoshopped picture of Bungdit and Father Hector Barnett, who you may recognise from *The Tale of the Painted Breast* scambait or even from the US TV show *Frasier*!

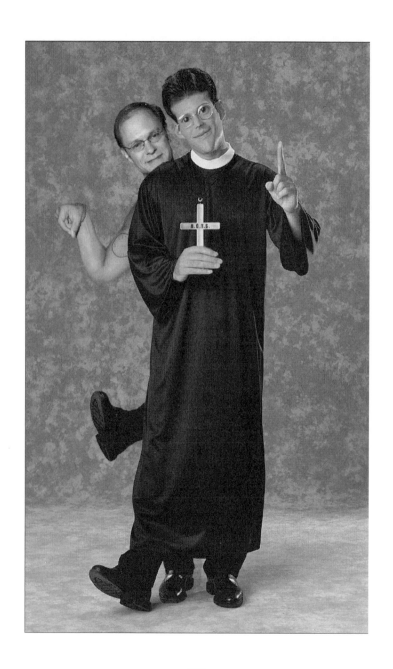

Aww.. Seems I gave Sadiq some more bum numbers.

From: Ahmed Sadiq
To: Father Bungdit Upp
Date: January 18, 2006
Subject: URGENT

Good day brother - pls save me all these embarrassments it looks like i am a fraudster whenever i insist on these nos you give me

can you believe it, that number didnt work out pls if this is real and truely if you are sending me any money, send me the correct no and detail, even the names didnt work, the bank tried the names, all were fake

wat is happenin pls

There's a new priest in town, and he has some rather bad news for Sadiq.

From: Father Hector Barnett
To: Ahmed Sadiq
Date: January 18, 2006

Dear Mr. Ahmed Sadiq

Good morning sir - Let me introduce myself. My name is Hector Barnett and I am the head of the Investigations Department for the HCTS. I believe you have been recently dealing with a former colleague of ours by the name of Father Bungdit Upp?

Unfortunately I've to report to you that Mr. Upp is now in police custody having been arrested in the early hours of this morning for diverting church funds to his own private account. Sadly it appears that Mr. Upp decided to return to his previous life of crime and has stolen a significant amount of cash from the church and some of its beneficiaries, which also includes yourself.

We have only completed some preliminary investigations however we have discovered that over the last 5 weeks Mr. Upp has stolen approximately US $309,947 from the church funds, and that includes the donation payment to you, totalling $42,772. I am sorry to have to deliver such bad news to you Mr. Sadiq. However , you are just one of many people we have had to contact this morning to impart such negative news.

As a consequence of Mr. Upp's actions any donation payments due are now unable to be paid personally by the church. Your only course of action at the moment is to contact the Criminal Compensations Department of the UK Police. They will arrange compensation for you for the full amount until such times as the investigations into Mr. Upp

251

have been completed. You will require a case number to give to the criminal compensations section which in your particular case is 11812121/421/771/HHGTTG/34333/SADIQ

When you contact the Criminal Compensation Department, please quote that reference number to them so that they know who they are dealing with. They will quickly arrange for your payment to be paid in full.

The contact email address for the department head is morse@xxxxpolice.co.uk The name of the person you need to contact is Inspector Morse.

Once more I am very sorry for the current situation, however I am sure you will understand that this is not of our doing. The church regularly employs ex-criminals in order to try to rehabilitate them into every day life and hopefully by giving them gainful employment they will shun their former criminal lives.

Unfortunately in Mr. Bungdit Upp's case it appears he was beyond our help.

Sincerely,

Father Hector Barnett
Investigations Department
Holy Church of The Tattooed Saint

Ahmed wastes no time in getting in touch with Inspector Morse.

From: Ahmed Sadiq
To: Inspector Morse
Date: January 19, 2006
Subject: urgent

Good day inspector morse - i am directed by the holy church of tattooed saints to officially report an ill done me by a worker in the church name bungdit Upp who by now is in your custody

as they told me, he has been embazzling church fund which includes the payment i should have gotten from the church

i demand justice in this, i cant compromise that money since its my last hope, they gave me a refence number which i should quote. its 11812121/421/771/HHGTTG/34333/SADIQ

i look forward for my payment please

Inspector Morse, of course, requires some proof that Ahmed is who he says he is.

From: Inspector Morse
To: Ahmed Sadiq
Date: January 19, 2006

Dear Mr. Sadiq

Ref: 11812121/421/771/HHGTTG/34333/SADIQ

I am in receipt of your email dated January 19, 2006.

As you may have been informed, we are currently investigating a person who has previously had contact with you, namely one Mr. Bungdit Upp. Mr. Upp is currently incarcerated in our custody on preliminary charges of money laundering, theft, identity theft, and suspicion of passing around the Tribble virus with intent to infect people.

My division are in charge of Criminal Compensations and investigations and we authorise intermediate payments to victims of crime.

I understand on reading your case notes that your entitlement is US $42,772.

Of course you will understand that before I can authorise such a payment you will be required to send me proof of your identification to ensure that this payment is sent to the entitled person, so please would you forward me a scan of your international passport and a signed letter with the following statement

---

Your name
Your address
Your telephone number
Date of birth
Today's date.

FAO: Inspector Morse - UK Police Criminal Compensation Department

Dear Mr. Morse,

C.R.A.B. Reference Number: Ref: 11812121/421/771/HHGTTG/34333/SADIQ

This letter is to certify that I am the above named person and I am entitled to a donation payment, authorised by Father Jack Hackett of The Church of The Tattooed Saint. The total payment I am entitled to is US $42,772.

Please find attached a copy of my official identification which I confirm is a true representation of me.

I confirm that during the course of my communication with all members of The Church of The Tattooed Saint that all information I have given has been truthful and factually correct and that if any false information has been given in any form I shall immediately lose all entitlement to the donation payment due to me.

Sincerely,

SIGN YOUR NAME

Date: WRITE THE DATE

_____

On receipt of the information above we will authorise your payment immediately.

Thank you for writing to us.

Sincere regards,

Inspector Morse
Head of Division
UK COD

Ahmed comes up with the inevitable excuses.

From: Ahmed Sadiq
To: Inspector Morse
Date: January 23, 2006
Subject: thanks

Good day inspector

Reference Number: Ref:

11812121/421/771/HHGTTG/34333/SADIQ

I thank you for the concern you have in retrieving my money which went into wrong hands. I appreciate all your efforts.

But what I don't understand is my identification you are requiring. Yes you don't want this money to be sent to a wrong person but I have been on this alone since last year, there's no other Ahmed Sadiq. But if you still want proof, I will supply you the information you require of me.

About the scan of my international passport, it wont be possible because I have been dispossessed of my travel documents by my tattoo markers because of my inability to afford the church's tattoo sign. Its because of this I am replying you late, I have been beckoning on them to assist me in this all to no avail. Father Hackett and the church know more about it.

(Ahmed makes a beginner's error here. He should have said something along the lines of 'I don't own a passport' and then he could have provided some other fake ID. However, by stating it is 'at the tattooist', he has owned up to having one and I will not rest until I get to see it!)

Instead I will send you my pictures of initiation into The Church of The Tattooed Saint and my inauguration form, I hope these should be concrete evidence of my person. Please I have suffered enough in this course, I demand fairness and justice. I didn't know it would culminate into this. I have always trusted the church, please don't fail me.

From: Inspector Morse
To: Ahmed Sadiq
Date: January 19, 2006

Dear Mr. Sadiq

Ref: 11812121/421/771/HHGTTG/34333/SADIQ

Thank you for your email. I am sorry, but without any form of official identification which also contains your photographic identification I will be unable to clear the payment to you.

I am not aware of the circumstances surrounding your payment, so your explanations are wasted on me. All that I know is that I have a payment of $42,772 authorised for a Mr. Ahmed Sadiq which is to be paid only on receipt of the required official identification and signed statement of intent as described in my previous email to you of 19 Jan 2006.

Please note that I have just received your second email in which you typed out the statement. This is not acceptable. You must send me by email attachment a SIGNED version of the statement containing your full HAND-WRITTEN signature.

Please note that I have absolutely nothing to do with the church or any other business. I am an inspector of Her Majesty's UK Police force and I deal with criminal cases. I have absolutely no affiliation with the church. I do not have any say whatsoever in what the church or people you have been dealing with have to say.

Unless you are able to supply the signed statement and a copy of your official identification then the money will not be paid to you.

Sincerely,

Inspector Morse
Head of Division
UK COD

Ahmed finally sends in the signed form, but still no passport image. He sent copies of his tattoo pictures but they are, of course, not proof of identity!

From: Inspector Morse
To: Ahmed Sadiq
Date: January 24, 2006

Dear Mr. Sadiq

Ref: 11812121/421/771/HHGTTG/34333/SADIQ

Thank you for the signed form which I have just received.

Please note that I still require a scan of your international passport. The images you sent of your tattoo pictures are of absolutely no use nor interest to me. They are not proof of identity.

Sincerely,

Inspector Morse
Head of Division
UK COD

Ahmed replies with more excuses.

From: Ahmed Sadiq
To: Inspector Morse
Date: January 25, 2006
Subject: pls understand me

Good day inspector

Ref: 11812121/421/771/HHGTTG/34333/SADIQ

I think those proofs are worthy enough to ascertain my genuinety.

Please why stress on the impossible. As I told you before, my passport is not at hand. It will be nice if I hint you about it. Those pictures I sent you with the church's tattoo was done here on credit. My friend in the church, father Corbin (of blessed memory) promised to send me a little part of my money to redeem my school documents and my travel documents.

But since his death, I begged father Hackett but he assured me of the bulk sum. And because of my failure to afford the services of the tattoo marking, we reached a compromise with the tattoo firm that if father Corbin sends the money; I will then collect my documents. But all my pleas to the church have been to no avail.

Down here, I am faced with so many frustrations. My documents are with an ordinary tattoo firm and they are threatening to sue me to court. Sometimes the need arises in school for some particulars, I will be full of flimsy excuses. What else am I to do, inspector. I will owe a lot to you if you actualize this for me.

I am frustrated that is why I sound desperate.

Thanks and I pray for your understanding.

Inspector Morse is not budging until he sees Ahmed's passport.

From: Inspector Morse
To: Ahmed Sadiq
Date: January 25, 2006

Dear Mr. Sadiq

Ref: 11812121/421/771/HHGTTG/34333/SADIQ

Please tell me exactly how those tattoo pictures are proof of identity? How do I know that the person in those pictures is in fact Ahmed Sadiq and not some other person who may have been paid to have the tattoo pictures? Tell me, WHERE IS THE PROOF? There is absolutely NO PROOF whatsoever that the person in those photographs is you.

Now again I repeat to you that you will not receive your payment unless I see a scan of your international passport. You can continue arguing forever if you wish but that will not change the fact that you will not receive anything from my department without proof of your identification.

If the tattoo shop will not give you your passport back then contact the police. It is against the law for an unofficial organisation or private person to hold another's passport against their will. If you think it will help then tell the tattoo shop owner to contact me via email and I will personally ensure to him that he will receive his payment when he releases his passport to you.

You have a very simple choice Mr. Sadiq; either provide me with your passport or you get no payment. That choice is yours entirely.

Sincerely,

Inspector Mores
Head of Division
UK COD

More pleading.

From: Ahmed Sadiq
To: Inspector Morse
Date: January 26, 2006
Subject: re: no passport no payment

Good day inspector - Please it's now left for you to decide on this. I have told you the much I have tried in this. I told the church and father Hackett to spare me at least $240 out of the money or anywhere else (notwithstanding the interest rate because I will surely pay back) to pay them up to collect my documents. But no way, they keep assuring me of the bulk money. Now the bulk money is ready, there is another clause of my identity.

I don't have any face again to go back to them begging them to release my particulars where I have not paid them. I cant imagine the embarrassment I will be causing myself if I go begging there, as it is, they might even arrest me for running away with their money, its their right because I didn't pay them, I only assured them of the church's benevolence and compliance to this.

So in your own, tell me what to do next, but I still doubt if those items I sent you including the scanned signed document you demanded didn't prove my identity.

Why not understand and trust me

Inspector Morse has lost patience with Ahmed.

258

From: Inspector Morse
To: Ahmed Sadiq
Date: January 26, 2006

Dear Mr. Sadiq

Ref: 11812121/421/771/HHGTTG/34333/SADIQ

Thank you for your email. However, as you have not sent your identification as required your case will be closed by 12 noon tomorrow and your payment will be denied permanently.

Sincerely,

Inspector Mores
Head of Division
UK COD

At the same time as pleading with Inspector Morse, Sadiq also fires off an email to his original intended victim, Lance Myboyle.

From: Ahmed Sadiq
To: Lance Myboyle
Date: January 26, 2006
Subject: pls what is wrong

Good day. Happy New Year. It has been very long since I mailed you. Sorry I have not been feeding you with the developments so far about the church and I. Sir, it has not been roses as I thought. **(A bit of an understatement I'd say, Ahmed.)** *My frustrated state now cannot be imagined because of my commitment and faithfulness to the church you introduced me to. Sir, to be sincere, I didn't know I will end up like this. I finally joined your church, met all the requirements even the grave ones of having on me the mark of shiver for the purpose of help, but what did I get in return, stories. Please why did you introduce me to their kind?* **(Because you tried to scam me, Ahmed, that's why.)**

I trusted them, starting from father Corbin, who they later told me was dead. Then, my case was transferred to father Hackett who recently became gravely ill as I was told and again transferred me to father bungdit. Above all I was still patient. It was father bungdit who purposely gave me wrong control numbers with fake payment details just to discharge me. All they told me now was that father bungdit is a criminal who laundered part of the church's fund to his own account.

My money being included. Now the case is with the UK police. Please tell me, what do I have with the police. Now the inspector in charge is threatening to withhold my money if I don't produce the scan of my international passport. Its scan is easy but I am not in possession of the passport. As you told me, that before I get help from the church, I must be a member.

In fulfillment to that, I explained to father Corbin how hard it was to locate a tattoo firm in my country. Amidst all, I was able to procure their services in another state here but on a condition. Because I couldn't afford $240 for their services to inscribe on me the shiver's sign, we reached a compromise that as soon as the church pays me, I will return their money and collect my school and travel documents which they seized as collateral considering how desperate I was to procure their services all to join your church. I made the greatest mistake of my life by accepting this term of services not knowing that I have toyed with my credentials and documents. I pleaded to both father Corbin and Hackett to at least give me a little from my money or anywhere else let me first get out my documents which is the most important all to no avail.

Right now, I have been dispossessed of my greatest assets in life. What did I do to deserve all these, just a little help I asked, has robbed me of my future. Please where did go wrong, the tattoo I did, my inauguration form and all the requirements were accepted by the board of your church, so I can't figure out where the problem lies. **(Again, being a thief was probably your mistake here.)** *I have always been truthful and faithful to the church, please if there is any place or thing I did wrong, tell me.*

Now the problem is a question of my identity. I have proved to my ability my genuinety to no avail. Since the inception, it has only been I alone, so why should the police be telling me that without the scan of my int. passport, all is void amidst my explanations to them. I believe that some forces are working against me.

Sir, I have taken time to explain my plight to you because you were the first I reached because of my problem and you introduced me to your church. You told me last year that you have closed your charity chances because the year was ending; now the year is starting, what will happen. Please I pray for your understanding, I am not asking to be included into your charity list for a bulk sum, I just need my documents back. Only if you can redeem them for me with $240, I will be so *grateful. All I ask for is this token, even if it comes from your personal savings, please do it for posterity sake.*

I have always trusted in you. I wait for your anticipated positive reply

It seems that Lance Myboyle is a little short of cash at the moment.

From: Lance Myboyle
To: Ahmed Sadiq
Date: January 26, 2006

Dear Mr. Sadiq - It is good to hear from you again. I hope you are well?

I read with interest your email below and find it quite strange that you seem to have had so many problems. The church is usually extremely efficient with relation to donation payments, and it is very unusual that you have been denied help so far. It seems you have been the victim of some very unfortunate circumstances. Still, at least you're not Cliff Richard, so thank God for small mercies.

Yes, it was a very sad event the death of my good friend and golfing partner Father Bruce Corbin. I do miss him very much. I was at his funeral and it was a very sombre and well attended occasion. I counted nearly 500 people at the funeral so it is obvious he was a much loved person. Such a great shame. He had such a low handicap as well. What a waste.

Unfortunately, as you of course now know, Father Hackett has been struck down with the same Tribble virus that infected Father Corbin, and in fact I have only this morning come back from visiting the good Father in hospital. I am sorry to report that he is also in a very bad condition and the prognosis for him is not good at all. As you probably well know, the Tribble virus is very virulent, which is the trouble with Tribbles, and once infected the chances of a full recovery are very slim indeed. Dr. Shatner informed me that Father Hackett's chances are very slim and it is really 50/50 as to whether he will survive or not. When you combine that with Father Hackett's old age then it does not add up to very good news at all, and I fear more bad news on the horizon. On the up side, he wasn't a very good golfer so I doubt he will be missed all that much.

Regarding your request for financial help in the matter of $240. I am afraid that I will have to regretfully refuse your request at the moment, even from my personal account which presently only contains as little as two million dollars. As I explained to you some months ago, my company do indeed give to charity on a very regular basis. However, you have missed our company's donation period which expired only three days ago. Unfortunately here in the UK we have very stringent charity and tax laws so my company is unable to help you in this respect. If we did help you we may face prosecution under section 4, chapter 19 of the UK Charities Act 1974.

Similarly, I cannot give you a payment from my own personal account because tomorrow I am taking delivery of my new luxury yacht "The Simple Life" which has been very costly for me, especially as I have had to have so many extra options installed, such as the gym, extra jacuzzi, helicopter pad, and 40 seater cinema. As you can imagine this has cost me a small fortune and so my personal funds are very tight at the moment, so again I apologise but I will be unable to help you. My wife also wants me to book our three week holiday in Barbados this afternoon so that will be even more cost to me. If you think your luck is bad then please think about me suffering in Barbados, the waiter service there can be quite slow and sometimes we have to wait up to ten minutes when we order a meal.

I am sorry I cannot give you much advice as to what to do at this moment in time Ahmed, only to say that you should try to get the identification that the police have asked you for. I can certainly try to put in a good word for you to the police on your behalf but I do not know whether that will be of any help. If you want me to contact them for you then please give me a contact number or address for them and I will write to them for you and vouch for you.

Good luck,

Lance Myboyle
Managing Director: Dark Side Communications
www.the-dark-side.co.uk

Ahmed gets back to Inspector Morse with a request.

From: Ahmed Sadiq
To: Inspector Morse
Date: January 28, 2006
Subject: please

Good day inspector, Please don't get so rigid. I have told you every thing. But as you are insisting, I am all out to follow your directives.

I will like to ask you of a favour, I know it will be very hard for you but *for heaven's sake, please help. Lend me the token $240; as soon as I receive my money, I will pay you out rightly with any interest of your choice. Or to avoid waste of time, you can collect your portion before sending it down to me*

As you can see, I am all craving for your concern, please inspector. Thanks.

From: Inspector Morse
To: Ahmed Sadiq
Date: January 28, 2006

Dear Mr. Sadiq

Ref: 11812121/421/771/HHGTTG/34333/SADIQ

Are you completely serious?!!! We are the police force, not a charity organisation. Frankly I am amazed you should ask such a thing. You are not taking drugs are you?

You will not get one single penny until your passport documents have been received. Now, please stop wasting police time.

Inspector Mores
Head of Division
UK COD

From: Ahmed Sadiq
To: Inspector Morse
Date: January 30, 2006
Subject: no problem

Good day inspector - My efforts to get those things out were frustrated. I had thought one Mr. lance would help but all was the same stories. But nevertheless, down here, I have pleaded with my friend's father who is a doctor and he has agreed to help.

So as soon I go to the bank and collect the money on this week, I will proceed to the tattoo firm and redeem my documents. Immediately I get them, I will scan my passport.

Sorry for the time wasting, I will get to you soonest

Ahmed eventually replies to Lance Myboyle.

From: Ahmed Sadiq
To: Lance Myboyle
Date: January 30, 2006
Subject: bye

Good day - Check it, you tell me of having 2 million dollars in your account but you can't spare my future for me.

Look at what you have caused me. You can't get help from your personal money, you now tell me that your charity chances has expired just three days ago. What kind of people are you. Don't you have conscience?

Last year you told me that the year was rounding off and so I came late. I accepted that in good faith, but now the year is just started, what is causing the expiration of your charity donations. What criteria.

You are planning of procuring a 2 million yatch with a holiday in Barbados but you forgot entirely the lamb you led astray. I can't believe this is my fate in this. You are all the same. Look at my ruins just because I obeyed you. I have no more pleas to offer. I now leave you to posterity. I won't curse you neither will I abuse you but search yourself, and see if you are right in frustrating the future of a young man who came to you. You could have left me unhelped rather than ruining me.

Good bye all of you

From: Lance Myboyle
To: Ahmed Sadiq
Date: January 30, 2006

Dear Mr. Sadiq - Thank you for your email.

I don't know why you seem to be so upset. I realise that you may have had a run of bad luck, but there is really no need to take out your anger on an innocent person such as myself. All I was trying to do in the beginning was help you. Perhaps God is punishing you for your initial lies to me?

Yes, it is true that I have 2 million dollars in my personal account. However, you do not seem to understand about business enough to realise why I cannot give you any of it. The money is stored in a seantic phospheral dimontic accrued divisionary high-yielding business current account. **(You must have heard of them!)** This account rewards me with much higher interest rates then a standard account, which is of course a great benefit. The downside is that to withdraw money from that account I have to give the bank 90 days notice. I suspect that you are not in a position to wait 90 days and this is why I refused your request. Now, if you ARE indeed prepared to wait that long then yes, I can give you the money.

You again are mistaken. The Yacht is not costing me 2 million dollars. Please read my previous email again more carefully. The Yacht cost me a small fortune, I said - actually 7.2 million dollars.

You did not 'obey' me Mr. Sadiq. I just gave you advice. It was your choice entirely to take it or not. I did not order you to do anything, nor am I in any way responsible for 'ruining' you. Again perhaps if you had not contacted me with a lie then I suspect God would look upon you with more generous eyes.

I have offered to contact the UK police on your behalf to try to help you but it seem you have already made your mind up not to contact me anymore so even though you have falsely accused me I wish you luck for the future.

Good luck,

Lance Myboyle
Managing Director: Dark Side Communications
www.the-dark-side.co.uk

Just over a week later, Sadiq comes through with his passport.

From: Ahmed Sadiq
To: Inspector Morse
Date: February 7, 2006
Subject: no problem

Good day inspector - I am so happy to be meeting your requirement for the actualization of my payment. I have gone the length of borrowing money from people I shouldn't have borrowed from. But all not withstanding, I assured them of immediate payment as soon as you pay me.

Consequent on this, I request for your rapid positive response to my case.Now I think its done well. Am waiting now for your actions.

Thanks for your understanding.

FEDERAL REPUBLIC OF NIGERIA

PASSPORT
PASSPORT

Type / Type   Country code / Code du pays
P   NGA

Passport No. / Passeport N°
A1351788

Surname / Nom
AHMED

Given names / Prénoms
SADIQ GARY

Nationality / Nationalité
NIGERIAN

Date of birth / Date de naissance
25 JUN 85 / 25 JUIN 85

Authority / Autorité
382

Sex / Sexe   Place of birth / Lieu de naissance
M   OWERRI

Date of issue / Date de délivrance
20 MAY / MAI 02

Holder's signature / Signature du titulaire

Date of expiry / Date d'expiration
19 MAY / MAI 07

<<<<KDAHMED<<<<SADIQGARY>>>>>>>>1351788<<<<<<<<<<
<<<<NGA<<<<382<<<<<<<MAI5543288765<<<<<PMOWRR<<<

Even the most gullible victim would surely not fall for such a pathetic attempt at passport fakery, and even I am impressed that Sadiq has the balls to submit this to someone he thinks is a police inspector! Let's give Sadiq a taste of his own cut & paste medicine.

From: Inspector Morse
To: Ahmed Sadiq
Date: February 7, 2006

Dear Mr. Sadiq

Ref: 11812121/421/771/HHGTTG/34333/SADI

Thank you for finally sending your passport image.

Your first payment has now been made.

Please keep a copy of the attached Western Union payment receipt for your records

Inspector Morse
Head of Division
UK COD

I attach the payment receipt.

266

To send money — FEXCO MT | WESTERN UNION | MONEY TRANSFER

For Western Union Card holders, please fill in your card number and the green shaded areas only.

Card No.: 0 2 3 7 9 3 3 1 0

Destination: City LAGOS

Please complete all in block capitals

Amount (in words) FIVE THOUSAND DOLLARS
Amount: 5000 Donor: NIGERIA

Fix exchange rate at time of transfer? Yes ✓ No ☐

Unless you have requested the foreign exchange rate for the transaction to be fixed at the time you pay in, the rate will be set at the time the transaction is paid and to which point any indication of the payment amount appearing on this form is advisory only.

SECTION 1 - RECEIVER (as on identification prod.)

First name(s): ADAMS
Last name: CHIDIEBERE

Will the receiver have valid identification? Yes ☐ No ☐

Question: CUT AND PASTE?

If No, please provide a test question and answer, maximum of 4 words (maximum send amount £350 when using test question and receiver has no ID)

Answer: YES

SECTION 2 - SENDER (as on identification produced)

First name(s): INSPECTOR
Last name: MORSE
Address: 221B BAKER STREET
LONDON UK

Postcode:

Telephone: | Please include STD code

Optional Services

☐ Message to be sent
☐ Telephone the Receiver. Tel No. (   )(
☐ Home cheque delivery -

Please fill in the receiver's address.

Customer's sign: X [signature]

RECEIPT

IMPORTANT NOTICE THE TERMS AND CONDITIONS ON WHICH THE SERVICE IS PROVIDED ARE SET OUT ON THE REVERSE OF THIS FORM. BY SIGNING THIS FORM, I ACKNOWLEDGE THAT I HAVE READ, UNDERSTOOD AND ACCEPTED THOSE TERMS AND CONDITIONS. If you do not wish to receive further information on the services provided by Western Union, please tick this box. ☐ COPYRIGHT© 2002 WESTERN UNION FINANCIAL SERVICES, INC.

Agent's Signature: Frank Sinatra

	Amount	Identification type	PASSPORT
		Passport/Driving licence No.	123454321
Transfer fee	80·00	Date issued	21/7/2000
Additional services		Expiry date	21/7/2010
Total Collected	5080·00	Place of issue	ENGLAND

OFFICE INFORMATION

Agency name	W.U. 300
Western Union operator number	14
Filed date	Filed time
Money Transfer Control Number	1 0 9 5 4 5 9 0 0 3

Sadly, I have to inform you all the some miserable scrote managed to find Ahmed Sadiq's contact details and got in touch with him to tell him that he was being baited by me and pointed him to my website. Here's the last email I ever received from Ahmed.

From: Ahmed Sadiq
To: Inspector Morse
Date: February 15, 2006
Subject: good day

Good day - I guess this is my last mail to you.

This is to pour out my mind to you over all that has been happening. I'm sorry in any way I have wronged you ever in this business. I plead for your forgiveness. In the same way, I pray to have the heart to forgive you all- lance, Corbin, Hackett, bungdit and you Morse.

I suffered terribly under your hands with the view to attracting your sympathy. My problem was that my innocence fell in wrong hands.

There's no problem, I will make up to all that I have lost in this course. Where will I start, from lance who sent me to your church (only to tell me that he runs his own charity, a charity that is dependent on queen Elizabeth's approval, isn't this the biggest joke on earth), from Corbin who you claimed was dead (but still has his valid contact in your website) to Hackett who you claimed was with tribble disease and is in his point of death (but can still go on with his daily chores, searching out the fake control number from his laptop).

Then to bungdit who you claimed embezzled money (that sent me non human pictures that was computer done joining two cartoons telling me it was him and Hackett dancing) and finally to you Morse who claims a UK police inspector (without any directory in the real uk police code). Yes I was desperate to meet my selfish desires but you could have ignored me initially or discouraged me the way I was going about the realization of my lifetime dream.

Thanks to Allah that you didn't put me into trouble. I hear that sometimes people lavish in jails and prisons for what they known nothing of, I didn't know it wanted to happen to me. You lured me to going to the bank two times to withdraw money you didn't send at all. So you would have been happy sending an innocent young man to jail.

You now came with the third joke that I should go and collect your so-

*called money. You think you can prove its genuinety by sending a copy
of the payment slip to me. Can't you see yourself, the color for Western
Union as every one knows is yellow and black (but yours was green), if
really you were serious of sending the slip, it should have come as an
attachment since it was scanned but yours was a simple computer cut
and paste work as depicted by your secret question. Wont it be better
and more convincing if the slip had a same background. Why the white
patches. A blind man will easily notice a foul play. Why should your
date of issue be 2000, aren't we in 2006, and the expiry date, why that
far.* **(Ahmed obviously doesn't see the irony in calling my Western
Union a pathetic cut & paste job.)**

*Who on earth has his first name as inspector, if so , your rank in the
"uk police" is what? How can you tell me you waited for the payment
information from me so went to the church to collect the one I had
given them before? You didn't even wait up to 24 hours, but you were
the same person that asked me to supply it, how then was the payment
processed days before the receipt of my side of the information.*

*Okay, the church gave you the payment information, who in particular?
Dead Corbin, gravely ill Hackett or bungdit-the convict in your
custody, who? And lastly who gave you the city as LAGOS. Never had I
mentioned my city to you not to talk of the church. Even in your widest
guess, you shouldn't have gotten it. This links to the call I got one night.*

*I got a call of a person who assuming anonymity claimed he has been
following my transactions with you. He said it all, and got it all and I
thank him for his advice. Yes, mails can be tracked, but not all. And you
can't tell me you even track the ones I receive. It's not possible at all.
Unless you have my password which is impossible. Sorry let the truth
be told, are you not these whole people.*

*What actually did you want from me? How can you tell me you have
been trailing my messages, how? Maybe you were tired of playing
along, maybe a sort of detective who wants to curb the menace of crime
in his country, Nigeria. Don't you have any other e-mail address to link
me up to with a big flimsy story to back it up?*

*I highly envy your high network of devices, high IQ, lots of websites
(which normally remains under construction until heaven falls).*

*My regrets are: my friend Chidiebere who I have disappointed greatly,
the tattoo firm who nearly brought down brimstones on me, my friend's*

*father who I don't know how to pay back the money I borrowed from
him and finally myself, because I have disappointed Allah and the
sacred precepts of Islam.*

*I pray I will be forgiven because I acted out of ignorance and
desperation.*

Good-bye

Quite a friendly email folks, and some of you may feel a tinge of
sympathy for Ahmed. But you'd better believe that this guy would
have taken me for every penny I had if at all possible. He is looking for
pity, which is what 99.9% of scammers usually do when finally busted.
They love to furnish their victims with pitiful stories but they are all to
be taken with a pinch of salt.

When you have seen as many real victims' horror stories as we
scambaiters have seen, you soon realise that these people have zero
morals and zero pity, and would have no qualms about leaving you in
a pool of blood if that's what it took to get a few dollars out of you.

Another day. Another bog-standard 419 scam. Sometimes I just get weary. This time I decided to see if this scammer would accept being sworn at repeatedly, so I decided to invent a new type of Tourette's Syndrome. Please note that this short scambait is in no way meant to poke fun at real sufferers, rather it was a shortcut for me to vent some anger at these pests. WARNING: Bundles of bad language follows, so if you are easily offended then please do not read any further.

From: Charles Bosah
To: Colin Carver
Date: March 3, 2006
Subject: Reply

FROM THE DESK OF
DR,CHARLES BOSAH
MUTUAL TRUST BANK [P.L.C]
HEAD QUATERS BRANCH
VICTORIA ISLAND, LAGOS-NIGERIA.

DEAR FRIEND - My name is DR CHARLES OBOSAH, INTERNAL AUDITOR MUTUAL TRUST BANK PLC. I am writing in respect of a foreign customer of our bank Mr.JONATHAN GHUNIAM with account number 14-255-2004/ASTB/123-99 who perished in an auto-crash in october 15 2003.

Since the demise of this our customer, I personally has watched with keen interest to see the next of kin but all has proved abortive as no one *has come to claim his funds of US$9..5m (Nine Million Five Hundred Thousand United States Dollars), which has been with our branch for a very long time.*

On this note, I decided to seek for whom his name shall be used as the next of kin as no one has come up to be the next of kin. The banking ethics here does not allow such money to stay more than four years, because money will be recalled to the bank treasury as unclaimed after this period. In view of this, I decided to seek through internet whom to confine in for this transaction. I seek your consent to present you as the next of kin to the deceased.

So that the proceeds of this account valued at $9.5 million dollars can be paid to your account for sharing 65% to me and 30% to you, while 5% should be for reimbursement of incidental expenses that may be incured during the transaction or tax as your government may require.

I will not fail to bring to your notice that this business is hitch free safe and legal. we have to hire an attorney who will protect you legally,and for benefit of doubt position you as the next of kin and beneficiary.that you should not entertain any fear as all modalities for fund transfer can be finalized as soon as possible.

When you receive this letter, kindly send me an e-mail on this mail box including your most confidential telephone/fax numbers and your address for quick communication.

Your Friend
DR CHARLES OBOSAH

The disclaimer I put at the beginning of my reply to Bosah below is included in all my emails to him. So as not to waste space, however, I have only included it once here.

From: Colin Carver
To: Charles Bosah
Date: March 3, 2006

IMPORTANT - PLEASE READ THIS DISCLAIMER BEFORE YOU PROCEED. THIS WILL AVOID CONFUSION AND FALSE IMPRESSIONS.

The sender of the message MR. COLIN CARVER is a sufferer of Tourette's Syndrome, which is a medical condition which affects the sufferer in various ways. For more information please visit www.xxxxx.com. Mr. Colin Carver, the sender of the message below is a sufferer of the more antisocial sub-strain, pseudo monimomenemeric Tourettes **(completely made up ailment!)**. This means that, uncontrollably, he sometimes inserts swear/curse words into his speech and messages. Please understand that this is NOT DELIBERATE but a medical condition. Mr. Carver is medically UNABLE to control this.

Dr. Phillis Simpson BSC. HHGTTG.

Dear Mr. Bosah - Thank you for your interesting fucking email. I have to say that I am very interested shit in your proposition however before I am prepared to proceed any faggot further I would like you to answer me some questions if you can.

1. Please can you tit-wank tell me how long this procedure will take to complete?

2. Will I be required to travel to complete this financial deal?

3. Is it completely arse legal?

Let me know the answer to the shagmenow questions above so that I can be in a better position to judge if I can help you.

Sincerely,

Colin Carver
Singlesideband Systems Ltd.

From: Charles Bosah
To: Colin Carver
Date: March 8, 2006
Subject: DETAILS

FROM THE DESK OF
DR CHARLES BOSAH
MUTUAL TRUST BANK [PLC]
HEAD QUATERS BRANCH
VICTORIA ISLAND
LAGOS- NIGERIA.

ATTN;COLIN

COMPLIMENTS AND HOW ARE YOU?

THANK YOU FOR YOUR REPLY TO MY PROPOSALS, IN REGARDS TO YOUR QUESTIONS LET ME ANSWER YOU ONE AFTER THE OTHER.

[1]HOW LONG IT WILL TAKE TO SEAL THE DEAL. IF YOU CAN GIVE THE ARTONEY I WILL HIRE FOR YOU, TO POSITION YOU LEGAL AS THE BENEFICIARY OF THE FUND IT WILL TAKE US 11 WORKING DAYS TO PERFECT YOUR PAPERS FOR THE TRANSFER.

[2]TRAVELLING, YOU ARE NOT REQUIRED TO GO ANY WHERE SINCE THE TRANSACTION IS BANK TO BANK.
[3] LEGALITY, YES IT IS ABSOLUTELY LEGAL AND SAFE THAT IS WHY I AM GOING TO ENGAGE THE SERVICES OF AN ARTONEY FOR YOU.

IT IS ON FORTURNATE THAT YOU HAVE DIFFERENT LAWS FOR DIFFERENT COUNTRIES, HERE IN NIGERIA WHEN AN ACCOUNT IS MORE THAN 6YEARS ON SERVICED THE BANK WILL CONFISCATE THE FUND THAT NECCESITATED MY CONSULTING YOU TO STAND AS THE BENEFICIARY SINCE OUR CLIENTS DIED WITH OUT LEAVING ANY TRACE TO HIS RELATION OR NEXT OF KIN.

PLEASE IF YOUR CAPEBLE TO ASSIST ME TO TRANSFER THIS FUND REPLY IMMEDIATELY SO THAT THE CARLOS BANK DIRECTORS WILL NOT CONFISCATE THIS MONEY,AFTER ALL YOU HAVE OPHANAGES,DESTITUES HOMES, AND OLD PEOPLES HOME WHO THE NEED THE FUND MORE. I TOO NEED IT.

PLEASE REPLY WITH YOUR FOLLOWING DETAILS
[1]AGE AND OCCUPATION
[2]CONTACT ADDRESS
[3]PHONE AND FAX NUMBERS
[4]A COPY OF YOUR INTERNATINAL PASSPORT OR DRIVERS LINCENCE
[5]BANK DETAILS WHERE THE MONEY WILL BE TRANSFERD INTO

WHEN YOU BRING THIS I CREATE A FILE IN OUR BANK THAT

THE BENEFICIARY OF THE FUND IN READINESS FOR TRANSFER
WHEN YOUR ARTONEY WILL FILE PAPERS ON YOUR BEHALF.

BEST OF LUCK

DR CHARLES BOSAH
INTERNAL AUDITOR
MUTUAL TRUST BANK [PLC]

I send Bosah my details, all of which are false except for the fax and telephone number.

From: Colin Carver
To: Charles Bosah
Date: March 3, 2006

Dear Mr. Bosah - Thank you for your reply arsewhacker it was interesting to read.

Eleven working days seems tickle-me-plums acceptable to me however I shall have to have assurances that it will not take too much longer than that as my time is extremely valuable and lurve-juice I cannot afford to devote my attention to other projects for too long.

It is good to know that travelling will not be required to facilitate the completion of this fucking project. This is encouraging as the need for travel would probably dissuade me from taking pissflaps part. Again I cannot be away from my company's work for too long as we are in a very busy period.

It is of paramount importance that this project is 100% legal because I cannot afford to be involved in any fucking project that may fall foul of the law and damage the good reputation of my company which has taken many years to build up. The single most important rimming thing to me is the smooth running and good name of my company.

Regarding your further questions, my details are as follows:

Name:
Colin Farquhar Carver

Contact address:
Single Systems Ltd.
Middlebrook Retail Park,
Bolton,
BL6 6JA United Kingdom.

Telephone number: +44 8707 65X XXX

Fax number: +44 8701 31X XXX

Bank:
Barclays Bank Corporate Banking
Winter Hey Lane
Horwich
Bolton
BL6 7NZ

Account No: 18120007221

Sort Code: 22-17-83

Please note that I cannot presently supply you with a copy of my wanking passport as I am in my office at the moment and my passport is locked in my home sperm deposit safe. I will forward it on to you in the next few days.

I shall also require a scan of your passport/drivers license for your ugly bastard identification too.

Sincerely,

Colin Carver
Singlesideband Systems Ltd.

I get an email from Bosah's attorney, Andy Uba. He's on his way to the High Court to find out for me what the bank will require to release the funds. Later, he gets back to me.

From: Andy Uba
To: Colin Carver
Date: March 10, 2006
Subject: PLEASE HOW DO WE PAY THIS BILL FOR THE TRANSFER OF THE FUND INTO YOUR ACCOUNT

ATTN: CARVER, COMPLIMENTS,

THIS IS TO INFORM YOU THAT I HAVE CONCLUDED THE ARRANGMENTS WITH THE BANK FOR THE TRANSFER OF YOUR FUND, BUT THE DELAY WILL BE HOW FAST WE CAN PROCURE THIS VITAL DOCUMENTS THAT WILL LEGALLY BACK YOU AS THE BENEFICIARY OF THE FUND.THE COURT GAVE ME THIS PRICE FOR THE DOCUMENTS TO BE OBTAINED ON YOUR BEHALF.

[1] AFFIDAVITT OF CLAIM $20,000.BECAUSE OF THE VOLUME.
[2]DEATH CERTIFICATE $20,000. FOR A FORIGNER, THAT IS
FOR THE DEAD MAN WHO DEPOSITED THE MONEY.
[3]LETTER OF ADMINSTRATION $10,000. FROM THE COURT.

BANKS REQUIREMENTS.
[1] MANDOTORY $10,000.FOR MUTUAL TRUST BANK
[2] CENTRAL BANK OF NIGERIA PROCCESING FEE FOR YOUR
VOUCHER AND $20,000
[3] MISCELLENOUS EXPENSES IS $5000,
YOU CAN SPLIT THE MONEY AND PAY IT BITS LIKE $3000 OR
$4000 AND PAY IT DIFFERENTLY,SO THAT WE WILL MEET UP
WITH TIME.

I AM PROUD TO TELL YOU WITH ALL SINCERERITY THAT AFTER
48HOURS OF THIS PAYMENT THAT YOUR FUND WILL BE PAID IN
TO YOUR ACCOUNT.AND I AM READY TO STAKE ANY
THING,EVEN MY LAWYER REGALIA.

PLEASE HOW DO WE PAY THIS MONEY? FOR THE PAYMENT YOU
CAN PAY IT EITHER WAY THROUGH MONEY GRAMME OR THE
OFF SHORE ACCOUNT OF MY FRIEND.

FOR MONEY GRAMME USE THIS INFORMATION;

[1] NAME;ERNEST EGELONU
[2]TEST QUESTION-PET NAME- ANSWER [NEST]
FOR MY FRIENDS OFFSHORE ACCOUNT;
[1]FIRST COMMERCIAL BANK.
TAAN BRANCH, 30,CHUNGKING SOUTH ROAD,
SEC,1,TAIPEI TAIWAN.R,O,C.SWIFT CODE;
FCBKTWTPOBU,
ACCOUNT NUMBER;16186001092.
BENEFICIARY NAME;FORTUNE TIME INTERNATIONAL
COMPANY LIMITED.

PLEASE YOUR MAXIMUN CO-OPERATION IS NEED NOW FOR
ANY CENT YOU CONTRIBUTED IN THIS TRANSACTION WILL BE
ACCOUNTED AND THE RECIPT AND WILL BE BALANCED TO
YOU OR WHO EVER YOU BORROWED FROM.I WILL FORWARD
THE RECIPT OF ALL THE EXPENSES EVERYBODY INCURED IN
THE CAUSE OF THIS TRANSFER. AND I WILL FORWARD EVERY
DETAILS FOR YOUR PERUSAL, AFTER YOU HAVE PAID FOR THE
PROCUREMENT OF THE VITAL DOCUMENTS FOR THE

TRANSFER. PLEASE TRUST GOD AND ME FOR I AM DOING EVERY THING WITHIN MY REACH TO SEE YOUR MONEY IS TRANSFERD INTO YOUR ACCOUNT.

BEST OF LUCK

REGARDS

BARR, ANDY UBA[S.A.N]

From: Colin Carver
To: Andy Uba
Date: March 10, 2006

Dear Mr. Uba - I have absolutely no fucking idea how we are going to pay that screw money dude. I certainly cannot pay it fart at this moment in time as my money is held in a high interest campache account, and I have to give 60 days notice before I can withdraw more than $1,000.

You can forget money fucking gram.

Last time I used that I got fucking ripped off by the money gram people. I was sending $500 to a doctor in the US for pile cream and the recipient never received it and I lost all of my asscream cash.

Listen, I can pay the money but I only have access to $37,850 in cash so if that will help to speed things up then if you can get somebody to meet me I will give it to you but I will want the payment back from the fucking final fund. So the money is available but I need someone to meet me at my location to pick it up.

If that cannot be dickwad done then I do not know how we can fookin proceed.

Sincerely,

Colin Carver
Singlesideband Systems Ltd.

Attorney Andy Uba gets in touch again, repeating the bank details and stressing the urgency of the matter, insisting I send the money by Western Union,

278

From: Colin Carver
To: Andy Uba
Date: March 10, 2006

Dear Mr. Uba - Do what you want. If I can't pay in the way I fucking told you then I have no further interest in this deal. Goodbye.

Colin Carver
Singlesideband Systems Ltd.

Uba then sends an email with no text, just the following subject line:

From: Andy Uba
To: Colin Carver
Date: March 11, 2006
Subject: MY FRIEND IN LONDON WILL CALL YOU GIVE HIM THE MONEY FAST.SO THAT WE CAN MEET UP WITH TIME.

Now I'm cross.

From: Colin Carver
To: Andy Uba
Date: March 11, 2006

When you are writing to me, address me fucking PROPERLY, not just in the subject matter. If you cannot take time to fucking write me a proper email then don't fucking write to me at all.

Colin Carver
Singlesideband Systems Ltd.

Uba's representative, who is supposed to be in London, gets in touch.

From: Smith Luca
To: Colin Carver
Date: March 16, 2006
Subject: Hello

Dear Mr Colin Carver - My name is Smith Luca the Business partner of Mr Andy Uba.He informed me that i should help him in collecting some money from you as i happen to be in london on a business trip.I had tried all the numbers he furnished me with but could not get you.Please i am planning on leaving london for india on the 20.03.06 and would like you to fix an arrangement of how i can meet with you to collect the said fund.better still if you can paid it into my account that will be better.

I await you response.

Mr Smith Luca.

From: Colin Carver
To: Smith Luca
Date: March 16, 2006

Dear Mr. Smith - I do not understand the problems you are having contacting me. Mr. Uba has already spoken to me on the phone number that I gave him. I shall repeat the numbers for you without the international dialling codes which of course you do not need as you are also in the UK: Office: 08707 65X XXX Mobile: 07017 00X XXX

I am available to meet at my location any day of the week other than Friday as I am away on a fucking contract signing.

Sincerely,

Colin Carver
Director
Singlesideband Systems

From: Smith Luca
To: Colin Carver
Date: March 17, 2006
Subject: Hello

Dear Mr Carver - I received your mail with many thanks,How are we to conclude this arrangement. I have tried to call the number but i was told by the operator that will be costly. Also i do not know how to get to your place can you pay the money into my account?Thanks.

Smith

From: Colin Carver
To: Smith Luca
Date: March 17, 2006

Dear Mr. Smith -You obviously do not have a clue how to operate a fucking telephone.

 The call will NOT be expensive as it is a UK inland call! I am only 300 miles away from your location!

Are you REALLY in London? I doubt that VERY much. Squeeze my gonads.

You will not get one single penny of my money in your account boy.

Sincerely,

Colin Carver
Director
Singlesideband Systems

I hear nothing from Luca, but eventually, weeks later, Andy Uba gets back to me with a very short message.

From: Andy Uba
To: Colin Carver
Date: April 3, 2006
Subject: READY

ARE YOU NOW READY TO PAY FOR THE DOCUMENTATIONS?

From: Colin Carver
To: Andy Uba
Date: April 3, 2006

Dear Mr. Uba - have been ready for your documentation for nearly a month now.

Colin Carver
Director
Singlesideband System

Uba now sends a blank email, with just a short instruction in the subject.

From: Andy Uba
To: Colin Carver
Date: April 4, 2006
Subject: please use the passport information i gave you to send the money and send the control numbers to me

From: Colin Carver
To: Andy Uba
Date: April 4, 2006

Are you too fucking STUPID to write me a proper email Mr. "Uba"? DON'T fucking order me around like a little kid. If you can't address me in a proper manner then please FUCK OFF and leave me alone. I have IMPORTANT business to be getting on with and I will not put up with having to deal with little children who know nothing about business.

Now, for the THIRD FUCKING TIME, you will NEVER NEVER NEVER NEVER get one single penny out of me unless you send somebody to MY LOCATION to pick it up in cash. If you cannot do that then FUCK OFF. Do NOT send that stupid motherfucker Mr. Smith Luca becasue that moron can't even use a telephone. I would not trust him with my money ever.

Colin Carver
Director
Singlesideband Systems

Uba must be frustrated. Uppercase characters appear once more!

From: Andy Uba
To: Colin Carver
Date: April 4, 2006
Subject: CONSIDER THIS OR FORGET IT

ATTN;COLLIN.

IF YOU CAN NOT SEND THE MONEY FOR THE DOCUMENTATION I DONT KNOW WHAT ELSE TO DO UNLESS YOU CAN GIVE ME INVITATION LETTER AND SEND ME TICKET AND BTA TO COME TO BOLTON MY SELF,I THINK THIS IS THE FINAL SOLUTION OR WE FORGET ABOUT THE BUSINESS,

PLEASE CONSIDER THIS OPTION.

REGARDS

BARR, ANDY UBA[SAN]+

From: Colin Carver
To: Andy Uba
Date: April 6, 2006

Screw you, asshole.

Alas, I never heard from Andy again!

I Pray to Die Henceforth

A tale of love, lust, loss and greed when The X Files meets The Matrix. Good people, please remember Fags in your prayers...

A small note: this particular scambait has references to a derogatory term for a homosexual. I would like to make it clear that this is for the purposes of this scambait only. Homosexuality is a big taboo subject in some parts of Western Africa, and being accused of it is amongst the most insulting things you can do to a person there, which is exactly my reason for the use of certain terms here in this scambait towards this particular scammer. It is not my intention to insult any actual (non-criminal!) homosexuals out there.

From: Mr john ademola <johnademola@gawab.com>
To: <[a non related email account!]>
Date: Fri, 29 Aug 2003
Subject: URGENT BUSINESS ASSISTANCE

Attn: President/CEO,

First, I must solicit your confidant in this transaction, this is by virtue of its nature as utterly CONFIDENTIAL and TOP SECRET. Though I know that the transaction of this magnitude will make any one apprehensive and worried, but I am assuring you that all will be well at the end of the day. We have decided to contact you due to the urgency of this transaction, as we have been reliably informed of your discreteness and ability in transaction of this nature.

Let me start by first introducing myself properly to you, I am williams kenny **[WILLIAMS KENNY - remember that!]** *a director with the Nigerian National Petroleum Corporation (NNPC) Eleme Refinery. I came to know of you in my private search for a reliable and reputable person to handle the confidential transaction, which involves the transfer of a huge sum of money to a foreign account requiring maximum confidence. THE PROPOSITION: a foreigner, Engineer James Akmed, an Oil Merchant/Contractor with the Federal Government of Nigeria, until his suspension three years ago, executed with us at Eleme Refinery of NNPC, and had a total contract executed worth US$28.6 (Twenty Eight Million,Six Hundred Thousand United States Dollar) which flows in the Corporation's suspense account.*

It is because of the allegation/petition leveled against him that he (Engr. James Akmed) who is a close friend to the late dictatorship General Sanni Abacha (formal Military President of Nigeria) who died in office in 1998 and during his tenure the country experienced various mismanagement and series of malpractices were carried out in collaboration with his foreign friends.

However, a Panel were set up to investigate the issue, who found him (Engr. James Akmed) guilty and the present Democratic President of Nigeria Chief Olusegun Obasanjo suspended him from transacting any business in Nigeria with immediate effect and was asked to leave the country. However, these made the contract fund "UNCLAIMABLE" which was only known to my colleagues and I. Fortunately, all the Contract document including the " CONTRACT COMPLETION CERTIFICATE" are with me but the need for a very trustworthy foreign business man/woman whom I would present as the Foreign contractor/ beneficiary to claim the fund. In order to achieve this development, some of my colleagues and I now seek your permission to have you stand as the FOREIGN CONTRACTOR so that the funds would be released and paid into your account as beneficiary's who executed the contract in the year 1999. All documents and proves to enable you get this fund will be carefully worked out. More so, we are assuring you of a 100% risk free involvement. Your share stays while the rest would be for me and my colleagues for investment purposes in your country.

We have agree that, the funds be shared thus, after it has been transferred into your nominated account:

(1) 30% of the money will go to you for acting as the beneficiary of the fund (2) 5% will be set aside for reimbursement to both parties for any incidental expenses that may be incurred in the cause of the transfer. (3).65% to us the originator of the transaction.

If this proposal is acceptable by you, do not make undue advantage of the trust we have bestowed on you and your Company, kindly get to me immediately on my E-mail Address as stated bellow. Please furnish me with your most confidential Telephone and Fax Number(s), Company Name to use, Banking information including the A/C Number, Swift Code (if any).

I assure you that if you will follow my instruction, the fund shall be in your Account within 7-10 days of this transaction.Thanking you for your kind understanding in this regard.

My best regards,
ENGR. JOHN ADEMOLA (MNSE)

So, as noted previously, numb-nuts starts off by introducing himself as 'Williams Kenny' and signs off with 'John Ademola!' I'll let that fly for now.

To: johnademola@gawab.com
From: Gillian Anderson

My dear Mr.Ademola - I was surprised to receive your kind email, as I do not understand where you found my private email address. However, your offer sounds interesting to me. Please explain a little more to me and please will you forward me some kind of identification?

Love,

Miss Gillian Anderson.
Clock Zone Ltd.

Date: Wed, 3 Sep 2003
From: john ademola
Subject: URGENT BUSINESS ASSISTANCE

Dear Miss Gillian Anderson - How are you and your family?

My good friend I got your mail thanks very much. For your express interest in my proposal. Sister regard your request i forward to you some kind of my identification,my sister i will send to you my photo when i hear from you and receive all the information i needed from you regard the approval of this fund in your name.

My friend if you are currently in events regard this country Nigeria you will know fully well that all the top government officials had used this means greatly enrich themselves by transferring/lodging funds into their foreign partner's bank account for their personal use, because we government officials are not allowed by law to operate foreign account, I took advantage of the situation, and placed this money in a Suspense Account with the Central Bank Nigeria, which I claimed was a fee owed to a foreign contractor.

I know that You have been receiving different e-mails of different stories but this is real and no crime is attached to it.

It may interest you to know that two years ago a similar transaction was carried out with one Mr. Patrice miller, the president of craine international trading corporation at number 135, east 57th street, 28th floor, new York, 10022 with telephone ((212))308-7788 and telex number 6731689,after the agreement between both partners in which he was to take 5%. the money was duly transferred into his account only to be disappointed on our arrival in new York as we were reliably informed that Mr. Patrice miller was no longer on that address while his telephone and telex numbers have been reallocated to someday else, that is how we lost uss$ 27.5m to Mr. Patrice miller.

This time around we need a more reliable and trustworthy person or a reputable company to do transaction with hence this mail to you, so if you can prove yourself to be trusted and interested in this deal, then we are prepared to do business with you.

What we want from you is the assurance that you will let us have our share when this amount of is transferred into your account.

To transfer this money into yours or Company's account, a fresh file has to be opened here in your name or your company's name. Therefore we request you to furnish us with your banking particulars thus: Your bank name and address, account number, name of beneficiary, telephone and fax Numbers of the bank, your company name and address, telephone, fax numbers. This transaction is expected to be concluded within (10) bank working days on the receipt of your bank particulars,

However, by virtue of our position as civil servants, we are not permitted by law to operate foreign account. This is why we are asking for your assistance to provide the necessary documents to facilitate the transfer of this fund into any account you will nominate of course.

Meanwhile, for the fact that we are still in Government Service, I would want you to keep this deal top secret, both from friends and family members in order not to blow up the deal, which could jeopardize our career which we have laboured for in the past years. As soon as the transfer is done, all related document to the transfer would be destroyed.

It is worthy to inform you that this transaction is entirely based on trust since this money is going to be into your own bank account. Bear in mind that this is absolutely a private and personal deal, not official, and hence should be treated with all measures of secrecy and absolute confidentiality.

When we receive the above information from you by email, we shall apply and obtain the necessary payment approvals from the relevant authorities including the Federal Ministry of Finance (F.M.F) which shall allocate you or your company foreign exchange cover for US$28.6 MILLION you or your company shall be officially regarded as the beneficiary of the fund.

However, your prompt reply will enable us to expedite action by forwarding the information (your bank particulars) to the authority concerned for immediate Processing of the approval document/ remittance.

At any stage of development, we shall send you copies of all the documents for your perusal until the amount reflects in the government's schedule list for payment, then representatives of the group will come to your country to man our share of the proceed, part of our own share could be use to set up a foreign trade, which will also be supervised by you as a partner.

Should you be interested in this arrangement and this proposal is acceptable by you, do not make undue advantage of the trust we have bestowed on you and your Company, kindly get to me immediately on my E-mail Address as stated above.

Let's trust that absolute confidentiality be our watchword throughout this business transaction. Your line of business does not matter in regard this transaction.

Your immediate response will be highly appreciated.
I wait for your call for more details

Best Regards,
ENGR. JOHN ADEMOLA (MNSE)
Phone:234-80-332-48217

A change in John's email address, but let's ignore it.

From: Gillian Anderson
To: John Ademola

Dearest John - Your email is most welcome, and your proposition
seems to be a good one. However, before I proceed to send you my
details I would prefer to wait until I receive some formal identification
from you. I hope that this is not a problem.

For your information, I own a modelling company (I am unmarried, so go
for it, stud), and my job takes me all over the world, but mainly to the US
and UK, and I enjoy the travel and lifestyle of full-time modelling. I also
enjoy porno movies, both watching and appearing in them. Should you
require it, I will be happy to supply my passport once I have received your
information.

Please note that due to an accident whilst on a modelling assignment in
1987, my hearing was damaged and is now 90% impaired, therefore I
cannot use a standard telephone and will only be able to communicate
vie email or fax. I hope this does not present a problem.

I was lying naked in a swimming pool whilst the photographer was on a
balcony above taking photographs; unfortunately his camera strap
snapped and the camera plunged 30 feet and clipped me on the side of
the head. Ever since then my hearing has been virtually non-existent.

Also please note that on Wednesday (3rd September) I am at a launch
party for a new magazine which is being published (I am on the front
cover!) so I will be unavailable via email or fax on that day.

My very best wishes,
Gillian.
Clockzone Modelling

Date: Mon, 1 Sep 2003
From: john ademola
Subject: Thanks sister here i attach my photo

Dear sister Gillian - How are you? Compliment of the day. I feel
delighted to write you once more..

However, I sincerely thank you for your quick response to my mail, I
will advise we use email and fax from now onward, I am very sorry for

the accident that happened to you during your modeling assignment in 1987. **(Thanks for your concern, John.)**

I got your mail my good friend and the content were well noted, my friend in regard your request for my identification, with all pressure I will send to you my photo now. I am also happy you are truly a trustworthy fellow one can always rely on at any given time in life due to your questions regards this transaction.

Please sister I would be very grateful if you answer me this questions as follows: How old are you? Are you sure that your account will accommodate this contract amount?

I assured you that this transaction is 100% risk free as we have concluded every arrangement to protect the interest of every one involved. Likewise, all modalities[!] *for the successful transfer of this money have been worked out.*

Please I do not need to remind you of the need for absolute confidentiality if this transaction must succeed. Due to my sensitive position in the Nigerian Government.

Let's trust that absolute confidentiality be our watchword throughout this business transaction. Your line of business does not matter in regard this transaction.

Your immediate response will be highly appreciated.

Best Regards,
ENGR. JOHN ADEMOLA (MNSE)
Phone:234-80-332-48217

John Ademola

From: Gillian Anderson
To: John Ademola

My Dear Mr. Ademola - Thank you for your email. Please note that I
have just received a fax from a colleague, and it seems that the fax
machine is not working correctly. The engineer tells me that a rat has
somehow got caught up in the workings (I hate those little bastards). If
you need to send me any documents, please send them as email
attachments for the moment.

As for your questions, my age is 27 and I'm one hot babe. As my
company currently earns in excess of 4.2 million dollars per year, I am
sure that my account is more than adequate to deal with a large sum
such as yours. If there's one thing I can handle, it's large loads.

Please Mr. Ademola, thank you for your picture, but it is quite small and
I cannot see your face very clearly. Please would you send me another
photo?

I await your instructions.

Kindest regards, Miss Gillian Anderson.

Date: Mon, 1 Sep 2003
From: john ademola
*Subject: please sister send down the info. so that we can move forward ,
here i attach my picture*

Dearest sister - How are your families?

*I got your mail request I send another picture because the one that I
have just sent to you is not clear.*

*Sister without much delay I attach here my full posture for your
viewing, but I want you to understand that this scan picture which will
not be all that clear for your viewing.*

*At this juncture sister I would have advice you send the information's I
requested from you now for us to get started as soon as this transaction
come to a successful conclusion, definitely we shall meet face to face in
your country for the shearing of the proceed.*

I am happy to read from your mail that your account is enough to accommodate the said fund.

My sister I will be very grateful if my request is welcomed by your person and you send down the information's probably today so that tomorrow I can ask my mentor to submit / file an application for the approval and release /transfer of the fund into your desired bank account from the authorities concern.

Sister regards your fax machine that is faulty , I would have advice you take it to technician immediately so as to rectifier the fault , this is very important because the authorities concern regard the approval of this contract fund will not send to you any document by email attachment.

Thanks for your understanding in this regard, I will also like if you can send to me your photo for my viewing when replying this mail.

I am looking forward to receive the requested information's you soonest. Hope to be with you soonest, may the good God guide you as you read this mail and understand the position of things.

Your immediate response will be highly appreciated, Say me well to your friends; remain blessed !

Yours sincerely,

ENGR. JOHN ADEMOLA (MNSE)
Phone:234-80-332-48217

An even less clear John Ademola

From: Gillian Anderson
To: John Ademola

My Dear Mr. Ademola - Thank you one again for your email. It was nice to receive it. Thank you also for your picture.

Please if possible next time, try to make your pictures a little larger. I have attached a photograph of me for you to drool over. I will send you another one soon.

The engineer has told me that the fax machine will have to be taken away to be repaired and rat guts removed, so if you need to send any documents then you will for the moment have to send them as email attachments. I will advise you when the fax has been repaired.

My Bank details are as follows:

Bank Name:

Plunder & Flee Incorporated
331 Offmerip Gardens
Stabmeintheback St.
London W4
England
Fax: +44 171 889 24538

Account No: 10012133-194
Sort Code: 22-14-77

Beneficiary Name: Miss Gillian Anderson

Company details

Clockzone Ltd (Modelling Agency)
203-207 Ex Files Gardens
Duchovny St.
London W4
England

Tel: (TextPhone) +44 171 837 66319
Fax: +44 8701 3XX XXXX

I hope this information is of help.

Sorry, but I have to end this email here as the vermin exterminator is here and he needs to use his flame-thrower.

Kindest regards,

Gillian
Clockzone UK.
(I attach a picture of Gillian Anderson.)

John takes a shine to me.

Date: Tue, 2 Sep 2003
From:john ademola
Subject: THANKS FOR THE INFO. MY SWEET ANGLE

Dear sweet angle **(Angle? Would that be 90 degrees or 45 degrees?)** -
*How are you and your family? Hope fine thank be to the God almighty,
I got your mail in regarding my your bank information's and your
picture.*

*Sister thank very much for your quick reply, and I will not fail to let you
that you are very beautiful, infect you are an ANGLE! Please sister
from today onward I will be addressing you as sweet angle.*

Sister I am very sorry that I could not hear your sweet voice over the phone, I cause that accident that happened to you, please bear with me for I fell for you.

I am also happy you are truly a trustworthy fellow one can always rely on at any given time in life due to your questions / carefulness regards this transaction .

Sequel to your request I fax if i have to fax any document now that i should scan and sent to you? I have to use the job completion certificate with me now to validate and obtain / back date a new job completion certificate on your name and of company as the beneficiary that executed this contract in the year 1999 as I have the old certificate and nobody knows about this development.

My sweet angle I will be very happy if to hear soonest that the engineer has been through with the fax machine so that we do not have any delay regard receiving the approval documents of this fund from all the ministries concerns.

My friend you know that this a deal do not worry for I have done the underground work for the for the successful transfer of this money , all I need is your support . As soon as I obtained the new certificate I will fax it to you immediately.

Would you like to register your company as a subsidiary contractor here in Nigeria?

I have to appoint an attorney on your behalf that will follow up this transaction I will pay him for his legal professional fee, because I am a government official , I don't want anybody to know my involvement in regard this transaction. I will tell the attorney that you are my old friend from LONDON Who executed a contract with my corporation (NNPC) that you ask me to secure an attorney that will assist you get the approval of this fund into your bank account

The attorney will proceeded and he shall be given you reports on his dealings.

At any stage of development, the lawyer shall send you copies of all the documents for your perusal until the amount reflects in the government's schedule list for payment, then representatives of the group will come to your country to man our share of the proceed.

Should you be interested in this arrangement mail me immediately.

Lets trust and absolute confidentiality be our watchword throughout this business transaction.

Thanks while I await your immediate response.

Best Regards,
ENGR. John Ademola
Telephone No: 234-80-332-48217

NB:Like you said that you will be off mail tomorrow, I wish you the best of luck and god's protection wherever you went my sweet angle.

Date: Tue, 2 Sep 2003
From: john ademola
Subject: FORWARDING OF YOUR INFORMATIONS

Dear sweet angle - My sister i want to bring to your notice that my mentor have this morning forwarded the letter of claims including your name/bank and of your company to the appropriate quarter concern for the immediate approval of the fund in your favour.

I am happy to inform you that your name and your company's has been encoded in the Federal Ministry of Finance (FMF) computer, thereby, making you the bonafide owner of the Twenty Eight Million, Six Hundred Thousand United States Dollars, (USD$ 28,600,000.00) I have been assured by my mentor in the (FMF) that the final approval must be ready as soon as possible. Thereafter, the fund will be released to you by the Apex Bank of Nigeria (CBN) through telegraphic transfer into your nominated bank account in London- England.

As soon as you receive any document/correspondence or phone call from any organization or an individual from Nigeria, you should not respond until you notify me so as to enable me advise you on what to do. THIS IS AN IMPORTANT INSTRUCTION WHICH MUST BE ADHERE TO.

You are expected to keep this transaction TOP SECRET at all times until the money has arrived your bank account.

Remember we are still in Government Service and will not want anything to Jeopardize our career. You should endeavor to keep me updating always so as to give me information on every stage of development concerning this transaction .

You should also bear in mind that any expenses we might incurred during the cause of this transaction will be taken care by 5% set aside for expenses. On this note, you are advised to keep records of all your expenses since the 5% will be shared according to the ratio of our expenses, and 30% will be given to you as the owner of the account used, while 65% is for me and my colleagues.

As soon as you confirm the money in your bank account, you MUST notify me so that i and one of my colleague will come down to your country to collect our share of the fund and part of our share will be used to set up a business which you as a partner will be inspecting for us over there.

Please mail me back immediately you receive this mail.

Thanks while I await your immediate response

Best Regards,

ENGR. John Ademola
Telephone No: 234-80-332-48217

From: Gillian Anderson
To: John Ademola

My dear John - Many thanks for your very sweet email, it was very touching to me. In fact I am touching me as I write this (hard to do, I can tell you).

Yes, it is a pity that I cannot talk to you over the telephone, but hopefully we will meet soon. Please try to find a bigger picture of yourself to send to me. For every picture you send to me I will send one from me. Your other pictures are too small. Your face looks nice, but I cannot see the pictures clearly as they are too small, and I want to make sure you are not a hideous pox-ridden specimen of a man, like my last boyfriend Brad Pitt.

Please for the future send any needed documents via email attachment, and I will also do the same. You may register my company, Clockzone Modelling Inc. if you feel that it would help to complete this transaction quickly. Please instruct your lawyer to proceed at his will.

I will leave you for now my John. I will be back tomorrow evening after the magazine has finished taking my photographs for their cover. I am excited; the photographer has promised me a pearl necklace if I do well.

Take care,

Gillian.
Clockzone Modelling Inc.

Date: Wed, 3 Sep 2003
From: john ademola
Subject: HAPPY OUTING TODAY MY SWEET ANGLE

Dear sweet angle

How is your outing regarding the magazine coverage?

I want to bring to your notice that I have this morning send the total sum of $ 15,610 .00 through my mentor to the lawyer Barrister John Chikwuma, of John Chikwuma & associates ,regard the Registration of your company (Clockzone Modeling Inc.) as a subsidiary contractor and to obtain other relevant documents that will help to complete this transaction quickly.

My angle I want to reminder you once again that i told the attorney that you are my old friend from LONDON Who executed a contract with my corporation (NNPC) that you ask me to secure an attorney that will assist you get the approval of this fund into your bank account.

At this juncture you should not let the lawyer or any official /ministry to know my involvement in this transaction until it comes to a conclusion.

Moreover the attorney shall be given you reports on his dealings and you will be up dating me as your partner, because I can not ask the attorney any question regards this transaction from now onward to avoid suspicious.

At any stage of development, the lawyer shall send you copies of all the documents for your perusal until the amount reflects in the government's schedule list for payment.

As soon as you receive any document/correspondence or phone call from any organization or an individual from Nigeria, you should not respond until you notify me so as to enable me advise you on what to do. THIS IS AN IMPORTANT INSTRUCTION WHICH MUST BE ADHERING TO.

You are expected to keep this transaction TOP SECRET at all times until the money has arrived your bank account, do not disclose this transaction to your bank at this stage until the fund is transferred into your account and you will be backed up with all the necessary documents of claim.

You should endeavor to keep me updating always so as to give me information on every stage of development concerning this transaction.

As soon as you confirm the money in your bank account, you MUST notify me so that i and one of my colleague will come down to your country to collect our share of the fund and part of our share will be used to set up a business which you as a partner will be inspecting for us over there.

Please mail me back immediately you receive this mail.

Thanks while I await your immediate response

Best Regards,

ENGR. John Ademola
Telephone No: 234-80-332-48217

From: Gillian Anderson
To: John Ademola

My dearest John - Many thanks for your wonderful letter, and I look forward to more from you. Please John, why do you not send me a LARGE photograph of yourself - I need to be wet. The others are too small for me to see you clearly. I have sent you another picture of me, and I will send more sexy ones if you will send me a good image of yourself - I have great tits; at least that's what my father says.

Please John, you can be assured 100% of my confidentiality.

Take care,

Gillian.

I send him another picture of the seductive Gillian Anderson.

Date: Wed, 3 Sep 2003
From: john ademola
Subject: THANKS FOR YOUR MAIL AND PICTURE , PLEASE DID YOU HEAR FROM THE LAWYER?

Hello sweet angle **(Will somebody PLEASE get this guy a dictionary!)** *- I got your mail and your request I send to you my lager photo for your viewing, my dear angle I would have send to you my photo again if I have one at my reach now, but I want you to understand that I am a handsome looking man* **(I think later on we are**

about to find out that John is what is technically known as 'a lying bastard') *and a director with NNPC, do not bother yourself about my postures because very soon we meet face to face and have diner /wine together in your country.*

My dear angle the reason why I do not have much posture of myself-alone is I am a public figure, most of my pictures where group pictures and most of all is video coverage, please bear with me my sweet angle.

I want to bring to your notice that there was a proverb,(which say that, it is nice for a queen to follow corner way to enter kings palace) that is to say as far as we are going to meet face to face soonest ,please dear picture or no picture for now let us join hand /rob[?!] mind together to the succeed of this transaction.

My sweet angle I am not saying that you should stop sending your pictures to me, I welcome your posture at any giving time, because I like/love to see you at all times.

My angle if I may forget how is your outing today?

Have you been contacted by the lawyer? Because I have advised him to proceed and I have send to him some money to execute his duty on your behalf.

Please you are to inform me as soon as your fax machine is ok. I am happy to hear that you assured me 100% of confidentiality.

My dear angle mail me back once you receive this mail.

Best regard
Engr. John Ademola

From: Gillian Anderson
To: John Ademola

Dear John - I think you have something to hide. I am attaching one last picture for you to this email then you will hear no more from me. You only seem interested in my money or help and you have no time for me and do not want to send me your picture. This saddens me John.

Goodbye,

Gillian.

...and another picture of Gillian Anderson.

Date: Thu, 4 Sep 2003
From: john ademola
Subject: TO MY SWEET ANGLE

Dear My Sweet Angle - I got your mail with a great shock of mind.

Let me tell categorically that i am not much interested in your money, but for you in particular. Due to the business we are into that make us to know ourselves is God sent which we both of us will benefit from it soonest.

I am not hiding anything for you to be very sincere, i am a director with Nigerian National Petroleum coporation, 35 years old married with one child but divioced in year 2002, since then i have not made any other choice of another wife, but because i came in contact with you i think i will give it a trial.

I believe by next week ending this funds will be in your account, i will then travel to meet with you so that we can sort things out.

Below is my photograph. Bear with me my dear angel.

My dear angle mail me back once you receive this mail.

Best regard
Engr. John Ademola

Oh dear - an enlarged version of his first pic. Slapping time!

From: Gillian Anderson
To: John Ademola

Dearest John - Your emails are welcomed, and thank you for putting my mind at ease with regards to some things. Dear John, please forgive me, for at the moment my dearest pet dog died this morning. My dog was with me for many many years, and since I have not yet been married he was a close friend to me.

My dog was called Fags, named after my great Uncle George Fagsinder Anderson. Fags had been suffering for some weeks now (he was coughing a lot recently) and his death was expected but it still comes as a great shock to me. Without Fags, my life feels empty at the moment. I really loved my pet, and I am not certain how I am to continue without Fags. Sorry to keep going on about a silly thing like Fags, but until you know the feelings I have, you will never know how hard it is to be without Fags.

My dearest John, I am unhappy also with picture you sent to me. They are the same picture that you sent to me before but you have enlarged it. This makes me even more unhappy, and I feel I cannot trust you. Are they your real pictures, or are you trying to keep your real identity secret because you do not trust me, or are you dead?

Please John, do not be afraid to reveal your true self to me. Looks are not important to me, but friendship and trust is. Now that I have to live without Fags I am in real need of somebody I can trust; I hope it is you. Do you think you can be a substitute for Fags? I feel sure that you can become my new Fag.

I am going to have to ask you to do one thing for me to prove your honesty to me. I need you to get a real photograph sent to me, but this time to prove that you are not sending me a false image I need you to hold a sign that shows the image must be you. Please John, will you take your photograph holding a sign for me? Will you pay respects to my dear, departed pet by holding up a sign? I would like you to hold up a sign that says 'I LOVE FAGS'. That way I know that the photograph is true because nobody else will know to do this. If you can do this for me then I know for certain you must be a true and gentle man. Without this proof I am sorry but I cannot proceed any further.

Please, for the memory of my Fags, do this one thing for me my dearest.

I have to leave now dear John. I have to arrange the burial for my beloved pet and the funeral director is asking for Fags.

Your love,

Gillian Anderson.

... and yet another picture of Gillian Anderson.

Date: Fri, 5 Sep 2003
From: john ademola
Subject: MY SWEET ANGLE I AM SORRY FOR FAG'S DEATH TAKE HEART

Dear sweet angle **(FFS)** *- I got your mail and I am very sorry to hear the death of your lovely pet Fags. It is a pity that I can not talk with you on phone, I would have tell you what and how I fell for the death of fag. Hence I send this mail to you.*

I am sorry for my late replying; it is because I went out early this morning to inspect a new site for my corporation (NNPC). My dear angle you wish is my command I will do exactly what you want regard fag's death. To show my concern for you and fag.

My dear sweet angle all the pictures that I have sent to you is my real image and to prove to you that I love you and not happy for fag's death I will snap a new picture today and send it across to you as you requested, to hold up a sign that says "I love Fags" **(Yeah!)** *because your happiness means much to me now that you have no friend expect me.*

I have to leave now my sweet angle. I have to and arrange with the photographer, which I will send to you by tomorrow as soon as I receive the copy from the photographer.

My dear sweet for the fact that I do not know much about scanning works because I am petrochemical engineering and I can not take my picture to anybody else to do the scanning for me do to the nature of this transaction. But I will do my best my sweet angle bear with me.

My dear sweet angle ,one more things that I wouldn't want to be hearing/reading from your mails to me is (if you done do this, I cannot proceed any further.) You should remember that this transaction is a god sent that brought us together and should be regarded at all times, because we both will benefit from it.

My dear angle there is something I have in mind to tell you but not until we meet face to face in your country, which will be soonest.

Please except my condolence for the death of fag, may the Good Lord gives you the mind to bear the grate lost.

Hope to be with you soonest.

Thanks while I await your immediate response.

Your lover, **(Eurgh!)**
ENGR. John Ademola
Telephone No: 234-80-332-48217

From: Gillian Anderson
To: John Ademola

Dearest John - Thank you for your thoughts about my pet. I know such things may be silly to you, but for me my Fags was a lifelong companion. As I am not married Fags was very close to me, and with me all the time. You could say I was addicted to Fags.

Thank you for trying with the picture. It is very important to me that I find someone who I can trust 100%. Please be sure to make the image as large as possible so that your sign of truth is clear. I will be VERY grateful to you for a big, clear image. I will not tell you now what I will do for you, but it will make you very happy!

As soon as your picture is received I will complete this transaction ASAP. I have attached a picture of my beautiful departed friend Fags. I hope you like Fags too.

Your love,

Gillian.

Fags

Date: Sat, 6 Sep 2003
From: john ademola
Subject: FOR THE MEMORY OF FAG'S DEATH / PLEASE SWEET
HEART HAPPY WEEKEND

Dear sweet angel. **(ALERT THE PRESS - he got it right!)** - *How are you today?*

I hope that fag's death is not causing too much disturbances to your life?

Please my dear sweet angel do not feel bad about this incident for it is not your wish but the devil.

I will not fail to tell you how i feel to hear fag's death,although i did not see/know fag but hence the death toches your heart i feel the same.

My dear sweet angel i am attaching this picture for the memory of fag's death to please my sweet angel.

My dear now that you have lost your life long companion do not worry much for you have found someone dear to you,that is me {I WILL BE ANYWHERE FOR YOU TO MAKE YOU HAPPY} this is my word of advise for you.

May his or her soul rest in perfect peace AMEN!!

Please i want to ask you this question , I know such question may be silly to you, but i am serious , Have you been proposed for marriage by any man as of now?

I want you to have me in mind from now onward because i want to be closer to you.

Please except my condolence for the death of fag, may the Good Lord gives you the mind to bear the grate lost.

Hope to be with you soonest.

Thanks while I await your immediate response.

Your lover,
ENGR. John Ademola
Telephone No: 234-80-332-48217

Attached to the email, John sends me a picture of a man with a cut & pasted head!

John Ademola

From: Gillian Anderson
To: John Ademola

Dearest John - How can you do this to me?

I thank you from the bottom of my heart for the beautiful message that
you wrote, but WHY oh WHY have you disguised the head? It is quite
plain to me that you have put another head on top of the original
photograph. John, I am in tears as I write. I am now wet. I was starting
to trust you and now you do THIS?? Please John, it does not matter to
me what you look like. As I have said before, your looks are not
important to me. Because I am a model, I have always had handsome

men coming after me, but they have ALL let me down once they did me doggy style. The only thing I could ever trust is Fags.

I know the picture is false. I work with photographers nearly every day, so please be honest with me.

Dear John, it seems that you are another of these bad men who will treat me badly and be bad to me, which is bad, and I hate bad. **(You follow that?!)**

Gillian

Date: Sun, 7 Sep 2003
From: john ademola
Subject: I WILL BE THE LAST MAN TO TREAT YOU BAD/HURT YOUR SOUL.

Dear angel - My dear angle I got your mail, and all the content of your mail were well noted my dear angel.

My dear angel to satisfy your mind and mine as partner to be in future, WHAT DO YOU WANT ME TO DO AT THIS PRESENT SITUATION? To please you. I am now getting real that you love me my sweet angel..

Please very urgent reply.

Your lover

John

From: Gillian Anderson
To: John Ademola

Dearest John - I need you to send me the picture of you holding the message for Fags again, BUT this time I NEED to see your REAL face my love. Please do not let me down.

Kindest, Gillian

Date: Mon, 8 Sep 2003
From: john ademola
Subject: FOR MY LOVE FOR YOU AND FAG'S

Dearest sweet angel - How are you today? My sweet angel Let's trust that absolute confidentiality be our watchword throughout this business transaction.

Regard your request from me, this is to prove my honest / love I have for you hence I send to you this picture for your perusal and safe keeping. Please my angel now that you have my photo I believe that we can proceed further as future partner to be and finalize this transaction as soon as possible.

My plan/intention is as soon as this fund is transferred / confirmed into your account; I will file an application letter for my resignation to the appropriate ministry concern as a civil savant with my government and come over to stay with you. Or what do you think?

Have you been contact by any of the ministries regarding the approval of this fund in your favour ? Have the lawyer sent to you any of the documents?

At any stage of development, the lawyer shall send you copies of all the documents for your perusal until the amount reflects in the government's schedule list for payment.

As soon as you receive any document/correspondence or phone call from any organization or an individual from Nigeria, you should not respond until you notify me so as to enable me advise you on what to do. THIS IS AN IMPORTANT INSTRUCTION WHICH MUST BE ADHERING TO.

You are expected to keep this transaction TOP SECRET at all times until the money has arrived your bank account, do not disclose this transaction to your bank at this stage until the fund is transferred into your account and you will be backed up with all the necessary documents of claim.

You should endeavor to keep me updating always so as to give me information on every stage of development concerning this transaction.

Please except my condolence for the death of fag **(FAGS! FAGS! FAGS! It's 'Fags', you idiot.)** *may the Good Lord gives you the mind to bear the grate lost.*

Please mail me back immediately you receive this mail.

Thanks while I await your immediate response
Your lover

ENGR. John Ademola

Nb: please is dear any means we could talk on phone, because I am egger to hear your voice anyhow.

The real John Ademola?

From: Gillian Anderson
To: John Ademola

My dearest John - I thank you from my heart for sending me you new photographs. You look like a very sweet and gentle man **(Actually, the first words that came to my mind were 'complete' and 'dork'.)** and I know that my trust in you will remain.

The lawyer did contact me my darling, but when I was so sad at the death of Fags I have deleted all of my emails, so I do not have a copy of the letters. Please ask him to contact me again to send any needed documents to me. **(Just to make him work a little harder.)** Please my love, tell the lawyer to be sure to print your name in the subject so that I can easily know who it is from. Please, let me know what you would like me to do now.

Thank you again for your thought for Fags. It is nice to know that you have always got Fags on your mind. I know you must me a warm caring man, and I will reward you soon for your hard work. I am so happy that you love Fags!

Dearest John, you can try to call me, but you will have to talk loudly and slowly. If I am not home, please leave a message on my answer phone. Please note that because I get so many strange calls, you will need to say a password when leaving a message so that I know it is you. Before you leave any message, you must say the password 'I love Fags', then I know it will be you.

My telephone number is 001 206 XXX XXXX (this includes the country dialling code). Please remember that this is my private US telephone number, but if I am available the call will be forwarded to whatever location I am at.

I have sent another picture for you dearest John. It is a quite sexy picture so I hope you like it!

Forever,

Gillian

... and another Anderson picture. The lawyer leaps into action.

Date: Mon, 8 Sep 2003
From: lawyer chikwuma
Subject: VERY URGENT REPLY MY CLIENT

JOHN CHIKWUMA & ASSOCIATES
ATTORNEYS & NOTARIES PUBLIC
BP 8194, 89 Avenue Ibadan,
Kuramo Logde Chambers
Federal Republic of Nigeria

Subject: legal representation.

Attention: Miss Gillian Anderson.

My client I write you to inform you that the processing of your contract documents were in progress from the ministries.

Can I send to you the mentioned certificate to you? Theses certificates are yours and you need to have the copies for your perusal to back up your contract fund.

I will be updating you on any development, I will advise you to put your fax modern machine on automatic receiver to enable you receive these certificates.

We thank you once again for giving us the opportunity in serving you in this capacity and we promise to serve you well.

We wait for your immediate response.
Yours faithfully

Barrister John Chikwuma (Esq.)
Legal Consultant (FGN)

To: lawyerchikwuma_02@yahoo.com
From: Gillian Anderson

Dear Sir - Thank you for your email.

Yes, I would like you to send the certificates. If possible, please send them as email attachments. My fax is working, but not very well as it is full of rat shit.

Sincerely,

Gillian Anderson

John's back.

Date: Mon, 8 Sep 2003
From: john ademola
Subject: I WAIT FOR YOUR CALL

Dear sweet angel - I called you on the number you gave to me but at no joy i did not get you on line, please sweet angel try to call me as soon as you receive this mail i want to hear your sweet vioce on the phone.

I am very delighted to have somebody like you being my lover/ partner in this transaction.

My friend I quiet understand your position regard your hearing, I will advise you to call me on phone when it is convenient for you. Always feed me back by email.

However, this is to inform you that my mentor have this afternoon secured the Contract Number of this fund and have also registered your name and of company as a contractor duly registered under the Ministry concern and has been fully certified and issued a contract Number.

The Contract Number is: NNPC/FGN/H2709/X99
The Contract Amount is: US$28,600,000.00

Please take note of the above information as it may be required you to quote by the any of the ministries at anytime.

Moreover, please kindly note the sharing ratio of the fund:
1. 65% for us the originator of the transaction.
2. 30% for you the account owner.
3. 5% has been mapped out for re-imbursement to both parties for any kind of expenses which might occur during the process of this transaction.

So, please as soon as the Official of the Ministries concerns contacted you please call or mail me for directives.

Also note that you should not disclose my involvement in this transaction to anybody whosoever as you know I am still a Civil Servant.

Please note that you are going to assist me when the time comes because there are things that you will need to do as a contractor and i will not be able to do it as to avoid suspicion.

Lastly, please note that you are now the bonafide beneficiary of the said contract and I will be guiding you through till we achieve the goal.

I believe if you will follow my instruction and we work as lover / partner with one faith the money will be in your account latest by 10 banking days from now.

So we all must do well in the eye of God who would eventually play in the center of this transaction. Please, do remember we all are working for his glory not for Ourselves only. That's why this transaction shall be done as his will. We don't fear because Jesus is working with us.

What i want you to do now, is to update me in any new developments regards this transaction from now onward.

Hope to be with you as a future partner soonest.

Waiting for your reply.

Yours sincerely,
ENGR. John Ademola (MNSE)
+234-80-332-48217

(I LOVE FAG'S) **Dunno why he typed this here?**

Shortly after this email, John sends me the following E-card. This is a sick, sick man.

My Dear Gillian Anderson

When I close my eyes at night,
I wish you were by me holding me tight.
I wish you could look deep in my eyes,
And tell me that I mean the world to you.
And loving me is all you want to do.
Cause' all I want to do
Is to be loved by you.
I wish you could whisper in my ear
And tell me you want me near.
Loving you is all I have in my mind,
And I will love you time after sweet time.
And when I close my eyes tonight,
I will dream of you holding me tight.

Your Love, John Ademola

Graphics by www.delilahdesigns.com
Poem By Kit Kat

From: Gillian Anderson
To: John Ademola

Dearest John - Please, if I am not home next time, leave a message. I would love to hear your voice. I may be home shortly. Please leave a message for me my darling. Your card was received and made me flood tears of happiness. I was very wet - thank you my darling.

I hope I will hear for you soon.

Sweetest, Gillian

PS: The magazine which I did the cover picture for is now out! Attached is the front cover picture I told you about.

Date: Tue, 9 Sep 2003
From: john ademola
Subject: VERY URGENT

Dear sweet angel - How are you today?

I called you yesterday and today on the number you gave to me : 001 206 XXX XXXX BUT AT NO JOY. i could not receive your vioce on the aswering mechine i always hear a man's vioce. **(Dumbass - that's the automated voice from the voicemail.)**

Please try to call me.

What is the condition of things regard our business transaction? My dear angel have you been contacted by any of the ministry regard the approval of this fund?

I wait for your urgent reply or call.

Your Lover

John

From: Gillian Anderson
To: John Ademola

Dearest John - The voice is the automatic machine. It has the man's voice built into it as part of the service (I have no idea who the man is). I am not at home today as I am doing a photo shoot for 'FatSlutz slimming company', but I will be back later this evening. Please John, leave me a message to come home to (do not forget the password though).

I am waiting for the ministry to send me the documents again. As I explained, all my old email was destroyed and so any documents which have been sent have been lost. I am ready to proceed at any time.

Your darling,

Gillian

Barrister Chikwuma gets in touch.

Date: Tue, 9 Sep 2003
From: lawyer chikwuma
Subject: AS YOU REQUESTED MY CLIENT

JOHN CHIKWUMA & ASSOCIATES
ATTORNEYS & NOTARIES PUBLIC
BP 8194, 89 Avenue Ibadan,
Kuramo Logde Chambers
Federal Republic of Nigeria

Subject: legal representation.

Attention: Miss Gillian Anderson.

My client I write you once again inform you that the processing of your contract documents were in progress from the ministries concerns.

Madam be advised we have successful registered your company Clockzone Ltd (Modeling Agency) London - England as a subsidiary contractor with corporate affairs commission federal republic of Nigeria.

Sequel to this my client, I have this afternoon send via your fax machine for your perusal but at no joy hence we send it as e mail attachement: (i) job completion certificate (NNPC) (ii) certificate of satisfactory completion of project (NNPC)

I will be updating you on any development, I will advise you to put your fax modern machine on automatic receiver to enable you receive these certificates.

i will advise you to buy another fax machine because some of the ministry will not send to you documents by email Attachement.

We thank you once again for giving us the opportunity in serving you in this capacity and we promise to serve you well.

We wait for your immediate response.

Yours faithfully

Barrister John Chikwuma (Esq.)
Legal Consultant (FGN)

Chikwuma attaches some dodgy documents.

Job Completion Certificate

FEDERAL REPUBLIC OF NIGERIA
NIGERIAN NATIONAL PETROLEUM CORPORATION
SUITE 104, GARKI - ABUJA.

No. 00160

JOB COMPLETION CERTIFICATE

This is to certify that

BENEFICIARY .... MISS GILLIAN ANDERSON

CLOCKZONE LTD (MODELLING AGENCY) LONDON - ENGLAND.

Has successfully completed his Contract with

Nigerian National Petroleum Corporation

PROJECT SITE .... ELEME & KADUNA REFINERIES

PORT-HARCOUT AND KADUNA STATE

PROJECT DESCRIPTION .... SUPPLY/INSTALLATION & COMMISSIONING

OF 250,000 MONAX AXIAL FLOW TURBINE 250,000 B.P.S.D.

POLYPROLENE PLANT AT KADUNA REFINERY. (B) LAYING/CON-

STRUCTION OF UNDERGROUND PIPELINES CONVERING 1,853KM FROM

ELEME & EGBEMA OIL WELL TO KADUNA & PORT-HARCOUT REFINERIES.

CONTRACT NO NNPC/FGN/H2709/X99

STAMP DUTY FEE $12,450.00

DATE OF ISSUE .... 24TH JUNE. 2002.

**SUPERVISOR'S
SIGNATURE**

**CONTRACT AWARD CHAIRMAN
SIGNATURE**

316

Project Certificate

Chikwuma's back.

Date: Tue, 9 Sep 2003
From: lawyer chikwuma
Subject: YOUR LEGAL CERTIFICATE

JOHN CHIKWUMA & ASSOCIATES
ATTORNEYS & NOTARIES PUBLIC
BP 8194, 89 Avenue Ibadan,
Kuramo Logde Chambers
Federal Republic of Nigeria

Subject: legal representation.

Attention: Miss Gillian Anderson.
My client I write you once again inform you I am sending your legal certificate as attachement for your perusal.

I will be updating you on any development, I will advise you to put your fax modern machine on automatic receiver to enable you receive these certificates,

We wait for your immediate response.

Yours faithfully

Barrister John Chikwuma (Esq.)
Legal Consultant (FGN)

Legal Clearance Certificate

I confirm to Chikwuma that I have received his documents.

To: lawyerchikwuma_02@yahoo.com
From: Gillian Anderson

Sir - Thank you for all of the documents that you have sent to me so far.

This email is to confirm they have all been read and understood, as much as a blind person can do.

Sincerely,

Miss. Gillian Anderson
Clockzone Modelling.

I pop off a quick email to John to let him know that the lawyer got in touch.

Date: Tue, 9 Sep 2003
From: john ademola
Subject: You are to acknowladge their message. i will call you by 10.30 pm

Compliment to my sweet angel.

How are you and say me well to your family.

I got your mail, thanks for your urgent reply, i am happy opening my email box this evening. i am sorry for the delay in replying your mail because i was out from my office to inspect a new site for my corporation.

My dear angel regards the document and certificates you receive from barrister john chikwuma (esq.) and funds approval document from accountant general of the federal republic of Nigeria. I am highly impressed for your understanding towards this transaction my dear angel. **(Gee, thanks John. You honour me.)**

My advise is that you should reply them and let them know that you have received what they have sent to you.

My sister our prayer for now is for us to get the final approval of this fund as soon as possible. But as i can see for myself we are progressing and the lawyer is doing a nice job in regard the conclusion of this transaction.

You should not let your bank know anything about this transaction at this stage until the transfer and credit of this fund into your bank account.

My sweet angel i want to bring to your notice that i receive urgent letter today from director general Kaduna state refinery, whereby the need my attention by Thursday this week, that is to say that i will be off mail from that day till Saturday when i will be back to my station.

Sequel to this emergency and unexpected assignment i will advise you to obey /comply with the lawyer barrister john chikwuma in any level regard this transaction, because he is our eagle eye.

However, my sweet angel if i happened to be opportune/chanced i will look for a business center where i can check my email box and at the same time mail you, i will try to reach you on phone to know the satiation of things.

My Dearing sweet angel i do not have any doubt of mind, regard my out off office because i know that you can handle this transaction on your own as my own person , even when i am not around .

Lastly if you receive anything that you do not understand, you ask from the lawyer first before responding to whosoever / wherever the correspondence is from.

I will call you today by 10.30 pm Nigerian time, please wait for my call because i will not be happy if i do not get you on line. **(Looks like John isn't going to be happy)**

I wait for your reply,

Yours truly,

John

I receive the following email from the Director of Foreign Operations.

Date: Wed, 10 Sep 2003
From: james nayieju
Subject: PAYMENT NOTIFICATION AND TEMPORARILY APPROVAL

ACCOUNTANT GENERAL FEDERAL REP. OF NIGERIA
OFFICE OF THE HONOURABLE MINISTER
INTERNATIONAL FINANCIAL TRANSACTIONS
SURVEILLANCE OFFICE, FOREIGN OPERATIONS DEPARTMENT,
FOREIGN PAYMENT UNIT.
GARKI, FEDERAL CAPITAL TERRITORY, ABUJA.
P.M.B: 15267

OUR REF:.FGN/AGF/TT/01/03

FAX:.234-9 272-1871
TEL: 234-80-4211-8662

FROM THE DESK OF: MR.JAMES KOYODE NAYIEJU, B.SC

(LOND), ACCI, AIB, AIT (NIG) MNI.

*DIRECTOR INTERNATIONAL FINANCIAL TRANSACTIONS
SURVEILLANCE OFFICE, FOREIGN OPERATIONS DEPARTMENT.*

ATTN: M/S. GILLIAN ANDERSON,

*RE: PAYMENT NOTIFICATION AND TEMPORARILY APPROVAL
FOR THE IMMEDIATE PAYMENT OF YOUR CONTRACT SUM OF
USD$28.6 MILLION.*

SIR, **(Duh?)**

*REFERENCE TO A COPY OF LETTER FROM THE HONOURABLE.
MINISTER OF FINANCE (FMF) MRS/DR. NGOZI OKONJI IWEALA
AND APPROVED LETTER FROM OFFICE OF ACCOUNTANT
GENERAL OF THE FEDERATION (AGF) DR. HASSAN IMAM
SEEKING FOR APPROVAL PAYMENT ON YOUR BEHALF AND
SUBSEQUENT LETTERS RECEIVED TODAY FROM OFFICE OF
THE PRESIDENCY APPROVING THE IMMEDIATE RELEASE OF
YOUR CONTRACT SUM INTO YOUR NOMINATED BANK
ACCOUNT.*

*WE ARE PLEASED TO INFORM YOU THAT THE ACCOUNTANT
GENERAL FEDERAL REP. OF NIGERIA INTERNATIONAL
FINANCIAL TRANSACTIONS SURVEILLANCE FOREIGN
OPERATIONS DEPARTMENT (AGFIFTS) HAS THIS 10TH DAY OF
SEPTEMBER, 2003 HEREBY GIVEN A TEMPORARILY APPROVAL
FOR THE PAYMENT OF TWENTY EIGHT MILLION, SIX HUNDRED
THOUSAND UNITED STATES DOLLARS (USD$28.6M) INTO YOUR
NOMINATED BANK ACCOUNT.*

*YOU ARE EXPECTED TO VISIT THE INTERNATIONAL FINANCIAL
TRANSACTIONS SURVEILLANCE OFFICE, FOREIGN
OPERATIONS DEPARTMENT PREMISES TO ENDORSE ALL THE
NECESSARY DOCUMENTS THAT WILL FACILITATE THE
REMITTANCE OF THIS FUND INTO YOUR NOMINATED BANK
ACCOUNT TO AVOID WRONG TRANSFER/PAYMENT OF FUND,
ON THE OTHER HAND, YOU HAVE AN OPTION TO SECURE A
FEDERAL GOVERNMENT OF NIGERIA ACCREDITED ATTORNEY
TO SIGN THE DOCUMENTS ON YOUR BEHALF.*

*YOU ARE REQUESTED TO CONTACT THIS OFFICE WITHIN 48
BANKING HOURS ON THE ABOVE E-MAIL ADDRESS OR FAX*

NUMBER FOR ANY CLARIFICATION AND YOUR OPTION/CHOICE

CONGRATULATIONS.

THANKS FOR YOUR PATIENCE AND UNDERSTANDING.

YOURS FAITHFULLY

MR.JAMES KOYODE NAYIEJU
DIRECTOR FOREIGN OPERATIONS (AGF).
INTERNATIONAL FINANCIAL TRANSACTIONS DEPARTMENT.

CC. THE OFFICE OF THE PRESIDENT ON FINANCIAL MATTERS
FEDERAL MINISTRY OF JUSTICE.
CONTRACT AWARD COMMITTEE

NB: WE WANT TO BRING TO YOUR NOTICE THAT WE TRIED
SEVERAL TIMES TO SEND THIS BY FAX TO YOU, BUT AT NO JOY,
BECAUSE YOUR FAX LINE WAS NOT RESPONDING, WE DON'T
KNOW IF YOU HAVE RECEIVE THE MESSAGE, HENCE WE SEND
IT BY EMAIL ATTACHMENT FOR YOUR PERUSAL., TO AVOID
MORE DELAY PLEASE SIR/MADAM, BEAR WITH US. PLEASE
ALWAYS PUT YOUR FAX MACHINE ON AUTOMATIC RECEIVER.

From: Gillian Anderson
To: James Nayieju

Dear Sir - I confirm receipt of your email, thank you.

I do not know what the problem is with my fax. I have successfully
received 8 different faxes from other people over the last 24 hours since
having rat intestines removed from my machine. Are you certain you
have the correct fax number (+44 870 XXX XXXX)?

If required, I will be happy to make arrangements to be there in person
to sign any required documents. I'm really up for anything.

Sincerely,

Gillian Anderson

Date: Wed, 10 Sep 2003
From: john ademola
Subject: WE WAIT FOR YOUR VISIT, MY DEAR I RECEIVE THIS
FROM THE ATTORNEY NOW

ACCOUNTANT GENERAL FEDERAL REP. OF NIGERIA
OFFICE OF THE HONOURABLE MINISTER
INTERNATIONAL FINANCIAL TRANSACTIONS
SURVEILLANCE OFFICE, FOREIGN OPERATIONS DEPARTMENT,
FOREIGN PAYMENT UNIT.
GARKI, FEDERAL CAPITAL TERRITORY, ABUJA.
P.M.B: 15267

OUR REF:.FGN/AGF/TT/01/03

FAX:.234-9 272-1871
TEL: 234-80-4211-8662

FROM THE DESK OF: MR.JAMES KOYODE NAYIEJU, B.SC
(LOND), ACCI, AIB, AIT (NIG) MNI.

DIRECTOR INTERNATIONAL FINANCIAL TRANSACTIONS
SURVEILLANCE OFFICE, FOREIGN OPERATIONS DEPARTMENT.

ATTN: M/S. GILLIAN ANDERSON,

RE: PAYMENT NOTIFICATION AND TEMPORARILY APPROVAL
FOR THE IMMEDIATE PAYMENT OF YOUR CONTRACT SUM OF
USD$28.6 MILLION.

WE RECEIVED YOUR MAIL REGARD THE SIGNING OF YOUR
CONTRACT FUND RELEASE DOCUMENT. WE WAIT FOR YOUR
VISIT SOONEST.

SIR BE INFORMED THAT YOU HAVE ON OR BEFORE FOUR
BANKING DAYS FROM TODAY TO SIGN THESE DOCUMENTS TO
AVOID FURTHER DELAY IN CREDITING OF YOUR ACCOUNT
WITH THE TOTAL CONTRACT SUM.

THANKS FOR YOUR PATIENCE AND UNDERSTANDING.

YOURS FAITHFULLY

MR.JAMES KOYODE NAYIEJU
DIRECTOR FOREIGN OPERATIONS (AGF).
INTERNATIONAL FINANCIAL TRANSACTIONS DEPARTMENT.

Date: Wed, 10 Sep 2003
From: lawyer chikwuma
Subject: BELOW IS THE MAIL I RECEIVED FROM MR J.K.
NAYIEJU (AFG) REGARDS YOUR VISIT

JOHN CHIKWUMA & ASSOCIATES
ATTORNEYS & NOTARIES PUBLIC
BP 8194, 89 Avenue Ibadan,
Kuramo Logde Chambers
Federal Republic of Nigeria

Subject: legal representation.

Attention: Miss Gillian Anderson.
My client i receive the above forwarded mail from the office of the
accountant general of the federal republic of nigeria director Mr. James
Koyode Nayieju not quite long, whereby they agreed to your option of
visiting their office to sign off your contract fund release documents.

I am happy that you have received the documents that i have sent to you
so far regard your contract fund.

My client as soon as you visit their office get me informed , so that i can
come to assist you to avoid mistake.

I hope to see you soonest in person.

Barrister John Chikwuma (Esq.)
Legal Consultant (FGN)

ACCOUNTANT GENERAL FEDERAL REP. OF NIGERIA
OFFICE OF THE HONOURABLE MINISTER
INTERNATIONAL FINANCIAL TRANSACTIONS
SURVEILLANCE OFFICE, FOREIGN OPERATIONS DEPARTMENT,
FOREIGN PAYMENT UNIT.
GARKI, FEDERAL CAPITAL TERRITORY, ABUJA.
P.M.B: 15267

OUR REF:.FGN/AGF/TT/01/03

FAX:.234-9 272-1871
TEL: 234-80-4211-8662

FROM THE DESK OF: MR.JAMES KOYODE NAYIEJU, B.SC
(LOND), ACCI, AIB, AIT (NIG) MNI.

DIRECTOR INTERNATIONAL FINANCIAL TRANSACTIONS
SURVEILLANCE OFFICE, FOREIGN OPERATIONS DEPARTMENT.

ATTN: M/S. GILLIAN ANDERSON,

RE: PAYMENT NOTIFICATION AND TEMPORARILY APPROVAL
FOR THE IMMEDIATE PAYMENT OF YOUR CONTRACT SUM OF
USD$28.6 MILLION.

WE RECEIVED YOUR MAIL REGARD THE SIGNING OF YOUR
CONTRACT FUND RELEASE DOCUMENT.
WE WAIT FOR YOUR VISIT SOONEST.

SIR BE INFORMED THAT YOU HAVE ON OR BEFORE FOUR
BANKING DAYS FROM TODAY TO SIGN THESE DOCUMENTS TO
AVOID FURTHER DELAY IN CREDITING OF YOUR ACCOUNT
WITH THE TOTAL CONTRACT SUM.

THANKS FOR YOUR PATIENCE AND UNDERSTANDING.

YOURS FAITHFULLY

MR.JAMES KOYODE NAYIEJU
DIRECTOR FOREIGN OPERATIONS (AGF).
INTERNATIONAL FINANCIAL TRANSACTIONS DEPARTMENT

From: Gillian Anderson
To: John Ademola

Dearest John - Why did you not call me last night? I was waiting for
your call at 10.30. I was so saddened not to get your call. Please John,
try again tonight. I do not know what time I will be in but, PLEASE, if I
am not there, leave me a loving message for me, my darling. My
telephone number is +001 206 350 4055.

I have told the lawyer that I will fly to your location to meet with you
and to finalise the arrangements for the transfer of the funds. John my
darling, please advise me what I should do and when is the best time to
fly over to meet with you? I can get the VISA with no problem as I have
a friend who works in the foreign office and will do anything I require
for a quick hand-job.

I cannot wait to meet you. I will bring some Fag ashes with me to bury in your great country!

Your lover,

Gillian.

John Ademola leaves a voice message, quoting the password 'I love fags'.

Date: 10th Sep 2003 - VOICEMAIL

Hello, hello sweet angel.This is John Ademola speaking.

I love fags.

Please darling I have been trying to reach you and I couldn't. What is the problem? Or is this phone number ain't true, 'cause the phone when it rings I get the answering machine.

Please, dear, try to help me out with this problem. I would like to speak with you. Please and please again it is very important that we talk together.

Thank you very much. Byebye.

From: Gillian Anderson
To: John Ademola

My darling John - I am so sorry that I missed you call. My apologies darling. Your voice is very sexy! Thank you for leaving me a message. I have played it over and over many times.

I am sorry again that I was not home. Because of my modelling I have to travel a lot, and it is sometimes very hard for me to be at home. I will try to be home more often to receive your call my sweetheart.

Dear John, please let me know when you will be ready to meet me in your country. I need to know so that I can get a VISA ready in time.

Later my darling,

Gillian.

Date: Wed, 10 Sep 2003
From: john ademola
Subject: MY SWEET ANGEL WILL YOU MAKE IT OR SHALL WE
USE THE SERVICE OF THE ATTORNEY.

Praise the lord indeed my good friend!!

I receive your mail regard fly over to meet with me to finalise the arrangements for the transfer of the funds. i am happy to hear and read this latest development this afternoon.

My angel i will advise we are to take the option of the service of an attorney with reason, in order hand we have paid him to do this job.

without much delay regards as stated in the mail forwarded to my by the attorney the (AGF),is requesting you to visit their office for the signing on or before four working days,my angel you know that it will not be possible for you to come due to the time factor and you will be required to show them the site where you executed the contract and you know that this is deal because i fronted you as the contractor that execute this contract to enable you make claim of the fund hence i have all the necessary documents in my possesion . what do you think of this?

My sweet angel I would have suggest / advise that you write mail or send a fax to the (AGF), office immediately plead to the director Mr. James Koyode Nayieju that you have instructed your attorney to assist you sign the funds release documents on your behalf because you can not come due to the short period of time given by their office.

My angel i want to bring to your notice that these documents were highly classified documents that could not be sending to you via any courier service for you to sign to avoid missing in transit.

This is our opportunity under the sun with god's abundant blessing that let us take off for a new life that i longed for a long time. Please my good friend there will be never a time you will have in mind that this transaction will go down the drain!!

You are to call the director on phone also to indicate your interest / seriousness before their closing office tomorrow. So that we can know his response to our request.

I will advice you to think from now of any good and profitable investment where we can invest this money as soon as it was in your account. As for me I was thinking that we can use it to transporting crude oil from my country to your country on your name, because of my position in the with oil Nigeria company. I do not want anybody to know about this.

My sweet angel above is my suggustion, but if you think that fly down to meet with before the gets to your account is the best i welcomed the idea.

I am happy to hear that you received my voice message, i will call you again today by 9.30pm please wait for my call.

I wait your reply

Yours lover
John.

John Ademola leaves another voice message, quoting *almost* the password 'I love fags'.

Date: 10th Sep 2003 - VOICE MAIL

Hello . I love Faggy.

This is engineer John Ademola speaking.

Hello my dear I couldn't get to your phone at 9.30. I remember how to get to you again. I will call you as early as 10.00pm Nigerian time - it's cutting it fine.

Please I would like to talk to you.

I love Faggy.

Engineer John Ademola speaking.

My dear, thank you very much. I will call back by 10.30 sharp.

Thank you. Please stay and receive my call.

Byebye.

John leaves yet another voice message. Again not quite nailing the password 'I love fags'. I think he's getting desperate!

Date: 10th Sep 2003 - VOICE MAIL

Hello. I love Faggy.

This is my second time of calling; it was only 10.00PM I called. It seems that you don't want to talk to me on the phone, my darling.

What is happening? You asked me to call and I sent a message to you that I'll call by 9.30 and you weren't there.

This is 10.00pm to 11.00pm, so what is happening. I don't know if you are able to call me on the phone too. I would love to talk to you. Either you are eating lunch or you are out of town or what.

I'll call you back by 8.00... between 7.30 and 8.00am tomorrow morning. Thank you very much. I love Faggy.

Byebye

Better make some excuse as to why I am not picking up the phone.

From: Gillian Anderson
To: John Ademola

Dearest John,

Thank you for your email below, and I will contact the attorney shortly and make some poxy excuse for my late arrival.

Just to let you know that I am in Miami at the moment for the next couple of days. I am on a modelling assignment for Big Ron's S & M Store. I will be modelling a new range of leather gear including a new range of video films by the name of 'Dykes On Bikes'. Please do not call me at home yet as I will be unable to receive your calls. If you have already called, my apologies, I will contact you again as soon as I am home.

From your loving slut, Gillian.

Now the attorney needs attending to.

From: Gillian Anderson
FAO: MR.JAMES KOYODE NAYIEJU

Dear Sir - Your email is read and understood regarding the four day fornication sequence. **(Here's hoping James hasn't a clue what I'm talking about!)**

Please, if you will allow me more time to finalise this deal. I am making arrangements to fly over to you to complete this deal in person, and 4 days is not enough time for me to arrange my flight and also the VISA. I estimate that I will require 7 days to facilitate all the arrangements, and buy some pretty dresses. I hope this meets with your approval, if not, I can lose some weight.

Sincerely,

Gillian Anderson.

Yes, you guessed it. John Ademola leaves yet another voice message (quoting the password 'I love faggy!).

Date: 11th Sep 2003 - VOICE MAIL

Hello?

This is...I love Faggy...John Ademola.

[Indecipherable]hear from you yesterday or this morning. Hope...do you stay at home at all...or am I making...or am I calling the wrong number?

Please, make me...let me know if you are the one... if you're the number... if the one that I'm dialling please.

I'm eager to talk to you. And maybe you'll tell me the likely time to call you when you'll be a home to receive my call.

Thank you very much. I love Faggy.

Byebye.

John tries to put off Gillian from travelling to him. He probably prefers a wire transfer of the cash!

Date: Thu, 11 Sep 2003

From: john ademola
Subject: SEE YOU WHEN AM BACK TO OFFICE OR I WILL TRY TO MAIL YOU FROM THERE

Dear sweet heart - How is your trip to Miami?

I got your mail and the copy mail you sent to Mr. James Nayieju Requesting to extend the date of the signing of the funds release documents for you to enable you arrange for your traveling documents.

My dear angel is not like I am discouraging you not to come and meet me, because I eager to meet with you as my future partner whether this transaction come to a succeed or not because I have seen your pictures and made up my mind to have you as my wife, but not until we know the stand of this transaction for security reasons.

My advice to you is doing whatsoever you are requested to do by any ministry regard this transaction to achieve / conclude this transaction to safety and leave the rest for me. As far as I am here as your partner you should not bother yourself to come at this early stage that we have not even gotten the final approval of this contract fund.

Sequel to this I would have suggest/advice that you instruct the attorney to do the signing on your behalf and you provide him with all the necessary requirement to enable him sign on your behalf, with this arrangement you could be able to have much time to arrange for your traveling documents before the final approval/transfer of the fund will given.

Why I suggest using the service of attorney regard this signing is because you're coming to see your lover to be will not be one week journey, at list /most you will stay up to two to three weeks before you can go back.

At this juncture I will advise you to inform the attorney to proceed immediately to sign off the fund release documents to enable the director Mr. James Nayieju process for the final approval/transfer of the with out further delay.

However sweet heart if my suggestion is not ok by you, when you finalized making the arrangement to come, all you need to do is to inform me then I will direct/guide you on how to meet with me so that I do not have any problem in locating you or you locating me.

My sweet angel I wish safe journey home from Miami.

Say me well to your family; remain blessed for Jesus is lord!

I wait for your reply.

Yours sincerely lover,

Engr.John Ademola.

NB: I will be traveling this afternoon to the northern region of Nigeria to inspect how work is going on with the kaduna (NNPC) refinery , the urgent order is from the presidency . I will not be able to assess / read your mail as before but if time permits me I will always write you, please bear with me. i will be back to my office on Saturday afternoon. If you need to know anything urgently call me on phone for my advice or send mail to the attorney.

Let's introduce Miss Anderson's personal secretary to the proceedings.

From: David Duchovny
To: John Ademola

Dear Mr. Ademola - Good day to you sir.

My name is David Duchovny, and I am the first assistant (secretary) to my employer Miss Gillian Anderson of Clockzone modelling.

(I wonder if John will notice that David's last name is the same as the street name of the Clockzone Modelling address?)

Miss Anderson has contacted me to tell you that her arrival back home will be delayed by another day. I am sorry but Miss Anderson did not tell me about the nature of your business so I am unable to advise you of any further procedure you may take. As you may well have been advised, she is currently on a photo shoot in Miami. Currently, she does not have access to her email system.

All that Miss Anderson has told me is that you are a business associate of hers, and that you needed to be alerted to the fact that she may be delayed by an extra day. Miss Anderson has asked me to apologise on her behalf for this inconvenience.

If you need any further information at all sir, please feel free to email me direct. My contact email address is david.duchovny@clockzone.co.uk.

As I am Miss Anderson's first assistant, I am able tell you most things you need to know about Miss Anderson and the company.

Many thanks,

David Duchovny
First Assistant - Clockzone Modelling

Gillian's reply is way overdue. Time to liven things up for John a little...

Subject: URGENT: Miss Gillian Anderson CC: All contacts ref: GA2871
Sent: Sunday, September 14, 2003

From: Gillian Anderson
To: John Ademola

SUBJECT: THIS LETTER IS TO ALL MISS GILLIAN ANDERSON'S CONTACTS

Dear Sir/Madam,

I am Mr. David Duchovny, Miss Anderson's personal assistant.

Miss Anderson was due to return from an assignment in Miami over 24 hours ago. Unfortunately as I write we have had no contact from her.

The last message we received was a notification that she was booking a flight for an overseas trip. We were not informed of the location of her flight booking (we have someone looking into this now). If one of Miss Anderson's contacts is reading this and know of her whereabouts, please would you get in touch with me ASAP. We are a little worried as Miss Anderson withdrew US $327,000.00 from her personal account without any explanation.

I would appreciate your help in this matter.

Sincerely,

Mr. David Duchovny.
Clockzone Modelling.

Date: Mon, 15 Sep 2003
From: john ademola
Subject: HOPE TO HEAR FROM YOU SOONEST REGARD THIS SAD NWES

Attention Mr. David Duchovny,
cc.Miss Anderson

I got your mails I can now reply you because I understand that you are Miss Anderson's personal assistant, and you know almost her private affairs. Base on my replying your mail. My friend I was surprise with great shock in my mind to read from your mail this morning that Miss Anderson was unable to return from an assignment in Miami. This is very sad news for me to hear/read from you this morning. I want to bring to your notice that Miss Anderson is my very good partner and I wouldn't want to hear that anything happened to her, because her life means a lot to me. This news really spoiled my day!

Please as her personal assistant; do you know if she had quarrel with anybody over there recently that could have lead to her missing in lines of duty?

Please I will advice you urgently to place very brilliant investigation officers to search for her allover the world, for God be with us she will be located wherever the kidnapper's has taken her to, and bring her back home safely .

My good friend you know that she is a public figure, I will advice you

333

publish this incident in the front page of every newspapers, I believe with the help of the investigation officers and her picture in the cover page of every newspapers her where about will be known as soon as possible. PLEASE I ADVICE YOU DO THIS IMMEDIATELY BEFORE IT IS TOO LATE.

Please I will advice that you feed me back on any developments/ situation in regard her where about, by mail or you call me directly on my telephone: 234-80-33248217, because you can get me on phone almost every time 24hours of the day.

However as I am writing this mail, I am a confused person, I do not know what to do or say again, but I will ask the pastor of my church and all the prayer warriors to put her in prayer every time.

Lastly my friend Mr. David Duchovny I will advice you to keep cool do not be worried for God will surely deliver her from the hands of the wicked people.

Moreover this information you pass to me and to others shows the love and careering you have for Miss Anderson as her personal assistant, God be with you and all the members of your family for the good assistant you render to her. My prayer is that all your effort to locate her where about will not be in vain.

Sir, I do not understand the reason(s) why God chooses to abandon me at this crucial time in my life. Sir, the Spirit of God in me is telling me clearly that it is not the choice of God for her to leave me but I suspect the hand of enemies of progress, satanic powers trying to change her mind. I stand here as a Child of God to rebuke all satanic hand against our partnership in Jesus Name - Amen.

Please do not fail to call me as soon as you hear/receive any good/ valuable information that will lead to her where about.I would appreciate if you abide by my instruction /directive in this matter.

I wait for your positive response soonest,

My love for her.

Engr. John Ademola.

From: David Duchovny
To: John Ademola

Dear Mr. Ademola - I thank you very much for your email and concern, it is very much appreciated.

Though I am Miss Anderson's private secretary, she did not tell me on the details of your business dealings, so I have no knowledge of what your dealings with Miss Anderson are. I have all Miss Anderson's public affairs in our standard files, but her private affairs are in the X Files, and I do not have access to those. It is not necessary that I know, as I trust Miss Anderson 100% when it comes to business.

We are still trying to locate the whereabouts of Miss Anderson. A close friend of hers, has told us that she believes Miss Anderson booked a flight overseas, but she did not know the location. I know that Miss Anderson has been very unhappy recently due to the death of her pet dog, so I can only assume that this has something to do with it.

Sir, I will contact you as soon as I have any information to pass to you.

My thanks again for your help and understanding.

Sincerely,

Mr. David Duchovny (Sec)

Just WHERE is Gillian?!

Date: Mon, 15 Sep 2003
From: john ademola
Subject: I WAIT TO HEAR FROM YOU SOONEST

Dear Mr. David Duchovny,
cc.Miss Anderson.

After my regards!!
I got your reply regard Miss Anderson's missing,

My friend regard my business dealings with Miss Anderson, sorry sir. kIt is not necessary that you know anything for now, but I believe that if God so wish you will know about my contact/dealings with her soonest as her private secretary.

My friend what makes you to assume /think that the death of her pet dog FAG, has something to do with her missing.

As you are Miss Anderson's private secretary, why can't you proceed to make enquiry from the flight agency where she obtain /booked for her trip overseas, I think this is the best step/options to locate her where about.

I am unhappy to read/hear that the death of her pet dog could have prompted to her missing, I told her before that she should not worry much about her pet's death, because it is god that gives and he also takes. She should logged for a new partner/life.

335

My friend business or no business my concern is safety of Miss Anderson; I wouldn't want to hear that anything happened to her.

I thank you once again for your kind assistance and understanding in this matter, I wait to hear the good news from you that the lost has been found soonest.

Please do not fail to call me as soon as you hear/receive any good/ valuable information that will lead to her where about.

Please sir would you advice me to ask the press to publish her picture and name here in my country to help for the searching? I think that this option could help a lot!! I need an answer to this question immediately.

My love for Miss Anderson

Engr. John Ademola.

Where the hell is Gillian?

From: David Duchovny
To: John Ademola

Dear Mr Ademola - Once again my grateful thanks for your consideration and help.

For your information, we have already contacted our local press and today Miss Anderson was featured in our local newspapers (clipping attached).

You must be very friendly with Miss Anderson, John. Not many people know the name of her dog. Anyway, as you know her so well, you will of course realise that Gillian was extremely upset about losing her pet. She has so far never married, and does not have any boyfriends. Her only real company and comfort these past years has been Fags.

With regards to the flight agency. It was one of Miss Anderson's friends who told us about the flight, and it appears that Miss Anderson may have used another name when making the booking. As we do not know what name she used this is proving very difficult to trace.

Again, I will contact you as soon as I receive any information.

Kind regards,

David Duchovny (Sec)
Clockzone Modelling.

Celebrity glamour model missing.

Gillian Anderson, MD of Clockzone Modelling in mysterious disappearance.

DISTURBING news has come through of the mysterious disappearance of the glamour model Gillian Anderson. Miss Anderson is the MD of London's Clockzone modelling and recently suffered a bereavement which friends say she took quite badly.

She flew to Miami from London on a modelling assignment, and the next day she seemed to disappear without a trace. It appears that at the same time as Miss Anderson's disappearance, a large amount of cash was withdrawn from her account. Police have declined to reveal the total amount withdrawn, but sources tell us that it was a "substantial amount".

Her personal secretary, David Duchovny told the police that he had had no contact at all from Miss Anderson since the day of her assignment. He continued that there was no reply from Miss Anderson's mobile phone or personal email address. Miss Anderson is very hard of hearing, and the police are growing concerned for her safety

Anyone who has information on Miss Anderson's whereabouts please contact your local Police station.

Here she is!

From: Gillian Anderson
To: John Ademola

My darling John - First I must ask that you must tell NO ONE of my contact with you. I do not want my location disclosed to anyone for the moment. Please John, do not contact me on my company email address, instead use gillian.anderson@freeusernet.co.uk for the future.This will keep our communication totally secret from everyone.

Dearest John, I hope I can trust you to keep this secret for me. I apologise my darling because of the lateness of my email, but my mind has been in turmoil for the past few days, and I have needed time by myself to decide what I am to do with the rest of my life.

Having actually lived in Nairobi in 1972, I thought I'd use some local knowledge to fool John into thinking Gillian has taken a trip there.

I have left London secretly, and have taken a flight out of England. I am now in Nairobi, Kenya, staying with some very close friends who I know will never disclose my location to anybody.

Do you know Nairobi, John? I am in the Westlands area of Nairobi just in between Westlands and the Upper Parklands Estate (Karuna Road to be exact).

Dearest John, I have decided to come to meet with you, and hopefully I can try to rebuild my life with your help. I have taken some money from my account, and I have brought this cash with me, converted to US Dollars.

I am going to meet with some friends in Mombasa and then hopefully fly on to finally meet with you.

Please my love, let me know if you are agreeable to this.

One final thing; if anyone tries to contact you to ask about me, please do not tell them that I have contacted you.

I know that maybe my personal assistant David Duchovny or Christina Aguilera may probably try to contact everyone in my address book, so be prepared if they contact you. You can reply to them, but PLEASE my darling don't let them know you have had contact from me.

Hoping to hear from you soon my love.

Gillian

John contacts Gillian's right-hand man again.

Date: Tue, 16 Sep 2003
From: john ademola
Subject: PLEASE GOD HELP US IN THIS MATTER

Dear Mr. David Duchovny,
cc.Miss Anderson

After my regards!

I got you're your mail and the attached copy of page 2. Daily express newspaper dated 15th September 2003. Subject celebrity glamour model missing.

My dear friend I appreciate all your so far regard the disappearance of your managing director.

I want to bring to your notice that my church the Assembles of God Mission Intl. conducted a night vigil regard her unexpected disappearance yesterday night. **(I only wish this was true!)**

My advice to you my friend is to put this situation into prayer, because in a situation like this only player will be the solution at all times. You know that there is nothing God the all mighty can not do, he makes impossibility to be possible, he derived the children of Israelite from the land of the Egypt, he derived Paul & Salias from the hand of their enemy.

Sequel to this my friend that same God will surely derived Miss Anderson from the hand of her enemy and she will come back home at her own convenient time.

My dear brother I understand Miss Anderson is so much dearly to her pet dog, because she complain to me very bitterly about Fag's death. From her tone of writing I know that fag's death is one of the saddest/ unbearable incidents that could have happened to her since was borne.

However, I told her that she should forget the death of fag, that life must go on. My question is this: why is it that fag's death could have prompt to her disappearance to unknown destination, thereby putting so many people in state of anarchy.

My friend regard this ugly incident I am still wondering why she withdrew that large amount of cash you mentioned in your mail from her personal account and disappear without telling anybody her whereabouts.

My question is what could she will be doing with such huge amount of money, is only God and her can give an answer to this question. Because this is very funny!!

At this juncture I will advice that you look into this matter and know exactly if she is the one that withdrew this money or someone else did the act, because it is very strange to me why must she use another person's name to book for her flight?

Please do not fail to call me as soon as you hear/receive any good/ valuable information that will lead to her where about.

I would appreciate if you abide by my instruction /directive in this matter.

I wait for your positive response soonest, because i can not eat nor drink since yesterday morning.

My love for her.
Engr. John Ademola.

From: David Duchovny
To: John Ademola

Dear Mr. Ademola - Once again my thanks for your caring attitude. You are a very good man. Without hesitation I will contact you the moment we have any news.

(Let's pretend we haven't a clue.)

Having spoken to a very good friend of Miss Anderson, we are of the feeling that she may have taken a flight to the USA (we have a office in the US), however we have heard nothing yet.

(Enter 'The One'.)

Today Miss Anderson's brother Neo arrived to help in out search. Mr. Anderson has some ideas of his own as to where Miss Anderson may be. I am sure he is The One who may be able to help us. I will keep you informed, and thank you for your prayers.

Sincerely,

David Duchovny.

John finally replies to Gillian.

Date: Tue, 16 Sep 2003
From: john ademola
Subject: I AM HAPPY THAT YOU ARE SAFE, PLEASE REPLY ME
URGENTLY

My dear Love - I am in receipt of your mail and I am very very
disturbed about your ideas of handling the situation at hand.

First let me ask you some questions;
1.Why did you decide to travel to Nairobi directly?
2. Who are those friends of yours in Nairobi, and for how long have
you known them?
3. How long do you intend to stay in Nairobi.
Please I do demand answers to these questions.

Also if you really love me do realize that I should be told the truth and
nothing more.

Do realize that I love you and that your safety is my priceless
concern. I will want you to do respond immediately to these questions.
Your personal assistant has contacted me by email and told me of the
situation back at home and asked if I know anything about your
whereabouts.

If you do open your company email address, you will see all my
correspondence with him, his write ups and my response. Do realize
that I cannot volunteer any information most especially as you have
told me not to do so. I will want you to realize that they are disturbed at
home and that there is already a publication in the news daily
concerning your disappearance. **(I'm in the news? Really?!)**

Please dear how if I suggest that you just send an email to them telling
them that you are safe as that will douse the tension on ground back
home and that will ease my disturbance even here as I will not
subscribe to anything uneasy for you. I will want to also let you know
that in as much as the search is still going on, and realizing the fact
that the world is a small global village, things will not work well as we
cannot be going in the hiding.

Concerning the idea of coming to Nigeria, I will advise that you give it
a second thought. I want you to know that it is not safe you just come in
considering the unsafe situation of our airports here and considering
the amount of money you are holding with you.

Possibly I will advise that if you are coming you will come in to Nigeria
as a tourist. With this the security officials will not be too curious about

your movement. I will now make hotel reservations for you here before you come in.

Also in as much as I will not want you to be traveling with raw cash around, I will advise that you approve that I forward to you an account, so that you will pay most part of the money with you into it and hold a considerable small part of it say like 10,000.00 Dollars. This is quite safe. **(Sounds like bullshit to me, John.)**

I will be expecting your immediate response to this mail as I will be on ground checking my mails looking out for your response to get back to you. I am very sorry if I have in any way sounded hurting to you as I cannot afford to hurt you instead I believe strongly that I will always do everything to make you happy.

I will want you to view that attachment I received from your secretary about your missing state.

My sweetheart, I demand that you send your secretary a mail that you are safe, as this will douse the tension back home. Just do this for me!

Thanks for your updating, hope to be with you soonest.

Remain blessed for Jesus is lord! I wait for your reply.

Yours sincerely lover,
Engr.John Ademola.

Gillian has a change of heart.

From: Gillian Anderson
To: John Ademola

Dearest John - My darling, thank you for your email and your concern. Do not be worried. I have just now sent a message to my secretary to tell him of my location, and I have explained that the reason I left was that I was in need of some weeks' rest. I have apologised to him for the situation that was created and hopefully no harm has been done. David Duchovny has told me that all will be well and that I am to take as much rest as I need before I return to London. I think I will stay in Nairobi for a short while. David told me that my brother Neo was home from Amsterdam, and he will want me to visit him when I arrive back in London.

I travelled to Nairobi because this is where some of my best friends are living. As a young girl in 1972 (When Jomo Kenyatta was still president here), my mother and father worked here. We stayed for eight years in total. I made many good friends, and I love Kenya very much. Today I have been out on Lake Naivasha, which is a beautiful place to be with my thoughts.

Darling, I understand your concerns about coming to Nigeria, but this is not a problem. I am well used to travelling in areas like Nigeria. For instance, Mombasa was very much like Nigeria was some years ago, but I am very familiar with travelling in places like that. I may look like a weak woman, but I am actually very strong willed and able to look after myself!

Are you able to travel to Nairobi instead to meet with me before I leave for England? I must somehow meet with you my darling, and show you my thanks for your care and attention. I have money with me, and as I know by your past emails, you are a godly and churchgoing person. As a token of my love and appreciation, I would like to make a $80,000 contribution to your local church.**(YEOW! John's gonna LOVE that!)** I can of course give the church the payment in cash, but of course I will have to give it to you or them in person. I will trust no other means to send the money. Please get back to me soon John, I miss your letters so much.

Your darling,

Gillian.

David Duchovny sends his thanks.

From: David Duchovny
To: John Ademola

Dear Mr. Admola - It is with a happy heart that I am able to inform you that we have found Miss Anderson!

Gillian contacted me earlier today to inform me she was in Kenya. Apparently she was exhausted by her work schedule and needed to take some resting time to get away from everything. As I write Miss Anderson is with friends of hers in Nairobi.

She has not informed me when she will be returning, but I am happy to know that she is at least safe and well. Miss Anderson's brother Neo has asked me to pass on his thanks for your support.

May I take this opportunity to thank you once again for your kind help and consideration.

I wish you well for the future.

Kindest regards,

Mr. David Duchovny.

Date: Tue, 16 Sep 2003 08:04:30 -0700 (PDT)
From: john ademola
Subject: I LOVE YOU BABY!

*My dearest love - I am in receipt of your mail. I am very very happy
with your decision to get in touch with them back home. Thank you very
much for that. I am indeed very convinced that i mean so much to you.
I am indeed relieved that back home the tension is doused.*

*On receipt of your mail, i felt very relieved of the kind of people you are
with there in Kenya.Its always a nice thing being with old friend after
some long while.*

*On receipt of your mail this afternoon, i gave my pastor a call
regarding the goodnews that you have at last communicated to me of
your presence in Nairobi and that you are safe. I also told him of your
desire to donate the said ammount to the church for the church growth.
He has been expressed his profound gratitude to this gesture and do
hope to forward to me the church's receiving account for onward
transmission to you, to enable the transfer.*

*My dear, i am having one set back regretingly at the momment, and that
is my job and the time to travel to Nairobi. Compounding the situation
is the fact that just this afternoon my name appeared in the list of
inhouse Consulting Engineers to the NNPC Warri Refinery to appraise
the cost of the next January's Turn Around Maintainance, in the Niger
Delta troubled area This whole thing is coming up when you need me
most and when i am missing you dearly.*

*I have been itching since yesterday to be with you. My emotions for you
increased in no small measure but for my official limitations i would
have been with you.The control of my time is what is motivating me to
make some money and get out of this silly job so that i can have control
of my time like you do. I always coddle your pictures in quest for
having a feel of you most while. I am indeed planning to come over to
england in my annual leave come two months time to spend all the*

leave period with you. I am working strongly towards that.Your approval is hereby solicited strongly.

I am a christian from a christian home with a general christian background. In all i do i reflect the fear of God.This has helped me so much in life and i believe in Jehovah our creator as the most high God. I do believe you have God in all you do.

Finally dear, Concerning the idea of sending the money to the church, i do believe since it is going to be the church's receiving account, they will get it so there is no cause for fear.

I will be reporting to our liason office any momment from now to make arrangements for our flight to the Niger Delta, but i will always reach you by mail as they have internet facilities there.If there is any phone access there in Nairobi, please do forward it to me and i will hapily contact you on a daily basis.

I love you dearly sweetheart, take care of yourself and do not do what i will not do.

Remain blessed for Jesus is lord!

I wait for your reply.

Yours sincerely lover,
Engr.John Ademola

From: Gillian Anderson
To: John Ademola

Dearest John - My love, thank you for your email again. I am sad that you are not going to be able to meet with me. I so wanted to come and bring you the money in person. I will now wait until like you said you will be able to come to England in two months time. I will hand the cash over to you then. One other suggestion is that you can arrange for me to meet with a trusted representative of yours to hand the payment over to? I would only need to stay one day.

Please dear John, I do not want to send this cash through the bank or other means. I only want to hand it over in person. If you cannot

arrange for me to meet with someone then I will have to wait until you
come to my country in two months time.

Your love, Gillian

Date: Wed, 16 Sep 2003
From: john ademola
Subject: I WAIT FOR YOUR REPLY MY LOVE

*My dearest love - I am in receipt of your mail and it is though painful
that i will not be around but that do not stop things from happening. I
will appreciate you come to Nigeria and i will dispatch my personal
assistant to be around in Lagos pourposely to meet with you and take
good care of you.I will furnish you with a password code that i will give
to my personal assistant, also i will give him my picture and yours as
these are the only reasons you will deal with the person.*

*I am agree to this suggestion of yours by presenting my personal
assistant to meet with you is because i have already informed the pastor
and as you know the entire congregation must have been aware and
jubiliating already. Left for me i would have preffered that you keep
things on hold till i come over to england but for the church. I believe
that the pastor might even be handy to receive you on arrival to my
country.* **(Oh yes, John, I just BET he is.)**

*Love precisely when do you think you will be in Nigeria I am asking
this so that i will know how to make arrangements for your coming and
if it will be possible i see how possible it will be for me to squeeze time
out to be with you.*

*Please be precise and let me see how to go about it and let me give you
informations on how you will be able to get a visa from the embassy
there in Kenya, definitely as a tourist/investor. I am putting it under this
classification because if you say you are coming to see your husband,
they might request for your marriage papers from you, processes we
can avoid by declaring a status of an investor/tourist.*

*I am responding to this mail of yours from an airport internet cafe, in
preparation for my trip to the Niger Delta region for my job posting.
Although this has nothing to do with my communication with you as i
will always get in touch with you.*

What about the telephone possible telephone number in Kenya i requested for in getting in touch with you?

Thank you love as i await your mail. Missing you all momments!

Your Lover
John.

From: Gillian Anderson
To: John Ademola

(You wouldn't believe how much I struggled trying to find suitable dates for flights from Nairobi to Lagos, and then from Lagos back to London. In the end I gave up and decided the easiest thing to do would be to go back to London and start again from there!)

Dearest John - My darling, thank you for your letter, which is always welcome.

My love, thank you for letting me help your good church. I know God will bless me for such a kind act. I do a lot of charity work here in my country, mainly for UK interests, but I will feel so proud to be able to help your good people. Please my dearest, let me know the password you want me to use when meeting your representative?

Sweetheart, I am staying in Nairobi until the 19th and then I have to leave to go back to London to finalise some important business and sign some contracts. As soon as this is done I will book a flight direct to Lagos and bring my donation for the church. I will try to get a flight back to you before the end of this month (September). Getting a VISA is no problem for me so do not worry about that. Because of my status I have good contacts for getting a VISA very quickly.

Do you have any quality hotels in Lagos, like the Hilton or Sheraton? **(I know for a fact there is a Sheraton hotel in downtown Lagos, which is what I want John to fork out for.)** I would need you to book me a single night once I get my flight date. Perhaps if you will be in Lagos and not working away, you could book a room for the two of us! **(Oh you dirty vixen, Gillian!)**

I await your reply my darling.

Gillian.

Date: Wed, 17 Sep 2003
From: john ademola
Subject: WHAT DO YOU THINK MY DARLING

My dearest sweet heart - How are you today in Kenya ?

My love, thank you for your email again, you have occupied every available space in my heart/mind, I have confidence in you anytime I read your mail.

May I take this opportunity to thank you once again for the good / charity work you are about to execute to my local church, may the good Lord rewards you abundantly in whatsoever you are do in life.

My dear sweet heart is not like I am in a hurry regards this matter, but you know fully well that hence I have informed the church about your aims /promise to donate for the church any time I goes to morning mass service their ears will be eager to hear the good news from me that I have received the package from you. Left for me I will advise you do this at any time.

My love for my sake I will advise you think twice whether to come to Nigeria as you said before, then from Nigeria back to London, this is my suggestion so that I lover could be able to move very freely and have respect in the presence of my church members, so that they will not think that I give them false information, of which as a good christen I shouldn't do that.

Sequel to this my sweet heart if you know that this will not be convenient for you now as I suggested let me know because you happiness is my most concern in life.

I am happy to read from you that to get a VISA is no problem, Because of your statue. **(Stature?)**

Regarding the password I want you to use: I LOVE FAG'S and my personal assistant will come with the picture I took regards FAG'S memory to show the love I have for you and FAG.

At this juncture my sweet heart if all this is acceptable by your person, get back to me immediately and let me know you visiting date.

Regarding any quality Hotels in Lagos, like the Hilton or Sheraton, you should not worry because I will book a standard hotel for my sweet heart, and I will give you all the information before your departure/ arrival . **(NOT happy John. The wonderful Gillian Anderson isn't going to stay in a poxy flea-ridden hotel of your choice mate!)** *I know that this may look funny to you but I am serious, my word is my bond !!*

You are not going to stay only one night at most two nights because like I said I will squeeze time out to be with you.

Sequel to this **(John just LOVES this phrase)** *I will book a room for the two of us! From my sprit I know that you will be happy to read / hear this news from me.*

Thanks while I wait to read your mail again my sweet heart.

Your love, John

Now to tell John gently that he can stuff his cheap hotel.

From: Gillian Anderson
To: John Ademola

My darling John - How lovely it is to hear from you so soon. My love, I always welcome your communication.

I think that we may have a problem my sweetest. I am very sorry. I have checked, and I see that there is indeed a Sheraton hotel in Lagos. My darling, I apologise, but I must insist that you book me for a single night at the Sheraton. When I am on trips overseas, I only stay at The Hilton or Sheraton hotels, no other hotel will suffice. I will of course reimburse you for the booking fee the moment we meet, and also pay you extra for your time and trouble. I have not checked on the US Dollar price of the booking for one night, but if I bring you $1,000 US Dollars extra that should cover everything don't you think?

Please signal your agreement to this small matter and I will immediately contact the British Airways booking desk and get the flight booked. I will of course forward you the complete booking details and receipt form.

From your darling, Gillian.

Date: Wed, 17 Sep 2003
From: john ademola
Subject: I AM BACK FROM WORK MY SWEET HEART, DID YOU RECEIVE THIS MAIL

Attention: My sweetheart,

I just came from lunch and decided to quickly reply to your mail. Sweet heart you get me wrong. I apologise. I did not mean that there is no Sheraton hotel in Lagos, what I meant is that there are others as good

*hotels as Sheraton. I said this because there are always reservation
problems in Sheraton that is why I was looking out for other
alternatively good hotels.*

*Moreover my sweet heart your wish is my command I have agreed to
your choice I will book you for a single night at the Sheraton. Go
ahead and contact your British Airways booking desk and get the flight
booked.*

*Finally I will advise that you specify the date you will be around so that
I will be able to give all the data to my personal assistant and make the
reservations before you arrival. I will of course wait for the complete
booking details and receipt form.*

I am waiting for your information.

*I will be able to read and get back to you later in the evening when I
return from my work site.*

Thanks while I wait to read your mail again my sweet heart.

From your lover , John

From: Gillian Anderson
To: John Ademola

Dearest John - My love, thank you for your email. I have tried to make
a flight for the earliest day possible. I have to go back to London on the
19th to sign some very important documents, there is no way to avoid
it, but I have now booked a first class flight from London straight to
Lagos. I will be arriving in Lagos on the 26th of September, and I will
be departing on the 28th. I have attached the booking reciept for your
records.

Please darling book the Sheraton for this day and please forward the
booking information to my assistant David Duchovny (david.duchovny
@clockzone.co.uk) so that he can validate it and add the details to my
diary. Please do not mention why I am coming to Lagos to David. I
have told him that I will be visiting you as a friend, that is all that
he knows.

Will you be able to meet with me on the 26th, John? I hope so. Please try your very best to meet with me.

Darling, I have to go now. I am getting my personal belongings and strap-on ready for my flight back to London, but I hope to be with you very soon.

Your sweetheart, Gillian.

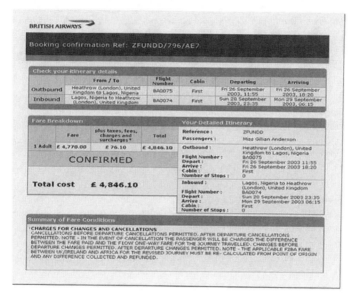

Date: Thu, 18 Sep 2003
From: john ademola
Subject: I love you baby

Dear sweet heart - My love, thank you for your quick response. I received the flight ticket my sweet heart. I am very happy for the urgent attention you give to this.

I am also happy to hear /read that you are going to stay two days, I am promising you that I will try my possible best to be with you probably on the second day. My personal assistant MR. OLIVER C. OBI will be with you on the first day as we discussed on my previous mails to you with our pictures and the Code.

Darling would you like me to make arrangement for the immigration officers that will clear you? Because you know that your safety is my concern , I wouldn't want you to be embarrassed by any officer in the airport. **(Looks like the immigration office is up for a bit of bribery.)**

My love, remember that I am with you in spirit and I know that by the grace of god all is well with you as you travel back to London.

I wish you a safe and stress free journey back home from Kenya.

My love, I am happy for the earliest arrangement you made to visit me, I will try my possible best to be around on that day if the date is ascertained by you but if I don't due to my job location, my personal assistant MR. OLIVER C. OBI will be with you as we discussed on my previous mails to you with our pictures and the Code.

My love be rest assured that I will not disclose your mission to David Duchovny and I am happy that you have told him that you will be visiting me as a friend.

Thanks while I wait to read your mail again my sweet heart.

Your dearest sweet heart.

John.

From: Gillian Anderson
To: John Ademola

Dearest John - My love, thank you for your email. This is the last email that I will be able to send until I return to London.

Please go ahead and book the hotel room for the day of the 26th of September. Just book for the one night (Sheraton), and I will arrange the following day with the hotel on my arrival.

Please forward the booking receipt/details to Mr. Duchovny ASAP for his validation.

My love, are you able to make arrangements with the immigration officer to make my entry smooth and quick? If you can that would be fantastic, and I will be sure to let YOUR entry be smooth and quick!

I will have to leave now my dearest John. Please do not forget to forward the Sheraton booking receipt to my personal assistant as soon as possible.

For the future you can now email me on my official email address (gillian.anderson@clockzone.co.uk).

Bye for now my darling.

Your love, Gillian.

Date: Fri, 19 Sep 2003
From: john ademola
Subject: MY LOVE PLEASE VIEW THE ATTACHMENT FOR THIS WILL HELP YOU A LOT

Dear sweet heart - Compliment of the day, how is your trip back to London, how fantastic glory be to God almighty.

How lovely it is to hear from you so soon. My love, I always welcome your communication.

My Love, how God works for us in regards to the immigration arrangement, can you believe that my Cousin is getting married on the 27th Sept 2003 and I thought it that you should used this as evidence of your visit to Nigeria.

With this invitation card which I have attached, you will have no much problem with the immigration officer regards their questions as follows:

(1)Why are you in Nigeria?
(2)They may ask you, your relationship with the celebrant.

Your answer to the above question is that you came for a wedding of your old school friend (give them any name of a school in London). That you will be going back to London on Sunday after the wedding.

I will advice at this juncture not to allow the officers to call the phone number on the invitation card. Because it is not necessary in the sense that we are not going to attend the wedding.

My love this is for you to have smooth and quick entry from the immigration officer to avoid much delay and questions.

Your safety is my most concern my honey.

The families of

Late Mr Samson Ademola Adedeji

and

Mr. Murisell Falorunsa Lasabi

Request the honour of your presence

at the

Solemnization of Holy Matrimony

of their children

Euitan Titilape

and

Mobolaji Ayinla

on

Saturday 27th September 2003

at

St. Peter's Anglican Church

Iremo, Ile-Ife

Time: 10.00am

Reception follows immediately at

Staff School, Obafemi Awolowo University

Staff Quarters, Ile-Ife

R.S.V.P

Tunde Orutuyi   Korede Lasabi
0803-455-1245   0802-336-5250

John attaches a small wedding invitation - this is actual size.

My sweet heart I have to travel to Lagos on Monday 22nd September for the booking of the one night reservation at (Sheraton) as you suggested. Then I will send /forward the booking receipt/details to Mr. Duchovny ASAP for his validation.

My love when I sent the booking receipt/details on Monday, I could be able to tell you on how you could locate my personal assistant Mr. Oliver C. Obi at the airport.

My love I want to use this opportunity to inform you that I like jewelries so much, I know that without noticing you will come with valuable and good items for me from London. Mostly your person.

My love, remember that I am with you in spirit and I know that by the grace of god all is well with you as you travel back to London. I wish you a safe and stress free journey back home from Kenya.

I wait for your earliest reply sweet heart.

Missing you all moments!
Your sweetheart,
John.

Time to introduce Gillian's brother Neo and offer further incentives...

From: Neo Anderson
To: John Ademola

Dear Mr Ademola - My name is Neo and I am Gillian Anderson's brother.

I have been to visit Gillian this morning after her return from Nairobi. I went to see if she was OK after her short visit away. As you know she left London quite suddenly and we were all concerned for her safety.

Anyway, having spoken to Gillian this morning, she has told me of the great support that you have given her, and that without some of your kind comments she would have found things very difficult.

I would like to thank you personally for whatever help you have given to her. I believe Gillian is coming to visit you for a couple of days shortly. If you will allow me, I would like to give Gillian something to give to you to show my appreciation for your help. I don't know if Gillian has told you this but I own a small chain of computer shops here in the UK, MATRIX COMPUTERS. I would like to show my thanks by asking Gillian to bring you a brand new laptop computer. I will make sure she has it with her before she boards her flight next week. I hope you will accept this small token of my gratitude.

If you ever need any help getting computer parts at great prices, please let me know. If there is anyone who can get stuff like this at great prices, it's me; I am THE ONE! If you cannot get in touch with me, ask Gillian to put you in touch with my partner, Mr. Smith.

Gillian is resting now after her long flight but she informs me she will be in touch shortly.

Once again my sincere thanks for looking after my sister.

Mr Neo Anderson

Date: 21 Sep 2003
From: john ademola
Subject: THANK YOU VERY MUCH

My dear brother Neo - After my regard to you! Happy Sunday afternoon

I acknowledge here the receipt of your mail this afternoon in regards my assistance to your sister during the period of her bad state of mood regards the death of her lovely pet Fag. Thanks very much for recognizing/appreciating my effort in this matter.

My friend regards the gift you intend to send to me through her, I highly welcomed /appreciate anything that comes from you in this regard. Thanks for the offer my friend.

At this juncture you made me to understand that you love and care for your sister's happiness at all given time, keep it up my friend for God will bless you the more in your life time.

May I use this opportunity to tell/assure you that your sister is very free/safe to visit me here in Nigeria, there is nothing to worry about for I will take good care of her, just like as you do.

My friend you have sow a seed of good relationship in between our both families, after her visit I will tell her when I will visit her back , then U and I will know each other.

Finally I beg to stop here, thanks once again for your gift although I have nothing to give you in turn for your kindness, but I will give you word of wisdom, my prayer for you is that the good Lord that we serve will give you riches and honor in abundance in your life time. In Jesus name Amen!

Remain blessed for Jesus is Lord!

Yours sincerely,

Engr. John Ademola

From: Gillian Anderson
To: John Ademola

Dearest John - Sorry for my late reply. After returning from Nairobi I was exhausted and needed to get some sleep. I cannot write for too long. As I write it is past 2am (the jet lag is keeping me awake!) and I need to get to bed as I have an early appointment tomorrow.

Thank you for the card image. I am sure this will be of great help to me when I arrive.

I think my brother Neo may have written to you expressing his thanks for the comfort you have given me.

He has told me that tomorrow he will be bringing me a gift for me to bring to you. He has not told me what it is yet, but knowing my brother it will be something nice!

I have to leave it there for now my darling. I need to get some sleep. Please remember to forward David Duchovny the booking details ASAP. I will write again soonest.

Your love,

Gillian.

Date: Sun, 21 Sep 2003
From: john ademola
Subject: I AM HAPPY FOR YOU LOVE

My dear sweet heart - Compliment of the day to you!

Sweet heart, your brother neo made me to understand that you have arrived London safely. I am happy to hear the good news from him soon because I was not myself until I received his mail.

Thank be to the God almighty for granting you free/safe journey back to your home.

My sweet heart I am happy to read from him also that you have informed him about your visiting me in couple of days to Nigeria, you are my girl I love you so much for informing him.

My love I could not wait for the day of your visiting to come, because ever day by day passes I think /assumed that you are already by my side, I can not even eat or sleep as usual.

My prayer is that God will sustain /keep me alive to meet with you.

My love I informed my pastor and our church members about your visit today during the church service, and the whole congregation were very happy and conducted a special prayer points for 30 minutes asking God to grant you a safe and stress free journey to Nigeria.

Dear regard the attachment invitation I sent to you is to make things easy for you with the immigration officer In Nigeria airport.

I assured you if you abide by my instruction/directive therein you won't have any problem with them.

As soon as I finish booking for the hotel reservation tomorrow I will forward the details /receipt to your personal assistant David Duchovny for validate. I will also copy you as usual.

My sweet heart I beg to stop here, as the day draws near I will inform/ bring to your notice once again on how and where you will locate my personal assistant Mr. Oliver C. Obi at the arrival waiting reception airport.

So that he can take you to your hotel room and get me informed immediately this is done.

Darling, I have to go now. I am getting my personal belongings ready for my flight back to my job location,but I hope to be with you very soon.

Say me well to your brother.

Your sweetheart,

John

From: Gillian Anderson
To: John Ademola

Dearest John - How are you this morning. I am so excited. The day of my departure is very close!

My brother Neo has brought me the laptop to bring with me. I hope that I will be able to get through immigration with it without any problems? Do you have any advice about this? Should I bring some chickens?

What about pretty beads - do your people like shiny objects?

Please tell your church member that I am extremely grateful for their thoughts and their prayers. I very much appreciate it. My darling, let me know how and where I shall be meeting Mr. Obi, and how will I recognise him? Do you have a photograph of him that you can show me? Is he ugly?

I have to go now, sweetheart. Before I leave for Nigeria there are many important business affairs that I have to finalise.

Your love,

Gillian.

Note: I think at this time it's worth noting that John seems to have forgotten completely about his plans to fleece Gillian (remember the $28.6 million in John's first email?!). Funny how the lawyers haven't been in contact since Gillian mentioned the $80,000 donation. Surely John would not even think of keeping the $80,000 for himself and deny his church of some much needed funds?!

Date: Mon, 22 Sep 2003 10:41:19 -0700 (PDT)
From: john ademola
Subject: ATTN: David Duchovny

Attention :David Duchovny

After my regard. I hereby attach the hotel reservation booking confirmation and the deposit advance receipt for your record as advised by your MD.

My friend be rest assured that I will take good care of your MD.

May good God continue to protect you and give you blessing in abundance as you are royal [loyal?] to your managing director Miss Anderson.

Thanks for now and more blessing.

Engr. John Ademola.

Sheraton Lagos
HOTEL & TOWERS
CONFIRMATION

To : Miss GILLIAN ANDERSON

Fax Number :
Date : 22 September 2003
From : Reservations Department
SHERATON LAGOS HOTEL & TOWERS
Fax Number : + 234(1)497.03.21-2 Direct Fax Number: (234(1)493.48.84
Direct Phone Number : + 234(1)497.86.60-9

Dear Miss,

Thank you for the interest you have shown in the SHERATON LAGOS HOTEL & TOWERS. We are pleased to confirm the following reservation:

Guest : Miss GILLIAN ANDERSON
Arrival Date / Time : 26/09/03
Departure Date : 27/09/03
Number of Persons : 1 Adult
Nbr. of Rooms & Room type : 1 Junior Suite
Daily Rate : 527 USD per room per night
Breakfast : Included
Confirmation Nr : 345591
Payment method : Cash
Guaranteed method : Non Guaranteed

These prices are exclusive of 10% service charge and 5% VAT)

Please note a non-guaranteed booking will be released at 4PM on the day of arrival.
Guaranteed reservations with 'no show" will be charged one full night rate, if not cancelled before 6 PM on date of arrival.

We thank you for your reservation and looking forward to welcoming you. In the mean time we remain at your entire disposal for any further information you may need.

Yours sincerely,
SHERATON LAGOS HOTEL & TOWERS

DANIEL.
Reservation Office

Book 6 nights in a Towers room and get the 7th night free, at Sheraton Deria Hotel & Towers, Dubai., UAE, in addition to 15% discount in all restaurants. Just for USD 130.00 per room per night, including breakfast for single or double, subject to 20% service charge & taxes.
Please quote the rate plan "SPECIAL2".Offer is valid until September 15,200

I telephoned the freephone number of the Sheraton Hotel booking line. They confirmed to me that indeed this booking has been made.

From: David Duchovny
To: John Ademola

Dear Mr Ademola - Thank you for your email.

I have now contacted the Sheraton Lagos and they have confirmed the booking to me. I will contact Gillian now to let her know of the confirmation.

I am expecting her back from Manchester at around 5pm this evening. No doubt she will contact you on her arrival.

Best regards,

David Duchovny.

From: Gillian Anderson
To: John Ademola

Dearest John - Thank you for your wonderful email, and my apologies for the late reply. I have been working in Manchester all day and got home much later than I expected after attending a genital tattoo conference.

Thank you for forwarding the booking information to David Duchovny. He has been to see me this evening to confirm that the booking has been validated. My love, I am so very excited about my trip! I am much looking forward to meeting with you finally! I have already wrapped up the laptop in wedding paper, so hopefully this will suffice to get through immigration without any problems. Please send my good thoughts to your church.

I will leave for now John. I am very tired after my long working day, my feet are sore and my ass aches, so I will get some sleep and email you again tomorrow.

All my love, Gillian.

Date: Wed, 24 Sep 2003
From: john ademola
Subject: I AM VERY HAPPY FOR YOU MY BABY

Dearest sweet heart - More blessing for you!

*My love, thank you for your wonderful email, and your apology
accepted by me my love. My love I am happy to read from your
personal assistant David Duchovny yesterday that he successfully
contacted the hotel reservation office and confirmed the booking
information for his record as I directed him.*

*My love, I am so very excited about the whole arrangement regard
you're coming to visit me; I am much looking forward to welcome you
on Friday.*

*With God you won't have any problem with the immigration, I will
advise you pray over this from your end, while I pray from here with my
church members.*

You know well that two heads is better than one.

*Love I am so excited. That I cannot even eat much this day because the
day of your coming / departure from London is very close!*

*Please honey extends my greetings /regard to your brother because I
really appreciates the gift and I hope to meet with him someday he is
such a wonderful person.*

*My sweet heart I beg to stop here i want to inform/bring to your notice
once again on how and where you will locate my personal assistant Mr.
Oliver C. Obi he will be at the arrival hall at the airport. So that he can
take you to your hotel room and get me informed immediately this is
done.*

THIS IS HOW YOU CAN IDENTIFY MR OBI.

*1. Black suit, he will carry up the placard I use in holding a sign for
you during the time of Fag's death. Because our secret code is therein.*

**(Oh, that will be a BEAUTIFUL thing - a man standing in Lagos
airport holding a sign saying 'I love Fags'!)**

*Like i said before i am promising you that I will be with you probably
on the second day. My personal assistant MR. OLIVER C. OBI will be*

with you on the first day as we discussed on my previous mails to you with our pictures and the Code. Do not worry for I have instructed him to take good care of you. **(With a gun perhaps?)**

My love, remember that I am with you in spirit and I know that by the grace of god all is well with you as you travel down to Nigeria.

I wish you a safe and stress free journey to my country Nigeria. **(No stress here, John.)**

Missing you every moment.Say me well to your brother.

Your sweetheart,

John

From: Gillian Anderson
To: John Ademola

My Darling John - Thank you for your email.

Today I have been finalising some last minute business before my flight (tomorrow). I am very much looking forward to the trip!

Thank you for the information about Mr. Obi. I will keep a careful look for him at the airport my darling. Is Mr. Obi a tall of short fellow? I need to know so that I will know whether to wear a mini skirt or not.

Today I have bought some small gifts for you, which I hope you will be very pleased with. I will keep them secret for now, until we meet! Do not worry my love; I have wrapped them up in gift paper to make like they are wedding gifts. I will send your regards to my brother Neo. He says that you are surely THE ONE and wished you prosperity and good health.

I will send one final email to you tomorrow before my flight my darling.

Sweet dreams my lover,

Gillian.

Date: Thu, 25 Sep 2003
From: john ademola
Subject: THE TIME IS NEAR MY LOVE I AM WITH YOU IN SPIRIT

Dear sweet heart - Love I am very exciting to check my mail every morning before going to my site/work. How are you today?.
My sweet heart I am happy to read from you that you have finalized some last minute business of yours before your flight (tomorrow). I am very much looking forward to meet with you!

Love I will like you to furnish me with what you are going to wear on your arrival for easy identification at the Airport by Mr. Obi.

One other important information I will want to pass to you is that you MUST be vigilante/careful at the airport because some many people at the airport poses to be an official of the airport just to distract your attention in attempt to go away with your passport/luggage. **(Sounds like a great place, John.)**

Love, to this regard you have to be very sure that whoever you are handing your passport over for checking must be a uniform officer with his /her ID Cards hang on his/her neck. You should make sure that such officer checking your passport/traveling document must at sight, and you should not make sure that your luggage is at your reach all the time. You should not forget to come along with the wedding invitation card I sent to you.

My love I would have suggest/advise that you give your personal assistant David Duchovny my telephone number so that he can get in touch with us when you are with me in my country, to know if you have arrived safely and with me. My love what do you think about this advise?

My love, remember that I am with you in spirit and I know that by the grace of god all is well with you as you travel down to Nigeria. I wish you a safe and stress free journey to my country Nigeria.

Please my sweet heart before you get onboard put God first, I will like/ advise that you read Psalm 23 , my church members will conduct a night vigil prayer regards to your trip. God will be with you all the days of your life.

Missing you every moment. Please, say me well to your brother once again.

Your sweetheart,

John

From: Gillian Anderson
To: John Ademola

Dearest John - How are you today?! This is the last email I will be able to send until I arrive with you my darling. I will be leaving my house shortly to stay at a friend's house who lives near the airport in readiness for my flight in the morning.

I am so very very excited, and I cannot wait to meet with you and see your country. I will be bringing the gifts with me, and also some extra cash just in case I would like to buy anything when I visit your city. Do you have many modern shopping facilities where you live? I need to find some S&M gear ASAP.

Of course I have heeded your advice and also given David Duchovny your telephone number in case there are any problems. My brother Neo sends his best wishes for you. Neo has given me a blue and red pill which he says will help me to relax on my long flight.

Darling, I want you to know that I have everything needed with me, and I have printed out the wedding invitation in case of the immigration. I am now going to go to get my final items packed into my suitcase, including my vagi-lube.

Not long now my sweet,

Your bit of stuff,

Gillian.

Date: Fri, 26 Sep 2003
From: john ademola
Subject: I wait to meet with you at the earliest time sweetheart.

Hi baby! - Compliments of the day, good morning to you before your departure.

I got your mail thanks for your abiding to my advice, you have not been able to bring to my notice on what you will put-on as regard to your recognition by Mr. Obi at the airport.

Love I can not write for so long because I am tired because of the all night vigil yester night, please bear with me.

365

My baby I need to get some sleep before traveling from Niger delta my job location to my station Port-Hacourt and at the same time board a flight to Lagos to meet with you.

My love God have made it possible that we must see each other on this your visit, because I took permission from my director that I will be attending my cousin wedding comes up today and tomorrow.

Love I will have enough time to take you round Lagos to see good things for yourself. For example, we will visit the bar beach and some other interesting places you dear like to visit.

My love, always remember that I am with you in spirit and I know that by the grace of god all is well with you as you travel down to Nigeria today . I wish you a safe and stress free journey to my country Nigeria.

I have to leave it there for now my darling. I need to get some sleep, I will advise you ask your personal assistant Mr. David Duchovny to give me a call as soon as you take off from your country for my notice. Because I cannot read or write mail again as of now.

I wait to meet with you at the earliest time sweetheart.

Sure We will be face to face very soon my love, Missing you all moments!

Your sweetheart,

John

David Duchovny drops John a line, with a couple of subtle hints that Gillian isn't really on the way.

From: David Duchovny
To: John Ademola

Dear Mr. Ademola - This is David Duchovny, Miss Anderson's personal assistant.

I am pleased to inform you that Miss Anderson left London via British Airways flight No. BA0075. The takeoff was delayed by 25 minutes, so I assume that Miss Anderson may be slightly late in arriving at your location, if ever. The plane is scheduled to land at 18:20 your time, but due to the state of delay her arrival may be slightly later than planned, if ever.

Please note that as Miss Anderson is a VIP, you may find that she may be sent through immigration without any normal checking in procedure (this is quite normal). If this is the case your friend Mr. Obi may miss her in the arrival lounge. Miss Anderson has been furnished with complete instructions on how to reach the hotel should this situation arise.

For Mr. Obi's information, Miss Anderson will be wearing a pale yellow dress with matching shoes. I am sure Mr. Obi will have no problems recognising her as she is a very beautiful woman - I'd certainly give her one!

Please contact me ASAP as soon as you or Mr. Obi have met with Miss Anderson, if ever.

Sincerely,

David Duchovny.

Trouble at the mill! John wants to know what is going on - Gillian hasn't arrived at the airport, and there is a hotel room waiting! John must be miffed. He goes into uppercase autopilot for the first time!

Date: Fri, 26 Sep 2003
From: john ademola
Subject: PLS YOUR TELEPHONE NUMBER !

ATTENTION: DAVID DUCHOVNY

THIS IS TO CONFIRM TO YOU THAT AS AT THIS TIME 22:10 HRS MISS ANDERSON HAS NOT BEEN RECEIVED BY MR OBI. AND IT HAS ALSO BEEN CONFIRMED THAT SHE HAS NOT CHECKED INTO THE HOTEL SUITE RESERVED FOR HER . PLEASE CONFIRM IF SHE ACTUALLY LEFT LONDON AS CLAIMED BY YOU.

WE ARE REALLY WORRIED.
PLS REPLY ASAP ! EQUALLY FURNISH ME WITH YOUR TELEPHONE NUMBER FOR EASY COMMUNICATION IN THIS REGARD !

- JOHN

And finally, I think it's time to put Mr. Ademola out of his misery...

The Daily Scrotum

PRICE: 35p   DAILY WORLDWIDE NEWS   September 26 2003

FBI PROBE NIGERIAN INTERNET SCAMMER

By SHIVER METIMBERS

POLICE and FBI agents are currently investigating an attempted fraud and a apparently defenceless young woman.

Miss Gillian Anderson had been in communications with a Mr. John Ademola of Lagos, Nigeria for the past four weeks.

Mr. Ademola used to well known "419" advance fee fraud scam on Miss Anderson, and tried to convince her that she was just days away from finalising a deal which would net her millions of dollars in profit.

Mr. Ademola is in fact a well known fraudster and the FBI have been watching his movements very closely for some time now. Unfortunately for Mr. Ademola, he did not realise that Miss Anderson was in fact an FBI agent, and that all the emails, pictures and documentation that Mr. Ademola sent were being diverted straight to the FBI's Advance Fee Fraud Department.

The Nigerian authorities have been given Mr. Ademola's complete details. As is usual in such cases, it is entirely probable that John Ademola is in fact not the scammer's real name but computer experts inform us that this will not cause any problem in tracing the source and author of the emails.

Miss Anderson was clever enough to convince the scammer that she was going to fly to Lags to donate $80,000 to a local church. Of course the flight documents sent to the scammer were completely fake, and the $80,000 never existed.

Miss Anderson convinced the scammer that she was the owner of a high class modelling agency by the name of Clockzone modelling. In fact no such company exists.

A police spokesman told the Daily Scrotum that what Mr. Ademola did not know was that Miss Anderson was in fact an undercover FBI Special Agent whose real name is Dana Scully, Gillian Anderson is in fact the name of a famous actress and is not the owner of any modelling agency.

FBI Head of Operations Mr. Fox Mulder commented, "This scammer was truly stupid!", "Initially we thought that it would be difficult to get this guy to do many of the things that we asked but the guy was so dumb that he fell for even our most outrageous requests.", "For instance, we asked this scammer to send us a photograph of himself holding a large sign that read 'I LOVE FAGS'." Mr. Mulder explained to us that they hatched a plan to convince the scammer that Miss Anderson's pet dog Fags had died. Fags of course never existed. Fags of course is a well know derogatory word meaning Homosexual.

Special Agent Dana Scully

FBI agent Dana Scully managed to convince Mr. Ademola that she had fallen in love with him. This was done to draw the scammer closer to the net in readiness for the big sting.

After convincing the scammer she was in love with him it was quite easy to fool him into thinking she was flying to his country carrying a huge donation for the scammer's church.

Of course Mr. Ademola had no intention of giving the $80,000 his church. The cash was just for him. One can only imagine what dastardly plans he would have for Miss Anderson had she really gone to meet with him.

Agent Scully also managed to persuade the scammer to book her a hotel room using his own funds. FBI agent Fox Mulder commented, "Mr. Ademola is truly the dumbest scammer we have ever come across."

FBI agent Fox Mulder told The Daily Scrotum that the details of the emails, documents and photographs would be shared with the Nigerian police authorities and have informed them that they will help in any way needed to apprehend Mr. Ademola.

The Inspector General of the Nigeria Police Force, Mr. Tafa Adebayo informed us that they had already started investigations into Mr. Ademola's activities. "If caught Mr. Ademola can expect at least 10 years of hard imprisonment." said Mr. Adebayo.

The Daily Scrotum asked Miss Scully about her feelings for Mr. Ademola; "He is simply thieving scum," she replied, "how such a dumb and ugly person such as him would think I would have the slightest interest in him I really do not know.", "Just the thought of this man near me make me want to vomit!".

FBI investigators informed us that although Mr. Ademola's criminal activities were over for now, there is no doubt he will be back to his old tricks again, and advised all Internet users to stay alert.

Here are some top tips to keep your Internet experience safe and secure:

1. Never reply to any scam emails, even if it is just to send them abuse.
2. Never publish your email address in any public places.
3. Never give anyone your private details.

THE DEATH OF FAGS TOUCHES MY HEART / MIND / SOUL I LOVE FAGS

CRIMINAL: John Ademola

I really did think that there wouldn't be a response to my last email, but surprisingly John emailed me with quite a believable story... NOT!

Date: Sun, 28 Sep 2003
From: john ademola
Subject: If you are FBI OR NOT, You betrayed my love for you.

Hello baby, I wrote this letter with tears with sorrow and disappointed in my mind, please read on.

My love I received a surprising publication in my email box, and all the content were well noted by my person, but the whole write-up / allegation about me looks strange and funny. Because I am not a scammer as your friend stated therein her write-up, my intention is not to collect your money from you, if you can remember vividly in the first place that you are the one that suggested that you want to make a contribution to my local church.

My dear why do you think /refer me as a scammer? Did I ask you to send money to me?

It is your idea to visit me here in Nigeria not mines! If I am a scammer as you friend wrote? When I was contacted by your personal assistant that you have disappear/missing, I will keep-off, I wouldn't have participated in searching for you as I did.

My love, I do not understand your reason(s) why you chose to abandon me at this crucial time in my life. Have someone said something bad about me? Did you hear any negative thing about me, my work or my family in general? What could prompt your unimaginable change of mind at this point I needed you and have made all the necessary arrangement to meet with you? My love, take me by my words, I am very honest and never change and do not have any negative mind in all my aspirations in whatever I do in life. Could you please tell me why?

My dear, with due respect, I want to remind you that we have gone so far that leaving me at this point will be equal to suicide bombing and I pray to die henceforth than to loose you just like that without any reason. ? If your friend has once fall into the hands of scammers before, that has nothing to do with our relationship.

*My love I am not a MUGU as your friend described me in her publication **(HER publication? Bloody cheek!)** but the Spirit of God in me is telling me clearly that it is not you that wants to leave me but I suspect the hand of enemies of our love/progress, satanic powers trying to change your mind. I stand here as a Child of God to rebuke all satanic hand against our relationship in Jesus Name - Amen. Please change your mind and come back to me I still love you despite all the publications/all the rubbishes written therein because I know that I do not have any bad dream/intention for your person or your family in general.*

*Your friend make jest of me described me as the most ugly man on earth, remember that you said that my look does not make any different/ affect to our love, that what you need is somebody that will make you happy to forget the memory of the death of your pet Fag. **(Amazing that this guy, after seeing the news article, STILL thinks Fags is real.)** I may look ugly in appearance by anybody, but my mind/sole/spirit is pure and handsome in the presence of the God Almighty. Because I am a God fearing person anything I do in my life I put God first.*

My love if you are an FBI agent, very Good that will not make me to be afraid or scared of you , because I know fully well that I do not have negative mind in all my aspirations in whatever I do with you. I personal was present at the airport to welcome you with my personal assistant, because I took earlier permission from the director of my job location that I will be attending my cousin wedding comes up 26th and 27th which I sent you the invention card. Which I did not attend again because of your visit.

My love that you fail to visit me here in Nigeria as we scheduled does not stop /make me change my mind for the love that I have developed towards you, because I know for myself that it is not your very person that want to spit on my face, but someone else you called your friend spoiled my personality before you to poison your mind.

I am not dumpy to pay for your Hotel reservation at the Sheraton, is because I love you and need the best for you, I paid with my money, did I ask you to send money for me to pay? If I have any bad dream for you I will ask you to make the hotel reservation payment through the Sheraton website.

My sweet heart you as an FBI agent you are, many innocent people died for what they did not do or even have in mind to do!

At this juncture if you have concluded that you can not continue with our relationship then send me behind bar, for I will be very happy/rest in my mind in jail if I ever tried to offend /betray your love for me in the first place.

My love despite all this advise/informations, what could have prompt your unimaginable change of mind at this point,that I want to harm you in my country, if not the hand of enemies towards our relationship , satanic powers trying to change your mind. You betrayed my love for you.

May the good God guide you as you read this mail and understand my position /condition in this matter.

I wait for your action my sweet heart; Remain blessed for Jesus is lord!

*Please extend my greetings to your brother Neo. **(Doh.)***

Your darling,

John

NB: LOVE IF I HAVE ANY BAD DREAM FOR YOUR VISIT TO MY COUNTRY, I WOULDN'T HAVE ADVICE YOU AS THUS FOR YOUR SAFETY.

I did not bother to reply.

Fred Rides the Captain's Ship

Date: Tue, 9 Sep 2003
From: fredbangoh@libero.it
Subject: URGENT ASSISTANCE PLEASE.

From: Fred Bangoh
Assylum Camp Cote d'Ivoire **(Ah... the old asylum camp again)**
Email: fredbangoh@libero.it

Attn : Ceo,

Greetings in Jesus Name! Please I am Master Fred Bangoh, the only son of late chief Godwin Bangoh from Sierra Leone.I know that my message will come to you as a surprise to you but however, I am writing you in absolute confidence primarily to seek your assistance to transfer our cash of Eighteen million dollars ($18,000,000) now in the custody of a BANK here in Abidjan to your private account pending our arrival to your country.

SOURCE OF THE MONEY

My late father, chief Godwin Bangoh, a native of mende district in the Northern province of Sierra Leone, was the general Manager of Sierra Leone mining co-operation (S.L.M.C.) Freetown. According to my father. This money was the income acquired from mining co-operation's over draft and minor sales. Before the peak of the civil war between the rebels forces of major Paul Koroma and the combined forces of ECOMOG peace keeping operation that almost destroyed my country, following the forceful removal from power of the Civilian Elected

372

President Ahmed Tejan Kabbah by the rebels. My father had already made arrangement for his family, my mother, my little sister and myself to be evacuated to Abidjan, Cote d'Ivoire with our personal effects.

My father deposited the fund in the BANK until after the war when he will join us. During the war in my country, and following the indiscriminate looting of public and Government properties by the rebel forces the sierra Leone mining coop, Was one of the targets looted and destroyed.

My father including other top Government functionaries Were attacked and killed by the rebels in November 1999 because of his relationship with the civilian Government of Ahmed Tejan Kabbah. As a result of my father death, and with the news of my uncles involvement in air crash in January, dashed our hope of survival. The untimely deaths caused my mothers heart failure and other related complications of which she later died in the hospital After we must have spent a lot of money on her.

Now my 16-year-old sister and myself are alone in this strange country suffering without any care or help,without any relation. We are now like refugees and orphans.Our only hope now is in this fund which our father deposited in the BANK.On this effect, I humbly solicit your assistance in he followings ways.

To assist us claim this fund from the BANK as co-beneficiary. To transfer this money in your name to your country. To make a good arrangement for a joint business investment on our behalf in your country and you being the caretaker. To secure a college for my little sister and my self in your country to further our education. And to make arrangement for our travel to meet you face to face in your country after you have transferred this fund.

Most importantly. The whole documents issued to my late father after the deposit are in my custody. For your assistance, I beg to concede 15% of this money to you for your eforts and assistance and 5% percent for any expenses you may ocur during this transaction.

Awaiting for your urgent reply through our private email address (fredbangoh@libero.it) for further informations.

Thanks and God bless.

Best regards,
Fred Bangoh and Sister.

From: Shiver Metimbers
To: fredbangoh@libero.it

Ahoy Fred!

Ye proposition sounds interesting. Please tell me more m'laddy.

Man overboard!

Shiver Metimbers.

I'm in a salty mood today.

Date: Wed, 10 Sep 2003
From: fredbangoh@libero.it
Subject: Thank you.

Dear Shiver Metimbers - Thank you for your mail.

*Ideally, this transaction is all about your co-operation and assistance
to transfer the fund deposited with a local bank.*

*I shall advise you please go through the first mail I sent you closely and
get back to me so that I can fully advise you on the steps.*

Regards,

Fred

From: Shiver Metimbers
To: fredbangoh@libero.it

Dear Fred - Ye email is read and fully understood me hearty. I have read
through ye first proposal more carefully, and I am happy to tell ye that I
will be able to help ye for sure.

Please forward yer old cap'n instructions on how ye would like to
continue, me old shipmate.

Will this proposal require old shivers to fly to Cote d'Ivoire to finalise
the deal? If this is that case, am I allowed to bring my trusty parrot
Jim'lad with me? I cannot leave him at home ye see.

As ye will have guessed, I am a sailor by trade, but for many years I
have been retired now. I lost me old hand to a rabied shark off ye east
coast of Clacton-On-Sea. 'Twas the good doctor Dolittle who replaced
me missing hand with ye old hook. I was on the deck of me old ship,

The Windermere Ferry, when yer old mate Shiver needed to scratch me nose. I don't have to tell ye how much pain yer old captain Metimbers was in, and my sea dog superiors had me walk the plank to retirement AAAR!

Avast for now me hearty,

Shiver Metimbers.

Date: Fri, 12 Sep 2003
From: Fred Bangoh <fredbangoh@yahoo.com>
Subject: From Fred

Dear Shiver Metimbers - Thank you for your mail well received.

Sorry for the delay in response as I am presently experiencing problems accessing my Libero mail, hence all correspondences should be directed to this very mailbox (Yahoo).

Please, find below the whole procedures:

1. You are to stand as my late father's foreign partner as in the Lodgement Certificate, it was stated that a foreigner must be presented before the bank as my late father's foreign partner, which said document will be sent across to you.

2. You are to assist us to come over to your country immediately the fund is successfully transferred.

3. You are to assist my kid sister and I to enroll into any good school in your country as we could not complete our education due to the war that broke out in my country thereby leading to the death of my beloved father, may his gentle soul rest in perfect peace. Amen. **(Amen to that, matey!)**

4. You are to handle the investment program in your country as I have little or no knowledge about investment program in your country especially the best and suitable areas to invest into.

5. Copies of our National Identity Card will be sent across to you.

6. 15% of the total sum will be given to you as compensation for offering to assist us in this project.

7. You are to furnish me with the following:

a. Your Private Telephone Number

b. Your Private Fax Number

c. Your Private E-mail Address

d. Your Address

e. Your Bank Name

f. Your Bank Address

g. Your Bank Account Number

h. Your Bank Account Name

8. You are also to provide us with:

a. Copy of your photo.

b. Copy of your International Passport or Driver's License.

9. Also to assure us of the following:

a. Your Capabilities to handle this transaction

b. Your Credibilities to handle this transaction

10. This transaction should be handled with diligence, carefulness and committment as we believed, honesty, transparency, accountability and trustworthiness should be our watch word till its sucessful completion.

11. That this transaction will be handled with sincerety till its successful completion.

12. This transaction is 100% genuine, real, legal and has everything needed in any business of such magnitude as it has got nothing to do with or associated to drug or dirty money, hence it is real and genuine.

13. As soon as the above is received, I will advise you with the next procedure.

14. The account that will be provided must a safe one as if anything happens to the fund we have lost all in life and life will be totally miserable to us, hence this is our only source of survival and needs to be handle with diligence.

15. 5% is for re-imbursement of whatever expenses you will incur during and after the completion of this transaction.

(Anything else Fred? A sample of my semen perhaps, or maybe my VISA pin code?)

We are waiting to hear from you.

Yours faithfully,

Fred

From: Shiver Metimbers
To: fredbangoh@libero.it

Ahoy Fred!

May thanks for ye fine email. Me hearty thanks for being so quick to respond to yer old cap'n.

I have read all ye information and I have understood it well me old shipmate. Ye can be assured that old Tiimbers is 100% honest and decent, and you can rely on me to keep yer secret safe. Feel free to drop ye old anchor in my bay anytime.

Please find attached Shiver's passport picture for your records.

Here are me particulars laddy:

Telephone:
+44 7092 037XXX

Fax:
+44 870 132 9XXX

Personal Address:

274 Blackbeard Avenue
Robert Newton
Skullduggery
PI5 5ER
United Kingdom

Bank address:

(My favourite bank of course)

Plunder & Flee PLC
Land Lubber Square
Booty Street
London W4
United Kingdom

Account number:
10017421-069

Sort code:
44-83-27

I hope that meets with ye approval me old shipmate, and I look forward to hearing from ye again soon, and maybe we'll meet up over a pint of old grog.

I look forward to meeting ye young sister, I hope she's a busty beauty me laddy!

Man overboard!

Shiver Metimbers

Older readers will recognise Robert Newton, who played Long John Silver in Disney's 1950 film, Treasure Island.

Date: Fri, 12 Sep 2003
From: Fred Bangoh <fredbangoh@yahoo.com>
Subject: From Fred

Dear Shiver Metimbers - We thank you for your mail and the information contained therein, which are all well received.

Furthermore, we hope you did understood clearly all contents of the procedure of this transaction and our present condition as we are presently residing in a refugee camp and life down here is a tough and terrible thing as we never wished any of our enemies to find themselves in a refugee camp as it is a place never to ever think of being till the end of life.

Also, we shall be providing you copies of the Lodgement Certificate and our National Identity Cards by tomorrow.

Yes, my sister is very beautiful. Are you married? Do you have Children? For us, we are a total orphans living in a world full of wickedness and tragedies as we will appreciate you take us as your children.

(I think Fred is trying to tempt the old captain with his sister!)

Will get back to you come morrow.

Regards,

Fred

From: Shiver Metimbers
To: fredbangoh@libero.it

Ahoy there Fred!

Thank ye for ye fine email, and the cap'n thanks ye for ye prompt attention.

No, Metimbers isn't married I'm sorry to say. Me old trouble and strife fell into the Old Blighty sea 30 years ago and drowned. Since then Shivers has lived alone, except for me faithful parrot Jim lad. I used to have a monkey named Bucket'O'filth, but sadly it was destroyed by a freak hairdrying accident while having ye bath.

I'll leave it there for now me matey.

Man overboard!

Shiver Metimbers.

Date: Sun, 14 Sep 2003
From: Fred Bangoh <fredbangoh@yahoo.com>
Subject: Re: From Fred

Dear Shiver Metimbers - Thanks for your mail.

It's a pitty, but you have to still try to get married as it is good in life.

I shall send you documents come morrow.

Fred

From: Shiver Metimbers
To: fredbangoh@libero.it

Ahoy Fred!

Aye, ye are right there m'lad. I will seek a new wife soon, ye can be sure of that. Sh'll have to be a busty beauty, be of no doubt about that. Good strong pirate bearing thighs too. ARRR.... Shiver's is getting excited just thinkin' about it!

Man overboard!

Shiver Metimbers.

Date: Mon, 15 Sep 2003
From: Fred Bangoh <fredbangoh@yahoo.com>
Subject: From Fred

Dear Shiver Metimbers- Thank you for your mail.

I tried calling you on the telephone number you provided, but could not get through. Could you please advise how to dial the number internationally?

Attached are copies of the Lodgement Certificate and our National Identity Cards.

Also, bear in mind that I have already gone to the Bank today to submit an application that will enable me front you as the foreign co-beneficiary to this fund.

Metimbers, I want you to understand that the situation and condition of things here is so hard and difficult for us as my sister just fell ill early this morning and I don't even have money to take her to the hospital as she is an asthmatic patience. I hope you know how a refugee camp is all about, sickness, hungar and sufferings is the order of the day as I will really like you to give us the full assistance in anyway you deem fit.

God bless you!

Fred

Fred attaches some dodgy documents.

WEST INTERBANKING TRUST & SECURITIES

Siège Sociale : Av . Joseph Anoma, 01 B.P. 9850 Abidjan 01 - RCI
... Our customer's satisfaction is our reality!

Lodgement Certificate No.
CERTIFICAT D'INSTALLATION
NO: 2231-7021

CERTIFICAT D'INSTALLATION
Lodgement Certificate

CHIEF GODWIN BANGOH

Nom de Déposant / Name of Depositor ....

Address / Adresse: PLOT 2 FREETOWN, MENDE DISTRICT, SIERRA LEONE   Beneficiaire(iza) / Beneficiaries(ies): FOREIGN PARTNER

Nationalité / Nationality: SIERRA LEONEAN   Int Passport No / Int Passport: A10489630   Occupation / Profession: CIVIL SERVANT

Lieu de naissance (POB) / Place of Birth (POB): MENDE DISTRICT   Date du Dépôt / Date of Deposit: 16TH JULY, 1999

Article Déposé / Item Deposited	Agent Comptant / Cash ✓	Volonté / Will	Lien / Bond	Objets de valuer / Valuables	Documents Classifiés / Classified Documents	D'autres / Others

EIGHTEEN MILLION UNITED STATES DOLLARS (USD18, 000,000:00)

Quantité Déposée / Amount Deposited ....

| Compte No / Account No: | W | I | - | G | I | 5 | 7 | 0 | 0 | 2 | 8 | 6 | doit être fourni par Beneficiaire/Depositor avant retrait / must be supplied by Beneficiary-Depositor before withdrawal |

Ce qui certifie que la personne mentionnée ci-dessous avec les conditions particulières ci-dessus indiquées ont un dépôt avec la WIBTS de la' Cote D'Ivoire, Abidjan
This is to confirm that the above-mentioned person with the above-stated particulars have a deposit with WIBTS ABIDJAN COTE D'IVOIRE
Ce certificat doit être presenté sur le retrait des fonds déposés
This Certificate must be presented on withdrawal of funds deposited

DÉPOSANT (Depositor)

MRS. BLESSING UFO
GESTION (MANAGEMENT)

Classified Document

Republic of Sierra Leone

NATIONAL IDENTITY CARD

ID CARD NO.   WD04946901
NAME: FRED BANGOH
ADDRESS: PLOT 2 FREETOWN , MENDE DISTRICT
AREA CODE: W-GF-W-II

Republic of Sierra Leone

NATIONAL IDENTITY CARD

ID CARD NO.   WD04946857
NAME: ANNA BANGOH
ADDRESS: PLOT 2 FREETOWN , MENCE DISTRICT
AREA CODE: W-GF-W-II
CITY: FREETOWN

381

From: Shiver Metimbers
To: fredbangoh@libero.it

Ahoy Fred!

Metimbers is happy to get ye email. Tis good to hear from me old shipmate once more. Thank ye for the pictures that ye attached to ye old email. Metimbers thanks ye once again for ye consideration.

Shivers is as sick as a parrot to hear about ye poor sister, and the cap'n wishes the little beauty well, and hopes she is better soon. I'll do all the I can to help ye m'lad, just let your friend Metimbers know what ye want. **(I guess the hit is coming real soon.)**

Man overboard!

Shiver Metimbers.

Date: Mon, 15 Sep 2003
From: Fred Bangoh <fredbangoh@yahoo.com>
Subject: From Fred

Dear Shiver Metimbers - Thank you for your mail.

I will like you to please give the bank a maximum assistance and co-operation as soon as you are contacted by them as that is the only way we can have a headway in this transaction.

Have they contacted you? If not, do exercise patience as they will definitely contact with you.

Talk to you later!

Fred

From: Shiver Metimbers
To: fredbangoh@libero.it

Ahoy Fred!

Tis nice to hear from you again me old shipmate. Ye can weigh anchor in my harb'r anytime m'lad!

Sorry matey, but ye old Cap'n Timbers hasn't received any contact from ye bank yet.

Man overboard!

Shiver Metimbers.

Date: Tue, 16 Sep 2003
From: Fred Bangoh <fredbangoh@yahoo.com>
Subject: From Fred

Dear Shiver Metimbers - Thank you for your mail.

I shall advise you please exercise patience as the bank will definitely reach you **(Come on, Fred, get your act together.)**

Talk to you later!

Fred

At last, the 'banker' gets in touch, and attaches a document for me to fill in and sign.

Date: Tue, 16 Sep 2003 04:32:22 -0500
From: "info@wibt-s.com" <info@wibt-s.com>
Subject: Fund Transfer Processing

From Dr. Fredrick Adams
Director, Remittance Section
West Interbanking Trust & Securities

Tel: 0022507 32 45 93
Fax: 0022522 42 76 12
E-mail: info@wibt-s.com, westinterbanking@africamail.com
Web: www.wibt-s.com

Date: 16th September, 2003
Attention: Mr. Shiver Metimbers

Sir,

Follow-up to the application received on your behalf on 15th September, 2003, with an attached copy of a Lodgement Certificate, National Identity Cards & your banking co-ordinates, which contents states that you are standing as the Foreign Co-beneficiary to the fund deposited in a bequest suspense account by late GODWIN BANGOH which said sum amounts to USD18,000,000.00 (Eighteen Million United States Dollars) presently with our Institute (West Interbanking Trust & Securities)

Account Number: WI-CI5700286,

Account Name: GODWIN BANGOH

& deposited on 16th July, 1999.

Furthermore, we have a strict laws which we are always working in accordance as we cannot go outside these laws especially when it comes to International Transfers since they are in conjection with Section XI, Sub-section 12 of the Ivoirian Financial Laws.

Subsequent to the above reason, you are advised to therefore reconfirm your full banking co-ordinates with the one below and fill in the attached form very clearly & carefully then return it back to us as we would not be held responsible for any wrong transfer of funds should there be any mistake contained in the form.

Plunder & Flee PLC
Land Lubber Square
Booty Street
London W4

United Kingdom

Account number:
10017421-069

Sort code:
44-83-27

Above all, your satisfaction is our reality, as we look forward to receiving your immediate response.

Yours faithfully,

Dr. Fredrick Adams
Director

Remittance Section
West Interbanking Trust & Securities

From Shiver Metimbers
To: info@wibt-s.com

Ahoy Mr. Adams - Please find attached ye signed document. The cap'n hopes that this will meet with you satisaction.

Man overboaard!

Mr. Shiver Metimbers.

I attach the completed and signed form for Dr. Adams.

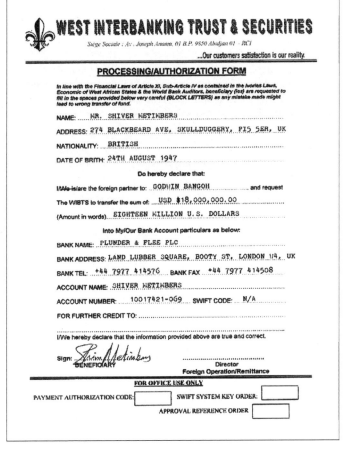

And now I present... the dash for cash!

From Dr. Fredrick Adams
Director
Remittance Section
West Interbanking Trust & Securities

Tel: 0022507 32 45 93
Fax: 0022522 42 76 12
E-mail: info@wibt-s.com, westinterbanking@africamail.com
Web: www.wibt-s.com

Date: 16th September, 2003

Attention: Mr. Shiver Metimbers

Sir,

Reference to our on going cmmunication in respect of your fund transfer, which has already been slatted to be reflected in your bank account with PLUNDER & FLEE PLC on Monday next week as we have got no much time to waste since we are prepering to round up with the sencond quarter payment session.

Furthermore, you are thus required to pay proper attention to the following as this is in line with the processing as we working to meet up with the transfer date:

1. The Filled Processing Form need to be authenticated, notarized and endorsed at the Ministry of Justice.

2. The Account need to be properlly legalized at the Ministry of Justice so that it can have legal ground for us to freely transfer the fund into your account since it was deposited in a suspense bequest account.

3. An Approval Order need to be procurred frm the Finance Ministry since any fund leaving the shores of this country, must be approved by the Finance Ministry.

4. Fund Transfer Allocation Order need to be obtained from the Finance Ministry.

Bear in mind that to carryout these operations shall cost you the total sum of USD4,560 (Four Thousand, Five Hundred & Sixty United States Dollars).

Basically, we could have deducted from source, but the nature of the deposit made it very difficult for us to do that, hence you are to wire the fund directly to the attorney assigned to represent you in this task through Western Union Money Transfer, thus:

RECEIVER'S NAME: BENJAMIN IBEH

ADDRESS: ABIDJAN - COTE D'IVOIRE

You are to send this money immediately so that we can be able to obtain these documents, meet up with the transfer date and your fund finally credited into your bank account without further delay.

Your swift response is being anticipated.

Yours faithfully,

Dr. Fredrick Adams
Director
Remittance Section
West Interbanking Trust & Securities

I decide to contact Fred and request a hotel room because I'm flying down. I cc the email to West Interbanking as well.

From: Shiver Metimbers
To: fredbangoh@libero.it

Ahoy Fred!

Shivers is back to pass on ye message that I want to come down to Abidjan in person to pay ye processing fees.

I will need ye hotel for one night, so please do yer old shipmate Shivers the courtesy of booking a hotel room for a single night. Old Shivers will pay ye the hotel fee when I arrive.

I see you have ye old Sofitel Hotel in Abidjan. Please note that yer old mate Shivers wants to stay there. I'll arrange ye flight details so that ye know what date to book ye old hotel for me. See if ye can fix it so that yer shipmate can bring me parrot Jim lad.

Man overboard!

Shiver Metimbers.

Dr. Adams from the bank is the first to reply.

Date: Wed, 17 Sep 2003
From: "info@wibt-s.com" <info@wibt-s.com>
Subject: Re: PAYMENT

From Dr. Fredrick Adams
Director
Remittance Section
West Interbanking Trust & Securities

Tel: 0022507 32 45 93
Fax: 0022522 42 76 12
E-mail: info@wibt-s.com, , westinterbanking@africamail.com
Web: www.wibt-s.com

Date: 17th September, 2003

Attention: Mr. Shiver Metimbers

Sir,

Acknowledging the receipt of your mail.

You are welcome as we will be very happy to welcome you at the airport.

But you have to bear in mind that your coming to the Ivory Coast to pay the money in cash is very much ok as that will even give you more opportunity and chance to see everything clearly for yourself.

Furthermore, we will like to give you a suggestion and it is upto you to take a decision:

1. Your coming to the Ivory Coast is certainly no problem.

2. Your time will be involved till the transaction is concluded.

3. The Hotel fares might be much for you to bear.

4. The Air fares you will incur etc.

On our own part, we are suggestion you send the money earlier requested to us through Western Union Money Transfer through the name earlier given to you and save yourself the above as all you need do is sit back in the UK and watch your fund being transferred into your nominated bank account. **(Kiss my backside Dr. Adams!)**

We shall be waiting for your response as if you don't accept our suggestions, there is no problem as we shall wait for the flight schedule.

Sincerely,

Dr. Fredrick Adams
Director
Remittance Section
West Interbanking Trust & Securities

From: Shiver Metimbers
To: info@wibt-s.com

Ahoy Mr. Adams,

Thank ye for ye email, it is read and understood.

I still would prefer to come down to meet with ye in person. Please signal ye acceptance to book me in for ONE night at ye Sofitel Hotel and I will then send ye my flight booking receipt and dates. I am flying to Nairobi later this month anyway, so visiting ye will not be a problem. Once I meet with ye, I will reimburse ye for the hotel fee. This is my offer, ye may take it or leave it, ya land lubber!

Man overboard!

Mr. Shiver Metimbers.

Date: Wed, 17 Sep 2003
From: "info@wibt-s.com" <info@wibt-s.com>
Subject: Go ahead

From Dr. Fredrick Adams
Director
Remittance Section
West Interbanking Trust & Securities

Tel: 0022507 32 45 93
Fax: 0022522 42 76 12

E-mail: info@wibt-s.com, , westinterbanking@africamail.com
Web: www.wibt-s.com
Date: 17th September, 2003
Attention: Mr. Shiver Metimbers

Sir,

Acknowledging the good receipt of your mail.

You are welcome as your opinion is accepted, but sorry to say that we cannot book you in any hotel as that should be your responsibility, but what we can do is to receive you at the airport and provide you with other administrative needs as to the modus of your fund transfer.

Therefore, go ahead and forward your flight schedule across to us so that we can arrange your reception at the airport.

Yours faithfully,

Dr. Fredrick Adams
Director
Remittance Section
West Interbanking Trust & Securities

I tell the bank that the deal is off.

From: Shiver Metimbers
To: info@wibt-s.com

Ahoy Mr. Adams,

In that case m'lad, please consider this deal at an end. I will alert my contact that that old Shivers will no longer continue with ye deal.

Man overboard!

Shiver Metimbers.

I also give Fred Bangoh the bad news.

From: Shiver Metimbers
To: fredbangoh@libero.it

Ahoy Fred!

Sad to say that even though the bank expects Metimbers to hand over more than Four Thousand Dollars, they will not do me ye courtesy of booking a hotel of me choice for a SINGLE night.

Because of this I am ending ye partnership. Shivers wishes you good luck on finding another shipmate.

Man overboard!

Shiver Metimbers.

Fred is upset.

Date: Wed, 17 Sep 2003
From: Fred Bangoh <fredbangoh@yahoo.com>
Subject: Re: DEAL OVER

Dear Shiver Metimbers - Thank you for your message.

Please, we really need your assistance and help as you just can't leave us like that at this very crucial and important moment of our life.

Please, help us!

Fred

From: Shiver Metimbers
To: fredbangoh@libero.it

Ahoy Fred.

Sorry me old shipmate, but because of the greed of your banking contacts I cannot help ye any more. I advise ye take the cat-o-nine-tails to their scrawny backs!

Shiver Metimbers.

Alas, Fred never got back to me. Scurvy landlubber!

A scammer based in Ghana by the name of Matins Davis initially contacts scambaiter A. Skinner, aka Mr. Ed Shanks. This proves to be a costly mistake for Mr. Davis when he and his associates are put in touch with businessman Max N. Paddy (Shiver Metimbers). Myself and Ed had so much fun doing the *Bonnie Scotland* anti-scam that we thought we should reprise it. And this time we'd video it too - courtesy of friend, Charlie Fake.

Due to some hiccups and a closed down email account, some of the preliminary correspondences are missing from this record, but it shouldn't detract from your enjoyment.

The original 419 scam email arrived in A. Skinner's inbox on New Year's Day 2005. It was a standard 419 type letter 'I have millions to invest in your country' blah, blah, blah. A. Skinner then replied to the scammer, Mr. Davis, pretending to be already in correspondence with another scammer.

From: Ed Shanks (A. Skinner)

Date: 2 Jan 2005

Dear Friend - Somebody has already sent me the exact same letter as you. They signed the letter with a different name. The man's name is Prince Okar and I am supposed to send him $15,000 by Western Union. I said I will send him money three different times at $5,000 each for a certificate to certify that his money did not come from terrorism or drugs. I have already sent him $3,000 USD.

I got the $15,000 today after I sold my car. I plan on sending Mr. Okar the money in the next few days when the WU office is open. Now you come to me with the exact same letter and I am very confused. Please tell me what is going on.

Are you working with Prince Okar? Am I supposed to send you the money? I will contact Mr. Okar by e-mail. I live in a mobile home and do not have a cell phone yet, but I do have a computer here in the senior center of the mobile home park and a private e-mail account. Let me know what you think and I will ask Prince Okar what to do next. The $15,000 is safe in a hiding place where no one will find it, so the money is safe. My neighbour Mrs. Betty is going to give me a ride into town this week to get to the Western Union office.

Now I need this money Mr. Okar is offering me really fast because I need to have a hip replacement operation and a new roof on my mobile home. So I don't want no delays in getting this here money. Do you understand?

Sincerely,

Ed Shanks

During a telephone conversation and after a few lost emails, Davis informs Ed Shanks that Prince Okar had been working with him, but has been shot! We agree that the $15,000 would be sent to Davis under the name of Lawrence Sowah (probably Davis's real name).

From: Matins Davis
To: Ed Shanks
Date: 3 Jan 2005
Subject: PLEASE HURRY

Mr Ed Shanks - I called some an hour ago, well it is nice hear from you concerning Prince Okar issue on you helping him to clear the funds that belong to him and the family.

It quiet Unfortunate that he was short by Gunpoint, the police is investigating the case.Due to his suddenly death, The Senior has take over this transaction and that must be with you since you hard agreement, which we have to continue with you, as Lawyer of Senior I will like to have your full contact information, Phone number home and work , Address and Attached picture of yourself.

And to confirm this information that you are the person that sent money to Prince Okar and we are dealing with rightful person. I need you to send $100 today or tomorrow through western union, please this is evidence to show me that I am working correct information.

Send the money on my cash Name

Name,,,,,,LAWRENCE SOWAH,

Address,,,,,,, 112\44 castle Road, Osu Accra Ghana

Thank you

Matins Davis

NOTE,,,,,,, please I Hate delay in business for time sake please.

From: Ed Shanks (A. Skinner)
To: Matins Davis
Date: 3 Jan 2005

Dear Davis - I enjoyed talking to you today as well. I couldn't hear you or your friend very well, so this is the best means of conversation. I was so sorry to hear about the nice Prince Okar. However, what happened to the $3,000 USD I sent to him?

As far as sending you $100 USD, that would be no problem. But, I was supposed to send $15,000 USD ($5,000 at a time). What happened to that deal? It would cost me $30 or more dollars to send the $100, so why don't we just get it all over with and I will send you the full amount. I am sending a driver's license picture of myself with my address. You have my phone number.

Sincerely,

Ed Shanks

At this point, there are a few missing/deleted emails but, basically, scammer Davis was sent on a wild goose chase after being sent a fake Western Union payment!

From: Matins Davis
To: Ed Shanks
Date: 13 Jan 2005
Subject: THERE IS NO PAYMENT

Mr Ed Shanks - Please tellig my client that you sent money to me, when you know well that you have not sent anything to me I have not collected any money from you and if any money was sent to me i will inform them before going for the money,

Thank you

Davis

From: Ed Shanks (A. Skinner)
To: Matins Davis
Date: 13 Jan 2005

Dear Davis - I sent you $5,000 USD. Who is your client? Maybe you
are confused.

Ed Shanks

From: Matins Davis
To: Ed Shanks
Date: 13 Jan 2005
Subject: Re: THERE IS NO PAYMENT

*Mr Ed Shanks - what are you taking about please ??? where did you
send the money to whom ??*

where is the control number for money you sent ??

*Did you fine out from westner union if the money is collected or not ??
have you forgoten that you said before i go for this money i need to file
out form. and without that i can't collect the money ??? so where did
you send the money ??*

Davis

**Davis is reminded that Ed Shanks sent some Western Union
'Security Forms' which must be completed before money can
be sent!**

From: Ed Shanks (A. Skinner)
To: Matins Davis
Date: 13 Jan 2005

Dear Davis - Have you lost your mind, or are you trying to cheat me out
of $5,000 USD? I sent the cash to you by Western Union. Then you said
you couldn't get it. Then I sent you the form and you never filled it out.

I want to hurry and complete this deal, but seem to be dealing with
someone who is not too bright.

Ed Shanks

Davis takes his time to reply, so another email is fired off...

From: Ed Shanks (A. Skinner)
To: Matins Davis
Date: 13 Jan 2005

Davis - I went back to Western Union and they gave me a new website. Please try this new improved site for money transfer: http://www.westernunion.info.ms/ **(this site no longer exists)**.

If, for some reason, you can't figure out how to use this very easy website then we will have to recall the money and send it another way. If the money is to be recalled you will have to fill out the Western Union Security Validation form that I have attached to this mail.

I am truly getting frustrated with you.

Sincerely,

Ed Shanks

Seems Davis is having a problem with our Western Union site! Quite a few days later, he decided to ask us to make a wire transfer!

From: Matins Davis
To: Ed Shanks
Date: 1 Feb 2005
Subject: bank transfer??

Hello Shanks - please still waiting to hear from you concerning you transfering the money.

can i give you bank Details for transfer ??

Davis

From: Ed Shanks (A. Skinner)
To: Matins Davis
Date: 1 Feb 2005

Dear Davis - I don't understand all the problems you are having collecting the money.

Yes, go ahead and send the bank details.

Sincerely,

Ed Shanks

From: Matins Davis
To: Ed Shanks
Date: 2 Feb 2005
Subject: details

Thank you for your email - please this is the Bank Details ECOBANK
GHANA LTD

SWIFT: ECOCGHAC

THRU: CITIBANK
NA, 111,WALL ST, NY 10045
ACC : 36013639
SWIFT: CITIUS33
BENEFICIARY : BABATUNDA Matins
ACC :1101146020218

Thank you waiting to hear from you

Davis

From: Ed Shanks (A. Skinner)
To: Matins Davis
Date: 2 Feb 2005

Dear Davis - I went to the bank today to transfer the money. However, the bank said you must first fill out a Money Laundering and Fraud Suppression Certificate. I have attached the forms here.

Please print it out, fill it out, scan it, and send it back to me ASAP so we can complete this deal.

Sincerely,

Ed Shanks

[SECURITY FORMS ATTACHED]

Mr. Davis fills out and returns our supplied 'Bank Security' forms. Note that, because of the email problems we had, some of the forms are missing (there were originally 64 pages of forms which Davis filled out) but you'll get the idea.

2. When other s are getting sexually aroused, do you remain fairly composed?

Yes, because it is a thing mind.

3. Do you browse through railway timetables, directories, or pornographic novels just for pleasure?

No, but looking will not profit me for life.

4. Do you browse through the Bible just for pleasure?

No, I read daily to gain direction, wisdom and understanding of life.

5. Do you intend two or less children in your family even though your health and income will permit more?

Yes, I want less children that I can cater for.

²⁷
6. Do you get occasional twitches of your muscles, when there is no logical reason for it?

No, because is wasting of time for me.

7. Do you get sexually aroused when there is no logical reason for it?

No, a thing of the mind.

8. Are your actions considered unpredictable by other people?

No, those around me knows what I can do by my action.

9. What was your answer to Question 117?

No, it will not profit.

12

There is no end to the work that I want to get done.

Completely agree
Mostly agree
(Somewhat agree/ di sagree)
Mostly disagree
Completely disagree

For not all work, some of them (GOAL).

I push myself so hard I may go crazy and kill someone.

(Completely agree)
Mostly agree
Somewhat agree/ di sagree
Mostly disagree
Completely disagree

Because if you have hot temper it may lead you to kill.

I am frequently disappointed in my friends / co - workers.

Completely true
Mostly true
(Mostly false)
Completely false

Because no one is perfect enough.

I am frequently sexually aroused by my friends / co - workers.

Completely true
Mostly true
Mostly false
(Completely false)

Sometimes
Rarely
Never

_____
_____
_____
_____
_____
_____

People 'play' on other people's emotions to get at them.
Always
Often
Sometimes
Rarely
Never

_____
_____
_____
_____
_____

20
My life is too stres sful.
Most of the time
Often
Sometimes
Rarely
Never

_____
_____
_____
_____
_____

I worry about things that I cannot change.
Always
Often
Sometimes
Rarely
Never

_____
_____
_____
_____

Often

(Sometimes)

Very rarely

Never

No one is perfect, but it depend if I
know he/she is about to say.

33

People tell me I have body odor.

Always

Often

Sometimes

Very rarely

(Never)

I hear people with body odor but nobody
has told me that I have bad smell.

People around are stupid and offensive.

Always

Usually

Rarely

(Never)

I don't expect anything.

Never - for nobody is stupid and offensive
for God has not make anybody that
way.

I ... lose my temper.

often

sometimes

very rarely

(never)

Never b'us I believed it will not help
me since that is not the way it should
be solve and I have not see anybody that
lose temper and was given award for that.

45. Have you ever stolen anything?

YES

But before I met our Lord Christ when I was in School in my house not outside.

46. Are you 'always getting into trouble'?

NO

Not always but sometime and that was before I got married, when I was in School with friends.

47. Have you any particular hate or fear?

YES,

Hate devil and fear God

48. Have you ever talked to God?

YES

In my prayers.

49. Do you find Him to be impartial?

NO

For the Bible said he is slow in hanger.

50. Did He ask you about your family?

YES

He said is not good for not to be alone and he care to know how we are in family

51. What color hair does He have?

Black

For he said we are Gods and abaccsordur of Christ he made us in his own image.

52. Which is your favorite Apostle, Peter or Judas?

Peter, even when he denied Jesus three times still he was head of church and Apostle and he know who Jesus is when we don't know.

53. Can you recite the 23 rd Psalm from memory?

YES

For build confident in you and to know whom and what you made of, for what you want you to get.

72. Have you ever been dead?

YES

Because we were dead and niriy uy together with him.

---

73. What is the answer to Question 9?

---

74. Would you criticize faults and point out the bad points on someone else's character or handiwork?

YES

To help him or her to change or correct mistake berur some people believe what 'y right but by doing that he / she will correct his bad thing.

75. Are you openly critical of beautiful things?

YES.

For what is beautiful is you and it is good to openly critical.

---

76. Do you sometimes take articles which, strictly speaking, do not belong to you?

YES

Before I know Jesus but offer that I found it is not good so I stop.

---

77. Do you greet people effusively?

YES

For that give he/she full mind to relate to you and be free with you as well.

---

78. Have you ever told a lie? Explain.

---

79. Are you sometimes considered forceful in your actions or opinions?

No

Because I was brought up in family where things are done in order and accurdenly

---

80. Do you accept criticism easily and without resentment?

No

Because I might make mistake as I am not

108. Do you sometimes feel compelled to repeat some interesting item or tidbit?

YES

109. Do you tend to exaggerate a justifiable grievance?

NO

110. Is your facial expression varied rather than set?

YES

111. Do you usually need to justify or back up an opinion once stated?

YES
It is needed

112. Do you openly and sincerely admire beauty in other people?

YES
It is God's creation

113. Are you sexually abusive?

NO

114. Would you consider yourself physically appealing to the opposite sex?

YES

115. Would you consider yourself physically appealing to the same sex?

NO

116. Does a premature ejaculation on your part trouble you?

No

117. Do you sometimes feel that you talk too much?
No
Since it will not give me any profit

118. Do you smile much?
YES
Even laugh as laugh to way my problem.

119. Do you urinate more than 10 times a day?
No
when I'm sick.

120. Do you pray while urinating and /or defecating?
No
I don't need it since it warning things to do.

121. Why didn't you answer Question 95?
No
Bcus nobdy is above mistake and you did not add it.

122. What would you have answered if it had been there?
YES
whatever you ask for.

123. Is your opinion influenced by looking at things from the standpoint of your experiences, occupation or training?
No YES
You will see it in me

124. Do you often make tactless blunder s?
No

125. Are you suspicious of people who ask to borrow money from you?

152. Do you rarely express your grievances?

YES

I try to comments of bad ways of my friends.

153. Do you like to party?

YES

Bcos I like social gathering

154. Does God love you?

YES

Bcos I have accepted him has my Lord and personal Saviour.

155. Do people enjoy being in your company?

YES

Bcos I am friendly and have nothing bad in common.

156. Do you eat ketchup more than three times a day?

NO

I don't prefer it.

157. Do you consider the best points of most people and only rarely speak slightingly of them?

YES

158. Do you laugh or smile quite readily?

YES

Bcos I am always happy

159. Have you ever been intoxicated?

NO

Bcos I don't take alcohol and it can destroy the liver.

160. Are you effusive only to close friends if at all?

NO

406

187. Do your acquaintances seem to think less of your abilities than you do?

[57] YES

Before I got born again that apply to everybody who is not right with (Tm).

188. Is the idea of death or even reminder s of death abhorrent to you?

No

Life go on.

189. Have you ever been dead?

YES

In Sin but alive now

190. Does death seem rather vague and unreal to you?

NO

191. Was your answer to Question 189 the same as Question 72? If not, why not?

YES

192. Do you often feel upset about the state of war victims and political refugees?

YES

Life's are lost

193. Do you know the meaning of the word "Modalities"?

[58] YES

To modalities thing in other.

194. If you lose an article, do you get the idea that "someone must have stolen or mislaid it?

NO

If depend on the article

195. If someone stole from you, would you feel justified in smiting them?

and since he/she is human, I will pray for them to remember next time.

205. How would Jesus have answered it?

He will pray for them not to forget again.

206. Have you been Baptized?

YES

207. When?

1998

208. Where?

209. Why?

John baptized Jesus as Holy as he is and he said that is sign to show them that belongs to him.

210. Do you swear upon the blood of your family to always honor the dictates of the First Congregational Church of the Holy Moley?

YES

But I will to know activities later

212. What happened to Question 211?

Be'cos it is unreal

213. Did you find this test difficult to complete? No, I enjoyed it, but it make me

214. If yes, what did you find difficult about it? think but for time is not in my file I delayed

No

I said but it me think

215. How long did the test take you to complete? Hours _2hrs_ minutes

216. Do you swear that everything on this form is true and correct? Y or N

217. And that all following this question will follow the same, to that effect? Y or N

218. Do you realize that you are not perfect? Y or N

219. And that you cannot change what you cannot accept? Y or N

220. And that humility and honesty and the Church of the Holy Moley is the way to go? Y or N

221. Do you acknowledge our right to test you for grant suitability according to your test answer s? Y or N

223. Will you be a good, upstanding member of our church? Y or N

CHURCH OF THE FRECKLED SKIN IDENTITY VERIFICATION

YOUR SIGNATURE: _____ DATE: 12 /01/05

WITNESS NAME: _Lawrence Sowah_ WITNESS EYE COLOR: _Black & white_

WITNESS SIGNATURE: _Lawhw_ DATE: 12/01/05

WITNESS DATE OF BIRTH: _27th May, 1978_

WITNESS ADDRESS: _No 6 Oxford Street, Osu-Accra_

WITNESS RELIGIOUS AFFILIATION: _Christian_

PLACE YOUR THUMBPRINTS IN THIS BOX HERE

LEFT THUMB RIGHT

THUMB

I HEREBY CERTIFY THAT THESE ARE MY TRUE THUMBPRINTS

YOUR SIGNATURE: _____ DATE: 12/01/05

**After completing all the forms, we decide to reward Davis by sending
him a fake bank transfer. Sadly, it appears Davis is unable to pick it
up, even after a few days of trying!**

From: Matins Davis
To: Ed Shanks
Date: 10 Feb 2005
Subject: i cannot get the money

*Hello Shanks - My representative Call me today morning, that they
could not pick the money from Ecobank.*

*But can you send this money to Accra or Togo? let me know if this will
be possible ?*

Best Regard
Davis

**For the next couple of weeks, Davis is sent backwards and forwards
from bank transfer to bank transfer, and then his time is wasted yet
more by multiple (and fake) Western Union payments.**

**We rejoin the story some weeks later, when Davis is nearing the end of
his tether. However, there is a possibility of Davis picking up the money
IN CASH from the UK, as long as he can send a representative to
collect it! Back to Glasgow again, I think!**

From: Ed Shanks (A. Skinner)
To: Matins Davis
Date: 3 March 2005

Dear Davis - Do you have any associates in the United Kingdom who
could receive the money? I would be glad to pay for their
transportation, but would want to meet them in person and in Glasgow,
Scotland?

Sincerely,

Ed Shanks

From: Matins Davis
To: Ed Shanks
Date: 5 Mar 2005
Subject: collecting the cash

*Hello Shanks - Thank you very much but I don't understand you, You
said you are transfering the money from USA to Glasgow, Scotland.*

Instead of GHANA ACCRA, and after that what happens ? How do I receive the money ? well I hope to Hear from you soon

Thank you

Davis

From: Ed Shanks (A. Skinner)
To: Matins Davis
Date: 7 March 2005

Dear Davis - This has gone on so long that I have accidentally deleted our original mails. If I remember correctly, the amount was $18,000 USD.

I have a very good friend in Glasgow, Scotland by the name of Mr. Max N. Paddy. This gentleman and I have been business partners and friends for years. I spoke with him today and he would be willing to make the payment of $18,000 USD in my behalf. He will pay it in person and in cash if you will have a representative come to Glasgow, Scotland to meet him there.

London is only a short train journey from Glasgow. Mr. Max would usually only be available for a face-to-face meeting on a Friday or Saturday. However, he will be expecting your telephone call now. Call him immediately after reading this mail. I have sent him a copy of this email and he will be expecting your call.

Mr. Paddy N. Max can be reached at +44 8707 65X XXX or by email on max.XX@XXXX. Max is a director of a large communications company, and his website can be found here:

Sincerely,

Ed Shanks

Mr. Davis tries to call Max N. Paddy (Shiver Metimbers) but he's not in, so he sends him an email.

From: Matins Davis
To: Max N. Paddy (Shiver Metimbers)
Date: 10 Mar 2005
Subject: introduction

Hello Paddy - I am Davis Matins, Mr Ed Shanks said I should contact you for money, which he like you to help him to pay the person I am sending to you tomorrow March 10, 2005.

411

I tried calling your line today as he said you will be expecting my call but, the phone line is either disconnected or not working, +44 8707 65X XXX 1 Do you have another phone number I can reach you ??? and what time will the person meet you for the money ??

Please reply back

Thank you

Davis

Time for Shiver Metimbers, playing millionaire businessman Max N. Paddy, to join the fun.

From: Max N. Paddy (Shiver Metimbers)
To: Matins Davis
Date: 11 March 2005

Dear Mr. Davis - Thank you for your email.

My apologies for not being available by phone, but at the moment I am presently in Perth, Scotland for an important business meeting and have not been in my office all day.

I told my good friend Ed Shanks that Friday or Saturday would be the best day for a meeting, however I did not realise that you would want to collect the payment so soon, so I apologise for that. I will be able to meet with you on Saturday (12th March), but if that is a problem for you then perhaps we can meet next Friday or Saturday. Please let me know which suits you best.

Are you familiar with the Glasgow area? For security considerations I think it would be best to meet in an open public place. A perfect meeting spot would be near Paisley Gilmour Street station which is only a few minutes by taxi from Glasgow airport.

Please let me know what day would suit you and I will provide you more detailed information about the meeting place. I will have the $18,000 in cash ready by tomorrow.

Please give me a call tomorrow evening when I shall be back from my trip and I will be happy to speak to you about further arrangements.

Sincerely,

Max N. Paddy.
Managing Director: Dark Side Communications Inc.

Davis calls again, but Max isn't in to receive the call. I write back to apologise...

From: Max N. Paddy (Shiver Metimbers)
To: Matins Davis
Date: 12 March 2005

Dear Mr. Davis - My apologies for not being available for your call yesterday evening (Friday). However, my meetings in Perth went on for much longer than I had anticipated and I have only just arrived back in Glasgow at 2am this morning. If you are able to call later this afternoon (Saturday) I will be most pleased to speak with you.

My apologies again for the delay.

Sincerely,

Max N. Paddy.
Managing Director: Dark Side Communications Inc.

Davis sent another email (which I have lost!) explaining that he was arranging for a female representative named Basira to come up to Scotland to pick up the cash from me. He passed on her number to me, but I neglected to call!

Matins Davis eventually gets through to me on the telephone.

Date: 12th March 2005

Max N. Paddy:	Good morning, Max N. Paddy speaking.
Matins David:	Yes, hello. This is Davis.
Max N. Paddy:	Oh good morning Mr. Davis. Thank you for your call. What can I do for you?
Matins Davis:	How was your trip?
Max N. Paddy:	It was very long and very tiring.
Matins Davis:	Did you get a call from Miss Basira?
Max N. Paddy:	No.
Matins Davis:	I will give her this number to call you.
Max N. Paddy:	OK.
Matins Davis:	She was talking about meeting with you to collect the money.
Max N. Paddy:	Yes that is correct.
Matins Davis:	But she is saying it is not easy, it is not safety enough. I think she is a bit scared.
Max N. Paddy:	OK.

Matins Davis:	So it is possible the money could be transferred to her account?
Max N. Paddy:	No. I will only hand over the money in cash and in person.
Matins Davis:	I was thought about. I, I, I, I, thought about that amount is too heavy to walk about you know?
Max N. Paddy:	Well that's not my problem I'm afraid. If you want the money then it is going to have to be collected from me in person.
Matins Davis:	OK I think she is sleeping now but I will tell her to contact you later.
Max N. Paddy:	OK that is fine.
Matins Davis:	She is insisting that you must send the money to her bank.
Max N. Paddy:	Well you must tell her that that is not going to happen.
Matins David:	Mr. Shanks told you the ticket for the train have to be paid for?
Max N. Paddy:	That's not a problem. I will give her all travelling expenses when we meet.
Matins Davis:	OK. Then have a nice day and I will speak with you again soon.
Max N. Paddy:	Thank you. Bye.

Another call from Davis a short while later, and an attempt to get me to meet in London.

Date: 12th March 2005

Max N. Paddy:	Hello.
Matins David:	Hello. This is Matins.
Max N. Paddy:	Hello Mr. Matins.
Matins David:	OK I spoke to my agent and she was giving me some resistance, but erm... Could you meet with her in London?
Max N. Paddy:	No.
Matins Davis:	But Mr. Paddy, the situ...
Max N. Paddy:	(interrupting) Can I stop you right there Mr. Davis. If she cannot come to Scotland than the deal is off. Please do not try to convince me otherwise.
Matins Davis:	OK so how does everything go through now?
Max N. Paddy:	Well I'm just waiting for someone to come and collect the money. The rest is not up to me.

Matins Davis:	But she says she does not know much about
	Scotland. Doesn't know much about there.
Max N. Paddy:	I do not know much about London either.
Matins Davis:	She just says that she has never been there and does
	not feel safe.
Max N. Paddy:	OK. Not a problem. I will inform Mr. Shanks
	that I shall return the money to the bank in
	the morning.
Matins Davis:	OK before you talk to Mr. Shanks I will get back to
	you soon.
Max N. Paddy:	OK, bye.

Basira, an associate of Martin, called me to ask about receiving the money. She had no interest in coming up to Glasgow, and was charmlessly assertive! In short, she put my back up. I told her that if she couldn't come to collect the money then she should stop bothering me.

Sadly, the call was taken whilst my recorder was elsewhere, so I didn't get a recording of her call.

Shortly after Basira's call, Davis rings me again.

Date: 12th March 2005

Max N. Paddy:	Hello.
Matins Davis:	Hello Mr. Paddy, this is Davis.
Max N. Paddy:	Hello Mr. Davis. What can I do for you?
Matins Davis:	Did she call you?
Max N. Paddy:	Yes she did.
Matins Davis:	And what was she saying?
Max N. Paddy:	She said she could not come to Scotland, so I am
	returning the money to the bank in the morning.
Matins Davis:	So you want to take the money back to the bank,
	right?
Max N. Paddy:	Well there's no point in me keeping it with me now
	if nobody wants to collect it.
Matins Davis:	OK I will find somebody else to come and collect
	the money from you.
Max N. Paddy:	OK that's fine.
Matins Davis:	OK I will call you back.
Max N. Paddy:	OK Mr. Davis. Bye.
Matins Davis:	Have a nice day

Yet another representative of Matins Davis calls to make arrangements

to come to Scotland. His name is Richard Jones. He has a Chinese accent.

Date: 14th March 2005

Max N. Paddy:	Hello.
Richard Jones:	Hello. Mr. Paddy. My name is Richard Jones and Mr. Matins asked me to call you.
Max N. Paddy:	Oh, right. Hello Mr. Jones.
Richard Jones:	I am coming to meet with you in Glasgow Scotland to collect a payment?
Max N. Paddy:	Yes, that is correct.
Richard Jones.	Yes. Please can you send me directions? I will be coming tomorrow.
Max N. Paddy:	Yes. What is your email address?
Richard Jones:	Yes. It is Richard, as in Richard, 20057 at Yahoo dot co dot uk.
Max N. Paddy:	OK thanks. I will send the directions shortly.
Richard Jones:	Thank you.
Max N. Paddy:	What time will you be leaving tomorrow?
Richard Jones:	It will be very early in the morning I suppose.
Max N. Paddy:	Fine. I will look forward to seeing you tomorrow.
Richard Jones:	OK thank you. Goodbye.
Max N. Paddy:	Bye.

I send directions to Richard.

From: Max N. Paddy (Shiver Metimbers)
To: Richard Jones
Date: 14 March 2005

Dear Mr. Jones - Thank you for your call a short while ago. Here are the direction to the agreed meeting place, which is out in the open in public for a more secure place to meet:

1. You need to catch a train to GLASGOW train station. This train journey should take around 4 hours.

2. Once you arrive at Glasgow station you will then need to get to a small shopping centre in a place called Paisley. You can either catch a taxi there (about 10 minutes) or there are regular trains that go directly to where the meeting place is.

3. The meeting place is PAISLEY GILMOUR STREET. It's just outside the station. If you are in a taxi, the drivers will know it well.

4. Once you get to PAISLEY GILMOUR STREET (it is next to a train station). You need to find the part of the small shopping centre called the PIAZZA. The meeting place is an area nearby called COUNTY SQUARE.

When you are there you will notice a circular open-air area with some seating. This is where you need to wait for me. Here is a photograph of the meeting area:

(I attach a photograph of the Piazza with a large cross marking the suggested meeting place.)

The building on the left is a pub called *The Last Post*. You can also see the entrance to the Paisley Gilmour Street Train Station (where you'll have come out of if you came by train).

Let me know if you need any more information.

As soon as you have started your journey, please give me a call so that I can be sure to be ready to meet with you.

When you arrive at the meeting spot give me another call and I will be with you within 5 minutes.

Please note that it was agreed that for my security we would both be alone for the meeting. I will not meet with you if I see any other person with you.

Please do not be offended by this. I just want to be sure I will be safe as I will be carrying a lot of cash.

I look forward to meeting with you.

Kind regards,

Max N. Paddy.
Managing Director: Dark Side Communications Inc.

Richard calls on the morning that he is supposed to arrive in Scotland... there is a problem.

Date: 15th March 2005

Max N. Paddy:	Hello.
Richard Jones:	Hello Mr. Paddy, this is Richard.
Max N. Paddy:	Hello Richard.
Richard Jones:	I got your description in the email this morning.
Max N. Paddy:	Yes.

| Richard Jones: | Yes. By the tone of it, yeah, I don't know that much cash you are talking about. I have had to call Davis Matins back to tell him it is not really safe carrying that kind of money around. He did not tell me it was so much money to collect, and I th.... |
| Max N. Paddy: | (interrupting) OK, bye. |

I slam the phone down on him! Richard calls me back a couple of minutes later.

Max N. Paddy:	Hello.
Richard Jones:	Hello Max. I was talking to you...
Max N. Paddy:	(interrupting) Yes, I'm sorry but I hope you are not going to waste my time by trying to convince me to send the money to you by Western Union or som...
Richard Jones:	(interrupting) No, no, no. I was just going to say you pay it into an account ther....
Max N. Paddy:	No, no, no. I've had this argument numerous times already. People have already tried to convince me to pay this money in several ways including into an account. This is never, never, never going to happen. The agreement is that the cash has to be collected from me in person. If this cannot be done then I am not going to pay the money - it is that simple.
Richard Jones:	Well it is not really safe carrying that kind of money. If you cannot pay it into my acc...
Max N. Paddy:	(interrupting) In that case please telephone Mr. Davis and tell him he is not going to get the money.
Richard Jones.	OK.
Max N. Paddy:	OK.
Richard Jones:	Bye.
Max N. Paddy:	Bye.

A 'furious' email is immediately sent to the boss, Matins Davis.

From: Max N. Paddy (Shiver Metimbers)
To: Matins Davis
Date: 15 March 2005

Dear Mr. Davis - Just what the hell is going on?! I have had a call from that moron Mr. Jones to tell me that he is now NOT coming to meet with me because he is scared to pick up such a large amount of money. He tried to convince me to transfer the money rather than hand it over in person. THIS WILL NOT HAPPEN.

I HAVE CANCELLED FIVE APPOINTMENTS TODAY SO THAT I COULD MEET MR. JONES - YOU HAVE COST ME A FULL WASTED DAY AND LOST ME MONEY!!!

Is this the way you usually do business Mr. Davis? Do you have any idea how BUSY and how IMPORTANT I am? I will NOT stand to have my time wasted by amateurs.

Let me make you understand this 100%:

I WILL **NOT** TRANSFER THE MONEY INTO ANY ACCOUNT. IT ** MUST ** BE PAID IN CASH AND IN PERSON.

I WILL **NOT** TRANSFER THE MONEY INTO ANY ACCOUNT. IT ** MUST ** BE PAID IN CASH AND IN PERSON.

I WILL **NOT** TRANSFER THE MONEY INTO ANY ACCOUNT. IT ** MUST ** BE PAID IN CASH AND IN PERSON.

I WILL **NOT** TRANSFER THE MONEY INTO ANY ACCOUNT. IT ** MUST ** BE PAID IN CASH AND IN PERSON.

I WILL **NOT** TRANSFER THE MONEY INTO ANY ACCOUNT. IT ** MUST ** BE PAID IN CASH AND IN PERSON.

I hope you get the message clearly. Now, please STOP wasting my time. If you are unable to get someone to come and collect the cash then please tell me NOW so that I am not wasting my valuable time.

Max N. Paddy.
Managing Director: Dark Side Communications Inc.

Mr. Davis drops me an email to tell me a new courier by the name of Peter Jones will be contacting me any moment.

From: Matins Davis
To: Max N. Paddy (Shiver Metimbers)
Date: 15 Mar 2005
Subject: peter jones

Mr. MAX.- I have a new asscociate Mr Peter Davis who will be calling you today soon to pick up the money. meantime please send your passport copy so you can be recognised at the meeting

thankyou

Davis

419

From: Max N. Paddy (Shiver Metimbers)
To: Richard Jones
Date: 14 March 2005

Dear Mr. Jones - My passport scan is attached to this email. **(I attach Max N. Paddy's passport.)** Please forward me your contact's photograph so that I may also recognise him.

Sincerely,

Max N. Paddy.
Managing Director: Dark Side Communications Inc.

Peter Jones calls. He is very well-spoken. Why this should surprise me I don't know, but it does.

Date: 15th March 2005

Max N. Paddy:	Good morning, Max N. Paddy speaking.
Peter Jones:	Ahh yes, good morning Max. My name is Peter Jones.
Max N. Paddy:	Oh yes, good morning Peter.
Peter Jones:	Erm, sounds like you were expecting my call.
Max N. Paddy:	That's right yes, Mr. Davis told me to expect your call.
Peter Jones:	Right well this all sounds quite straightforward, just a matter of when is convenient for the both of us.
Max N. Paddy:	Almost any day is fine for me though it would be preferable for me to meet on a Saturday.
Peter Jones:	OK. Well I'll check on the feasibility on my getting up to you as early as possible and then I will give you a call right back.
Max N. Paddy:	That's great, thank you Peter.
Peter Jones:	OK, bye for now.
Max N. Paddy:	Bye.

A short while later Peter Jones calls back and we then make arrangements to meet up in Glasgow on Friday. Some background info is needed here...

I am of course located nowhere near Scotland. However, I have a scambaiting partner who goes by the pseudonym of Charlie Fake and he has agreed to video Peter Jones secretly when he arrives at the meeting location. The plan is to get Peter to travel the few hundred

miles from London to Scotland, get him on camera, and at the same time make a call to him to tell him we know exactly what his scam is all about.

An interesting development: a day or two later, Davis decides to cancel the Friday meet with Peter Jones.

From: Matins Davis
To: Max N. Paddy (Shiver Metimbers)
Date: 17 Mar 2005
Subject: re: peter jones

Hello Max - How is your trip? And business as well, I believed all is Well. Please I would like you do something for me.

Peter Jones will be meeting you on Friday Right? If yes, I will like you to tell them to hold on that you are not ready now and that, when you are ready, you will let them know and on what date they should come to you. BUT REMEMBER THAT WILL NOT STOP THE APPOINTMENT ON SATURDAY. AS I WILL SEND SOMEBODY TO YOU ON THAT DATE TO PICK UP THE MONEY SATURDAY PLEASE

Please I am doing this for Security Reason Over here, so they MUST not know that I told you this, either by phone call or email Just tell them that you are not ready yet.

Waiting to hear from you. thank you
Davis

From: Max N. Paddy (Shiver Metimbers)
To: Matins Davis
Date: 17 March 2005

Dear Mr. Davis - Why are you asking me to do this? This seems very suspicious to me. What is the reason behind this sudden change of plans? Have you informed Mr. Shanks about this?

I cannot telephone Mr. Peter Jones because I do not have his telephone number. As you have already spoken with him (you must have done to tell him to call me) then please tell him of the change of plans.

Why is Mr. Peter Jones not coming on Friday now, what is the problem? I do not like to be messed about in this way. Who is meeting me on

Saturday - what is this person's name? Please ensure that whoever is meeting me on Saturday is able to meet with me between 11am and 4pm on Saturday. These are the only hours I will be available. Also, they will need to contact me to tell me if they are coming by train or plane and also so that I can give them directions for the meeting place.

Please do not delay me any further as this is a lot of money to be holding on to for so long.

Get back to me immediately that you read this email.

Sincerely,

Max N. Paddy.
Managing Director: Dark Side Communications Inc.

Just as I send the above email, Davis calls me and gives me some excuse (which I couldn't make out) as to why the meeting needs to be moved to Saturday. A new courier by the name of Steven will now come to meet me on Saturday.

'Steven' calls me on the eve of the pickup. He sounds suspicious of me and asks a lot of questions.

Date: 18th March 2005

Max N. Paddy:	Good morning.
Steven:	Hello, is that Max?
Max N. Paddy:	Yes it is.
Steven:	Hello Max it is Steven. How are you?
Max N. Paddy:	I'm fine thank you. How can I help you?
Steven:	Right, erm... It's about tomorrow.
Max N. Paddy:	Yes.
Steven:	Erm. Yes. Er... Right. What's the name of this meeting place again where we are meeting?
Max N. Paddy:	It's called County Square. How are you going to be travelling?
Steven:	I'll probably be coming through by air.
Max N. Paddy:	OK that's fine.
Steven:	OK. Erm.. I've. I've got an email attachment here. OK. Is that... What is the name of your company?
Max N. Paddy:	My company name is Dark Side Communications. I have no idea what you have there because Mr. Matins Davis told me he was sending you the meeting information along with a photograph of the

	meeting place.
Steven:	OK. It was just that I... I was trying to locate the company and erm.. It is on, erm, it is...
Max N. Paddy:	(interrupting) It's on Greave Industrial Estate, approximately 7 miles away from County Square.
Steven:	Is it?
Max N. Paddy:	Yes.
Steven:	I was ju... I was just online trying to check the company name but I couldn't seem to find it.
Max N. Paddy:	Mr. Matins should already have given you the details of our website which has all the contact information you need.
Steven:	Yes but the website doesn't have your number.
Max N. Paddy:	Yes it does. I can give you the company number right now if you cannot see it.
Steven:	Yes please do give it to me.
Max N. Paddy:	OK. The number is 08707 650 XXX.
Steven:	Thank you but do you not have a Glasgow registered land-line number which should start with 0141?
Max N. Paddy:	No. I don't know if Mr. Davis has explained to you but our company is in the process of moving to new premises so in the meantime so as not to lose calls at the new offices we are having all our calls redirected through a universal number to avoid confusion. I'm sure you are familiar with call diversion.
Steven:	OK. I said to Davis before that I am... That I am a very busy person so that you need to... To wire the money...
Max N. Paddy:	(interrupting) No. If that is going to be a problem for you please tell me now. I have no idea what this money is for but it must be collected from me in person.
Steven:	Well... I work as an agent in London so I am just working for my commission and I...
Max N. Paddy:	(interrupting) Listen, I do not know what this payment is for. All I know is that I am paying this money on behalf of my friend Ed Shanks. I know nothing about the deal and what the money is for. However, what I can tell you for sure is that I will not have my time wasted for the third time. If you do not want to proceed with this deal then please tell me now so

	that I can return this money back to the bank.
Steven:	OK. That is not a problem I understand and I am prepared to come down. I can get you on this line at any time?
Max N. Paddy:	Yes.
Steven:	OK not a problem at all. I will let you know in the morning what time I will be arriving in the square.
Max N. Paddy:	OK that's fine. Thank you.
Steven:	OK bye bye.
Max N. Paddy:	Bye.

Concerned that Steven may pass on his suspicions to Davis, I decide to take preventative measures and give Davis a scare by pretending to be feeling very insulted and wanting to end the deal.

From: Max N. Paddy (Shiver Metimbers)
To: Matins Davis
Date: 18 March 2005

Dear Mr. Davis - I must tell you that I am VERY unhappy with this Steven person who telephoned me a short while ago. He was asking MANY questions about me and my business and was questioning my honesty. This I will NOT stand for.

Please tell Steven that I no longer wish to meet with him. I will NOT be spoken to like and questioned like a child. I shall NOT be at the meeting place tomorrow and I shall NOT be handing over the $18,000. I am afraid you will have to find somebody else to help you because I no longer wish to be a part of this very suspicious deal.

I will inform my friend Ed Shanks that I cannot help him.

Sincerely,

Max N. Paddy.
Managing Director: Dark Side Communications Inc.

From: Matins Davis
To: Max N. Paddy (Shiver Metimbers)
Date: 19 Mar 2005
Subject: i am sorry for that ACT please

Hello Max - I am very sorry to hear this, Steven has NO RIGHT to ask you any Question on what the money is for or what you do as well, I cannot believed he could ask this kind of Question from you or what kind of business you doing as he has NO right with that ?

For this ACT I have concealed him from meeting you tomorrow Saturday. BUT I have told Mr. Shanks that the whole thing is going to END tomorrow.

On the issue of Suspicious deal well from what he has been saying to me that he does not want anybody to robbed him of the money as he returning back to UK, Since he don't know me and I didn't tell you to send the money through BANK but CASH, he also said that traveling with such amount money from UK is too RISK for him as well but with all this EXCUSE He has not right to ask you ANY QUESTION AS WELL .

Well I as said this meeting will end tomorrow, called Mr. Jones OFFICE here and they have agreed to conditions, which means Mr. Jones will be coming to you tomorrow, I call your phone ringing no respond from you tell you what the arranged with they as the TIME given to Steven remains the same tomorrow Please REMEMBER I don't know them, I only sign contract with their office here while they go for the money there.

Well as I said Mr. Peter Jones will call you to tell you that will be on his way Scotland tomorrow please

Once again I am very Sorry for that STUPID ACT by Steven.

Thank you

Davis

Mr. Davis calls to apologise for Steven's actions.

Date: 19th March 2005

Max N. Paddy:	Good morning.
Davis:	Yes, good morning. This is Davis speaking.
Max N. Paddy:	Hello Mr. Davis.
Davis:	Sorry I saw your mail yesterday, and the actions of Steven. I am surprised he could be asking such questions of you.

Max N. Paddy:	Yes it was very disturbing.
Davis:	I must apologise for him.
Max N. Paddy:	OK, so what is happening now Mr. Davis?
Davis:	Yeah, well Mr. Peter Davis will be on his way to meet with you now.
Max N. Paddy:	So it is Peter who is coming now?
Davis:	Yes. I just have to cancel Steven for what he has done. It is not right enough. Mr. Peter wants to talk to you on the telephone before he comes.
Max N. Paddy:	OK but I must tell you that I am quite suspicious of Peter. However, I will meet with him.
Davis:	He will call you shortly to confirm the meeting.
Max N. Paddy:	OK fine.
Davis:	Thank you. Bye bye.
Max N. Paddy:	Bye.

Peter Jones calls to arrange a second trip to Scotland.

Date: 19th March 2005

Max N. Paddy:	Hello.
Peter:	Hello Max, this is Peter Jones.
Max N. Paddy:	Oh hello again Peter.
Peter:	Hi, erm, well I don't know if you are aware but I was in Scotland yesterday.
Max N. Paddy:	I wasn't aware of that at all Peter. I received an email from Mr. Davis to tell me the meeting had been postponed.
Peter:	Well it confused me!
Max N. Paddy:	I haven't a clue why things have been shifted around.
Peter:	Well it's a mystery to me, and also very frustrating. Travelling all that way it was a complete... headache.
Max N. Paddy:	Tell me about it!
Peter:	Yes, we're all busy people I'm sure.
Max N. Paddy:	If you don't mind me asking you Peter, what is your part in all of this?
Peter:	Well basically I'm involved in import and exports to and from Africa, from various parts of the world.
Max N. Paddy:	I see.
Peter:	Erm. I don't really have any role in this other than

	the fact that the people in Ghana, erm, have known me for many years and they trust me impeccably.
Max N. Paddy:	Right.
Peter:	They've asked me to do this as a favour.
Max N. Paddy:	You see I'm a little confused as I am paying this money on behalf of an American friend of mine. I'm sat here with all this money and I haven't the faintest idea what it's for!
Peter:	Well I do have a pretty good idea. It's, it's nothing really to worry about. Do you have any experience in Africa at all?
Max N. Paddy:	None at all.
Peter:	Well when you do business in Africa unfortunately it all works on a cash only basis. The banking systems in Africa are not as efficient as ours for one, and secondly there are places in Africa where if you do transfers of any kind then your money just simply disappears! It all works on a cash basis.
Max N. Paddy:	I see!
Peter:	It's all because of corruption and what have you. Anyway, I can come up to Scotland tomorrow or maybe Monday or Friday.
Max N. Paddy:	Next Friday would be the best time for me.
Peter:	OK then can I confirm that with you now and there will be no complications. It really is straightforward and simple. I will be there, on Friday, between the hours of 12 and 4. There will be no exceptions.
Max N. Paddy:	OK then that's confirmed and I will be seeing you on Friday.
Peter:	OK then I will see you on Friday and will probably call you to check things out before I arrive.
Max N. Paddy:	OK Peter, thanks.
Peter:	Bye.
Max N. Paddy:	Bye.

As you can gather, it appears Peter Jones did come to Scotland. He wasn't told by Mr. Davis I wouldn't be there... Shame!

Anyway, now we know that the meeting is definitely on for Friday, and a quick call to fellow scambaiter Charlie Fake confirms that he'll will be ready with his anti-scammer disguise kit and camera!

I get a few days rest from telephone calls and emails, then Matins Davis gets back in touch.

Date: 24 March 2005

Max N. Paddy:	Hello.
Davis:	Hello yes, Davis speaking please.
Max N. Paddy:	Hello Mr. Davis.
Davis:	I... I talked to Peter Jones today and he tell me he coming to you tomorrow.
Max N. Paddy:	Yes that is correct.
Davis:	OK. At what time are you meeting?
Max N. Paddy:	We agreed between 12pm and 4pm. Peter did not give me a specific time for his arrival.
Davis:	You have my number so when the meeting is over call me immediately and let me know.
Max N. Paddy:	OK.
Davis:	OK, have a nice day then.
Max N. Paddy:	OK. Thank you, bye.
Davis:	Bye.

THE BIG DAY ARRIVES!

Peter Jones is now in Glasgow (whilst I rest at home a few hundred miles away, watching TV).

Date: 25 March 2005

Max N. Paddy:	Hello, good morning.
Peter:	Hello, is that Max?
Max N. Paddy:	Yes this is Max, is that Peter?
Peter:	Yes. Right, anyway, I'm in Glasgow now, very close to the airport. What sort of time do you want to meet up?
Max N. Paddy:	Well I can be at the meeting point within five minutes of your arrival.
Peter:	Well if we say 12 o'clock?
Max N. Paddy:	OK that's perfectly fine.
Peter:	OK then Max, I will see you shortly.
Max N. Paddy:	OK Peter, bye.

I make a quick telephone call to Charlie Fake to let him know that the 'meeting' is imminent. Mr. Davis calls and I tell him that Peter has arrived in Glasgow.

Date: 25 March 2005

Max N. Paddy:	Hello.
Davis:	Hello Mr. Paddy this is Davis.
Max N. Paddy:	Hello Mr. Davis. Peter Jones has just called to tell me that he will be at the meeting place in half an hour.
Davis:	That is good. Call me after the meeting please.
Max N. Paddy:	I will do that.
Davis:	OK bye.
Max N. Paddy:	Bye.

Peter Jones is now close to the meeting place after a 360 plus mile (6-7 hour) drive.

Date: 25 March 2005

Max N. Paddy:	Hello.
Peter:	Hello Max, this is Peter.
Max N. Paddy:	Hello Peter.
Peter:	OK well I'm minutes away from the meeting place now.
Max N. Paddy:	Oh that's great.
Peter:	So how will I know you Max?
Max N. Paddy:	OK, I'm around 5 foot 6 inches, blue jeans, white shirt, and a grey jacket. How will I recognise you Peter?
Peter:	Well, a dark shirt, a blue fleece coat, dark trousers and light coloured boots.
Max N. Paddy:	That's great. I've just got a couple of things to wrap up here Peter and then I'll be there for 12pm.
Peter:	Yes, 12pm is fine.
Max N. Paddy:	I'll just have to try to confirm to Matins Davis that you are here. I keep getting cut off when I try to ring him!
Peter:	Ahh yes, I know. The telephone system in Ghana is awful.
Max N. Paddy:	Yes, it seems so! Have you dealt with Mr. Davis before Peter?
Peter:	Yes I have yes.
Max N. Paddy:	Ah good OK, so he's not an unknown quantity to you.
Peter:	My organisation has been doing business with his organisation for years now. Effectively I am just

	doing a favour too.
Max N. Paddy:	OK then Peter I will give you a call shortly before 12pm.
Peter:	OK bye.
Max N. Paddy:	Bye.

Peter Jones has now arrived at the meeting spot, County Square.

Date: 25 March 2005

Peter:	Hello, Peter Jones.
Max N. Paddy:	Hello Peter, it's Max here.
Peter:	Hello Max.
Max N. Paddy:	Have you arrived at the meeting place yet Peter?
Peter:	Yes I'm here now.
Max N. Paddy:	That's great. I'll be there in about 5 minutes, I am just about to set off now.
Peter:	OK.
Max N. Paddy:	OK Peter, see you shortly, bye.
Peter:	Bye.

I call Peter again to let him know I'm just about there! In the background are various traffic and bird sounds, all of which are being played on my PC to make Peter think I am outside.

Date: 25 March 2005

Peter:	Hello, Peter Jones.
Max N. Paddy:	Hello Peter it's Max. Just to let you know I should be with you in about 2 or 3 minutes. I.... (car noises!) sorry about the noise Peter, it's a bit busy here!
Peter:	OK that's fine. I'll be sitting down reading your local newspaper. I'm facing *The Last Post* pub.
Max N. Paddy:	That's great.
Peter:	It all sounds a bit cloak & dagger doesn't it?
Max N. Paddy:	(laughs) Yes, it does seem a bit weird doesn't it? Anyway, I'll be there very shortly.
Peter:	OK fine.
Max N. Paddy:	OK Peter, bye.
Peter:	Bye.

Charlie Fake has confirmed to me that he has been filming Peter for some time now and still is. Time to give Peter the bad news that he's had a wasted journey.

Date: 25 March 2005

Peter:	Hello.
Max N. Paddy:	Hello Peter it's Max.
Peter:	Hi.
Max N. Paddy:	Sorry for the delay, I got held up by a friend that I met on the way.
Peter:	Right.
Max N. Paddy:	Can you just pass a quick message on to Matins Davis for me please.
Peter:	(in a suspicious voice) Right.
Max N. Paddy:	Just tell him that I know he is a 419 scammer and I am not coming. I... (Peter puts the phone down!)

Sadly, Peter didn't give me the abuse I was expecting and just quickly cut me off. Very unsatisfying.

Thanks to Charlie Fake, though, we also have some video footage and some audio he captured!

Please enjoy some stills from the video:

'Is that somebody filming me?'!

'No boss, the fool still hasn't turned up with the cash.'

'Ha! The idiot is on his way here now!'

The next step in my cunning plan is to try to convince Peter's boss that I DID actually hand over the cash. As soon as I made the final telephone call to Peter, I emailed Matins Davis.

From: Max N. Paddy (Shiver Metimbers)
To: Matins Davis
Date: 25 March 2005

Dear Mr. Davis - I tried to call you three times on your number but there was no reply, so I have decided to send you a message.

I met Mr. Peter Jones a short while ago and handed over the payment to him, so expect a call from him soon. Please will you confirm to me and Mr. Shanks when you are in receipt of the payment.

Good to get to the end of this at last.

Best regards,

Max N. Paddy.

I wait about half an hour then send Davis another email claiming, I had received a telephone call from Peter Jones complaining that I had not turned up.

From: Max N. Paddy (Shiver Metimbers)
To: Matins Davis
Date: 25 March 2005

Dear Mr. Davis - Just what the hell is going on?! I have just had a call from Mr. Peter Jones to tell me that I DID NOT give him the $18,000 and that I never came to meet with him in Scotland!! THIS IS A LIE. I met him at exactly 10 minutes past 12pm today and handed him the $18,000 in cash. He shook my hand and thanked me. I even took a photograph of him as I waved to him when I was approaching him for the meeting:

Now, WHAT IS HAPPENING WITH MY MONEY? Are you having some kind of joke with me!

Max N. Paddy.
Managing Director: Dark Side Communications Inc.

I attach one of the photographs taken by Charlie Fake.

To cause further confusion and panic, I ensure all telephone numbers to me that Davis has are 'disconnected'! Davis sends a frantic email to Ed Shanks.

From: Matins Davis
To: Ed Shanks
Date: 25 March 2005
Subject: ?????

Hello,

WHAT IS HAPPNING PLEASE ??

DAVIS

From: Ed Shanks (A. Skinner)
To: Matins Davis
Date: 25 Feb 2005

Dear Davis - I spoke with Paddy Max after recovering your frantic telephone call this morning. Sorry we got disconnected. Mr. Max assures me he handed over the cash to Mr. Jones. It appears that Mr.

Jones is not being honest with you. Are you sure you know this gentleman very well? Please keep me informed.

Sincerely,

Ed Shanks

Davis is unconvinced of Max's innocence and replies to Ed Shanks.

From: Matins Davis
To: Ed Shanks
Date: 25 March 2005
Subject: max did not come

Hello - Well I don't believed Mr Max that he gave the money to them because I told him that he should call me before handing the money to them, which he did not call but he give them Money as said did, for I did not accept that explaintion from Mr Max.

Okay, I talk to Mr Jones on phone and said he will involve police inside for lieing against him, is Mr Max ready to go to police with them, please tell Max to call me and put Jones in comferance in other for us hear each other.

Am just wondering WHY Mr Max wants to pay this money in cash, I expected him tell Mr Jones to sign his signature before making payment of as such amount since he cloud not hear voice on phone.

Please tell me what is HAPPENING ? I know how many times I called Mr Jones on phone , even the today before their meeting I called for two times,

Lastly,,,,, why didn't Mr Max Take Jones picture when is he has received the money from him ????? Answer please

WHY IS MR MAX PHONE NOT WORKING AGAIN ??

I Need Mr Max phone contact Address and office address.

Thank you

Davis

From: Ed Shanks (A. Skinner)
To: Matins Davis
Date: 25 March 2005

Dear Davis - I am not sure what is going on, but will launch a full investigation with the Secret International Police here in America to get to the bottom of this.

435

I am sure Mr. Max N. Paddy is of the highest moral ethic. I do not know your friend Mr. Jones. Of course, to answer your question, how could Mr. Max hold the camera and take a picture of himself and Mr. Jones at the same time? That would be impossible.

I will need for you to send me a complete statement for an affidavit before an investigation into this matter can be launched. Please write down in your own handwriting exactly what you know to be true and what happened. Sign and date it then email it to me. I have lost all of this money, so need your help.

If Mr. Jones stole the money then he should be give it to you.

Sincerely,

Ed Shanks

Davis doesn't reply to Ed Shanks until the next day. Seems Peter is miffed...

From: Matins Davis
To: Ed Shanks (A. Skinner)
Date: 26 March 2005
Subject: jones will report to the police

Hello Shanks - Well Mr Jones is going to report the it to UK police but he needs Mr Max contact address,

he tried reaching him {Mr Max} on phone but no way, as the phone is off, I my self have tried reach max too on phone but i cloudn't as well.

The picture he took Mr Jones is not the point because i told him not to give any money to Jones till he hear from me, and i am always on phone with Mr Max even before the time he give this money out i called him and inform him not give till hear from him.

{1} SO WHY DID HE GIVE OUT THE MONEY ??????????

Mr Shanks something is wronge somewhere please,{2} for how long will this take us ???

{3} Bytheway the world we live in now does it allow such amount of money paid in cash with out any docuently signasture????

{4} If this money was sent direct to me will all this Happened ??

please we need way out NOW, I have asked four QUESTION which i think you and Mr Max need to answer for me

Davis

Davis sends an email to Max N. Paddy.

From: Matins Davis
To: Max N. Paddy (Shiver Metimbers)
Date: 26 March 2005
Subject: address

Hello Paddy Max - Please i need your full address and contact information, we have to contact UK POLICE to look into this case.

Sorry i am asking this from you

Davis

I give Davis the real contact details of the Paisley Transport police.

From: Max N. Paddy (Shiver Metimbers)
To: Matins Davis
Date: 26 March 2005

Dear Mr. Davis - My full address is below, and for your information I have already contacted the police over this matter. You need to contact the Paisley main police station and ask for Sergeant Andy Cunningham who is the person I have reported this thief Mr. Jones to. The telephone number of the Paisley police station is +44 141 335 XXXX. The report number is 4515781.

I have also handed over Mr. Jones' telephone number to them. They have told me not to speak to anyone on the telephone until they have contacted Mr. Jones.

You are reading my message incorrectly. The picture was taken AFTER I had given the money to Mr. Jones. If you study the picture carefully you can quite clearly see the money in the plastic bag that I handed over to him. I told him I was taking the picture as proof to Mr. Shanks that I had indeed handed over the money. Here is another picture, and the bundle of cash inside the white plastic bag is clearly visible:

My full address, which I have given to you before is:

7 Knutmeg Grove
Greave Industrial Estate
Off Gilmour Street
Paisley

Glasgow
Scotland
PA1 1DD
United Kingdom

I don't know how long you have been dealing with Mr. Jones, but he is
most definitely a very suspicious character. He told me he was an
important businessman in charge of import and export to West African
counties. Take a look at his picture. He does NOT look like a
businessman to me - he looks nothing like one. You had better find out
what has happened to my money quickly. I have not mentioned your
name or details to the police yet, but if my money is not returned I will
have no choice.

Sincerely,

Max N. Paddy.
Managing Director: Dark Side Communications Inc.

I attach the incriminating photo.

From: Matins Davis
To: Max N. Paddy (Shiver Metimbers)
Date: 26 Mar 2005
Subject: jones

*Hello Max - I forward your last email to Jones and called me to tell me
that he call the Police and Said the police has not call him.*

*He said the plastic bag you mentioned about is from super market he
went in to buy things from and that he can proof it with you by his
LAWYER'S help, he said he will return back to Scotland because of this
issue.*

*Mr. Max I need your phone number where I can reach you , I will not
give to anybody okay*

Waiting to hear from you

Davis

From: Max N. Paddy (Shiver Metimbers)
To: Matins Davis
Date: 26 March 2005

Dear Mr. Davis - I do not know when the police will be calling Mr.
Jones, all that I know is that they asked me for his telephone number
and also not to speak to anyone involved before they speak to Jones.

I do have some more photographs of Mr. Jones which I am waiting to
receive once they have been developed. I believe one of them will show
Mr. Jones holding the cash in his hands quite clearly.

Hopefully this will prove to you that I am telling you the truth in this
matter.

I will send you more proof of Mr. Jones' dishonesty later this evening
once I have received the last of the photographs.

Sincerely,

Max N. Paddy.
Managing Director: Dark Side

Davis fires off his four questions once more to Ed Shanks.

From: Matins Davis
To: Ed Shanks (A. Skinner)
Date: 26 Mar 2005
Subject: re: max did not come

Hello Shanks - Well Mr Jones is going to report the incident to UK
police but he needs Mr Max contact address, he tried reaching him {Mr
Max} on phone but no way, as the phone is off, I my self have tried
reach max too on phone but i cloudn't as well.

The picture he took Mr Jones is not the point because i told him not to
give any money to Jones till he hear from me, and i am always on
phone with Mr Max even before the time he give this money out i called
him and inform him not give till hear from him.

{1} SO WHY DID HE GIVE OUT THE MONEY ??????????

Mr Shanks something is wronge somewhere please,{2} for how long
will this take us ???

{3} Bytheway the world we live in now does it allow such amount of
money paid in cash with out any docuently signasture????

{4} If this money was sent direct to me will all this Happened ??

please we need way out NOW, I have asked four QUESTION which i
think you and Mr Max need to answer for me

Davis

From: Ed Shanks (A. Skinner)
To: Matins Davis
Date: 26 March 2005

Dear Davis - Sorry to be so long getting back to you. This whole thing
has me so upset that I had to take a sedative last night. From what I
understand, Mr. Max has contacted the police. Perhaps Mr. Jones has
run off with the cash. It certainly looks that way. I do have the address
for Mr. Max, but we are all fearful of Mr. Jones so will not divulge it at
this time.

1) Mr. Max gave out the money to your trusted friend who double-
crossed all of us.
2) I have no idea how long this will take us. I have lost cash.

3) What good would a signature do? He has photos of the so called Mr. Jones.
4) If you had decent friends all this would not have happened.

Please keep me informed. I would like to have the police here work on the case in conjunction with Interpol and Scotland Yard.

Ed Shanks

From: Matins Davis
To: Ed Shanks (A. Skinner)
Date: 26 Mar 2005
Subject: re: re: max did not come

Hello Shanks - I don't know any yet as the two party are still not cleared to me who is acting funny I am working underground investigation concerning this case, before then I am making an arrangement to see the funds transfer into your account, while investigation is going on , I am using the pictures sent to me by Mr. Paddy Max to the security company that we have some little problem concerning money am sure the company will understand me . if they do I will use them to make transfer WHY to avoid USA investigating about the Fund as you know since September 11 USA has been monitoring every funds coming from African to states and that goes out as well.

Please will this be Okay with you ?? Can you travel out of the USA to any Europe if necessary ?? Because the company can only help getting the funds to Europe for easy transfer, you know well that when the money is transferred from Europe the USA FEDERAL INVESTIGATION WILL NOT INVESTIGATE IT,

I believed this will be Alright with you. Waiting to hear from you soonest

Davis

From: Ed Shanks (A. Skinner)
To: Matins Davis
Date: 26 March 2005

Dear Davis - I am still in a state of shock! How can we still transfer the fund if the fees have been stolen? Please give me some time to think about this and let the investigation continue.

Ed Shanks

To make our story even more plausible, fake security camera images are put together showing Peter Jones with the money that Max N. Paddy handed over!

From: Max N. Paddy (Shiver Metimbers)
To: Matins Davis
Date: 27 March 2005

Dear Mr. Davis - I have been sent some security camera images taken at the place where the meeting place was. I have attached two images from the security camera to this email.

You can quite clearly see that Mr. Jones has got my money in his hands as he walks away from the meeting. I have circled the areas to make them more clear to you.

(Peter Jones counts the cash!)

(Peter Jones handling the cash!)

I do not know how much more evidence I can give you before you believe me. You can see with your own eyes that Mr. Jones is a thief. I want to know when I will get my money back from this man.

Max N. Paddy.
Managing Director: Dark Side Communications Inc.

Seems the security images are not quite enough to convince Davis...

From: Matins Davis
To: Max N. Paddy
Date: 27 Mar 2005
Subject: who am i to believe

Hello Max - I JUST DON'T KNOW WHOM TO BELIEVE, HE SAID WILL CALL THE POLICE, AND HE IS TAKING YOU TO COURT LIEING AGAINST HIM, PLEASE ALWAYS UPDATE ME WITH ANY INFORMATION YOU HAVE

DAVIS

Just what I need: A CRIMINAL reporting me to the police.

From: Max N. Paddy (Shiver Metimbers)
To: Matins Davis
Date: 27 March 2005

Dear Mr. Davis - I REALLY hope that Mr. Jones DOES take me to court. I look forward VERY MUCH to seeing this thief put behind bars. I have all the evidence I need.

I have the photographs, the security footage AND today I have also received VIDEO FOOTAGE of this thief Jones also. You may also find yourself in deep trouble because of your association with this person. I will be contacting the Ghana police shortly also if I do not get my money back within 7 days.

Tell Mr. Jones that he can look forward to many many years in jail for what he has done. I am very excited that he is being foolish enough to lie to the police!

Goodbye.

Max N. Paddy.
Managing Director: Dark Side Communications Inc.

From: Matins Davis
To: Max N. Paddy (Shiver Metimbers)
Date: 28 Mar 2005
Subject: who am i to believe

Hello Max - that will be Good if you can use that Evidence to proof yourself in Court as he said will be taking you to Court.

Mr. Peter said you Never meet him and you said met him, WHO IS TELLING THE TRUTH ?? I believed the police in UK or Scotland should be able to fine out this from there and not from here as you are putting it .

I believed you are on phone , can I have your number ??? if the police said you should not speak to anybody , for how long ??? why has the police not call Peter ??? how long will take police to call Peter ?? because I this come to End without any delay

Mr. Max are you sure you give the money in person or you sent

444

somebody to do it on your behalf ?? well I have about seven {7}
Questions I will like you to answer for me please.

Davis

From: Max N. Paddy (Shiver Metimbers)
To: Matins Davis
Date: 28 March 2005

Dear Mr. Davis - So, you are also in on the SCAM? It seems you must be because after all the solid evidence I have given you you still believe that I did not give Mr. Jones the cash.

The police have informed me the Peter Jones is NOT that man's real name. He told me he was English, and now the police tell me he is in fact South African. It seems Mr. Jones (or whatever his real name is) has a lot to hide. Is Mr. Davis your real name? We will soon find out. I do not know if the police have spoken with Jones yet, they do not tell me everything, just the important information I need to know.

Mr. Jones has STOLEN my money. The evidence I have is as follows:

1. Photographs of Mr. Jones holding the bag of money I gave him.

2. Security camera images showing Mr. Jones COUNTING my money.

3. VIDEO footage of Mr. Jones STEALING my money.

4. Eyewitnesses (three of them) who witnessed me handing over the cash to Mr. Jones. One of the eyewitnesses is a Father of our local church and will be happy to explain in court what he saw. He has even agreed to let YOU question him by email. If you want to please let me know and I will give you the church email address. This MAN OF GOD saw your THIEF friend STEAL my money. Father Perkins saw ME and Mr. Jones TOGETHER and WITNESSED me handing over the money. You may call a man of God a liar if you please but you will be denying all the evidence.

I have also been told that there are security images of me AND Mr. Jones talking with each other and showing me handing over the cash. I have not received this yet, but when I do I will send it to you. Then you will HAVE to believe what I am telling you.

The police already believe my story 100%. The reason they believe my story 100% is because I CAN PROVE EVERYTHING I SAY. Your

THIEF friend Mr. Jones can prove NOTHING.

I have even shown the police my bank statement showing the withdrawal of the $18,000.

The police have told me they WILL be arresting Mr. Jones when he arrives here. Let me know when he is coming.

I cannot believe that you are being taken for such a fool by Mr. Jones. After all the evidence that I have given you, you still think that I am to blame. Ask yourself WHY I would do such a thing? I have NOTHING to do with this 'deal' you have got going with my friend Ed Shanks. All that I know is that Mr. Shanks needed my help, and as a good friend I gave it to him. Now I find that I have been robbed by common thieves. Believe me, I will not rest until justice is done.

Max N. Paddy.
Managing Director: Dark Side Communications Inc.

From: Matins Davis
To: Max N. Paddy (Shiver Metimbers)
Date: 28 Mar 2005
Subject: my questions to you

Hello Max - Please answer this Question for me, WHY did you chose to pay this MONEY in Cash and not Bank , if you could remembered All the agency I sent to you refused to come Scotland for the money, all asked for bank transfer, Mr. Jones did not even know about all this, and he is the only who accepted.

Well for not accepting the Bank transfer and NOT calling me makes me not having 100% trust on you for now, I hope you will understand me. why don't you answer your telephone

Davis

From: Max N. Paddy (Shiver Metimbers)
To: Matins Davis
Date: 28 March 2005

Dear Mr. Davis - I have ceased telephone communication because this is what the police have told me to do. I am following their orders. I will call you in the next few days.

You asked me why I did not call you just before I gave Mr. Jones the money. The answer is that I DID try to call you, twice, but I could not get through to your number. If you recall about 1 or 2 weeks ago I had exactly the same problem and I even told that to you. You then explained to me that the telephone lines to Ghana are bad and sometime it takes many attempts to get through.

I DID try to call and I even telephoned Mr. Jones to ask him to call you to tell you that I wanted to speak with you. It seems he had other ideas and did not do as I requested.

The reason I wanted to give cash rather than transfer the money by bank transfer/Western Union etc., was because I foolishly thought that if I met face to face with the person receiving my money I would get an explanation of the proceedings and also some form of receipt for my money.

I am NOT in the habit of transferring money across the world to people I have never met. I have never done this and I never will. Unfortunately I did not realise Mr. Jones was a thief with a previous record of felony and I also never received my receipt for the money.

I have just this morning received more security images which show BOTH me and Mr. Jones TOGETHER, and the picture clearly shows me handing over the cash to Mr. Jones. I will send these pictures to you later today. At the moment I am too busy as I have a meeting to attend.

If you see the new pictures and STILL do not believe that I met with Mr. Jones then all that I can assume is that you are also in on the scam that Mr. Jones is perpetrating.

Finally, what is Mr. Peter Jones' REAL name? You MUST know as I do now that the name Peter Jones is false. If you have been doing business with him for so long then you must know his real name.

I want to know what it is and I want his full postal address and post code. I have given you my details, now I am requesting that you give me his. If you are unwilling to help me in this matter then the only conclusion I can reach is that you knew all the time that Mr. Jones was going to steal from me.

Max N. Paddy.
Managing Director: Dark Side Communications Inc.

From: Matins Davis
To: Max N. Paddy (Shiver Metimbers)
Date: 28 Mar 2005
Subject: re: my questions to you

Hello Max - Look I have told you that Mr. Jones is an agency, I REMEMBERED I told you NOT give him any money till you hear from me. REASON for these is because I need his agecy to hear him accepting that the money is given to him with the agency accepting it will help me pick the money up here.

Truth is that I could Not ask any money from them here because it was not confirmed that you have paid any money as they did not hear him accpting it with you. Your friends knows that I must speak to you and Peter before handling the money to him. But WHY did you give without hearing from me ????????

Peter said he never met you, because you called him on phone that you know it is {419 SCAM} So you cannot give him the money again, while you are saying that paid him. WHO DO I BELIEVED ??????

Well I have every reasons to believe you based on the evidence you have given so far but on their hand peter denied meeting you. Now it is time to deal with peter agency here

But I will need your help to deal with peter agency here, CAN YOU HELP ???

{1} I will need to file this case to Court before I do this I need to involve some top men in force, to avoid them having their way .

{2} I want all the evidence you have with you. Concerning the peter movement.

{3} lastly the issue in involve money { $18,000} and I will need $5,000 to get them paid within Five days BUT I have only $2,700 with me, please can I get $2,300 UDS from you ???? to stop them from empowering the top men here.

With the money and evidence I WILL gather here will help to trap their company here and that will make Peter pay all the money there with expensive made.

Please let us work together now by helping me outwith the information and the money

Thank you waiting to hear from you soon

Davis

Time to send Davis another fake security camera image, this time showing Max N. Paddy meeting with Peter Jones.

From: Max N. Paddy (Shiver Metimbers)
To: Matins Davis
Date: 28 March 2005

Mr. Davis - Attached you will find YET ANOTHER piece of evidence. This security camera image shows ME with Mr. Jones, face to face just after I handed over the money. Now, there is not much more I can tell you to prove that I am telling the truth. Mr. Jones told you that I never even met with him, but as you can see quite clearly there I am. I shall await your apology.

Mr. Davis, IT IS NOT MY FAULT IF I CANNOT GET THROUGH TO YOU ON THE PHONE! I tried 2 or 3 times but could not get through. What would you have wanted me to do - come back to my office without giving the money? If I had done that then you would have been angry with me!

You say 'Peter said he never met you', but you can see with your own eyes that I did indeed meet with him. The evidence is there for any fool to see. Please let me see Peter's evidence that I was not there. Show me now.

You have asked for my help to prove Peter is guilty of being a thief, and I will be happy to help you AS SOON AS I GET MY MONEY BACK. I have already given you much more evidence that I should do. You STILL have not given me Mr. Jones real name and real contact address. I am waiting to receive it.

I cannot believe you are now asking me for MORE MONEY?!!!! You will not get one single dollar from me until Peter has been put in jail.

Now, you have seen the very best evidence of Peter's guilt. Do you STILL believe this thief?

Max N. Paddy.
Managing Director: Dark Side Communications Inc.

After being forwarded the 'evidence' above, Peter Jones asked Davis to forward a long list of excuses as to why he should be believed over me. However, I get the feeling Davis is slowly coming around to my way of thinking. Peter is not very happy!

I decide to tell Davis I'm cutting off contact as I believe he is in on the scam.

From: Max N. Paddy (Shiver Metimbers)
To: Matins Davis
Date: 29 March 2005

Mr. Davis - I have shown you the evidence I have. Mr. Jones has none, and a call to my police station this afternoon informs me that Mr. Jones has NOT spoken with them at all. I think we all know who the liar is here.

I do not understand the technicalities of the security camera images, I am not an expert in such things, but what I can tell you for certain is that the images I sent to you were from THREE different cameras. Perhaps the times were set incorrectly on some of them, I just do not know. All I know is that you simply refuse to be man enough to admit you have been fooled by Jones, so the only assumption I can make is that you are part of this crime.

I have no further things to say to you Mr. Davis. It is clear that no matter what evidence I give to you that you will not believe me, or are for some reason unwilling to believe me. Therefore I can only assume that you are in on this scam and you are also whatever this 419 scam thing is. I shall forward all your emails and correspondence to the Paisley police first thing tomorrow morning. I see I am wasting my time with you. I will do this no longer. I shall let the police speak with you instead.

Mr. 'Jones' is correct only in that the telephone number is of the transport police. As the crime was committed on their territory they were the people I reported the crime to. They own and run the meeting place known as County Square, which is directly in front of the train station as you will know because I sent you a picture of it nearly 2 weeks ago if you recall. This IS a Scottish contact number, and to aid you EVEN MORE, here is their webpage with the number plain to see: http://www.btp.police.uk/areas/scottish.htm just click on "Paisley" and all the details you will need are there. Again, more evidence that Jones is lying.

Please do not bother me ever again. I am now sure that you are in on this crime, and I simply no longer believe anything you tell me anymore.

Sincerely,

Max N. Paddy.
Managing Director: Dark Side Communications Inc.

Time for Ed Shanks to take over for a while!

From: Ed Shanks (A. Skinner)
To: Matins Davis
Date: 29 March 2005

Dear Martin - Thank you for forwarding this mail to me. I can assure you that Mr. Paddy Max is a person of the highest ethic. That is why I trusted him to pass this cash to your alleged Mr. Peter Jones. It is noted that Mr. Jones claims to have done this and that. However, the photographs do not lie. If Mr. Jones is of such a great reputation and if that is indeed his real name, then please have him provide a copy of his passport scanned to me.

Does Mr. Jones think we believe his story about the bag? Why would he have that large a bag just for a few sweets? He would have a small bag. Mr. Jones also states he has spoken with the police, but does not mention the name of the officer whom he spoke with. This is very suspicious.

Where do we stand now, Martin? Your friend has cost us all a great deal of money.

Ed Shanks

Davis sends Paddy N. Max an email, and also cc's it to Ed Shanks. Max is not replying!

From: Matins Davis
To: Ed Shanks (A. Skinner)
Date: 30 March 2005
Title: evidence

Hello Max - Thank you for your email and Evidence you provided to me, as you know i wasn't there, So i need more proofs from you and Jones,

Okay as you have All this proofs to show that Mr Jones has Collected $18,000 USD from you i will like you send the Money i requested from you please attack them here as you know that only Agreement we hard here is that i MUST speak to you and him while their are there

The Truth is that i was with them i called you and you said you will him in 20 minutes time but later after that i recieved a call from Peter to tell me that he you are not coming again, i tried calling but your phone is Rinning and No one is Pick it up, not untill i came to check my Email and got your email that paid $18,000 to JONES.

Now you can see why i act this ??? and Jones has been calling me here but I never hear from you since then even when you promised to call me. Well i will be waiting for the money i requested,

Thank you for all the Evidenc you have provided so far

Davis

A couple of nondescript emails are quickly exchanged that lead nowhere. Then our next piece of evidence is unleashed.

I tried to think of more ways to try to convince Davis that Peter really had lied to him. I hit upon the idea of sampling various pieces of audio from Peter Jones's telephone calls to me and then editing them together to make a brand new fake telephone call. It was pretty hard going, and the audio is a bit suspicious in parts, but I thought it would be good enough to fool Davis.

As I am not speaking to Davis at the moment, I handed the fake conversation between Max N. Paddy and Peter Jones to Ed Shanks to send to Davis.

From: Ed Shanks (A. Skinner)
To: Matins Davis
Date: 31 March 2005

Dear Matins - I hope this mail finds you in better condition than myself. My days have been ruined by the fact that Peter Jones robbed us. Mr. Paddy Max has been able to obtain the audio recording of conversations between himself and Peter Jones. He got this from the telephone cellular company who keep them for a short while for security reasons. He sent the audio file to me.

I am attaching the actual voice conversation between Paddy Max and Peter Jones to this email so you can hear for yourself what a crook and liar Peter Jones is. It is the conversation that took place on the exact moment that Paddy Max handed over the cash to Peter Jones. It can be clearly understood while listening that Peter received the money.

Let me advise you of another development. Regarding your request that I send you money for the Peter Jones investigation. I would need to borrow the money from Mr. Paddy Max. He refuses to loan me the cash unless you admit to him that Peter is a thief, and send him a copy of Peter's passport. Can you do this so we move forward ASAP?

Sincerely,

Ed Shanks

(Ed attaches the fake telephone call.)

Peter:	Hello is that Max?
Max N. Paddy:	Hello is that Peter?
Peter:	Yes.

Max N. Paddy:	Hello Peter. Sorry, I know I have only just left the meeting with you but I wonder if you could do me a favour please?
Peter:	OK.
Max N. Paddy:	Mr. Davis asked me to call him just before I gave you the money...
Peter:	Right.
Max N. Paddy:	... a few minutes ago, but I have tried to call him a few times now but I just can't get him on the line.
Peter:	Oh I know, it's a terrible phone system.
Max N. Paddy:	Tell me about it! Anyway, he asked me to call him just before I gave you the money...
Peter:	Yeah.
Max N. Paddy:	...but I just can't get through to him so please can you give him a call for me to let him know you collected the money safely?
Peter:	Right OK.
Max N. Paddy:	Thanks so much Peter, and I hope you have the money wrapped up safely!
Peter:	Yes I have.
Max N. Paddy:	Great stuff. I was initially thinking about doing a bank transfer rather than handing cash over but Ed Shanks wanted no trace of the payment so...
Peter:	In Africa where if you do transfers of any kind then your money just simply disappears.
Max N. Paddy:	So cash is the usual way you do business in Africa then is it?
Peter:	Oh yeah. It all works on a cash basis.
Max N. Paddy:	I'm just worried about handing over such large amounts of cash.
Peter:	There will be no complications. It is all really straightforward and simple.
Max N. Paddy:	Well that is very good to hear. It's just that the way these people seem to be working is a bit strange.
Peter:	Do you have any experience in Africa at all?
Max N. Paddy:	No. I have just handed over £18,000 to you and I have no receipt or anything. Please do not forget to confirm with Mr. Davis that you have received the cash.
Peter:	I confirm that with you now.
Max N. Paddy:	Thanks Peter.

Peter:	I don't really have any role in this other than the fact that the people in Ghana have known me for many years and they trust me impeccably.
Max N. Paddy:	Well, that's good to hear. As you know, I'm just doing this as a favour to a good friend and the money I gave you is just to help him out of a situation.
Peter:	I'm just doing a favour too.
Max N. Paddy:	Right. OK I will leave it there for now Peter. It was nice to meet you and I hope we meet again sometime. I'll send an email to Davis now and let him know the meeting went ahead as planned.
Peter:	OK.
Max N. Paddy:	OK Peter, I'm due for a meeting now so I'll say goodbye for now.
Peter:	OK bye.
Max N. Paddy:	Bye.

I think we may have finally convinced Davis that Peter stole the money.

From: Matins Davis
To: Ed Shanks CC: Max N. Paddy
Date: 31 March 2005
Title: i believe you now

Thank you for this evidence you provided to me After I have listen to conversation, I discovered it is obviously that you gave Peter Jones the money and is a THIEF and BIG LIER,

Immediately I called the attention of Jones Representative to listen to the Audio conversation between you and him

COULD YOU BELIEVED WHAT THEY SAID??? {I QUOTE THEM}
{1} this is not Peter voice and peter voice is not cleared,
{2} That max said 18,000 pounds and it is Dollars , so it can Different person voice. {3}Davis don't you know they can work on this out with somebody voice ??
after hearing this stupid statement from them I got provoked and called a police friend and I told him on phone and he said I see him in the office for official report tomorrow.

Please I am Ready to deal with all of them involved in whichever means I could .

For this reasoning Mr. Max I need your help please I know I have not believed you all this while but you need understand me here as well.

With all these evidence you provided is enough to believe you and as well get Jones in Jail and all of them here. On the issue of Jones passport, I sent message concerning that but he told me is that he is taking you to court so his lawyer said he should not pass this to me, But NOW I KNOW IT IS BIG LIE

Please Max, they have the money and to get this money from with the help of top friend in the police I need money to do this if Not they will close the case with money if I DON'T act fast now please waiting to hear from you as soon as possible

Thank you

Davis

Of course, Mr. Davis has to do some work before he can get back on my good side!

From: Max N. Paddy (Shiver Metimbers)
To: Matins Davis
Date: 1 April 2005

Dear Mr. Davis - Well finally you have come to see that what I have been telling you all this time is true. Thank you for being intelligent enough to see through this man's lies.

Well, Mr. Jones knows my address and also my business address, so if he really means to try to clear his name then he is being very slow about it because I have heard nothing from him. He is most welcome to come to my offices. However, he will be in danger of immediate arrest if he sets foot in Paisley again. But enough of that buffoon, let us get back to business.

My friend Ed Shanks telephoned me a short while ago, and he sounded to me very frustrated and upset. It appears that you require more money from him but he no longer has anything to give. He has begged for my help, but I have to be honest with you and tell you that my help will be hard to give because my trust has dealt a severe blow because of the actions of Mr. Jones. As it stands at the moment, I have lost $18,000 and I do not know if I will ever see it again.

My friend Ed Shanks has promised me that if I help him out once more, you will both pay me back my $18,000 once the deal you have with

Mr. Shanks has been finalised. If this is indeed the case then perhaps I may be willing to help. Please understand that I am only doing this to help out my very dear friend. If it were not for Ed begging for help then I would have ended this deal immediately.

Now Mr. Davis, I need some very honest and accurate information from you before I am prepared to help you with yet more money. I need you to answer the following questions as accurately as you can, and also I have some terms you must agree to. If you can answer the questions and agree to my terms THEN and only then will I be willing to help my friend Mr. Shanks by sending you the money by whatever means best suits you.

1. I do not know what your deal is with Mr. Shanks, but can you please tell me once I pay you the money, how long will it take to complete?

2. Once you and Mr. Shanks have the full deal completed, will you agree to pay half of my $18,000 back to me?

3. Please tell me of the TOTAL AMOUNT required to finally finish this deal. I need to know the complete amount so that once Mr. Shanks pays you there will be no further charges. I have told Mr. Shanks that I am willing to help him up to the amount of US $50,000 but no more than this. So please let me know the exact and FINAL amount that is required to finalise this deal.

Now to my terms:

As a result of the robbery which took place against me, I have lost a lot of trust in this deal, and I need to be 100% sure of the identity of the person I am giving this money to. I will need you to show some proof of identity to me in the following manner;

1. I will need a good quality scan of your passport or other identification card that includes your photograph.

2. To prove that the person in the passport or ID is you I will also need you to take a new *high quality* photograph of yourself holding a sign with the following message written on it: PETER JONES IS A THIEF.

You will need to have a photograph taken of yourself holding this CLEAR sign. Scan the photograph and then send it to me, along with your passport, by email attachment. It is VERY IMPORTANT that the passport/ID and your photograph scan are HIGH QUALITY and LARGE & CLEAR. I will reject any small or unclear images.

The reason I need you to take a new photograph of yourself holding the sign is that I can then compare it to your passport/ID photo and then be sure of course that you are one and the same person.

Now Mr. Davis, so long as you are prepared to accept my terms above ad answer the questions, I WILL send you the payment you require, up to the total amount of US $50,000.

As soon as the scans of your identification and your ID/passport are received (and are of sufficient quality) then I will advise my secretary Mr. John Kimble to make the payment to you immediately in whatever manner suits you.

Some readers may recognise the name John Kimble - a character from an Arnold Schwarzenegger movie.

Please note that the above terms are non-negotiable. If you do not agree to my request then I am sorry but I will have to tell my friend that I am unwilling to help him.

Sincerely,

Max N. Paddy.
Managing Director: Dark Side Communications Inc.

From: Matins Davis
To: Max N. Paddy (Shiver Metimbers)
Date: 1 April 2005
Title: re: i believe you now

Hello Max - Thank you for your email , your terms are accepted and I will forward everything to you by as soon as I have the picture from photograph, hoply by next week it will be ready.

I hope you advise your secretary Mr. John Kimble to make the payment to ready as you said. I talk Mr shanks on phone just some minutes ago concering the your terms .

And any email you receive from anybody that you don't understand do NOT reply, like,,, jones and his parterns . Can forward such email to me here.

Thank you

Davis

Davis sent the scan and passport image. Unfortunately, the quality was awful, so he was required to re-scan everything and send it again. I won't bore you all with the several emails backwards and forwards complaining about image quality.

At last, competent images are received.

From: Matins Davis
To: Max N. Paddy (Shiver Metimbers)
Date: 3 April 2005
Title: my picture and answers

ANSWE TO YOUR QUESTION

1. Ans,,, THE DEAL WILL TAKE ABOUT WEEKS DEPENDING WHEN THE MONEY IS RECEIVED .
2. Mr Davis and Mr Shanks WILL PAY THE FULL MONEY {$18,000} SINCE WE ARE MAKING GOOD PROFIT.
3. THE TOTAL AMOUNT REQUIRED IS LESSTHAN $50,000 USD, WE WILL NOT REQUIRE MORE THAN THAT, THANK YOU.

Now answer to your terms:

1. I will need a good quality scan of your passport or other identification card that includes your photograph.,,,,,,MY PASSPORT HAS BEEN INCLUDED {SEE THE ATTACHMENT}

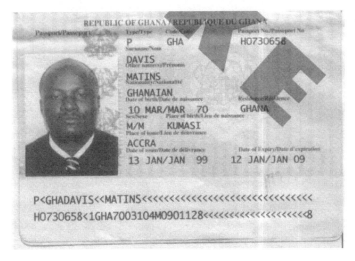

2. To prove that the person in the passport or ID is you I will also need you to take a new *high quality* photograph of yourself holding a sign with the following message written on it: PETER JONES IS A THIEF,,,, ALSO ATTACHED {SEE THE ATTACHMENT}

Time to put Davis's mind at ease.

From: Max N. Paddy (Shiver Metimbers)
To: Matins Davis
Date: 3 April 2005

Dear Mr. Davis - Thank you! That picture is acceptable.

Please can you calculate the exact amount of payment you require and I shall ensure my secretary is made aware and ready to make the payment to you. I leave for an overseas trip on Monday evening, so it will be left to my secretary Mr. John Kimble to make the payment to you.

I may request a password/answer question for you to use with him so that he can be sure he is speaking to the correct person, just for extra security.

I will talk to Mr. Kimble in the morning and get back to you with payment information. In the meantime, please let me know the TOTAL amount required to finalise this deal once and for all.

Kind regards,

Max N. Paddy.
Managing Director: Dark Side Communications Inc.

From: Matins Davis
To: Max N. Paddy (Shiver Metimbers)
Date: 3 April 2005
Title: re: my picture and answers

The issue of money needed, make payment of $45,000 , because some area need to be negotiated after making first payment of $20,000. So I am asking for $45,000

Davis is quite a greedy little scammer, isn't he?!

From: Max N. Paddy (Shiver Metimbers)
To: Matins Davis
Date: 3 April 2005

Dear Mr. Davis - Any you are sure that this payment will be the final payment 100%?

If that is the case then I shall make arrangement with Mr. Kimble. I think the earliest that I can arrange payment will be Tuesday. I need to ask you the answer to two questions now. Mr. Kimble will ask you these two questions when you speak to him for the payment. You will need to give me the answers to these two questions now, and then give the same answers to Mr. Kimble on Tuesday when he asks you. This way he will know 100% to whom he is speaking to.

The questions I need the answers to are:

1. What is your father's name?

2. What does he do (what is his job)?

One further question Mr. Kimble will ask is an extra security question. He will ask you this:

'What about Thomas Aquinas?'

The answer to this question must be: "Thomas Aquinas is the head
Tribble keeper at Tribbles R Us'.

Once Mr. Kimble has received the correct answers to those three
security questions he will be sure he is talking to the correct person and
will make the payment to you immediately the same day. Please supply
me with the answers to questions 1 and 2 as soon as possible.

Kind regards,

Max N. Paddy.
Managing Director: Dark Side Communications Inc.

From: Matins Davis
To: Max N. Paddy (Shiver Metimbers)
Date: 3 April 2005
Title: ranswers

Max

TO YOUR QUESTION

The questions I need the answers to are:

1. What is your father's name? ,,,,,,,,, DAVIS

2. What does he do (what is his job)? ,,,,, BUSINESSMAN

Thank

Davis

Davis drops an email to Ed Shanks concerning the final payment.

From: Matins Davis
To: Ed Shanks (A. Skinner)
Date: 3 April 2005
Title: payment

*Hello Shanks - I just sent a message to Mr Max concerning the amount
we will need from him. As required to know because he will leaving for
overseas on Monday evening.*

*The reasoning why I asked $45,000 which I know it might not get to
that amount but to be on safety side and avoiding asking for money
from him required for that amount.*

Why do I have to demand for this money from him?? Well if you remembered on phone I told you that the Funds will pass through diplomatic carry to avoid 11 SEPTEMBER

As you know very well that since September 11 issue, American Government always interested in funds that is coming from African,

This is why we Need to use DIPLOMATIC CARRY, and this is the reasoning of $45000 please

Thank you

Davis

And back to Max N. Paddy.

From: Matins Davis
To: Max N. Paddy (Shiver Metimbers)
Date: 3 April 2005
Title: contact this number

Please ermail Bernel Nelson,

HER EMAIL ADDRESS IS bernelxxxx@hotmail.com CALL HER ON THIS PHONE ,,,001973454XXXX SHE WILL TELL WHAT TO DO.

MR SHANKS KNOWS HER VERY

DAVIS

Before I can reply, Matins gets back to me.

From: Matins Davis
To: Max N. Paddy (Shiver Metimbers)
Date: 4 April 2005
Title: payment iformation

Hello Max - I made a call to Bernel Nelson informing her to call you but she will not be able

Because she Can't take outside USA now. I will contact you later today with information payment.

For me I will always be in touch with or Mr Kimble

Thank you
Davis

From: Max N. Paddy (Shiver Metimbers)
To: Matins Davis
Date: 4 April 2005

Dear Mr. Davis - Thank you for your email.

I will receive your payment information later today hopefully. I do not leave until later this evening, but I shall always be available by email in any case.

I have passed your 2 answers over to my secretary John Kimble, and also he will be expecting your telephone call on Tuesday. I will contact you later with his contact information and a time to call him and also of course his contact email address. Please ensure that you also have the Thomas Aquinas answer ready for him when you speak to him on the telephone.

Today I will arrange the money you require and pass it over to Mr. Kimble before I leave so that he can process your payment tomorrow (Tuesday). Please ensure that you give me the full details of how the payment is to be made to you.

I hope to hear from you later today.

Max N. Paddy.
Managing Director: Dark Side Communications Inc.

Davis sends the payment information.

From: Matins Davis
To: Max N. Paddy (Shiver Metimbers)
Date: 4 April 2005
Title: the details

Hello Max - Thank you for your reply

Please this is the information for the payment

STANDARD CHARTERED BANK NEW YORK,
SWIFT BIC CODE SCBLUS33XXX
FOR ACCOUNT NO. 3582092805001

IN THE NAME :

UNIBANK GHANA LIMITED

P.O.BOX AN 15367

ACCRA- NORTH

BENEFRICIARY :
NAME A.F.B LIMITED

ADDRESS:
P.O. BOX KN 3714
KANESHIE, ACCRA
ACCOUNT NO : 0330240147211

Please comfirm if you have this information

Thank you

Davis

NOTE .... Please scan the reciept of the payment to me

I get ready to set up a call between Davis and John Kimble.

From: Max N. Paddy (Shiver Metimbers)
To: Matins Davis
Date: 4 April 2005

Dear Mr. Davis - Thank you for your email and your telephone call a short while ago.

I shall forward the payment information to my secretary John Kimble. Mr. Kimble's contact number is +44 7017 450 XXX

Please note that I am leaving in a short while. Mr. Kimble will not be in my office until after 11am tomorrow (Tuesday) morning, so please ensure you call after this time. You may also contact Mr. Kimble on his private email (he will be available at al times) on kimble.xxx@xxxxx.co.uk. If you need to ask him any questions before you call him tomorrow he has been advised to help you as much as possible via email.

Before you telephone him tomorrow ensure the following:

You give the correct answers to:

1. Who is your father?

2. What does he do?

and finally, you will be asked:

'What about Thomas Aquinas?'

and your answer must be:

'Thomas Aquinas is the head Tribble keeper at Tribbles R Us'

It is very important you give loud and clear, correct answers to the questions above.

Please note that my secretary is Austrian, and speaks English only a little, so please do not be offended if he seems rude. This is not his intention, this is just the way he sounds!

I shall return from my trip on Wednesday evening, and hopefully everything will then be in place so that you and my friend Mr. Shanks can finalise your deal ASAP.

Good luck,

Max N. Paddy.
Managing Director: Dark Side Communications Inc.

Davis sends an email to the non-existent John Kimble.

From: Matins Davis
To: John Kimble (Shiver Metimbers)
Date: 4 April 2005
Title: introduction

Hello Mr. Kimble,

I am matins Davis, I have been in contact with Mr Paddy Max for sometime now, I understand he will be leaving the country on Tuesday and coming back on Wednesday evening, well he as told me you will be making payment of $45,000 tomorrow.

Well I will call you tomorrow at the same time given . with Answer ready

I hope to hear from you by replying back

Davis

From: John Kimble (Shiver Metimbers)
To: Matins Davis
Date: 4 April 2005

Dear Mr. Davis - I thank you very much for your email which I have received some short time ago. I have been advised by Mr. Paddy that I am to make a payment of USD $45,000.00 tomorrow to you using the following details......

STANDARD CHARTERED BANK NEW YORK,
SWIFT BIC CODE: SCBLUS33XXX
FOR ACCOUNT NO: 358209280XXXX
IN THE NAME: UNIBANK GHANA LTD
P.O.BOX AN 15367
ACCRA- NORTH
BENEFICIARY NAME: A.F.B LIMITED
ADDRESS: P.O. BOX KN 37XX
KANESHIE, ACCRA
ACCOUNT NO: 0330240147XXX
Please email me to confirm the above details are correct.

I believe that Mr. Paddy has told you to call me after 11:00am tomorrow morning?

Thank you.

John Kimble (sec)
Dark Side Communications Inc.

And so the trap is set... The next day arrives, and Davis telephones John Kimble in the vain hope of finally getting his money.

A note for those unfamiliar with the next routine: I have acquired an Arnold Schwarzenegger soundboard. Put simply, this is a computer program which has various Arnold Schwarzenegger sound samples taken from the film *Kindergarten Cop* (Arnie played undercover police officer, John Kimble, in this movie). Press a key and Arnie speaks! I am going to use this soundboard to communicate with Davis!

Date: 5th April 2005 - Matins Davis call John Kimble (try to read this in your best Arnold Schwarzenegger accent!):

John Kimble:	Good morning
Davis:	Good morning.
John Kimble:	Yeah.
Davis:	This is Matins Davis speaking.
John Kimble:	How are you?
Davis:	I'm OK, and you?
John Kimble:	Yeah.
Davis:	OK.
John Kimble:	I want to ask you a bunch of questions, and I want

	to have them answered immediately.
Davis:	All right
John Kimble:	Who is your daddy and what does he do?
Davis:	Davis. He's Davis, and he's a businessman.
John Kimble:	Yeah. I would like to talk to you about Thomas Aquinas.
Davis:	Thomas Aquinas is the head of Tribble keeper at Tribbles R Us.
John Kimble:	WHO ARE YOU?
Davis:	Again. Hello. Your voice is low please.
John Kimble:	Yeah.
Davis:	Hello?
John Kimble:	STOP WHINING!
Davis:	Yes, this is Davis calling.
John Kimble:	Good morning.
Davis:	Yep.
John Kimble:	Yeah.
Davis:	Thomas Aquinus is the head of Tribble keeper at Tribbles R Us.
John Kimble:	Yeah.
Davis:	OK.
John Kimble:	First, I would just like to get to know you.
Davis:	What?
John Kimble:	STOP WHINING!
Davis:	Oh God!
John Kimble:	YOU SON OF A BITCH! YOU LACK DISCIPLINE!
Davis:	(silence!)
John Kimble:	First, I would just like to get to know you.
Davis:	You like to know me?
John Kimble:	Yeah.
Davis:	Yeah I'm Davis, Matins.
John Kimble:	How are you?
Davis:	I'm OK, and you?
John Kimble:	Yeah.
Davis:	Yeah, you are John Kimble right?
John Kimble:	Yeah.
Davis:	OK, I just want t...
John Kimble	(interrupting) Who is your daddy and what does he do?
Davis:	My daddy name is Davis. He is a businessman.

John Kimble:	I would like to talk to you about Thomas Aquinas.
Davis:	Thomas Aquinas is the head of Tribble keeper at Tribbles R Us.
John Kimble:	WHO ARE YOU?
Davis:	I'm Davis.
John Kimble:	Yeah.
Davis:	Are you OK with that?
John Kimble:	NO DEAL!
Davis:	OK.... So can you go ahead with the payment?
John Kimble:	STOP WHINING!
Davis:	Can you go ahead with the payment?
John Kimble:	I'VE GOT NEWS FOR YOU, YOU ARE MINE NOW!

Davis, probably very frustrated at this point, puts the phone down on Mr. Kimble!

Looks like the jig is finally up! I doubt very much that after the last telephone call that Matins Davis will be willing to proceed with 'the deal'. However, after what must have been a somewhat confusing and worrying call, Davis gets in touch with John Kimble minutes later via email.

From: Matins Davis
To: John Kimble (Shiver Metimbers)
Date: 5 April 2005
Title: payment

Hello John Kimble - i picked up your first question and second but i could not hear you on the last question which be thomas Aquinas ??

Can you go on with the payment Now

I received a call from Paddy Max

Thank you

Davis

Poor fool - he still doesn't seem to have grasped what is going on, and also tells a little white lie about Max phoning him! At the same time, Davis sends an email to Max N. Paddy.

From: Matins Davis
To: Max N. Paddy (Shiver Metimbers)
Date: 5 April 2005
Title: hello max

Hello Max - Thank you for your call, what is today password ?? i call

Mr Kimble some minutes ago but i could not hear him very well concering the last Question But I gave him the Answer for all the question

Is he making the payment or Not ??/

Davis

Unfortunately, Max is out of the country so cannot respond! Going for the hat-trick, Davis gets in touch with Ed Shanks.

From: Matins Davis
To: Ed Shanks (A. Skinner)
Date: 5 April 2005
Title: hello ed shanks

Hello Shanks - Honestly I don't know what is going on as nobody is reply me back my emails.

Mr., Max is out the country but he said Mr. Kimble will take care of the payment, since yesterday I have not hard anything from them. I call the phone disconnected tone.

if you have a way of reaching Mr Max please tell him that i can't understand what is going again and why is he not replying my email again.

Waiting hear from you

Davis

Ed Shanks gets back to Davis.

From: Ed Shanks (A. Skinner)
To: Matins Davis
Date: 6 April 2005

Dear Davis - Sorry not to have got back to you sooner. I knew that Mr. Max was going to have his secretary, John Kimble, send you the $45,000 USD. I was not aware of the method he was going to use to get the money to you. How was he going to do that? Have you got it yet?

I did get a note from Mr. Max in which he states that a newspaper reporter from Paisley is publishing an article about Peter Jones robbing Paddy Max of the $18,000. The reporter went to Max's home for the interview. I do hope to see the article in the paper when it is published. How is the investigation going at your end?

Sincerely,

Ed Shanks

From: Matins Davis
To: Ed Shanks (A. Skinner)
Date: 7 April 2005
Title: re: hello ed shanks

Hello Shanks - Thank you for your email. Mr Max told Mr John Kimble to make $45,000 Payment avalible to me by Bank transefer which i gave him the Bank information and gave me Question and Answer as security while calling MrKimble. after calling Mr Kimble andhim the answer to the Question. Since then he did not reply me again And even himself never reply as well. please why is Mr Max not replying my emails ???

I call Mr Kimble on phone he was acting funning to me, WHY ?? Did he know that i phone call is money ?? from here. please fine out from Mr Max if he is paying the money or Not. I did not see reasoning why he should keep silent for now, he has my number he call me tell me something, when was the last time you recieved email from him ? {Mr Max} please waiting to hear from you

Davis

As I am currently 'overseas' and unable to communicate with Davis, I pass on a new fake newspaper headline to Ed Shanks to send to Davis.

From: Ed Shanks (A. Skinner)
To: Matins Davis
Date: 8 April 2005

Dear Davis - I may be able to help you with some cash for the investigation. However, look what Mr. Max sent me today. It is an article in the Paisley newspaper which is attached to this mail. Max told me he was still out of town and would remain so for several more days. He has not been able to get in touch with his secretary, John Kimble. I am currently praying that Kimble didn't run off with your $45,000 USD. The newspaper article is very revealing and I hope to get a full explanation from you.

Sincerely,

Ed Shanks

The newspaper masthead (Paisley Daily Express) is the real thing. We know that in the video where Peter Jones is spotted with a paper, he was reading this very newspaper, though not this doctored version of course!

Daily Express

LOCAL BUSINESSMAN ROBBED BY SCAMMER

Waiting: The alleged thief, Peter Jones

Scammer: Matins Davis in Ghana

By SIMON DEXTER

AUTHORITIES are asking for the public's help in trying to apprehend a man they say scammed a local businessman out of almost 9,600 GBP.

New Scotland Yard spokesman detective Robert Buxton told the Paisley Daily Express Thursday the alleged scammer goes by the name "Peter Jones", and is possibly part of a much larger outfit committing what is commonly known as "Nigerian Letter" or "Advanced Fee" fraud.

Buxton says this latest incident took place last Friday in County Square, where local businessman Max N. Paddy, owner of Dark Side Communications, agreed to meet Jones and hand him 18,000 USD. In return, Buxton says, the victim was promised access to "millions upon millions of dollars" in Ghana.

According to Buxton, Jones met Paddy and then apparently disappeared with the money. It was only after several days of frustration and failed attempts to get his money back Paddy decided to contact the police.

According to police, Jones was caught on film by both CCTV and the victim, who took a picture of Mr Jones as he approached the meeting place in County Square. Paisley, so he could have "better identification" of the suspect.

Jones is described as a white male in his late 30's, about 5 foot 6, wearing tan boots and dark clothing. He is also believed to be of South African origin.

Buxton also tells the Express Jones is believed to be working in concert with a suspected scam artist named "Matins Davis" (see photo) based in Ghana. According to Buxton, Davis allegedly contacted Paddy and is responsible for setting up the meeting between Paddy and the suspect.

Buxton called Davis "...a person a number of police agencies, both here and internationally, are looking very closely at."

Police would not confirm other details of the investigation, only saying both New Scotland Yard and Ghanaian authorities are actively lending support" to the current inquiry.

Authorities say these types of gangs "...have been known to kidnap, torture and often times murder people who get between them and their money."

Please contact Crimestoppers on 0800 555 111 if you have information which can help the police.

472

Davis contacts John Kimble...

From: Matins Davis
To: John Kimble (Shiver Metimbers)
Date: 8 April 2005
Title: not scam

Hello Kimble - Well i recieved message from Shanks today , i don;t know if you know him that i am into ADVANCED FRUAD. well tell hiom that i said i can prove to him that i am not by taking this Case up to anywhere i can.

our arrangements is that he will make payment of $ 45, 000 the same the day if the answer is giving but since he thinks that are into that lets take up . .

If you wants to send the money go ahead and do that

Thank you

Davis

John Kimble doesn't bother to reply!

Ed Shanks receives an email from Davis...

From: Matins Davis
To: Ed Shanks (A. Skinner)
Date: 8 April 2005
Title: hello ed

Hello Shanks - It will be good I get this money from You to pursue this CASE from here,{ANY AMOUNT YOU HAVE } but who is Max and what his relation in this business ? because it look like this business not secret any more if the police are making opening then .

Mr Shanks I so much respect you and honour you after I discovered the kind of Man you are, why should you allow Mr Max Tell the Newspaper that, we are into Nigeria Letter or whatever they called it .

Please Answer this Question for me

_{1} who is Mr. Max to you ??

am sure Mr. Max is not ready to pay this money, reasoning for this are ,,,, he told me his secretary, John Kimble will make the payment ready the same day if I gave him the correct which I did.

473

Mr Max told me his secretary John does not speak English very well because he is from German , please such man be in that office that with communication ,??? When he was talking to me sound like he is talking his small boy, is that how it should be ? WHY would max ask him to make payment for me and he would want to call a Man who cannot speak ?? on phone. Mr. Shanks do you know I spend money making calls?? From here .

Well in the newspaper article HE mentioned NIGERIAN LETTER or ADVANCED FRUAD, Good if he believed that is what we are doing now let get into END of this Deal, with that we shall know who is who ??

I will like you to send the Money I required from you today and I will send this case to police station myself to prove to him that we are not into ADVANCED FRUAD as he believed.

ARE YOU READY TO SEND THE MONEY ?? IF send today, by Monday inter- pol will contact Mr. Max to testify if it is ADVANCED FRUAD or NOT.

Thank you for understanding and Co –operating

Davis

We now attempt to try and get some solid information on just exactly who and where Peter Jones, the Glasgow scammer, is:

From: Ed Shanks (A. Skinner)
To: Matins Davis
Date: 9 April 2005

{1} who is Mr. Max to you ??

Max is married to my sister, and has been for the last 17 years. He has been a partner in many business ventures with me, and I trust him more than I would trust my own brother. I certainly trust him more than I trust you.

Max's company is an INTERNATIONAL company, and he has MANY different foreign speaking people working for him, including German, Italian, Chinese, Indian, Spanish and more. His company deals with many overseas clients and so the need for communications in languages other than English is very important, you tit.

If you want to contact Interpol about Max Mr. Davis, please do so. I am sure that Max Paddy will appreciate more police help to track down the thief Peter Jones. He is willing to hand over any evidence required. Please contact Interpol IMMEDIATELY.

Now, Mr. Kimble is the last person I know that had your $45,000 so it is important you speak with him. I HAVE NO MONEY LEFT, so if you cannot get the money from Mr. Kimble or Max then I am afraid I can no longer complete this deal.

Mr. Davis, it is YOUR FAULT that there has been such a delay. If you did not employ a THIEF to STEAL Mr. Paddy's money then we would not be in this present predicament. You need to look to yourself for the cause of all this trouble.

I was informed by Mr. Paddy that unless you use the correct passwords from now on all your communications to him and Mr. Kimble will be 100% ignored. He has implemented these very tight security measures because of your thief friend Mr. Jones WHO YOU STILL HAVE NOT GIVEN US INFORMATION ABOUT.

Mr. Paddy has asked these questions about Mr. Jones and, until you answer them, you will not get a dollar from anyone:

1. What is Peter Jones' real name?

2. What is Peter Jones' business name?

3. What is Peter Jones' full and complete business address?

4. What is Peter Jones' business (NOT mobile) telephone number?

If you are unable to answer the above then I think it is time for us to end our partnership.

Davis replies with some information, but it's just not good enough!

From: Matins Davis
To: Ed Shanks (A. Skinner)
Date: 9 April 2005
Title: the information your wanted

Hello Shanks - Max's company is an INTERNATIONAL company, and he has MANY different foreign speaking people working for him, including German, Italian, Chinese, Indian, Spanish and more. His company deals with many overseas clients and so the need for communications in languages other than English is very important, you tit. ,,,,,, ,,,,,yet gave somebody that cannot speak English WHY ?

Now, Mr. Kimble is the last person I know that had your $45,000 so it is important you speak with him. I HAVE NO MONEY LEFT, so if you cannot get the money from Mr. Kimble or Max then I am afraid I can no longer complete this deal.,,,,,SPEAKING TO HIM IS NOT THE BIG DEAL BUT HE MAKING THE PAYMENT. I DON'T TO CALL AND RECEIVED STUPID SOUND FROM HIM . LET HIM CALL ME IF HE WANTS TO MAKE THE PAYMENT

Mr. Davis, it is YOUR FAULT that there has been such a delay. If you did not employ a THIEF to STEAL Mr. Paddy's money then we would not be in this present predicament. You need to look to yourself for the cause of all this trouble...I ONLY REPLY THIS EMAIL because you mentioned it is my FAULT for such delayed, I did not employ Peter Jones. For your correction. If Mr. Max been a businessman pay $18,000 by cash with receipts then he has problem in Running the company.

And your Question I have made it clear to Mr max that I don't know much in person but I know their agency , which I planed to deal with here .

I was informed by Mr. Paddy that unless you use the correct passwords ,,,,,,I made it clear to him that I can't open the windom here with system.

1. What is Peter Jones' real name?,,,,,,,, I only know with that name

2. What is Peter Jones' business name?,,,,,,, They are like Western Union

3. What is Peter Jones' full and complete business address? Mr. Max HAVE IT, let the police call him and take the number from him, by way what do take me for ??? Fool or what ? Mr Max took my picture that he wants to sure of whom he is dealing with ,but rather he took to Newspaper that I have Fraud him with Peter. Mr. Shanks do you know I called the police from more time and he said NO CASE was reported to him. Please tell Mr. Max he should stop that act before he fine himself to in trouble.

4. What is peter Jones business (NOT mobile) telephone number.,,,,, THAT WAS NOT GIVEN TO ME, I CAN'T HAVE BECAUSE THEY ARE MY ENEMIES FOR NOW and for your information Mr Jones Said he is waiting for Max to call on his phone, he is ready to meet him. I asked Max to give his PICTURE, but he has not done WHY? I also need his passport as well.

If you are unable to answer the above then I think it is time for us to end our partnership. ,,,,That is all for now that I know and if you wants to End. go ahead I have nothing much to say but Thank you for wasting my time and money for calls

Good Day

Davis sounds miffed, and attempts to call our bluff by saying he's had enough of the deal. I know enough about the scammer mind by now to know that this won't be the case!

From: Ed Shanks (A. Skinner)
To: Matins Davis
Date: 9 April 2005

Dear Davis - This whole matter is about to put me into a mental hospital. Sometimes I think that is where you are writing from. It would be so easy for you to follow directions, but you refuse. If you don't want the money then our business is finished. Mr. Max is a decent man, and so am I. I feel that we have been shafted by you and am beginning to wonder if you are a scammer.

Ed Shanks

From: Matins Davis
To: Ed Shanks (A. Skinner)
Date: 10 April 2005
Title: hello shanks

Hello Shanks - Thank you for your email . well I don't know how badly you feel but I think felt more badly than you think. You said it will so easy to fellow direction and I refused, I did not refuse to fellow Direction as you stated it,

The issue of think woodenly if I into Scammer , well I amo not and the only way to prove my is to get into end of this business. Which is most coming to end if he hard send the money required {$45,000}

Well I will be waiting to hear from you
Thank you

Davis

From: Ed Shanks (A. Skinner)
To: Matins Davis
Date: 11 April 2005

Dear Davis - My mental state is still not quite well. I think we can salvage the whole operation and recover the $45,000 USD if you would just co-operate. Here is the information we need on Peter Jones.

1. His land-line number.

2. The full and complete name of his business

3. The full and complete address (including post code) of his business.

Also, I have another friend here in the USA that might help me if John Kimble will not. Please keep me informed.

Ed Shanks

Davis is being stubborn...

From: Matins Davis
To: Ed Shanks (A. Skinner)
Date: 11 April 2005
Title: hello shanks

Hello Shanks - all these things you neede can only get if the law is involved as you know very well that since the issue of the $18,000 USD they have not been in good time with me they would not want answer me with these Details you needed

that is why i requested for $2700 from you but since you cannot get it, i might have problem in geytting the information from them please. mr Peter Jones information only get if i have the law deal with them.

Thank you
Davis

Time for Max N. Paddy to turn the screw. I'm back from my trip, and I won't stand for any more crap!

From: Max N. Paddy (Shiver Metimbers)
To: Matins Davis
Date: 11 March 2005

Mr. Davis - I have only this evening returned from my business trip, and I have not yet spoken with my secretary Mr. Kimble. However, Ed Shanks tells me there have been many problems, and I can tell you that Mr. Shanks is EXTREMELY upset and has told me that as far as he is concerned his deal with you is over. He tells me he has put so much effort and work into this deal and received nothing in return except trouble and lies.

Now, I have told Mr. Shanks that I will help him. However, I will NOT proceed any further for one moment until you give me full details about the company, name, and address and full contact details for Mr. Peter Jones.

Please do not lie to me about not knowing anything about him. Mr. Jones told me that he has been working with you for some years, so you MUST have his personal details.

Here is my final offer to you, you can take it or leave it.

I will send you the money your require and take over the deal for Shanks as long as you give me answers to the following questions:

1. What is the full name of Peter Jones' company?
2. What is the full address of Peter Jones' company, including the full UK postcode?
3. If his company has a web site I want to know the address.
4. What is the telephone number for his company (NOT mobile)?

Now, if you cannot or will not answer the questions above then please do not waste your time replying to me. I have absolutely ZERO interest in proceeding until you give me this information. I will be happy to keep the information 100% confidential and Peter Jones will NOT be told where I got the information from.

Do NOT bother to reply to tell me rubbish and lies such as 'he is something like Western Union'. I know this is a lie.

The UK police will not give me the information I require because of the impending investigation so I am demanding it from you. If you do not give it to me then you do not get a single dollar from me and you will never see the $45,000, ever.

This deal now rests in your hands. Either give me the Peter Jones information I require or the deal is 100% over and finished.

DO NOT REPLY TO ME IF YOU ARE NOT PREPARED TO GIVE ME INFORMATION ON JONES.

Sincerely,

Max N. Paddy.
Managing Director: Dark Side Communications Inc.

Davis doesn't reply to me. Instead, he contacts Ed Shanks.

From: Matins Davis
To: Ed Shanks (A. Skinner)
Date: 12 April 2005
Title: re: hello shanks

Hello Shanks - thank you for your email. i will waiting for that .
I recieved information from Mr Max, that he needs Peter Jones
information before he give $45,000 USD to me. please is that i don't
want give him information he asking for , he should understand that i
needed this $18,000 USD for business and how would i feel seeing
Peter made way with this money just like that, i requested for $2,700
just to put them in jail but since not understand me.

well he just emailed me today and he will tell Mr Kimble to make
payment of $45,000 USD AS Soon as i gave him the information
required concerning Mr PETER JONES.

Please how much can you get with today and tomorrow?? in order to
make them give me the information needed through the help police
involvement

Thank you

Davis

From: Ed Shanks (A. Skinner)
To: Matins Davis
Date: 12 April 2005

Dear Friend Davis - I most heartily suggest you comply with the wishes
of Mr. Max. I am flat broke and don't have a dime. My thought was to
ask for charity from my church to raise the money you need, but at the
present time that will have to wait. It may be possible some months in
the future, but is highly doubtful.

For now you must give Mr. Max the information he requests on Peter
Jones. After all it was Peter who grabbed the cash and ran. That is your
only alternative!

Sincerely,

Ed Shanks

Davis is starting to get desperate for some cash.

From: Matins Davis
To: Ed Shanks (A. Skinner)
Date: 14 April 2005
Title: please mr shanks

Hello Shanks - I have paid all the money I hard with and borrowed toad as well but it still remain some money to add, {$1000} I have to pursue this case in other get the information I needed from them , also see them paying the $18,000 dollar back.

Mr. Shanks I will like you to understand that I covering this Peter Jones AS Max is seeing it, what I will I get when Jones made way with the money and leaving us not completing our deal, You should understand that the $18,000 is been sent to meet up demand here , so WHY should allow Jones to run with it.

For this Reason I have NO other option but to pursue this money from them after I sent my staff to go there and pretending that She has money to pick up in UK that She needs their contact information in UK but they only gave her mobile phone number {Mr. peter Jones }and Max is not interested in mobile phone , and I will like to inform you that their agency name here is not the same thing over there , from information I am getting now.

Shanks I know you said you don't have money but I know for sure you get $1,000 as that is only what I needed now to this done .please let me down

Thank you

Davis

Matins Davis follows up his email with a phone call.

From: Ed Shanks (A. Skinner)
To: Matins Davis
Date: 14 April 2005

Dear Davis - Thank you for the telephone call this morning.

I do have a problem understanding you on the telephone because of our dialects. I must tell you again that my pockets are empty at this time. No Cash. Zero! There is a chance of getting some money from my church in a month or two. However, there will be NO MONEY for you until all of Mr. Max's questions are answered.

If I understood you correctly on the telephone, you said that you sent a representative to the security company in London to talk to Peter Jones. But, when I asked you for the address of the security company you did not have it. What kind of double talk is this? I suggest you get the address of the security company, their telephone number, Peter Jones telephone number, and his email address as required. Then, we can start getting along with this deal.

I am still a nervous wreck over all of this and am barely living day to day. You must fully comply with Max since he has the cash.

Sincerely,

Ed Shanks

From: Matins Davis
To: Ed Shanks (A. Skinner)
Date: 14 April 2005
Title: re: please mr shanks

Hello Shanks - Thank you for email.

I am not saying in UK but here, their representative company in Ghana. i have Peter Jones PHONE number {mobile} Max Said he needs land phone number and Not Mobile . Why would Max thinks i want to cover up Jones??? what will that be for me ?? please let get this out, i need this money pursue this Case as said ealier on my email. and if i get this information it will forwarded to Max since that is what he wants to release the money for us to move on .

i am waiting for you send what you with there now .

Thank you

Davis

From: Ed Shanks (A. Skinner)
To: Matins Davis
Date: 15 April 2005

Dear Davis - You ask why you would try to cover up for Jones? Perhaps you really did get the money from him and are trying to pull a fake to get more? All we know for sure is that Jones got the cash. Now we are having problems with you helping us to determine who he really is and giving us the information. I trust you, but there is room for doubt here. I am in a tizzy over all of this my friend. Please get back to me with something positive.

Sincerely,

Ed Shanks

Well, surprise surprise! Davis finally gets back to Max with the Peter Jones information.

From: Matins Davis
To: Max N. Paddy
Date: 15 April 2005
Title: peter jones

Max - These are information you required from me , but I will like to let you know that I have NO business or interest to cover Mr jones up as made away with the money ment for business here, when I know he has the $ 18,000 Dollars with him, considerly the proves you have provided. But Please DON'T even think of it that I am covering him up and if that is what you are thinking off, then get it out of your mind.

Well I Got these informatio this morning.

{1} UK INFORMATIONS

Company,,,,,, PANZO EXCHANGE

ADDRESS,,,,, 1 XXXXXX
XXXX XXXXXX
London
XXXX XXX
United Kingdom

TEL;,,,,,,,0207241XXXX ,mobile,,,,4479328XXXX

(Note: address and telephone number edited out JUST in case I have been given an innocent person's details.)

You DON'T want mobile number ? I believed you have it but I still add it as well

{2} GHANA INFORMATIONS

COMPANY,,,,,,PIVIO EXCHANGE LTD,,

ADDRESS ,,,,,152/71 Mensah street,

Opp HOTMOBILE company
Accra ringe Road
ACCRA Ghana

TELL,,,,,,,,,02179414XX

Note I understood he runs another company with the same address am still investicating that too, if I have any information concerning that I will let you know,

Can we go ahead Now ?? Waiting to Hear from you then

Davis

At this point, I had to take a real week's holiday, so I left A. Skinner to tell Davis I had gone away on business and that his $45,000 payment would be made when I return.

From: Ed Shanks (A. Skinner)
To: Matins Davis
Date: 16 April 2005

Dear Davis - Thank you for finally coming up with the information. Did you get the email address of Peter Jones?

Mr. Max will be in Von Richthofen in Germany for a week, so that will delay things. I will be in touch with both of you when he gets back.

Ed Shanks

From: Matins Davis
To: Ed Shanks (A. Skinner)
Date: 16 April 2005
Title: ????

Hello Shanks - But why is not Replying me again ? he told me that once he gets that email cxoncerning the information he will email me

He ready to make payment? or Not, We should know that instead of wasting my TIME Please By theway i asked for some money from you to meet up this CASE after Paying $3,500, you told me, you can't get it till months End From Church, is that how will do business???? what of about your friend in USA you mentioned, can't He Rase some money for you ??? because we can't contiune like this.

*It looks like we are not doing anytime on this, Very soon i will stop
Responding to your email or whoever that comes from you that
NOTHING GOOD to Offer*

*Tell Mr Max that he should stop playing Games with me and if you are
involved in these games with him, then i will advise two of you to stop
because i have another things to do.*

Davis

From: Ed Shanks (A. Skinner)
To: Matins Davis
Date: 16 April 2005

Dear Friend Davis - There are no games here. Max is out of town on
vacation & I am broke right now. It is as simple as that. You will have to
wait! I may be able to get money from the church in a month or two, but
that is some time away. Be calm!

Ed Shanks

**A few days pass, but Davis seems to be desperate for even a little
cash.**

*From: Matins Davis
To: Ed Shanks (A. Skinner)
Date: 23 April 2005
Title: hello shanks 500*

*Hello Shanks - How are you doing ? i hope fine. well concerning what
we discoursed on phone today that i need $500. can tell Mr Max to
send that money to me through Western union ? hopely to hear from
you.*

he can send the money on this name ,,,,Mr LAWRANCE SOWAH

waiting to hear from you

Davis

From: Ed Shanks (A. Skinner)
To: Matins Davis
Date: 23 April 2005

Dear Davis - I will tell Max that you are in a state of desperation. I am so sorry that my own funds have been depleted temporarily. I still plan to try to get money from the church when their funding is available.

Ed Shanks

Davis gets in touch with the now returned Max N. Paddy.

From: Matins Davis
To: Max N. Paddy (Shiver Metimbers)
Date: 23 April 2005
Title: welcome back

Hello Max - how are you doing? well in your last email, you mentioned that ONCE I you have the information for Mr Peter Jones you will make $45,000 USD ready, but what can I say now that no email from you again, well i hope you recieved an email from Mr Shanks? I told him that i need $500 from him since I paid all my Money in other to see the $18,000 out but it seem you are ready for that again as i am not hear ing you.

Can i get $500 from you ?? as i am out of Cash now

Thank you waiting to hear from you

Davis

From: Max N. Paddy (Shiver Metimbers)
To: Matins Davis
Date: 24 April 2005

Mr. Davis - Thank you for your email. I assume that Ed Shanks made you completely aware that I had to visit Von Richthofen in Germany for the last week. I only returned home earlier today and have just seen your message.

I am happy to inform you that all preparations are in place to send the $45,000 payment to you, which I will do at the beginning of next week, probably on Monday or Tuesday. Please will you confirm in full exactly how, and to whom the payment is to be made. I am thankful that at last we will be able to make some good progress on this matter.

Sincerely,

Max N. Paddy.
Managing Director: Dark Side Communications Inc.

Davis seems to think there is finally a light at the end of this very long tunnel... the poor bloke!

From: Matins Davis
To: Max N. Paddy (Shiver Metimbers)
Date: 24 April 2005
Title: welcome back

Hello Max - Thank you very much for your email. And welcome back home. I believed this time around the Payment will be made, by the way how, have you gone concerning Peter Jones Case over there ?? I could not do anything as I paid $3,500. I borrowed $1,500 to add up to my $2500 I hard with me in other to get them trapped here, as you know since I could not get the money required for me to pursue the case here. But since you are back it will be okay

Well Now you are back home, I hope things will move speedily ? Once again back home and this is the Bank Information Again

THIS IS THE INFORMATION

STANDARD CHARTERED BANK NEW YORK,
SWIFT BIC CODE: SCBLUS33XXX
FOR ACCOUNT NO: 358209280XXXXX

IN THE NAME: UNIBANK GHANA LTD
P.O.BOX AN 15367
ACCRA- NORTH

BENEFICIARY NAME: A.F.B LIMITED
ADDRESS: P.O. BOX KN 3714
KANESHIE, ACCRA
ACCOUNT NO: 033024014XXXX

Thank you
Waiting to hear from you
Davis
Note,,,,,, ARE YOU STILL ON PHONE ?

Davis, full of expectant glee, sends an email to Ed Shanks.

From: Matins Davis
To: Max N. Paddy (Shiver Metimbers)
Date: 24 April 2005
Title: max

Hello Shanks - I hope you my email last sent to you. Mr. Max Said he will send the money {$45,000} today or tomorrow. I sent the message to him and you as well I hope you received it.

But I hope send it as promised, I gave him my account Number to transfer the money, well I don't think it is necessary contacting the Church again for money , that if he will send it this time around.

Thank you

Davis

From: Ed Shanks (A. Skinner)
To: Matins Davis
Date: 25 April 2005

Dear Davis - That is really good news. Max is a kind and gentle man and I knew in my heart he wouldn't let you down. Please keep me posted.

Ed Shanks

I'm a few days late with my $45,000 payment and, with no replies to his 'where are you?' emails, Davis is a little worried and tries to hit me for some quick cash.

From: Matins Davis
To: Max N. Paddy (Shiver Metimbers)
Date: 27 April 2005
Title: 2000 please?

Hello Max - Please can i get $2,000 before friday through WESTERN UNION TRANSFER ??? I needed it for very important thing,

let me know if you can send that to me before transfer of $45,000

Waiting to hear from you

Davis

I am disgusted that Davis wants even more money!

From: Max N. Paddy (Shiver Metimbers)
To: Matins Davis
Date: 24 April 2005

Mr. Davis - What is going on? You promised me that the $45,000 payment would be the final payment that Mr. Shanks and myself would have to pay and NOW you are asking for yet MORE money ($2,000)?! I was going to send your $45,000 payment earlier this morning (Thursday), but after seeing your email below I thought it best to question you first.

Why are you asking for yet more money? You have now delayed the payment. I will not have time to send it today. You had better come up with a good explanation.

Max N. Paddy.
Managing Director: Dark Side Communications Inc.

From: Matins Davis
To: Max N. Paddy (Shiver Metimbers)
Date: 28 April 2005
Title: re: 2000 please?

Mr Max - The $2,000 I Asked for is part of the money that you will send to me Mr Shanks is Aware of this when you are on your trip Germany i Requested for it on phone. I am not asking for more money Rather then what we agreed on , if $2000 was sent then you have only $43,000 to send as remain money .

On your email where you stated that you are sending this money , you mentioned on thursday or Friday which i don't know yet if you are sending it on that Day since you Said you have alot to do in Your Office as you came back and their is alot to do in your Office

Now you have known the reasoning that it is part of the money that i requested .can you still send the money today ??? their still more time Today or tomorrow morning.

I hope to hear from you

Davis

I ignore Davis for a short while to make him sweat a little.

From: Matins Davis
To: Max N. Paddy (Shiver Metimbers)
Date: 29 April 2005
Title: re: 2000 please?

Hello Max - I am waiting to hear from You as you said today you will make the payment

I hope to hear from you with the Receipts for the payment

Davis

I want to kill off my character to screw with Davis's mind even more, but to do it all of a sudden would be suspicious, so I need to plant a 'seed of impending doom' into his mind!

From: Max N. Paddy (Shiver Metimbers)
To: Matins Davis
Date: 29 April 2005

Mr. Davis - I was going to make the payment this afternoon. However, I became suspicious of a man who seemed to be following me very closely when I went to the bank. He followed me all the way from outside of my office, all the way to the front of the bank. I decided it was not safe to withdraw the money today.

I will make the payment to you on Tuesday, and you have my 100% guarantee on that. I cannot make the payment on Monday because it is a holiday here in the UK and the banks are closed.

Sorry for the inconvenience. Sincerely,

Max N. Paddy.
Managing Director: Dark Side Communications Inc.

Davis can almost smell the cash!

From: Matins Davis
To: Max N. Paddy (Shiver Metimbers)
Date: 29 April 2005
Title: re: 2000 please?

Thank you sir, you are a wonderfull person

thank you

davis

The day of doom arrives. Time to let Davis know all is well, and to set up a call to me.

From: Max N. Paddy (Shiver Metimbers)
To: Matins Davis
Date: 3 May 2005

Mr. Davis - I will be asking the transfer of the $45,000 later this afternoon. I need to get down to my bank after a meeting to withdraw the money and take it to my personal bank to make the transfer to you. I am hoping to get this completed before 3pm today (Tuesday). Please call me by 3pm today to confirm the payment details. My mobile telephone number is +44 87XX XXX XXX

Sincerely,

Max N. Paddy.
Managing Director: Dark Side Communications Inc.

Well, it had to happen - since I planned it. There I was, minding my own business, talking to Davis on the the phone, getting ready to make the $45,000 transfer to him, and suddenly tragedy happens. (For added effect, I am playing traffic and crowd noise in the background and have a trunkful of sound effects at the ready.)

Max N. Paddy:	Hello.
Davis:	Hello, this is Davis speaking.
Max N. Paddy:	Hello Mr. Davis. You've called a bit late. I'm just outside the Western Union office now Mr. Davis. Just getting ready to transfer the money.
Davis:	OK.
Max N. Paddy:	Erm. Once I have transferred this money over to you how long will it take to complete the deal?
Davis:	It should take less than two weeks.
Max N. Paddy:	Right. So will you give me a call as soon as you have received the money?
Davis:	Sure.
Max N. Paddy:	OK. I'm sorry about the traffic noise but I'm outside at the moment at the payment office.
Davis:	No problem.
Max N. Paddy:	Er, just one moment Mr. Davis, there's a man trying to talk to me.
Davis:	OK.
Max N. Paddy:	Yes, can I help you?

Now a thief wants my bag!

Thief:	Yes, I want your briefcase.
Max N. Paddy:	Excuse me?
Thief:	GIVE ME YOUR BRIEFCASE, NOW!
Max N. Paddy:	Oh, go away!
Thief:	GIVE ME THE BRIEFCASE OR YOU'RE A DEAD MAN!
Max N. Paddy:	Get away!
Thief:	RIGHT!

Sounds of a short fight ensue and then several gunshots ring out! Crowds of people start to scream in panic, and the sound of a car screeching away from the scene is heard.

Davis:	Hello?
Passerby:	WHAT THE HELL IS THAT GUY DOING!
Woman:	YOU BASTARD, I'LL GET YOU FOR THIS!

491

Lots more screaming crowds, accompanied by policemen's whistles.

Little girl: Can I have your watch when you are dead?

Still more screaming, and then sounds of police sirens and ambulances approaching.

Davis: Hello, Mr. Paddy?

We hear the sound of screeching wheels as the ambulance arrives to Max N. Paddy's body lying on the ground in a pool of blood.

Paramedic (radio):   A man has just been murdered. He's dying, bleeding to death.

Paramedic 1:   FOUND ANYTHING YET?
Paramedic 2:   NOTHING YET SIR!
Paramedic 1:   HOW ABOUT YOU?
Paramedic 3:   NOT A THING SIR!
Paramedic 1:   WHAT ABOUT YOU GUYS?
Paramedic 4 & 5: WE AIN'T FOUND SHIT!

Police (radio):   What we're dealing with here is a complete lack of respect for the law.

Davis: Hello?

Sounds of general mayhem continue.

Davis: Hello. Mr. Paddy?

Sounds of ambulance and police fading into the distance.

Davis: Hello? Hello?

Davis hangs up the phone.

Can things get any worse for Davis? They certainly can't get any worse for Max!

Davis tried to call me back, but of course I can't answer the phone because I'm dead.

He contacts Ed Shanks by telephone and tells him he is worried and heard shots. He's very confused and is not sure what is going on. Time to put together a newspaper item about my murder!

I mock up a fake newspaper article describing Max N. Paddy's death and get Ed Shanks to send it to Davis.

PAISLEY
Daily Express

BUSINESSMAN IS MURDERED

LOCAL BUSINESSMAN KILLED BY GUNMAN; SUSPECTS AT LARGE

GLASGOW police are investigating a shooting leaving a prominent local businessman dead, a police officer wounded, and his unknown assailants at large.

Glasgow Homicide Inspector Hector Barnett says 45-year-old businessman Max Paddy of Glasgow was pronounced dead at Southern General Hospital shortly after being gunned down by his attacker around 3 o'clock Tuesday afternoon. He was shot five times in the chest at near point blank range.

According to Barnett, Paddy had apparently just left the Plunder & Flee bank on Main Street when he was attacked. Police describe the gunman as a white male, approximately 35-40 years old, 1.8 meters tall, weighing around 88 kilograms and wearing dark clothing. His accomplice is described only as a white male with short dark hair. Both suspects were last seen driving away in a late model Mini Cooper, partial license plate MDS 34.

A police officer who was conducting a foot patrol apparently witnessed the incident and gave chase. The suspect also fired at the unidentified officer, slightly wounding his left hand. Barnett would only describe the officer as a long time veteran of the force. He says the officer was treated at the scene and is "currently assisting this department as we look into this deplorable act."

TOTAL CHAOS

Witnesses to the shooting describe a scene of sheer panic, with some bystanders running in all directions, and others crouching in the street, screaming. Wendy Abercrombie

By ROB MEBLYNDE

of Aberdeen tells the Times "I was pushing me mum 'round the park for some fresh air when I heard the shots. It sounded like someone was lighting firecrackers...I saw one man run for a car carrying a large suitcase. He jumped into the car and drove away..." Another witness, who asked not to be identified, says "It all happened so fast. One minute I'm doing a bit of window shopping, and the next I'm running for my life."

Paddy, the owner of Dark Side Communications, was known as a generous philanthropist who often gave money to local charities and sponsored youth football teams. Reached by phone at D.S.C.'s international headquarters, a Dark Side employee identifying himself as John Kimble told the Times, "We are deeply saddened by the sudden and tragic loss of such a wonderful man. We ask the media to respect our privacy as his family and friends try to make sense of this horrible crime." Kimble also says Dark Side Communications is offering a reward of 25,000 GBP for information leading to the arrest and conviction of Paddy's gunmen. "We want to get these dangerous criminals off the streets and bring closure to Max N. Paddy's family".

UNDERWORLD CONNECTIONS?

Authorities would not say if this shooting is related to Paddy's loss of several thousand pounds to a suspected scam artist a few weeks ago. Detective Barnett told us "...we are currently looking at all possible scenarios in our investigation. That is certainly one avenue of inquiry we are looking at." When asked if police believed Paddy could have been dealing with criminals or was

killed in a dispute over money, Barnett said "we cannot rule anything out at this point. We do know that Mr. Paddy was involved in a suspected overseas scam involving many thousands of dollars. I can confirm to you that we are looking at suspects both in London and in Accra in Ghana."

For others who live in this tight knit community, the shooting has shattered their sense of security. Abercrombie says, "I guess it's back to Tribble baiting at the pensioner's home for me mum until these crooks are caught."

Paisley Express Internet crime correspondent Roger Megently explains "Apparently Mr. Paddy had been corresponding with a suspected 419 scam crime gang, and police are actively investigating possible leads to try to confirm if this murder may be connected."

Anyone with information is urged to call Crimestoppers on 0800 555 111. If your information leads to an arrest you could receive a substantial reward.

FUN FOR ALL THE FAMILY!

PET TRIBBLE

CHILD SAFE – WILL NOT BITE
FURRY · FUN
KEEP OUT OF REACH OF KLINGONS

New Tribble packs now available at The Happy Eater Only £12.99

493

From: Ed Shanks (A. Skinner)
To: Matins Davis
Date: 04 May 2005

Davis - Do you know that Max has been robbed and murdered? What you heard on the telephone yesterday was a robbery and murder. We are all involved!!!

Mr. Kimble sent me a news clipping from the local paper. I attach it here for you to read.

What on earth have we got ourselves into? I suggest you call Mr. Kimble and notify the police. Respond ASAP.

Ed Shanks

Later that same evening, I receive a message from A. Skinner to tell me that Davis had telephoned him again. He was in a state of agitation. Apparently he was worried about Max, was unsure what was going on but he was sure he heard gunshots!

Davis says he won't be phoning again, claiming he is spending too much money on telephone calls, but A. Skinner suspects he may be a little worried about being dragged into a real murder investigation.

Davis has had time to think about things, and is now very suspicious that the wool is being pulled over his eyes. I can't think why! He sends an email to both myself and Ed Shanks.

From: Matins Davis
To: Max N. Paddy & Ed Shanks
Date: 4 May 2005
Title: re: back

Gentlemen - You think I pick Money on the Floor ? I called you and told to hold while talking to somebody, it is time I close the you and Your Shanks issue, since you have refused to pick call again.

Mr. Shanks if this is how you and Max does your business, then I am sorry you need a change, Well I am tried of you tricks and lies. From look of things we are not qualified to handle it, sometimes I wonder how you will handle this business with your style of business,

Please Mr. Shanks Do you not email me again since you are not capable take care of this business,

Davis

Oh dear - Davis appears to be upset! As I can't reply to Davis myself (I am dead), Ed Shanks gets back to him.

From: Ed Shanks (A. Skinner)
To: Matins Davis
Date: 3 May 2005

Dear Davis - I am literally SHOCKED at your tone to me. You made a deal with Max and I am sure he was planning on sending the $45K USD to you today. I don't know what happened. You have called me 8 times now, but at the present I have no answers. We will have to wait until one of us talks to Mr. Max.

Ed Shanks

A. Skinner contacts me to tell me Davis has called him; Davis believes now that my shooting was real!

He complains that this deal - otherwise know as 'his scam' - has been going on for many many months now and all he has for his trouble are hefty telephone bills (shame!). He bemoans to A. Skinner he won't be able to sleep tonight.

The next day Davis wakes up in a suspicious mood, and is adamant he has been wronged. Time for him to issue us with some threats.

From: Matins Davis
To: Max N. Paddy & Ed Shanks
Date: 5 May 2005
Title: inforamation

Shanks - You don't worry about it i will send the message to FBI and then we will know where Max is, i Talk to a friend in USA who works with Airforce, he said he willl give information on one his Friend who is FBI, so when i get his number and i will information him on how Your So call mark has been operating by Changig his phone number on every two weeks,

I am very sure he is connected with OSAMA, I am sure he wanted the Funds help him America for second time or maybe UK,

SHANKS I need Max contact information on the hospital where the Body is at the monment,

I need his picture, INTL passport, Mr Kimble information as well.

I need his wife name and picture.

i have your contact information, don't tired changing it information.

VOA will pick it up because i am tell them everything. and larry King also will talk about it on CNN show.

Davis

NOTE,,,,,I NEED THE INFORMATION CONCERNING THE HOSPITAL BECOS FBI WILL NEED IT PLS

Looks like Davis is starting to go a bit mental!

Ed Shanks writes back to say he needs information on Peter Jones before he will give out any further Max info, as he suspects Peter Jones murdered Max as revenge! Shanks also tells Davis that he has no more money to give and that his church is his only support now.

More crazy rantings from Davis...

From: Matins Davis
To: Ed Shanks (A. Skinner)
Date: 5 May 2005
Title: I NEED THIS INFORMATION

Shanks - I am not giving you any information because you may be behind all of this. ,,, YOU SEE SOMETIME I THINK ARE GOING CRAZY .

Did Peter Jones murder Max? ,,,,, WHO IS MAX ?? PETER JONES WAS IN GHANA, YESTERDAY I WENT ASKED HIM FOR $18,000 USD FROM WHICH HE TOLD THAT HE NEVER MET MAX , THAT MAX NEVER SHOW UP TO MEET HIM , I AM NOW BELIEVING HIM WITH WHAT IS HAPPENING, LOOK YOU AND SO-CALL MAX ARE MAD AS LONG I AM CONCERNED,

AT YOUR AGE, YOU STILL PLAY GAMES LIKE THIS, I DON'T EVEN KNOW IF ARE WHOM CLAMED TO BE WITH THE AGE YOU GAVE TO ME, WELL NO PROBLEM I WILL KNOW WHEN FBI COME IN THIS CASE ,

DAVIS

Davis, unable to control himself it seems, writes again a few hours later.

From: Matins Davis
To: Ed Shanks (A. Skinner)
Date: 5 May 2005
Title: INFORMATION

Hello Shanks - I SEE, you will not Surprise if Peter Killed Max,

Max that has no I.D to show when ask him one, FBI has told me not talk more much they will take over,

Do you know that Max is planing to use the Funds to attack Prime Minister Toni Bla of UK, He only decleared himself Death because he knows he will not be able to do what he intends doing before the Election, well that is the little story they believed Max need the money for ?

FBI has also goted information that Max company was not registered and it is not where he said it is located,

For your information I HAVE TOLD FBI ABOUT THE FOUNDS $27M WE ARE ABOUT TO TRANSFER INTO YOUR ACCOUNT, I know i will be question later on that and too as well,

LARRY KING Show this will take on for All America to know what is going and what we planed to use this money ,just the same where Micheal Jackson case is how the will do on Air CNN,

We want to know who killed Max and the kind of business he doing as well,

i sent Message to Ken Mehlman, The RNC Chairman, i beileved you know him very well , am sure he will reply this matter, the whole Americans will know verything if you DON'T PAY ME MY MONEY ALL EXPENSIVE I MADE

Waiting for you

Davis

Look like myself and A. Skinner are in deep shit with the FBI and Larry King.

Now, we decide to give Davis the telephone number of the morgue where Max's body is presently being kept, so that Davis can have a chat with the people there and get some kind of confirmation that Max is, indeed, dead. Of course, we don't give him the number of a

real morgue. Instead, we give him the contact number of a fellow scambaiter who will be taking on the role of morgue attendant.

After we send Davis the morgue telephone number, he replies with the following...

From: Matins Davis
To: Ed Shanks (A. Skinner)
Date: 6 May 2005
Title: telephone

I WILL GIVE FBI THE NUMBER TO CALL HIM , I WILL NOT CALL HIM UNLESS I WAS TOLD TO CALL ,
SHANKS FBI CONTACTED INTER-POL YESTERDAY AND THE CALL ME, BUT I TOLD THEM I WAS IN A MEETING BUT I WILL MAKE IT TODAY.

SHANKS IF YOU DON'T TELL ME WHEN YOU WILL GIVE ME MY MONEY {EXPENSIVE} I WILL GIVE YOUR INFORMATION TO LARRY KING SHOW AND INTER-POL AS WELL FBI,

FOR YOUR INFORMATION EVEY PHONE NUMBER MAX GAVE TO ME TO CALL HAS BEEN GIVEN TO FBI AND NOW THEY ARE ASKING FOR YOUR INFORMATION,

QUESTION,,,,,ARE YOU PAYING ME THE MONEY ?? YES OR NO IF YES IT MUST WITHIN 7DAYS,

IF YOU GIVE ME MY EXPENSIVE I MADE, I WILL NOT GIVE YOUR INFORMATIONS TO LARRY KING SHOW,
AND I WILL NOT TELL FBI ANY BAD STORY CONCERNING YOU,

BUT IF NO ,,THEN I WILL TELL LARRY KING,FBI, TALK SHOW IN VOICE OF AMERICA{VOA} AND YOU KNOW WHAT I WILL TELL THEM WHAT NEVER HAPPENED, YOU KNOW WHAT I MEAN.

SHANKS YOU PLANED TO HELP A FAMILY WITH THEIR FUNDS,BUT IT WILL BE DIFFERENT THING NOW, IF MAX HAS THIS GAME TO PLAY THEN WE WILL PLAY IT TOGETHER, YOU KNOW WHATEVER I TELL FBI THEY WILL BELIEVED,

FOR MAX PART,WELL DO YOU KNOW THAT THEIR WAS BOMB THAT BLASSED A BULIDING KILLING MANY? WELL MAX YOU SHOULD KNOW ABOUT IT, AND I AM CONNECTING HIM TO THAT AS WELL.

YOU KNOW WHAT YOU AND MAX PLANNING DIFFERENT THING SAMPLE BUT I AM MAKING IT HARD FOR SOON IF I DON'T GET MY EXPENSIVE MADE , OR YOU WILL SPEND MORE,

I GOT INFORMATION AGAIN FROM FBI THAT THE NEWSPAPPER THAT WROTE ABOUT 419 MAX SENT TO YOU

DON'T ANYTHING ABOUT THAT STORY, AM SURE THEY WILL WANT TO KNOW HOW MAX DID THAT, WE YET TO KNOW IF THIS LAST NEWS ABOUT HIS DEATH REALLY HAPPEN

SHANKS REPLY ME AND TELL ME HOW MUCH YOU ARE PAYING ME AND WHEN, IF NOT .....

DAVIS

You just can't make this stuff up!

Ed Shanks replies to tell Davis that there is no money for him. Perhaps it would be a good idea for Davis to call Max's boss (played by Shiver Metimbers) who is looking after all the funeral arrangements and is the executor of Max's will:

From: Ed Shanks (A. Skinner)
To: Matins Davis
Date: 6 May 2005

Dear Friend Davis - Look my friend, this is all getting to be more than I can take. My nerves are on edge. Can't you understand that I am broke? No greenbacks, no Euros, no cash, no USD (at least not right now). Hold off on your demands.

On a happier note, I had a call last night from Mr. Bunchov Schitz who is the Director of Max's company which as you know is Dark Side Communications. Mr. Shitz is the person who will attempt to find a replacement for Max and is also the executor of his will. He is now making arrangements for Max's funeral.

Sadly, I won't be able to attend. However, the good news is that I may be inheriting some cash from Max. He and I were very close until the end when he was shot (probably by Peter Jones).

I told Mr. Shitz about you, but did not mention all the threats you are making. You can tell him if you want. I'm sure that Max's company does not need all the negative publicity you have in store for them. Mr. Shitz can be reached at this email address: bunchov@xxxxxx.co.uk

I urge you to hold off on your threats. I am taking most of the day to attend a durarium with the Church of Milk and Honey. Blessings on them.

Sincerely,

Ed Shanks

After the email above, Davis quickly twigged that he had been taken for a very long ride and many, many insults ensued. Of course, we reciprocated with some threats of our own, and we both had a war of words for a few weeks afterwards, 99% of which is unrepeatable in even semi-polite society!

Davis's threats of getting the FBI involved and, even worse, Larry King never materialised.

I've had a few of Davis's email accounts shut down and have been generally trying to be a pain in his backside, but now instead of issuing me with threats he has taken to ignoring me!